THE CHARLES ELIOT NORTON LECTURES
1940–1941

LITERARY CURRENTS IN HISPANIC AMERICA

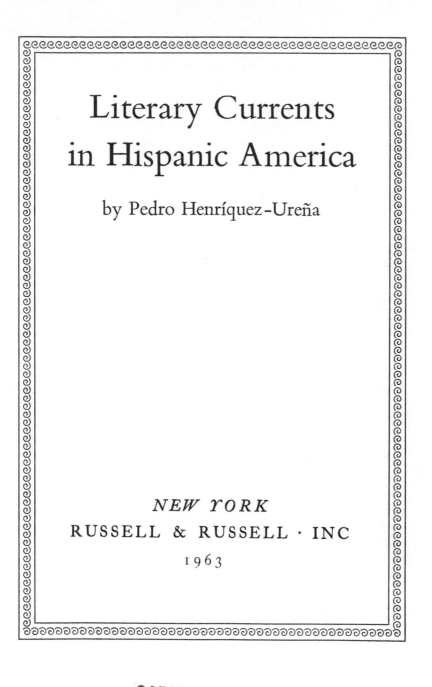

Literary Currents
in Hispanic America

by Pedro Henríquez-Ureña

NEW YORK

RUSSELL & RUSSELL · INC

1963

FOREWORD

THE PRESENT BOOK contains the Charles Eliot Norton lectures for the academic year 1940–1941, delivered at the invitation of Harvard University, in the Fogg Museum of Art, on the nights of the sixth, the thirteenth, and the twentieth of November, the eleventh of December, the eleventh, the eighteenth, and the twenty-fifth of February, and the fourth of March. I have devoted two and a half years since then to rewriting and enlarging the text of the lectures and adding notes.

At first I intended to limit the scope of the lectures to the literature of Hispanic America (I prefer this designation to the more popular though less satisfactory "Latin America"); afterwards I decided not to exclude the arts, in order the better to convey a sense of the unity of culture in the countries reared in the Hispanic tradition in this hemisphere. However, I could hardly do more than venture a few remarks on art, since it is not my own special field of study, and a thorough acquaintance with all the important works would require, besides the adequate technical knowledge, a personal visit to all the Hispanic American countries — and, so far, I know slightly more than half of our twenty separate political entities, including Puerto Rico, which retains its linguistic and cultural allegiance to the Hispanic tradition. My survey of art movements, therefore, should be taken merely as a supplement to the survey of literature. Fortunately, the excellent collection of slides in the Fogg Museum enabled me to show to the public who attended the lectures a number of characteristic examples of architecture and painting, and I hoped they would express more than I could tell.

As my subject was not familiar to the majority of the audience to whom I addressed my lectures, I felt compelled to include a large amount of information that might otherwise have been omitted. But I have tried to consign as much of it to the notes as seemed feasible. At the same time, I have given the reader, both in notes and in the brief general bibliography at the end of the book, many references that will allow him to go farther into the field, should he so desire.

These lectures have no pretension to be a complete history of Hispanic American literature. My intention has been to follow the currents related to our "search for expression." The lectures, in fact, were announced under the title, "In Search of Expression," which I thought best to change afterwards. The poets and writers I mention were chosen as examples of such currents but they are not the only ones that might claim to represent them. This purpose will explain many omissions, especially in the twentieth century: the literary movements have become so ample that any attempt to mention most of the significant names of the present day would crowd the pages and confuse the reader. There is no critical intent in any omission.

I desire to thank Mrs. Paul Phelps Morand (formerly Miss Ruth Shepard Phelps), Professors Howard Mumford Jones, of Harvard University, and Hayward Keniston, of the University of Michigan, Messrs. Lincoln Kirstein, Arthur Szathmary, James Monroe Smith, Alan J. Ansen (Harvard '42), and Boice Richardson (Harvard '43) for their kindness in reading my manuscript, wholly or in part, and making suggestions, especially in matters of language. I am especially indebted to Mrs. Morand for her unusual kindness in seeing the book through the press and completing the index. I desire also to thank Mr. Keyes DeWitt Metcalf, Librarian of Harvard University, and Messrs. Robert Hammond Haynes, Assistant Librarian, and Homer Halvorson for their kind assistance in the Widener Library.

P. H.-U.

CONTENTS

1. THE DISCOVERY OF THE NEW WORLD IN THE IMAGINATION OF EUROPE   3

2. THE CREATION OF A NEW SOCIETY: 1492–1600   30

3. THE FLOWERING OF THE COLONIAL WORLD: 1600–1800   58

4. THE DECLARATION OF INTELLECTUAL INDE-PENDENCE: 1800–1830   94

5. ROMANTICISM AND ANARCHY: 1830–1860   112

6. THE PERIOD OF ORGANIZATION: 1860–1890   137

7. PURE LITERATURE: 1890–1920   161

8. PROBLEMS OF TODAY: 1920–1940   185

NOTES   205

BIBLIOGRAPHY   285

INDEX   297

1

THE DISCOVERY OF THE NEW WORLD
IN THE IMAGINATION OF EUROPE

IN ONE of the letters he wrote towards the end of his life, Charles Eliot Norton congratulated his friend Horace Howard Furness, the great Shakespearean scholar, on the voyage he was about to undertake in "the treacherous southern waters" of the Atlantic. His unfaltering curiosity, that had taken him over so many fields of human endeavor, was still awake in his eightieth year and prompted in him the desire to visit the seas and lands once ravaged by pirates and buccaneers, much as the European humanists of the sixteenth century were eager, in Frampton's phrase, for "joyfull newes of the newe founde worlde." "I wish I were to be with you," he says, "to sail over that Spanish Main which was once the sea-field of adventurers."

It is not perhaps unfitting that now, in the course of these lectures that were instituted to honor his memory, we should travel over those lands and seas to discover what human endeavor has achieved there, in the field that was nearest to Norton's heart, that of letters and the arts, and to show what may still make them interesting to a humanistic curiosity.

In a time of doubt and hope, when political independence had not yet been fully achieved, the peoples of Hispanic America declared themselves intellectually of age, made their own life their "proper study," and set out on the quest for self-expression. Our poetry, our literature, was to be a genuine expression of ourselves. Europe was old; here was a new life, a new world for freedom and enterprise and song. Such was the intent and the meaning of the great Ode, the first of the *Silvas americanas*, published by Andrés Bello in 1823. Bello was not an improviser, not a romantic upstart; he was a scholar, a great grammarian, a translator of Horace and Plautus, a pioneer explorer in the still virgin forests of medieval literature. His program of independence was the outcome of careful thought and assiduous labor. Since then, our poets and writers have persisted in the quest; in recent years, musicians, architects, and painters have joined in it. How such a duty has been fulfilled, how far such hopes have been attained, is to be the subject of these papers.

Centuries before this search for expression became a conscious effort of men born in Hispanic America, Columbus had made the first attempts to interpret in words the new world he had found. As a navigator, he opened it to explorers and conquerors; as a writer, he discovered it for the imagination of Europe — in the words of Dr. Johnson, "he gave a new world to European curiosity." He is the source of two ideas which soon became commonplaces: America as the land of plenty, and the Indian as "the noble savage." In artless but picturesque language, his *Letter on the Discovery* (1493) describes the islands of the Caribbean Archipelago as a paradise of abundance and perpetual spring:

> This island [Hispaniola] and all the others are very fertile, to an extraordinary degree, and this one extremely so. In it there are many harbors on the coast of the sea, and many rivers, good and large, which is marvellous. Its lands are high; there are many sierras and lofty mountains. . . . All are most beautiful, of a thousand shapes, and all easy to walk through, and full of trees of a thousand kinds, and tall, so that they seem to reach the sky; and I am told that the trees never lose their foliage, and this I can believe, for I saw them as green and fine as they are in Spain in May, and some of them were in flower, and some with fruit, and some at another stage, according to their nature. The nightingale was singing, and so were other birds of a thousand kinds, in the month of November, wherever I went. There are six or

eight kinds of palms, which are a wonder to behold, on account of the beautiful variety of their shapes, but so are the
other trees and fruits and plants. In it [the island] are marvellous pine groves, and there are very wide plains, and there
is honey, and birds of many kinds, and fruits in great diversity. . . . Hispaniola is a marvel; the sierras, and the mountains, and the plains, and the meadows, and the lands so fine
and rich for planting and sowing, for breeding cattle of
every kind, for building towns and villages. . . . It is a land
to be desired, and, once seen, never to be left.[1]

In his *Journal* of the voyage of discovery — or what remains of
it in the extracts made by Father Las Casas — Columbus is in
constant rapture about the landscape of the New World. The
description of the first island, Guanahani, is surprisingly brief,
perhaps because Las Casas shortened it: "They [the sailors who
went ashore] saw trees very green, and much water, and fruits of
various kinds." The next day (October 13) Columbus describes
the island at greater length, and fortunately we have his actual
words, without any abridgment: "This island is quite large, and
very level, with very green trees, and much water, and a very large
lake in the center; there is no mountain, and everything is so green
that it is a pleasure to gaze upon it." Then, four days later, the
little island Fernandina

is very green and level, and very fertile, and I have no doubt
that all the year round they sow and reap grain and all the
other things too. I saw many trees very unlike ours, and
many of them had branches of different kinds, and all coming from one root; one twig is of one kind, and one of another, and so unlike that it is the greatest wonder in the
world. How great is the diversity from one to another! For
example: one branch has leaves like those of a cane, and
another leaves like those of a mastic; and thus, in a single
tree, there are five or six different kinds, and all so diverse
from each other. Nor are they grafted, so that it cannot be
said that grafting does it; on the contrary, they are wild, and
these people do not cultivate them.

In this statement, Columbus was led into error by the number of parasitic plants that may assault a tropical tree. He then adds: "The fishes here are so unlike ours that it is a marvel; there are some shaped like dories, of the finest colors in the world, blue, yellow, red and of all colors, and others are painted in a thousand ways, and the colors are so fine that there is no man who does not wonder at them and take great delight in seeing them." From then on, his tone is persistently hyperbolic, as for instance (October 19): "I saw this cape so green and so fine, like all the other things and lands of these islands, so that I do not know where to go first, nor do my eyes ever tire of seeing such beautiful verdures. . . . There came from the land the scent of flowers or trees, so fine and soft, that it was the sweetest thing in the world." Or, later (October 21): "The singing of the little birds is such that it seems one could never wish to go away from here; the flocks of parrots darken the sun." Then, speaking of Cuba (October 28), he says that "the island is the most beautiful that eyes have ever seen." And of Hispaniola (December 11) that "it is the most beautiful thing in the world."

Columbus describes the native islanders of the Bahamas and the Greater Antilles as simple, virtuous, and happy beings. In his *Letter on the Discovery* he says: "The people of these islands all go naked, men and women, as their mothers bore them." This nudity was one of the most striking novelties for him, as for all later explorers, coming from overclothed Europe. He adds:

> They have neither iron nor steel nor weapons, nor are they fitted to use them. This is not because they are not well built and of handsome stature, but because they are very marvellously timorous. . . . They are so guileless and so generous with all that they possess, that no one would believe it who has not seen it. Anything they have, if it be asked of them, they never refuse; on the contrary, they offer it, and they show as much love as if they would give their hearts. . . . They do not hold any creed, nor are they idolaters; they all believe that power and good are in the heavens

and are firmly convinced that I, with these ships and men, came from the heavens, and in this belief they everywhere received me after they had mastered their fear. This belief is not the result of ignorance, for they are, on the contrary, of a very acute intelligence, and they navigate all those seas, so that it is amazing how good an account they give of everything. It is because they have never seen people so clothed or ships of such a kind.

And in the *Journal of the Discovery* (October 11): "They were very well built, with very handsome bodies and very good faces. . . . They do not bear arms or know them, for I showed them swords and they took them by the blade and cut themselves through ignorance." Then (October 13): "Very handsome people. Their hair is not curly, but loose and coarse like the hair of a horse. . . . Their eyes are very fine, and not small. They are not at all black, but of the color of the Canarians [the old Guanches] . . . their legs are very straight . . . and no fat belly, but very well shaped." And later (October 16): "I do not know that they have any creed, and I believe they would be speedily converted to Christianity, for they have a very good understanding." And in his *Journal*, as he was already thinking of how he was to describe his discovery to the sovereigns (December 25), he wrote: "I assure Your Highnesses that there is no better land nor people. They love their neighbors as themselves, and their speech is the sweetest in the world, and gentle, and always with a smile."

All Indians were not, indeed, "noble savages" like the Tainos he found in the Antilles. He learned from them about their enemies, the ferocious tribes of the small islands to the South, who were said to eat human flesh. The name of those warrior tribes — Caribs, or Canibs, or Cannibals — eventually became a fearful symbol.

The letter of Columbus on the Discovery was read throughout Europe. In 1493, immediately after its publication in Spanish, it was translated into Latin by the Catalan Leandro de Cosco and

had at least eight editions, besides a paraphrase in Italian verse
by the Florentine theologian Giuliano Dati.

The imagination of men in Europe found in these descriptions,
along with many strange novelties, the confirmation of immemo-
rial tales and dreams, *la merveille unie à vérité*, in the quaint expression of Mellin de Saint-Gelais. Columbus himself had visited
our tropical islands in a transport of Platonic reminiscence; in his
travels he was constantly recalling what he had heard or read
about real or imaginary lands and men — Biblical or classical or
medieval legends and inventions, especially the marvels in Pliny
and Marco Polo. The manatees, in the sea, he takes for sirens,
although he does not find them "as beautiful as they are painted."
The Indians tell him, he fancies, of Amazons, of Cyclops, of men
with dog faces, of men with tails, of men without hair.[2] Even the
song of a tropical bird becomes for him the song of the nightingale.

Columbus has often been praised for his pictures of nature in
the tropics. No less a master of description than Alexander von
Humboldt finds in them "beauty and simplicity of expression" together with a "deep feeling for nature." Menéndez Pelayo, the
eminent Spanish critic, attributes to them "the spontaneous eloquence of an untutored soul to whom great things dictate great
words." But Cesare de Lollis, in his scholarly edition of Columbus' text, declares them monotonous and artificial; by a forced
enthusiasm, he thinks, Columbus tries to prove the importance of
his discovery. There is a note of excess, no doubt, in the writings
of Columbus, but it is native to him. It is also true that in his
letters to the sovereigns and to his supporters Santángel and Sánchez — which are practically one letter — he suppresses the un-
pleasant features of the islands; his *Journal* here and there speaks
of the uncomfortable heat he suffered in the Bahamas, but his
letters are silent about it. And his language becomes monotonous
t times, with repetitions of hyperbolic formulas, because he was

not a man of letters and had no wealth of words at his command; but he achieves delightful effects with his scanty vocabulary, as when he speaks of trees that "ceased to be green and became black from sheer greenness," or of "the chirping of crickets all through the night," or of the smile that accompanies the speech of the islanders, or when he says in simple words: "The nightingale was singing." Again, his pictures may seem artificial, but only because he paints them according to the literary fashion of his times — he obeyed it, even though he was no great reader. To be perfect, a landscape had to be a garden of perpetual spring. Paradise itself had been so conceived for many centuries. And the islands of the Caribbean happen to be green and full of flowers, fruits, and singing birds all the year round, even while it is winter in Europe.[3]

By their agreement with the then current ideal of beauty in nature, his descriptions left a lively impression upon the European mind. Later on, they were confirmed and developed by many chroniclers. The New World, or at least its tropical zone, has retained in the imagination of most men the essential features that appear in the famous letter of 1493 — the unlimited wealth and fertility, the perennial spring of the tropics, now somewhat altered through more prosaic experiences into a perennial and not very genial summer. Many new regions were discovered and explored after Columbus; men found that the Americas contain deserts, jungles, grassy treeless plains, formidable mountain ranges, two zones with a round of seasons, and even a polar zone. But the change in popular notions has been very slow. At present, North America is known to be roughly similar to Europe in climate; the rest, the vast and variegated territories of Hispanic Middle and South America, are often vaguely conceived as a jumble of more or less torrid lands, although, owing either to height or to latitude, a very large part of that area is temperate. No small amount of popular sociology is based upon this geographical misconception.

Columbus' portrait of the Tainos as noble savages is partly a poetic figure, composed under the influence of a literary tradition and with the desire to enhance the value of his discovery. But, again, the portrait did resemble the Tainos. Its fortune was not similar to that of his landscapes; but it contained the seed of the complex problem of "natural man" which engaged the mind of Europe for three hundred years. We find in it even a preference for the natives of America, on account of their physical beauty, as against the natives of Central Africa — a preference that recurs in many vindications of the Indians and is still quite common, in spite of Count Keyserling's eloquent praise of black beauty.

After the short-lived excitement of the news conveyed by Columbus' letter, there came a lull. For a time, the Discovery seemed a failure. Great hopes had accompanied Columbus on his second voyage (1493), when he came to Hispaniola with seventeen ships and twelve hundred men of various ranks and professions. But dissensions broke out. And there was very little gold. We know the rest. In Spain, according to Ferdinand Columbus, the Discoverer was dubbed "the Admiral of the Mosquitoes, who has found lands of vanity and delusion, the grave and ruin of Castilian gentlemen." Fifteen years went by, and the Spaniards had settled only Hispaniola.

Explorations were carried on, however, though without plan or method. And then the account of Amerigo Vespucci's voyages, when he set out "to see a portion of the world and its marvels," reawakened the interest of European readers. His descriptions of Brazil read like mere variations on themes from Columbus, although he is often censorious regarding the Indians:

> They go about wholly naked, men and women alike. . . . They are of medium stature, very well proportioned. Their skin is of a color which inclines to red, like a lion's mane; and I believe that if they went clothed they would be white like ourselves. They have no hair at all on the body, except

long and black hair on the head, especially the women, which renders them beautiful. . . . They are very swift of their bodies, in walking and running, both men and women. . . . They swim past all belief, and the women better than the men. . . . Their weapons are bows and arrows. . . . They have neither king nor master, nor do they obey anybody, for they live in their individual liberty. . . . They do not practise justice, nor punish the criminal, nor do father and mother punish their children; and . . . we never saw any disputing among them. . . . They are people neat and clean of person, owing to the constant washing they practise. . . . We did not learn that they had any religion. . . . I deem their manner of life to be Epicurean [a strong condemnation at that time]. . . . They engage in no barter; they neither buy nor sell. . . . They are contented with what nature gives them. The wealth which we affect in this our Europe . . . they hold of no value at all. . . . They are so liberal in giving that it is the exception when they deny. They eat little meat, other than human flesh. . . . They eat all enemies whom they kill or capture. . . .

What shall we say of the birds, which are so numerous, of so many varieties and colors of plumage that it is a wonder to behold them? The land is very pleasing and fertile, full of huge forests and woods, and always green; and it never loses its foliage. The fruits are so many that they are beyond number, and altogether different from ours.[4]

Vespucci speaks also of new skies and new stars: "Already [in his third voyage] we had utterly lost the Ursa Minor, and the Ursa Major stood over us very low. . . . We guided ourselves by the stars of that other, southern pole, which are many, far larger and more lucent than those of this pole of ours. I drew the figuration of most of these."

Columbus had already said, in his pathetic letter to Doña Juana de la Torre (ca. 1500): "I made a new voyage to the new sky and world, which until then were hidden." The new sky and stars, which had been no more than a scientific datum in astronomical treatises from Aristotle to Alphonso the Wise, became a literary topic in the sixteenth century. They reappear in the Decades *De Orbe Novo* of Peter Martyr of Anghera; in the *Itinerarium* of the Italian humanist Alessandro Geraldini, first bishop of Santo Domingo and probably the first man to write Latin verse and prose in the Americas ("alia sub alio caelo sidera"); in Gonzalo Fernández de Oviedo's *Historia general y natural de las Indias* ("estrellas no vistas sino por acá"); in Girolamo Fracastoro's poem *Morbus gallicus* ("diversum caelo, et clarum maioribus astris"); in Étienne de La Boétie's Epistle on Columbus *Ad Belotium et Montanum* ("alio fulgentia sidera caelo"); in Mellin de Saint-Gelais's sonnet in praise of the *Voyages aventureux* of Jean Alphonse de Saintonge ("et autre ciel s'y voit d'autre nature"); in Camoëns' *Os Lusiadas* ("lá no novo hemisphério nova estrella"); in Ercilla's *Araucana* ("climas pasé, mudé constelaciones"); in Juan de Castellanos' *Elegías de varones ilustres de Indias* ("otras estrellas ve nuestro estandarte y nuevo cielo ve nuestra bandera"). During the seventeenth century, they survive at least in Bernardo de Valbuena, who mentions them many times.[5]

After Vespucci, Europe never ceased to look Westward. Information flowed from many sources. The richest of all was Peter Martyr's *De Orbe Novo*. A man of genius in his way, a humanist with a journalistic vocation, Peter Martyr (1457–1526) offered to his readers a full and brilliant pageant, as in Benozzo's frescoes, with exotic kings, gold, birds, trees. His general descriptions of nature are few but impressive:

> The Spaniards declare that there is not in the universe a more fertile region.[6]
> They planted all kinds of vegetables. . . . Sixteen days after the sowing, the plants had everywhere grown; melons, pumpkins, cucumbers, and other similar products were ripe for picking thirty-six days after they were planted, and nowhere had our people tasted any finer flavor. Throughout the whole year one might thus have fresh vegetables. . . . Some of the trees were in flower, and the sweet perfumes

they exhaled were wafted across the sea, while others were weighted with fruit.[7]

Perpetual spring and perpetual autumn prevail in this fortunate island [Hispaniola]. During the entire year the trees are covered with leaves, and the prairies with grass. Everything in Hispaniola grows in extraordinary fashion. . . . What greater happiness could one wish in this world than to live in a country where such wonders are to be seen and enjoyed? Is there a more agreeable existence than that one leads in a country where one is not forced to shut himself in narrow rooms to escape cold that chills or heat that suffocates? A land where it is not necessary to load the body with heavy clothing in winter, or to toast one's legs at a continual fire [Peter Martyr's own habit, no doubt, as he wrote so much], a practice which ages people in the twinkling of an eye, exhausts their force and provokes a thousand different maladies. The air of Hispaniola is said to be salubrious, and the rivers, which flow over beds of gold, wholesome.[8]

He devotes many pages to descriptions of fauna and flora, and many more to the inhabitants. He speaks with horror about the habits of "the odious Cannibals," those "rapacious wolves," but praises the placid Tainos:

The islanders of Hispaniola, in my opinion, may be esteemed more fortunate than were the Latins. . . . They go naked, they know neither weights nor measures, nor that source of all misfortunes, money [a reminiscence of Saint Paul — "the love of money is the root of all evil"?]; living in a golden age, without laws, without prevaricating judges, without books, satisfied with their life, and in no way anxious about the future. Nevertheless, ambition and the desire to rule trouble even them; and they fight among themselves.[9]

It is proved that amongst them [in Cuba] the land belongs to everybody just like the sun or the water. They know no difference between *meum* and *tuum*, that source of all evils. Little suffices to satisfy them. . . . It is indeed a golden age; neither ditches, nor hedges, nor walls enclose their domains; they live in gardens open to all, without laws and without judges; their conduct is naturally equitable, and whoever injures his neighbor is considered a criminal and an outlaw.[10]

It is likely that this Arcadian picture held the attention of only a humanistic minority. The common man in Europe, like the many simple-minded explorers who saw the Indians and wrote about them, conceived them as little better than wild animals, harmless or dangerous as the case might be. In the Americas the Spanish and Portuguese settlers soon accustomed themselves to deal with them, as either friends or enemies, but in any case as neighbors; they became a normal part of the common life of the colonies. But in Europe thinkers and writers found in them an absorbing problem, related to one of the great questions that the mind of the Renaissance was debating, the age-old contrast between nature and culture. Deeper still lay another problem, the very concept of nature, taken over from antiquity and remodelled. Was man naturally good? Was the Indian "the natural man"? Did he live in a state of innocence? Was his a happy life? Were its blessings higher than the doubtful blessings of European civilization? Were even the worst habits of Cannibals more criminal than the practices of Christians, who did not eat their fellows, but tortured, mutilated, and burned them?

When Sir Thomas More looked for a distant and safe corner of the earth where he might build his *Utopia* (1516), he deliberately chose a vague island, visited by an imaginary companion of Vespucci. The utopian ideal, one of the great inventions of the Greek genius, one of the fine flowers of Mediterranean culture, could not fail to have a new birth in the Renaissance; it was "discovered again, along with the New World." [11] Machiavelli depicts political Europe as it is; More, to whom it is distasteful, conceives a perfect *politeia* and places it in new and unspoiled lands. Following his example, Campanella builds his *City of the Sun* (1623) in another vague country under the equator, but gives it a few traits that he probably draws from either the Aztec or the Inca civilization. Bacon removes his *New Atlantis* even farther from actuality, but it is significant that its inhabitants speak Spanish.

While these theoretical questions were being asked in Europe, the Spaniards and the Portuguese in the Americas were facing the practical problem of how to deal with the Indians. For the conquerors, the issue was clear: the native populations were to be subdued and set to work for their new masters. In the early years of the Conquest, the Indians were classed in two groups: the Caribs who resisted and fought the Europeans, and the Guatiaos, who were friendly to them. And yet, so harsh and so thoughtless was the treatment accorded by many of the conquerors to the Guatiaos on the islands that men and women died by thousands. A few rebelled, but failed to maintain their independence; at last, the revolt (1519–1533) of Enriquillo, a Christianized Taino of Hispaniola who read and wrote Spanish and knew the use of European weapons, succeeded in saving a few thousands, who were declared free from any masters by a decree of Charles V.

As early as 1510, the brothers of the Order of Saint Dominic, upon their arrival in Hispaniola, had looked with angry astonishment upon the behavior of the privileged settlers, the *encomenderos*, to whom Indians were entrusted, technically as wards but practically as serfs. After long thinking and praying, the friars decided on their course of action. The event is one of the greatest in the spiritual history of mankind. The preachers gave again to Christianity its ancient role of religion of the oppressed. Friar Pedro de Córdoba (1482–1521), the vicar of the Order, instructed Friar Antón de Montesinos, their best orator, to preach a sermon on the fourth Sunday of Advent. Montesinos took as his text the words of the Gospel, "The voice of one crying in the wilderness." After a brief introduction, says Las Casas,

> he began to show the sterility of the wilderness of men's consciences on the island, and the blindness in which they

were living, with great danger of their damnation, not realizing the very grave sins in which they were steeped. . . . "In order to make them known to you I have come up on this pulpit, I who am a voice of Christ crying in the wilderness of this island, and therefore it behooves you to listen, not with careless attention, but with all your heart and senses, so that you may hear it; for this is going to be the strangest voice that ever you heard, the harshest and hardest and most awful and most dangerous that ever you expected to hear." He spoke at great length of that voice, with penetrating and terrible words, which made their flesh tremble. "This voice says that you are in mortal sin, that you live and die in it, for the cruelty and tyranny you use in dealing with these innocent people. Tell me, by what right or justice do you keep these Indians in such a cruel and horrible servitude? On what authority have you waged a detestable war against these people, who dwelt quietly and peacefully on their own land? . . . Why do you keep them so oppressed and weary, not giving them enough to eat nor taking care of them in their illnesses? For with the excessive work you demand of them they fall ill and die, or rather you kill them with your desire to extract and acquire gold every day. And what care do you take that they should be instructed in religion? . . . Are these not men? Have they not rational souls? Are you not bound to love them as you love yourselves? . . . Be certain that, in such a state as this, you can no more be saved than the Moors or Turks who lack and reject the faith of Christ." . . . He left them astounded, and many felt as if they were out of their senses; some were too hardened, a few felt some compunction, but none was converted.

The *encomenderos,* after a troubled Sunday dinner, flocked to the house of Diego Columbus, the viceroy of the Indies, and required him to demand a disavowal from the Dominican Order. They all went together to the poor wooden building of the monastery and held a long conference with the friars, but the only promise they obtained from the firm and discreet Friar Pedro de Córdoba was that Montesinos would preach again on the following Sunday, dealing with the same matters, and would try to satisfy them, if possible. There is no need to describe at length what he said. It is easy to conceive it, knowing that he took as the text for his sermon a passage from the Book of Job, "I will repeat my knowledge from the beginning. . . . For indeed my words are without a lie." [12]

A new type of crusade had begun. The spirit of charity tried to subdue the rapacious violence of the will to power. Perhaps for the first time in history, men of a powerful conquering nation discussed the rights of conquest. Great ethical and political principles, the right of every man to freedom and the right of every community to independence, were implied in the controversy and were later brought into it by the contestants. Córdoba and Montesinos carried their battle to the court of Spain. It is generally believed that the Laws of Burgos (December 27, 1512), designed to improve the condition of the Indians, were the result of discussions between Ferdinand the Catholic and Montesinos. A few months later a supplementary decree, the Clarification of the Laws of Burgos, seems to have been obtained by the personal influence of Friar Pedro de Córdoba.

But the enforcement of the Laws was unsatisfactory, and the controversy did not end there. In the year (1510) when Córdoba and Montesinos arrived in Hispaniola, a young lawyer who had received his degree of Licenciado from the University of Salamanca, Bartolomé de Las Casas, was ordained in the city of Concepcion de la Vega; he was the first priest to say his first mass in the New World — "la primera misa nueva en el Nuevo Mundo." Like any Spaniard of distinction in the Antilles, he had Indians assigned to him. He treated them well and saw nothing essentially wrong in the *encomienda* system. Once a Dominican friar to whom he had gone for confession reproved him for exploiting the natives and denied him absolution; he then went to a more lenient confessor and obtained it. After his ordination he continued to have Indians at his service. But four years later, in

Cuba, while preparing himself to preach a sermon on Whitsunday, his eyes fell upon chapter xxxiv of Ecclesiasticus:

> He that sacrificeth of a thing wrongfully gotten, his offering is ridiculous; and the gifts of unjust men are not accepted. The Most High is not pleased with the offerings of the wicked. . . . Whoso bringeth an offering of the goods of the poor doth as one who killeth the son before his father's eyes. The bread of the needy is their life: he that defraudeth him thereof is a man of blood. He that taketh away from his neighbor's living slayeth him; and he that defraudeth the laborer of his hire is a blood-shedder.

From that day he devoted his life to the protection of the Indians and became the impetuous and indomitable Quixote of the brotherhood of men. His campaign is well known. It lasted fifty years and helped to bring about two great events: one, the New Laws of 1542, which finally determined the status of the Indians; the other, the legal theories expounded at the University of Salamanca by Friar Francisco de Vitoria, the reformer of theology and political doctrine.[13] The Laws, it has often been said, were not greatly honored in practice, but their good results, however we measure them, cannot be disputed. And the doctrine of Vitoria asserts the rights of all peoples to freedom, even when they are not Christians, even if they live in sin — and their unbelief, when due to ignorance, is not a sin. The Indians were "true owners" of the territory they occupied; they were not naturally subjects of "the Emperor," but the Spanish king might rule them, solely for their own good. No man is a slave by nature: Vitoria explains away Aristotle's theory on the subject as a theory of "civil and legal slavery, wherein none are slaves by nature." His greatest disciple, Friar Domingo de Soto, went still farther and preached abolition. War is justified by Vitoria only as a means of redressing injuries, as when Christians who peacefully seek the propagation of the faith or the right to trade are attacked by heathen populations. It is not difficult now to be a more radical pacifist, and in

the sixteenth century itself Vives was more radical than the great
Dominican,[14] but, as usually happens, the influence of Vitoria's
theory was not due to its old elements — the dead weight it carried from the past — but to its innovations. His doctrine of the
right to independence, if not new in essence, had a new ring
through its connections with new circumstance. And its gradual development through the sixteenth century ultimately led
to Grotius' theory of the law of nations, which meant "a progress in the moral life of mankind." [15] Sixteenth-century Spain,
however much she may have erred, has the right to be called, as
Karl Vossler calls her, the mentor of ethics among European
nations.

The efforts of Las Casas produced, unfortunately, another result. One of his many suasory writings, the *Brief Relation of the
Destruction of the Indies* (printed in 1552), was seized by the
jealous enemies of the mighty Spanish empire and used by them
as the main foundation for the "black legend" of Spain. It contained little that might not have been gathered from many chroniclers, including Oviedo, Las Casas' pertinacious antagonist; [16] but
it was found useful because it was very short and very forceful,
with the eloquence of anger. And Las Casas had the peculiarly
Andalusian gift of exaggeration, by no means confined to his controversial pages. In recent times, much generous effort has been
spent in dispelling the black legend. No small part of that effort
is due to historians of the United States. But even today it is difficult to convince the man in the street that the Spanish conquest,
in spite of the evils from which no conquest is free, had a unique
human quality. In fact, the Spaniards, and the Portuguese too,
soon came to feel that the Indians were men, after all, not very
unlike themselves, and mingled with them, and treated them as
they treated one another — not better, as Las Casas wished, but
seldom worse. The tyranny of many a nobleman over his subjects
in Europe until the end of the Middle Ages, and even afterwards
(the tyranny of, say, any one of the *comendadores* portrayed by

Lope de Vega), was fully as harsh as that of the *encomenderos* over the Indians in the Americas.[17]

  While this long battle was being fought, the explorers were discovering new lands and searching for many more that belonged to the chimerical geography of the Middle Ages and survived in the credulous minds of navigators: the country of the Amazons; El Dorado, the country of the Golden King; the enchanted City of the Caesars, where the only metal to be had was silver, and houses were made of it; the site of the fountain of perpetual youth. Both the real explorations and the visionary quests gave a new impulse to that European literature of "extraordinary voyages," of which the first great modern example is found in Rabelais.[18]

Then Mexico and Peru were discovered and conquered. At last, Columbus' venture proved a success. In an incredibly short time, the two vast and opulent empires fell into the hands of Spain. The European mind, which was devoting so much attention to the reports about savage tribes, was not yet ready to understand those strange and magnificent civilizations, even after reading many extensive and precise descriptions of their cities and customs; it only drew a chaotic impression of wealth, power, multitudes of men, not the revelation of new types of culture. Charles V, for example, seems to have been indifferent to the rare beauty of the Inca jewels chosen for him by the Pizarros. Even the much later *Royal Commentaries* of the Inca Garcilaso (1609) were very slow in producing their effect. It was only in the eighteenth century, after the discovery of Chinese culture, that an interpretation of Mexico and Peru was attempted. The Spaniards who took part in the conquests and saw the two empires in their full splendor were never in doubt as to the magnitude of their civilizations — there is ample proof in the writings of Cortés, Bernal Díaz del Castillo, Francisco de Jerez, Cieza de León, as well as in chroniclers like Sahagún, who saw only the ruins of the glorious past.

But this was the result of immediate experience and seemed to be incommunicable to Europe.[19]

The European thinkers and writers of the sixteenth century did not read the accounts of discoveries and voyages in search of new forms of culture which might be contrasted with their own. Their main concern was Nature. Columbus, Vespucci, Peter Martyr, Las Casas, had informed them about savages who lived in a "natural state," in an age of innocence. The philosophical opposition between nature and culture, the comparison between the natural man and the civilized man, feeds on the inexhaustible material provided by the New World. It persists and grows more and more complex through the centuries.

In Spain the Indian is seldom mentioned in this connection; to defend him would have meant at least a theoretical rejection of the Conquest, and the authorities would probably have frowned upon such an attitude after the controversy started by the Dominican friars had been settled by legal provisions.[20] The Indian appears, then, only as a picturesque exotic figure in such works as Tirso de Molina's trilogy of the Pizarros, where the Amazons are introduced — a surprising bit of fancy for a poet who had actually lived in the New World. Could he really believe, like Spenser, that "the Amazons' great river" had "proved true"? On the whole, the Americas occupy much less space in Spanish (and Portuguese) literature than might have been expected.

Even while the controversy about the Indian was on, the Spanish humanists did not look to the savage as the embodiment of nature in opposition to culture; they looked, instead, to the peasant, either laborer or shepherd, in accordance with the classical tradition — for example, Antonio de Guevara, in his *Dial of Princes* (1528), with its famous tale of the Danubian rustic, and in his *Scorn of the Court and Praise of the Village* (1539). The dream of a perfect and simple life, a sort of utopianism that assumes a wide variety of shapes, pervades Spanish literature in the sixteenth century, from Juan and Alfonso de Valdés to Friar Luis de León. When the Renaissance faded away and the prosaic, typically modern era began, Lope de Vega, a city-born poet, who loved the pomp of cities, felt also the fascination of country life and frequently opposed the simple and heroic virtues of the peasant to the proud tyranny of the nobleman and the scheming duplicity of the courtier. At times he ventured farther, and we hear the familiar motif of the golden age when he introduced savages in such plays as *The Guanches of Tenerife, The New World,* and *Arauco Subjugated.* With dramatic impartiality, Lope makes the savages defend their rights with arguments that Las Casas would have approved. Cervantes, too, who entertains no delusions as to the perfections of modern society and regretfully looks back towards the medieval ideal of chivalry and the Renaissance ideal of learning, now and then turns his eyes towards the golden age, as in the famous speech of Don Quixote when resting in the company of the goatherds. And Quevedo, a bitter censor of his times, writes in praise of More's *Utopia,* translated into Spanish by his friend Jerónimo de Medinilla (1627). Finally, Gracián presents in his *Criticón* (1651–1657) a "natural man" in accordance with the model invented by the Spanish Arab of the twelfth century, Aben Tofail, in his *Self-Taught Philosopher.* Gracián's Andrenio knows no society, not even that of savages, and no speech; after Critilo teaches him to speak, he shows that in his solitude he had discovered the highest and simplest religious and moral principles. Andrenio's desert island was not placed by Gracián in the New World (was it by design?) but near Africa — it is Saint Helena.

In France the Indians were discussed with greater freedom. The French had met with little or no success in their first colonial ventures. André Thévet, who came to Brazil with Villegaignon's expedition (1555), in his *Singularities of Antarctic France* (1558) describes the Indians, with more pity than anger, as "marvellously strange and savage people, with no faith, no law, no religion, no civility whatever, living like irrational beasts just as nature has

produced them." But Jean de Léry, who also accompanied Villegaignon, feels moved to ask whether many of our reasons for
despising savages are not simply prejudices, and even confesses
that their nudity is chaste — a daring thought for a Calvinist
theologian. And Jodelle, who wrote a laudatory poem for Thévet's book, remarks that if barbarism exists in Rio de Janeiro,
"the Antarctic France," it exists also, under another guise, in his
own "Arctic France." Ronsard, commenting upon Villegaignon's
expedition in his *Discourse Against Fortune* (1559), condemns
all conquests and all attempts to impose European civilization
upon savages. The Indians live in a golden age; why teach them
"the terror of the law which makes us live in fear"? Let them live
happily; "I should like to live thus."

The discussion reaches its highest point with Montaigne, in two
famous essays — one on cannibals, the other on carriages — and
in many scattered remarks. Montaigne carries the criticism of
European civilization, as compared with the savage state, to its
extreme consequences. He had read a number of chronicles of
travels and conquests; he had, besides, held converse with travellers, sailors, merchants, and even with Brazilian savages taken
to Rouen during the reign of Charles IX.[21] "I finde," he says in
his essay *On Cannibals* (I, 30),

> there is nothing in that nation that is either barbarous or
> savage, unlesse men call that barbarisme which is not com-
> mon to them. . . . They are even savage as we call those
> fruits wilde which nature of her selfe and of her ordinarie
> progresse hath produced: whereas indeed they are those
> which our selves have altered by our artificiall devices and
> diverted from their common order we should rather term
> savage. In those are the true and most profitable vertues
> and naturall properties most lively and vigorous, which in
> these we have bastardized, applying them to the pleasure of
> our corrupted taste.[22]

And later: "It is a nation that hath no kind of traffike, no knowledge of Letters, no intelligence of numbers, no name of magis-

trate, nor of politike superioritie; no use of service, of riches or of
povertie; no contracts, no successions, no partitions, no occupation
but idle; no respect of kinred, but common, no apparell but nat-
urall, no manuring of lands, no use of wine, corne, or mettle."
Shakespeare, it is well known, adopted this passage in *The Tem-
pest*, a play so full of echoes from books of travel, to describe
Gonzalo's utopian commonwealth (Utopia again!):

> No kind of traffic
> Would I admit; no name of magistrate;
> Letters should not be known; riches, poverty,
> And use of service, none; contract, succession,
> Bourn, bound of land, tilth, vineyard, none;
> No use of metal, corn, or wine, or oil;
> No occupation; all men idle, all;
> And women too, — but innocent and pure;
> No sovereignty. . . .

"The very words," Montaigne goes on to say, "that import lying,
falshood, treason, dissimulations, covetousnes, envie, detraction,
and pardon, were never heard of amongst them" — as, later, they
were unknown amongst Aphra Behn's Caribs of Surinam or
amongst Swift's Houyhnhnms. It is true they eat human flesh,
but "I am not sorie we note the barbarous horror of such an action,
but grieved that prying so narrowly into their faults we are so
blinded in ours." In fact, "we may call them barbarous in regard
to reasons rules, but not in respect of us that exceed them in all
kinde of barbarisme." The defense of the savage, we see, benefits
not only the peaceful tribes, like the Tainos found by Columbus
in the Antilles; it boldly includes the man-eaters also. And Montaigne, leaving no problem untouched, not even the economic
organization of European society, relates that when he spoke to
the Brazilian savages in Rouen they told him "they had perceived
there were men amongst us full gorged with all sortes of com-
modities, and others which, hunger-starved, and bare with need
and povertie, begged at their gates: and found it strange these

moyties so needy could endure such an injustice, and that they tooke not the others by the throte, or set fire on their houses."

In his essay *On Carriages* (III, 6), or *coaches*, as Florio called them, he says: "Our world hath of late discovered another. . . . It was an unpolluted, harmlesse world." He condemns, in the manner of Las Casas, the European invasion: "the richest, the fairest and the best part of the world, topsiturvied, ruined and defaced for the traffick of Pearles and Pepper. Oh mechanicall victories, oh base conquest!" And he realizes — he is one of the first few men to do so in Europe — that there were great civilizations in the Americas when the Spaniards came. These civilizations he praises as very few men have done before the twentieth century: "Nor Grece, nor Rome, nor Aegipt, can (bee it in profit, or difficultie, or nobility) equal or compare sundrie or divers of their workes." But, with the foreboding that civilizations are mortal (according to M. Paul Valéry's dictum), he says: "And, as wee doe, so judged they that this Universe was neare his end: and tooke the desolation wee brought amongst them as an infallible sign of it." And he ventures a startling prophecy: "This late-world shall but come to light when ours shall fall into darknesse."

Montaigne's meditations show the trend of future developments.[23] During the two following centuries, the Americas do not hold a very prominent place in French imaginative literature, in spite of Voltaire's *Alzire* (1736) and *L'Ingénu* (1767), Marmontel's *Les Incas* (1777), and Florian's *Camiré*; nor, for the matter of that, in English literature, in spite of Dryden's *Indian Emperor* (1665) — Dryden, by the way, seems to have invented the expression "noble savage" in his *Conquest of Granada* (1670). But the literature of travel and description of new lands grows steadily, and the names of many French explorers are still familiar to us: Champlain, Lescarbot, Claude d'Abbeville, Yves d'Evreux, Mocquet, Sagard, Lejeune, Brébeuf, Du Tertre, Marquette, Hennepin, Lahontan, Charlevoix. After them, La Condamine and Bougainville have a strictly scientific outlook.

All these books described the life of the Indians, and the judgments of the authors often followed Montaigne's tradition. Whether favorable or unfavorable to the savages, they gave fresh nourishment to avid philosophical thought. In the eighteenth century, the European mind was at last taking possession of the earth and surveying mankind from China to Peru. We know how the old quarrel about nature and culture became then a passionate contention. Diderot and Raynal, without renouncing the benefits of European culture, expressed a deep sympathy for oppressed peoples; Voltaire, like Dr. Johnson in England, was actively in favor of civilized life and contemptuous of the virtues attributed to savages; Rousseau, on the opposite side, is the great denier of European civilization, although his "natural men" have only a negative superiority, due to the lack of incitements to evil in their environment — they are neither wolves, as in Hobbes, nor lambs, as in Locke, two of the masters who taught him the doctrine of the social contract. Rousseau's ideal is not the savage but the man who, like his Emile, is brought up in harmony with the dictates of nature. And that was the light which led, along one road, to the romantic conception of life and art, along another, to social and political revolution.[24] More generous than any of his forerunners, Condorcet, shortly before his death on the guillotine, asserted in his *Outline of the Progress of the Human Spirit* (1794) his unconquerable faith in the future and proposed to the civilized nations a plan for the peaceful enlightenment of backward peoples.

The dispute about nature and culture ran through the nineteenth century and still goes on. To single out a conspicuous example: D. H. Lawrence, weary of the many repressions that stifle the soul in civilized communities, tried to go back to the true life through the road of essential emotions and communion with primitive nature. In *The Plumed Serpent*, his "natural man" is a visionary Indian who, incongruously enough, tries to revive the spirit of the old and complex Mexican culture that existed before the Spanish conquest. But it is significant that his many critics, as a rule, do not defend Western civilization, of which they themselves have drawn acidly satirical pictures (e.g., Mr. Aldous Huxley in *Point Counter Point*, where Lawrence is portrayed); they merely point out that the return to nature through contact with savages or with peasants is nothing but a delusion.

From another point of view, the modern "diffusionist" theory of culture gives us a new image of primitive man as free from both the advantages and the disadvantages of civilization: "Natural Man," says Mr. G. Elliot Smith, "displays no innate desire to build houses or to make clothes, to till the soil or to domesticate animals. He has neither religion nor social organization. . . . Organized warfare, brutality, and most kinds of violent behavior are due to the circumstances of civilization and are not found among really primitive peoples." [25]

Besides giving Europe so much matter for speculation and fancy, the Americas gave it many new words and things. The explorers, on their return, carried the words. As early as 1493, Columbus and his companions spoke of the Indian canoes, and Nebrija, the great humanist, immediately recorded the term (*canoa*). New words appeared also in the writings of the innumerable chroniclers and in the poems of Ercilla, Juan de Castellanos, Eugenio de Salazar, and Juan de la Cueva.[26] Many spread to the whole world and were adopted even in very remote languages: tobacco, potato, maize, hammock, savannah, cannibal, from the Taino of the Antilles; hurricane, from the Quiche of Yucatán through the Antilles; pirogue, manatee, from the Carib; cocoa, chocolate, chicle, tomato, tamale, coyote, from the Nahuatl of Mexico; quinine (derived from *quina*), alpaca, guano, pampa, from the Quechua of Peru; coca, from the Aymara of what is now Bolivia; ipecac, from the Guarani of Brazil and Paraguay. It is astonishing to find that at least one of the words, *aje*, which appears constantly in the first chroniclers from Columbus to Bernabé

Cobo, now represents nothing; no one today is sure which plant it was; there are only opinions.[27]

And then the things themselves, both living and inert things, that transformed economic life. Above all, the metals, "the most important cause of the price revolution [in Europe] of the sixteenth and seventeenth centuries."[28] The Indies, Peru, Potosi, Xauxa, become in Spain household words for wealth. In England, as Virginia Woolf says, in her beautiful essay *The Elizabethan Lumber Room*, "we find the whole Elizabethan literature strewn with gold and silver; with talk of Guiana's rarities, and references to that America — 'O my America! my new-found-land' — which was not merely a land on the map, but symbolized the unknown territories of the soul." And there were the precious stones, the birds, the plants, whether for food, medicine, building, ornament, or recreation. The now humble root of the sweet potato was once one of the most prized delicacies on European tables, as many Spanish and Portuguese writings prove, and when Falstaff dreams of a sumptuous reception for one of the ladies of Windsor he exclaims: "Let the sky rain potatoes!" Every one knows the story of the lowly beginnings from which the white potato rose to its present tyrannical position. The story of tobacco is no less picturesque — let it only be remembered that the early Spanish settlers on the Antilles felt unspeakable horror when they first saw the Indians smoking.

A few of the animals and plants of the Americas have adapted themselves so well to new lands and climates that their true origin is at times forgotten. The opulent but insatiable Orient has, even in name, appropriated the turkey (which Europeans taught the Turks to raise) and maize, the Indian corn, which the Italians call Turkish grain, *granturco*. Victor Hugo was deceived by the transference, and in the poem on the stele of Mesa, "Inscription," in the *Légende des Siècles*, he attributes fields of maize to Chaldea. Flaubert, after all his archaeological pains to give in *Salammbô* a flawless reconstruction of Carthage, inadvertently adorns the

African landscape with our thorny cactus, which is a newcomer there. Today we must attribute to whimsical humor M. Jean Giraudoux's ancient Greek tomatoes in his *Electra*.

Our plants and birds have been adopted by European pictorial art from the earliest times — witness Raphael's cartoons for tapestries. The cactus, after it was transplanted to the Old World, soon began to appear in pictures of the life of Christ, with the arid landscape of the Holy Land as a background. Ornamental figures of savages, too, are introduced in architecture — for instance, the giants armed with clubs in the College of Saint Gregory at Valladolid. Columbus expected to find the site of the Terrestrial Paradise in his voyages,[29] and in 1498 he even thought, after exploring the northern coast of South America, that "the land whence he came is a great continent where the Terrestrial Paradise is located"; Vespucci thought it could not lie very far from Northern Brazil; after them, many men seem to have thought that the plants and birds of tropical America must have existed in the lost home of our first parents. Thus, Skelton calls the parrot "a bird of Paradise." [30] When Rubens copied Titian's painting of Adam and Eve in the Garden of Eden, he introduced among the trees a macaw, a flaming red parrot. Comparing Titian's original with Rubens' copy, it has been remarked, we see how the art of the Renaissance passes into the baroque. Very appropriately, the symbol of that momentous change in the history of art is a bird from the fantastic forests of tropical America.

2

THE CREATION OF A NEW SOCIETY
1492–1600

THE CONQUEST and settlement of the New World by the two
Hispanic nations gave rise to a new society, probably unlike
any that had been seen before and certainly never equaled in
the magnitude of its territory.[1] Its structural lines were traditional and familiar: on the one hand there were the conquerors,
and on the other, the conquered peoples. As usual, the conquered
were expected to work for the conquerors. The fate of the Indians
had been sealed as early as 1500 by a generous decision of Queen
Isabella in accordance with old Roman principles — they were
not to be enslaved; they were to become vassals. The queen's
decision was reinforced afterwards by a series of laws which
were the outcome of the great controversies of the sixteenth
century. In practice, the Indians were often exploited as serfs
(the custom has not died down as yet); but their legal status
was clear.[2] They had to work under the *encomenderos* to whom
they were assigned, or, if they lived under their old chiefs, the
caciques, they had to pay a fixed tribute to the crown. They
were to be taught the rudiments of Christianity and of European
culture; a selected minority were to receive college education, beginning with Latin.[3] The Inquisition was not allowed to institute
any prosecution against them; their errors in the interpretation of
the Faith were to be condoned as due to mere ignorance. If they
were often oppressed by greedy masters, they were also pro-
tected and defended — now and then by conscientious government officials, and much more frequently by the priests, especially

the members of the monastic orders, who wished to make persuasion do the work of fear.

It is mostly from such protectors that we learn of the abuses of which they were the victims. The efforts of the priests in behalf of the Indians make an extraordinary story of devotion, courage, and self-sacrifice. The campaigns of Friar Pedro de Córdoba and Friar Antón de Montesinos established an evangelical tradition for the Order of Saint Dominic in the New World. Las Casas himself joined the Order in 1523, after several years of secular priesthood, and kept up the tradition, together with such energetic preachers and organizers as Friar Tomás de Berlanga, Friar Domingo de Betanzos, and Friar Pedro de Angulo. But the members of the Franciscan Order were the first men from Europe who taught in the New World; they began about 1505 in Hispaniola. In Mexico they were known for their charity and humility, especially Friar Pedro de Gante (ca. 1479–1572), who founded the first school (1523), and Friar Toribio de Benavente (d. 1568), whom the natives nicknamed Motolinía, "the poor little one." Friar Juan de Zumárraga (d. 1548), the eminent first Archbishop of Mexico, devoted much of his energy and intelligence to the education of the Indians. Vasco de Quiroga (ca. 1470–1565), the bishop of Michoacan, organized his flock by villages, each with its own handicraft and the lands held in communal ownership; he drew his inspiration from More's *Utopia*.[4] Two of the priests who devoted their lives to the welfare of the natives of South America have become saints in the Catholic Church: the Franciscan Friar Francisco Solano (1549–1610)[5] and the Archbishop of Lima, Toribio Alfonso de Mogrovejo (1534–1606). And the work of the Jesuits in Paraguay is well known — how they organized a theocratic society, in which there was no division of property and the Guarani were taught to work and pray, to build and paint, to sing and dance, and even to print books from wooden type made by themselves. But the Jesuits forgot to choose and educate leaders from among the native population, and when they were suddenly expelled from all the Spanish dominions (1767) their work crumbled away and soon the very churches they had built were in ruins; this disaster, however, was partly due to the maladministration of the officials who replaced the Society.[6]

The natives of the Greater Antilles and the Bahamas, the peaceful Tainos, were decimated and reduced to a remnant which slowly dissolved through interbreeding. In one of his few poetic moments, Las Casas tells how he had seen the islands thronging with multitudes of men and how, thirty or forty years afterwards, they seemed empty — at times, he says, I think I must have dreamed. The causes of that strange ethnic tragedy have yet to be made clear. Neither the cruelty of the conquerors nor the plagues they brought with them from Europe seem more than partial explanations. Was there a race suicide? Both Las Casas and Oviedo give us reasons to make us believe it. Life probably did not seem worth living after the old happiness vanished, the golden age in which Columbus found them. Meanwhile, in the Southern Antilles, the warlike Caribs were mostly exterminated or deported. In all the other countries the Indian accepted the rule of the conqueror, although there were sporadic revolts; only in Chile and Argentina did he survive as a permanent menace to the Spanish-speaking population until nearly the end of the nineteenth century.

Brazil did not seem to present very great problems to the Portuguese. The Indians were rather few; they retreated before the invaders, or fought against them — with no great persistence — or submitted to them. In the diffusion of Christianity the Society of Jesus had the cardinal role. A Brazilian historian, Ronald de Carvalho, says that "the Jesuit worked with refined wisdom, instructing the Indians in Christianity, subduing them through gentleness or through force to the discipline of religion, and preventing their enslavement by the *maganos of Portugal.*" Another historian, Pedro Calmon, thinks that "the rural college of the Society was the first organized *fazenda* in the country, the first rational enterprise, the first attempt at a methodical exploration of natural resources." And the Jesuits compelled the Indians to adopt Guarani as a common language, a *lingoa geral*, above the Babel of native tongues: a language that became, according to the brilliant sociologist Gilberto Freyre, "one of the most solid foundations of the unity of Brazil."[7]

There were also slaves, brought at first from Europe — a number of whom were white — and afterwards, in great masses, from Africa. They, too, found protectors, such as the Catalan Jesuit Pedro Claver (1580–1654), the apostle of New Granada, now a saint of the Catholic Church like Toribio de Mogrovejo and Francisco Solano. Las Casas, who at first had tolerated black slavery as a means of saving the Indians, repented afterwards, saying he had come to realize that the Portuguese, the first exploiters of the African slave traffic, were just as cruel in enslaving the natives of the dark continent as the Spaniards in subjecting the natives of the Americas. Slavery subsisted until it was abolished during the wars of independence or not long after; but there were abolitionists in colonial times, such as the Jesuit Diego de Avendaño in Peru, and Antonio Vieira and Manoel Ribeiro Rocha in Brazil.[8]

The new society so constituted is often described as governed by a rigid code of customs and a no less rigid set of laws. Such a description does not seem to me quite faithful to the facts. Nominally, the social structure was a hierarchy built on aristocratic principles. The principles were there, but their application was not strict. The laws, as we have seen in connection with the Indians, were frequently violated. And the legislation that governed economic activities was often so ill-conceived and so inimical to the development of natural resources and to the fulfillment of common desires, that its violation became a necessity. In trade, contraband became normal, including the circulation of forbidden books. Even after independence, contraband remained for many years one of our typical customs. There remained, in fact, a general and enduring discrepancy between the law and actual life.[9]

Nor were social rules any more strictly observed. In Spain itself there was little rigidity outside the court of the Hapsburg monarchs. The Spaniard has always shown a tendency to be a law unto himself. Every Spaniard, says Unamuno, feels equal to the king, "though with less money" — *dineros menos*. The last centuries of the Middle Ages are filled with the loud noise of the strife between the noble and the plebeian, the king usually siding with the poor in order to break the power of the lords. The very Spaniards, either plebeians or impoverished gentry, who had seen and perhaps contrived the downfall of the power of the nobility, flocked to the newly discovered lands. There was no real transplantation of the traditional class divisions, rather a new division of social groups: racial discriminations appeared as a sequel to the legal slavery of the negroes and the virtual serfdom of the Indians, but without the sharp cleavage that has made the "color line" a seemingly insoluble problem in the United States. Interbreeding gave rise to a curious subdivision of castes that eventually received a sort of legal sanction, but, as a modern writer remarks, interbreeding itself, by its persistence, naturally tended to destroy the very discriminations that had sprung from it, making them purely nominal.[10] When independence was proclaimed, not only were they abolished by law, but they gradually lost all weight in custom.

Thus, the new society of Hispanic America now and then fell back into medieval ways which were already disappearing in Europe, but on the whole it was in a fluid condition, because of the frequent changes in people's fortunes, their mobility, and their adaptation to new circumstances. There was a constant flux and reflux between Spain and her colonies, a general movement of society brought forth by the new possibilities of travel and gain, and all this helped to break down old social rules on both sides of the ocean.[11] Any man who had taken part in the Conquest, any man who grew rich after it, felt entitled to whatever distinctions might be granted him — he might not even wait for the grant.

In the sixteenth century, it became the custom in Spain to call any woman of decent behavior and not too humble station a lady — the title of *Doña* might precede her Christian name. It was only in the seventeenth century that the privilege of using the title of *Don*, formerly accorded to the nobility alone, was accorded to the men. But in the Americas the custom began quite early. Any man who held Indians in *encomienda*, for instance, was likely to assume the title. From a letter of Saint Theresa, dated 1576, we learn that when her brother Lorenzo de Cepeda (d. 1580) returned to Spain from Quito, with great wealth, after thirty-four years of absence, he let himself be called *Don*, as he was wont to do in America. Since the Cepeda family belonged to the gentry, not the nobility, this act of Lorenzo was a matter of much gossip in the provincial society of Avila, and the Saint herself was grieved by such vanity and presumption that bordered on usurpation. Imagine Mr. Carnegie returning to Scotland as Sir Andrew, self-styled! Again in the early seventeenth century, one of the signs of madness of Cervantes' hero is that he changes his name from plain Alonso Quijano to Don Quixote. Significantly enough, in Spain one of the first recorded cases of the use of *Don* by a man well born but with no clear right to it is that of the Mexican poet Juan Ruiz de Alarcón.

Even in grave matters of nationality and religion the royal decrees were disregarded. At first, only the subjects of the Queen of Castile were allowed passage to the New World; but, by hook or by crook, the subjects of her astute husband, the King of Aragon, frequently obtained passage too. Foreigners were barred, but they came, either by special permission or by stealth. To name a single example: one of the conquerors of Peru was a

Greek, Pedro de Candía, born in El Greco's own island. The Jews — real or feigned *conversos* — were thousands, the Protestants not a few. Many converted Moors came also in the sixteenth century: two hundred of them took part in the conquest of Peru. There is record even of a Mohammedan Turk, who went back to his native country a rich man.[12] If matters went thus in the Spanish domains, in Brazil they were still easier, since the colonial legislation of Portugal was far less stringent than that of Spain. The country was open to all foreigners, provided they were Catholics; and their orthodoxy was not minutely scrutinized.[13]

And so, although the social structure was formally aristocratic and there were many theoretical discriminations of class or caste, exceptions and irregularities were common. The Church, of course, made no such distinctions.[14] The usual divisions came from wealth and education, as they still do.[15] Although the settlers might see fit to exploit the Indian whenever they found it profitable, we know they came to feel that he was a man like themselves. During the first hundred years the European often took to himself an Indian wife, by marriage or otherwise; the oldest families were so begun, the aristocracy not excepted — several conquerors married ladies of Inca or Aztec royal blood. Intermarriage of the different races was not forbidden.[16] Men fully or partly of Indian race became writers and artists of distinction during the colonial period. Ruy Díaz de Guzmán, or Juan de Espinosa Medrano, or Miguel Cabrera may serve as examples. A few displayed with pride their Indian names — the Inca Garcilaso de la Vega, Juan Zapata Inga (i.e., Inca), Tito Cusi Yupanqui (heir to the Inca throne, who also bore the Spanish name of Diego de Castro), Hernando Alvarado Tezozómoc (a son of the Aztec emperor Cuitláhuac), Fernando de Alba Ixtlilxóchitl (a descendant of the kings of Texcoco), Felipe Huaman Poma de Ayala. The display was really excessive in the case of Juan de Santa Cruz Pachacuti Yamqui Salcamayhua and Domingo Francisco de San Antón Muñoz Chimalpahin Quauhtlehuanitzin.[17] In fact, any Indians who had belonged to, or were descended from, the native ruling classes were entitled to respectful treatment and received the title of *Don* in colonial documents. Among the Portuguese of Brazil, the absence of deep social and racial prejudices seems to have been still more common than in the Spanish colonies. And such prejudices as did exist dwindled or disappeared — at least as much as in the most unprejudiced community anywhere else — once independence was achieved and they lacked the support of legal precept. However, it would be a delusion to imagine that the Conquest was anything but a tragedy for the natives. Only a minority escaped subjection, and the benefits they reaped from education were usually scanty. The men who achieved distinction in intellectual or artistic pursuits may seem many in number, but they are only scattered exceptions among the submerged millions. With the Conquest, as Justo Sierra says, "a spiritual slumber of the Indian race begins."

Not all the countries were similar in their social development. There were the countries in which the mines were the foundation of wealth and the countries in which the basis was agriculture, or cattle, or even industries, such as the sugar industry in Brazil. There was a vast difference between populous and opulent cities like Mexico or Lima, equal or superior to Toledo, Madrid, or Seville, with a large leisure class of a decidedly aristocratic tone, and cities that throve on sea trade and rose to prominence only in the eighteenth century, like Havana and Buenos Aires — the capital of Argentina is described by López and Mitre as a mercantile democracy.[18] There were cities of the Bostonian type, where the Church and the University took the lead, as in Córdoba of Argentina, or Charcas, the Sucre of modern Bolivia, or Santo Domingo, once "the Athens of the New World," in Hispaniola. Learning counted for so much in that former "capital of the Caribbean" that in the seventeenth century a man of African blood, Tomás Rodríguez de Sosa, who had been born a slave and was freed by his master, became a renowned theologian and orator — according to an official report from the archbishop Francisco Pío de Guadalupe y Téllez, he was often invited by the Spanish president and judges of the Real Audiencia to preach in their private chapel.

José Ortega y Gasset maintained in a recent lecture at Buenos Aires (1939) that the Spaniard — and the same thing may be said of the Portuguese — became a new man as soon as he settled in the New World. The change did not require centuries; it was immediate. The march of time only served to reinforce it. The Englishman, says the distinguished Colombian writer Sanín Cano, is eminent for his ability to settle in the most diverse lands without adapting himself to them — a shining example of Gourmont's "insurrection of the vertebrates." But the Spaniard readily responds to his environment. Not that he did not choose, having so much from which to choose in the Americas. He naturally shunned the deserts and the hot, thick, tropical forests; he shunned the bitter cold of the Northern lands and of Patagonia, and even, at first, the mild chill of Buenos Aires, where the conqueror Irala, writing to the king in 1545, complains that "the land is very cold." If we look at a climatic map of this hemisphere, we soon discover that most of the territory where Spanish is spoken consists of high table-lands between mountain ranges, like enlarged reproductions of Castile. But all sorts of territories were explored — witness the tragic journey of Álvar Núñez Cabeza de Vaca from Florida to the Pacific coast of Mexico. The Spaniard, to be sure, succeeded in settling many tropical areas — the islands of the Caribbean Archipelago, the coasts of Mexico and Central America, of Venezuela and the countries now called Colombia and Ecuador, the inland plains of Paraguay; he eventually accustomed himself to Uruguay and to what is now the central portion of Argentina; he even occupied the dry lands from Texas

to California. But the largest part of the truly tropical lands fell
to the Portuguese.

The Spaniards and the Portuguese brought to the New World
their own culture, their religion and their laws, their literature
and their art, their science and their industries, their plants and
their domestic animals, thus modifying the environment and
the native life and producing a fusion and mutual interchange
of influences. For, at the same time, they adapted themselves to
the Indian, while they taught him European ideas and customs.
They learned to eat his food and to cook it in his fashion; to
enjoy his drinks and to use his medicinal herbs; they learned
from him to smoke, to make and use his canoes and pirogues,
his pottery, his fabrics, his hammocks; they adopted his methods
of hunting wild animals, his system of protecting crops on a slope
by dividing the land into terraces. They used his roads and
canals. They took hundreds of words from his many languages;
furthermore, as Cuervo has shown, from early times they gave
new meanings to old Spanish words, in keeping with new needs
— such words as *estancia*, which became the name for large
landed estates.[19] In short, the native cultures were decapitated,
and all the "higher learning" of the Indians disappeared — even
the ability to read the Aztec and Maya codices — but the common
techniques of everyday life survived and blended with the
European. At the same time, not a few of the Spaniards and
Portuguese undertook the task of studying the Indian tongues.
For the missionaries this was a labor of love, which produced a
vast and wonderful collection of grammars, dictionaries, readers,
and catechistic works. Some of the most important languages
were taught, mainly for priests, in theological seminaries and in
universities — as in Mexico and in Lima.

The Indian — the sedentary Indian, at least — gave a peculiar
tone to the new society of the Americas. In spite of the instinctive
belief in human equality which is typical of Hispanic people,
there was a greater distance between master and servant when

the servant scarcely spoke Spanish or Portuguese and hardly understood European customs. And yet Indian habits influenced the whole body of society. Indian courtesy and reserve, for example, pervade the life of Mexico and Peru to this day. In Brazil and in Cuba, besides, the African slaves made a distinct contribution to common life.[20]

In several ways, people in the colonies did not enjoy as much freedom of movement as they had in Europe. Besides the legal restrictions on economic activities, there was rigorous control of public order. The danger of political disturbances was ever present, from both *criollo* and Indian sources. The first period of the Conquest had been at times anarchical. There were dissensions among the early settlers in Hispaniola; there were troubles in Mexico, which only the energy and tact of Cortés managed to overcome; the conquest of Peru degenerated into bloody civil war. Many conquerors were suspected of disloyalty to the crown — there was everywhere a natural temptation to break the allegiance. And in private life there was as much turmoil. The authorities, therefore, soon decided to keep order by means of stern police ordinances. While men in Spain or Portugal moved about freely at all times of the day and, according to Madame d'Aulnoy's rather fanciful report, three hundred duels were fought every night in Madrid under Charles II, in the colonies all controllable activities were kept within tight bounds.

The essential weakness of this society lay in its latent disorganization. It was held together mainly by the external force of the distant European governments. The political rights of the colonists were very limited. The relations of the Spaniards and the Portuguese with the Indians were spontaneously human, but they were anarchical, and their relations with the African slaves even more so. As a consequence, the customs of the poorer classes were disorganized, save where isolated native tribes or "forgotten villages" preserved their ancient ways of life. Social ascent for men of ability was mostly a matter of chance. Only the cultured groups had real and permanent standards and traditions. It was they who succeeded in preserving and furthering civilization through their effort and example, even though they were blind to the evils they brought upon society with this conduct toward the subject groups. The great problem of Hispanic America was — and still is — social integration.[21]

However, that originally heterogeneous society of Hispanic America eventually produced a new type of man, a predominant type, although not general as yet — "the new man," *o homen novo* of the sociologist Euclides da Cunha; "the new autochthonous man," *el nuevo indígena* of the poet José Joaquín Pérez. It is not a race, of course, nor even a particular racial mixture, but the result of many generations of men of different origins living together under similar conditions. The result, as Ricardo Rojas puts it, not of an *ethnos*, but of an *ethos*. Bolívar had already remarked on it: "We differ," he said, "from all the other varieties of the human species." And when he said "we" he thought, as usual, of all Hispanic America.

In colonial times, strange as it may sound to unsuspecting ears, one of the guiding principles of that society, after religion, was intellectual and artistic culture. It was the crown of social life, just as sanctity was the crown of individual life. That culture was not progressive — it was based on authority, not on experiment — and it was not based on popular education, as the modern ideal requires; Charles Péguy remarks that the ideal of popular education did not emerge for the peoples who live within the Latin tradition until the French Revolution. But it was in no way aristocratic; learning was practically — though not nominally — within reach of all that might aspire to it, only it was not expected that all would aspire, and much less was it conceived that knowledge should be imposed upon all. Music, painting, and sculpture, especially, were often taught to people of very humble station.[22]

Spain gave to her colonies as complete an organization of

culture as she had herself. Not so Portugal: perhaps because Brazil was so much nearer to Lisbon than most of the Spanish dominions were to Spain, institutions of higher learning, if theological seminaries are excepted, were not established in the vast colonies, and most Brazilians of note went to Coimbra for their studies. But in the Spanish possessions, as soon as the new settlements became towns and cities of the European type, schools were founded, both for *criollos* and for Indians.[23] Before the city of Santo Domingo, in Hispaniola, was fifty years old, it had two universities: in 1538, by a bull of Pope Paul III, the college of the Order of Saint Dominic became the University of Santo Tomás de Aquino, with privileges similar to those of Salamanca and Alcalá de Henares (the friars had probably begun to teach in their monastery shortly after their arrival in 1510); in 1540, a royal decree of Charles V authorized the erection of the University of Santiago de la Paz, with funds granted by a wealthy settler from Estremadura, Hernando de Gorjón (d. 1547), its basis being a college founded before 1530 by the active bishop Sebastián Ramírez de Fuenleal. In 1551, the Emperor created two great universities, in Mexico and Lima, the only ones that became official crown institutions.[24] New ones were established at Bogotá (1580), Quito (1586), Cuzco (1598), Charcas (1624), Córdoba del Tucuman, Huamanga (1677), Guatemala (1687), Caracas (1725), Havana (1728), and Santiago de Chile (1738). A few more colleges aspired to the category of universities and even obtained it for a time; the privilege was often disputed between two monastic orders — in Quito, in Bogotá, and even in Córdoba there were for a time rival institutions. The leading universities had the four traditional schools of the Middle Ages — the Arts, Theology, Law, and Medicine. The medieval tradition prevailed in them, as in the universities of Spain, and after the first century it was only by exception that they opened their doors to modern learning. When the colonies heard of Galileo or Descartes or Harvey or Locke or Condillac, it was as a rule through individual researches or even, paradoxically enough, through the independent theological seminaries. Modern science was first introduced in the colonies by free private initiative, and only in the latter half of the eighteenth century did it come through such official channels as the research expeditions paid by the royal treasury (which is said to have spent two million francs on three botanical expeditions) or through special institutions like the Mexican School of Mines (1792), which counted among its faculty the Basque chemist Fausto de Elhúyar (1757–1833), the discoverer of tungsten, and Andrés del Río (1765–1849), the discoverer of vanadium and a pioneer in geology and paleontology. By the end of the century, however, the crown was not as liberal as it had been before and refused its approval to several projects for new institutions of learning.

Printing was introduced into Mexico around 1535 (the earliest book extant bears the date of 1539); into Peru, in 1584. During the seventeenth century it appeared in Guatemala (1660), and, according to the American historian Isaiah Thomas, in Santo Domingo, where books were certainly printed in the century following. Later dates are 1703 for Argentina and Paraguay (the printing plants of the Indians in the Jesuit Missions), 1707 for Cuba, 1739 for New Granada, 1754 for Ecuador, 1780 for Chile, 1806 for Venezuela, 1807 for Uruguay and for Puerto Rico. Brazil, again, lags behind, although its colonial literature is far from scanty; printing appears there at the beginning of the nineteenth century — a clandestine press had existed before, but it was suppressed (1706). Books, however, real books to be read and not mere school texts or devotional pamphlets or government publications, were printed only in the two viceregal cities, Mexico and Lima, at least until the last years of the colonial era.

Before 1600, news sheets were occasionally printed in Mexico and in Lima — the first vague attempts at newspapers, before most European cities had them. Such news sheets became frequent in the next century. In the eighteenth century several periodicals were published in the Mexican and Peruvian capitals — excellent literary and scientific reviews, besides the official government gazettes. The first daily papers appeared at a time when they were still a rarity anywhere — the *Diario de Lima* (1790–1793), edited by Jaime Bausate, and the *Diario de México* (1805–1817), founded by the *oidor* Jacobo de Villaurrutia, from Santo Domingo, and Carlos María de Bustamante, who in later years became a prolific historian. They gave scanty news: most of their space was devoted to public affairs, to economic problems, to essays on scientific topics, literature, or art (including translations from Winckelmann and Lessing), and to poetry. In the early nineteenth century, when printing spread to all the colonies, newspapers and periodicals were published in many cities, together with pamphlets, which became a very popular vehicle for the diffusion of ideas.[25]

Still another cultural institution — we may so call it — made a very early appearance in Hispanic America. The permanent public theatre, with its own buildings, acting companies, and paying audiences, then a new thing in Europe, began in Mexico in 1597, with the *casa de comedias* of Don Francisco de León, and in Lima shortly afterwards, in 1602 or before. The first public theatre in Europe, we know, was built in Paris in 1548; the first in London opened in 1576; the first in Madrid, in 1579. They nurtured the marvellous development of modern drama in France, England, and Spain.[26] In Hispanic America, religious drama in the medieval manner had been transplanted by the missionaries at least as early as 1525, and it was developed in Spanish and Portuguese as well as in many Indian languages, very often combining the European with the native dramatic technique;[27] the modern drama was imported as soon as it began to develop in Spain. Early in the seventeenth century, Mexico had three acting companies and "new plays every day," according to Bernardo de Valbuena in his poem on the greatness of that city (1604); Lima had two companies. Later, the wealthy mining

town of Potosi, in the country now called Bolivia, and perhaps
Puebla, in New Spain (i.e., modern Mexico), had theatres. New
ones were built only towards the end of the colonial period — in
Buenos Aires, as the capital of a new viceroyalty, in 1771, under
the auspices of the viceroy Vértiz; in Havana, 1776; in Montevideo, 1792; in Bogotá, also the capital of a new viceroyalty, 1805;
in Santiago de Chile, 1815, just before the country achieved its independence.[28]

It is not often remembered that writers of all ranks came in
great numbers to Hispanic America during the sixteenth century
and at the beginning of the seventeenth. The discoverers themselves, the explorers, and the conquerors, even though they were
not men of letters, often wrote about their own experiences —
thus, after Columbus, whose knowledge of literature was of the
scantiest, and Vespucci, who had literary leanings and wide reading, there were Hernán Cortés, who had studied at Salamanca,
Bernal Díaz del Castillo, Álvar Núñez Cabeza de Vaca, Pedro
Pizarro, Pedro de Cieza de León, Pedro Sarmiento de Gamboa,
and Pero Lopes de Sousa. At times the writer was a mere
adventurer, like Alonso Henríquez de Guzman, "the distressed
gentleman" — el caballero desbaratado — or even an adventuress,
like Catalina de Erauso, the incredible "nun ensign"; at times,
he was a government official, like Gonzalo Fernández de Oviedo,
or Francisco de Jerez, or the oidor Alonso de Zorita, or the cor-
regidor Juan Polo de Ondegardo, or Gabriel Soares de Sousa;
most frequently he was a priest, from Friar Ramón Pane, the
first ethnographer in the Americas, who came with Columbus in
the voyage of 1493, down to the innumerable chroniclers of the
monastic orders. Once, at least, a conqueror was a great poet,
Ercilla. It is only natural that professional men of letters should
not be common in the expeditions of exploration and conquest.
But when the new lands were settled, and the new society
organized, scores of writers arrived. Among a host of dii minores,
there came Gutierre de Cetina, the author of sugared sonnets

and madrigals, one of them the "Ojos claros, serenos" that our youths still know by heart (he died in Mexico, probably the victim of a jealous husband); Francisco Cervantes de Salazar, a typical scholar of the hopeful humanistic period of Charles V; Micael de Carvajal, one of the best dramatists of the formative period preceding the age of the *comedia*; Friar Alonso de Cabrera, most original of preachers, whose depiction of customs was so peculiarly lifelike that it was copied by novelists; Eugenio de Salazar, a master of humorous prose and a rather prosaic but unusual poet of domestic life; Juan de la Cueva, the well-known pioneer in the historical chronicle-drama; Diego Mejía, the translator of Ovid's *Heroides*; Friar Diego de Hojeda, whose *Cristíada* is the most beautiful religious epic in post-Renaissance Spanish literature;[29] Enrique Garcés, a translator of Petrarch and Camoëns; Luis de Belmonte, an erratic dramatist of the school of Lope de Vega; Álvaro Alonso Barba, the best metallurgist of the seventeenth century, whose treatise on mining, *Arte de los metales*, is still read for its masterly prose; Bento Teixeira, who sang of Brazil, in his *Prosopopéa* (1601), in the manner of Camoëns;[30] Francisco Manoel de Mello, the historian of the Catalonian war (1645), a master equally of Portuguese and Spanish, who was sentenced to confinement in Brazil (1655–1658) and wrote there his best work, the *Apologos dialogaes*.[31] There were even such unusual writers as Luis de Carvajal, *el Alumbrado* (*ca.* 1566–1596), a Jewish martyr consumed by a strange mystic fervor, and Lázaro Bejarano, a restless follower of Erasmus, with an irrepressible satiric vein — he governed the island of Curaçoa, by reason of his marriage to the daughter of Juan de Ampíes, treated his Indians with paternal care and wrote in their defense a philosophical dialogue — now unfortunately lost — against the brilliant Sepúlveda.[32] The greatest men, besides Ercilla and Mello, were Mateo Alemán, the true begetter of the picaresque novel, and Tirso de Molina, the creator of Don Juan and author of many splendid dramas and comedies. Alemán came to Mexico in 1608 and published there two short works, a narrative of the voyage and death of Archbishop García Guerra and a treatise on orthography, in which he shows his acquaintance with the fine but now little-known Spanish tradition of technical phonetics. After a few years of activity, all traces of him are lost; he must have died in Mexico, for when he arrived there he was already past threescore. Tirso de Molina came to Santo Domingo in 1616, still a young friar some thirty-three years of age, and until 1618 taught theology at the Convent of Our Lady of Mercy and took part in poetry contests. Cervantes himself applied for official posts in the colonies, but fortunately for us was never appointed; in the new environment, where the printing of novels was forbidden and where he would have had much else to keep him busy, he probably would not have written *Don Quixote* or even the *Exemplary Novels*. Three other eminent men of letters in the sixteenth century also wished to come but did not — Diego Hurtado de Mendoza, Friar Luis de León, and St. John of the Cross.

Artists were no less numerous than writers. The catalogue of their names, though extensive, is not yet complete. It includes the Franciscan Friar Diego de Valadés, who taught the Indians in the school founded by Friar Pedro de Gante in Mexico; Alonso de Narváez, the creator of the miraculous image of Our Lady of Chiquinquirá, in New Granada; the· Basques Francisco de Zumaya and Baltasar de Echave Orio (1548–1620); Sebastián de Arteaga (1610–*ca.* 1655), who painted in Mexico the impressively shadowed *Incredulity of the Apostle Thomas* and the delicate golden *Marriage of Joseph and Mary;* Pedro de Reinalte Coello, a son of the court painter Sánchez Coello; Gabriel Murillo, a son of the famous artist of Seville; the Roman Matteo Piero d'Alessio, a reputed disciple of Michelangelo; the Neapolitan Angelo or Angelico Medoro, whose euphonious Ariostean name sounds like a deliberate invention; the Fleming Simon Pereyns, who, being suspected of heresy, was condemned by the Mexican

Inquisition, in 1568, to paint the image of the Virgin Mary (his masterpiece is the Saint Christopher of the Cathedral); the Dutchman Frans Janszoon Post (1612–1682), who came to northeastern Brazil about the middle of the seventeenth century and contrived "the first American landscapes" according to "an artificial formula, a stage-set of tropical flora and fauna with a background of luminous blue vapors"; still another and far greater Dutchman, Albert Eckhout, who drew and painted in masterly fashion the flora, the fauna, and the inhabitants of Brazil.[33]

Among the sculptors whose names have been retained, Diego de Robles and Luis de Rivera were pioneers in Quito, and Matías de la Cerda in Mexico; Ignacio García de Ascucha fashioned the reliefs of the high altar in the Franciscan Convent at Bogotá; Diego de Ortiz made the miraculous figure of the Virgin of Copacabana in Peru.

And there were the innumerable architects, beginning with Zafra, who came to Hispaniola with Columbus in 1493. Among the builders of the first churches, palaces, and fortresses in the city of Santo Domingo, the outstanding personality is that of Rodrigo Gil de Liendo, to whom we are indebted for the church of Our Lady of Mercy, the now ruined convent of the Franciscan Order, and part of the Cathedral (the original creator of that masterwork is unknown). Occasionally, the conquerors themselves were builders, as in the case of Pero Ansúrez Henríquez de Camporredondo, who personally planned the city of Charcas (1538). And a knowledge of architecture was quite common among the members of religious orders. The first builder in Brazil was the Portuguese Jesuit Francisco Dias. The Fleming Jodoco Ricke, a Franciscan friar, opened a school for architects, sculptors, and painters in Quito; it became in 1553 the College of San Andrés, the first of its kind in the Americas. Francisco Becerra is called "the best architect that came to the New World in colonial times" — he built, wholly or partly, the Cathedrals of Puebla, Lima, and Cuzco and the convents of the Dominican and the

Augustinian Order in Quito, as well as palaces, fortresses, and bridges. The ubiquitous Italian brothers Antonelli built fortresses in Havana, Santo Domingo, Puerto Rico, Guatemala, Cartagena of the Indies, Chagres, Portobelo, and the Straits of Magellan. Finally, the two most imposing architectural monuments of the colonial period, the twin Cathedrals of Mexico and Puebla, are to be classed as mainly the work of Europeans.[34]

Not a few of the writers who came to the New World discovered their vocation in the new environment. Bartolomé de Las Casas, when he arrived in Hispaniola (1502) as a young lawyer, following the footsteps of his father (who accompanied Columbus on his second voyage), was perhaps a mere fortune-seeker. In the Antilles, as we know, he became a priest and afterwards embraced his arduous task, the protection of the Indians. He thereby developed into a copious writer and left us, together with his controversial pamphlets and letters, two gigantic books — the *History of the Indies*, a narrative of events from the Discovery until 1520 (he had carried it as far as 1540, but lost his own manuscript), and the *Apologetic History of the Indies*, in which he vies with Oviedo in the geographic, botanical, and zoological description of the western hemisphere. Alonso de Ercilla grew from an obscure captain into a poet while fighting the indomitable natives of Arauco. His *Araucana* met with amazing success in Spain, like a novel of chivalry, and begot many imitations and replies (he was found, by some, too chary of praise for the youthful chief of the Spanish army, García Hurtado de Mendoza); today it lives mainly as the national epic of Chile. With Homeric impartiality, Ercilla evenly distributes the pride and pomp of war between the two contending peoples. But, since the Spaniards did not acquire in Chile any territory comparable to that they had won from the Aztecs or the Incas or even entirely subdue their pugnacious foes, the resistance of the Indians stands out all the more vividly. The sturdy *caciques* of the poem — Lautaro, Caupolicán, Tucapel, Galbarino, Colocolo (whom even Voltaire admired and compared to Nestor) — have become statuesque legendary figures appropriately represented today in the picturesque parks and avenues of their native land. It has been suggested that Ercilla's impartiality may be partly due to the influence of Las Casas; perhaps a sufficient explanation is that such impartiality was a tradition of classical epic poetry, accepted even for history by writers like Diego Hurtado de Mendoza when dealing with the Moors. Moreover, Ercilla insistently condemns greed as a motive for war and shares the belief in the moral purity of savages; when he describes the inhabitants of Chile south of the Araucanians, he says (canto XXXVI) that "malice, theft, and injustice had not yet entered there nor polluted the natural law." [35]

Cieza de León came to the Indies in his fourteenth year. Later on, as a follower of Pizarro, he became the unsurpassed chronicler — equaled only by Garcilaso — of the majesty and fall of the Inca Empire. Bernal Díaz del Castillo, who had followed Cortés, felt compelled in his old age to reconstruct the story of the conquest of Mexico from the archives of his capacious memory, which retained the looks and the ways of every conqueror and the color of every conqueror's horse. Juan de Castellanos, like Cieza, was a stripling when he came, but a mature priest when he began to write his astonishingly circumstantial *Elegies of the Illustrious Men of the Indies*, the longest poem in Spanish literature. Not only do the events he reports belong to the New World; his very language is a clear mirror of Spanish as it came to be spoken in the Caribbean zone during the latter half of the sixteenth century.

All this literature, from Columbus to Palafox, belongs to Hispanic America much more than to Spain and Portugal. It is the work of men whose new life, as Ortega says, has reshaped them. A few pages from it revealed the New World to the imagination of Europe, which took from them only a few striking topics. But the prodigious mass of writings that flew from the pens of the early chroniclers and poets contained the actual discovery of the New

World by European eyes. Its direct vision could be fully understood only in the Americas; for them it was an imaginative and intellectual act of appropriation.[36]

The universities and the convents, the learned men at the head of the dioceses and the *audiencias*, the viceroys themselves in the great capitals, together with the presence of so many writers, painters, sculptors, and master builders, produced a favorable environment for literature and the arts. It was to be expected that the children of the conquerors, and of the conquered too, should very soon try to write in Spanish and Portuguese, to paint and to build houses and churches in the European manner. By the middle of the sixteenth century we begin to hear names of writers and artists born in the Americas. Fifty years later they are plentiful: in Mexico, three hundred poets competed for prizes in a contest of 1585.[37] The writers produced religious works, history, lyric, and epic poetry, and plays; novels were seldom written, because it was forbidden to print them, but they were read in spite of prohibitions.[38] Most of this early literature is lost; printing was still new and insufficient. But we know of the Mexican poet Francisco de Terrazas, a conqueror's son, who wrote refined verse in Spanish, in Latin as the language of learning, and in Italian as the language of fashion.[39] Pedro de Oña (1570–*ca.* 1643), of Chile, left us four long poems — one of them, *Arauco Subdued* (*Arauco domado*, 1596), a variation of and perhaps a correction to Ercilla's *Araucana*. Oña writes fluent and at times very elegant verse; while he lacks the architectural power of his eminent rival, he is a master of artificial scenes in the manner of the Renaissance, from which he carefully omits the real wild flora and fauna of the country he is describing — his own. Not that he suppressed the native landscapes entirely — his pictures of desert lands are quite realistic. In his last work, *The Golden Vase* (*El vasauro*, 1635), he shows himself a far greater poet and displays not only fluency and elegance but energy and brilliancy as well. By the time he wrote *El vasauro* he was already under the — for him — beneficent influence of Góngora.[40] Cristóbal de Llerena, of Santo Domingo, and Juan Pérez Ramírez, of Mexico, show a surprising ingenuity of construction and style in their short plays. Not all women were mentally idle, either: Eugenio de Salazar mentions "the illustrious poet and lady Doña Elvira de Mendoza, born in the city of Santo Domingo," but gives no sample of her work. Fortunately he copied six delightful poems of her compatriot the nun Doña Leonor de Ovando (d. after 1609), who rose to such devotional conceits as these:

> I know that He would have suffered His passion for me alone, and would have redeemed me alone, if He had created me alone in this world.[41]

Pedro Gutiérrez de Santa Clara, born either in Cuba or in Mexico, Cristóbal de Molina "of Cuzco," Luis Jerónimo de Oré (1554–1627) and Blas Valera (ca. 1538–ca. 1598), of Peru, Juan Rodriguez Freile (1566–1638), of New Granada, Baltasar de Obregón, Hernando Alvarado Tezozómoc (ca. 1520–ca. 1600), Diego Muñoz Camargo (ca. 1526–ca. 1600), Baltasar Dorantes de Carranza, Juan Suárez de Peralta, and Fernando de Alba Ixtlilxóchitl (ca. 1568–ca. 1648), of Mexico, and Ruy Díaz de Guzmán (ca. 1554–1629), of Paraguay, are good historians, and their work combines with that of the chroniclers of European birth to give us a complete picture of our first colonial century.[42] The archbishop Agustín Dávila Padilla (1562–1604) is the first historian of a monastic order — the Dominican — in the Americas, as well as a pioneer archaeologist. These are not yet, however, the men and women who represent the flowering of the colonial world.

Besides, our sixteenth century does not derive from them its most characteristic originality: this it owes to such works in architecture and drama as show a blend of European and Indian cultures. The New World caught the last lingering rays of the art of the late Middle Ages, together with the first blush of the Renaissance, in painting — witness the oldest pictures in the

Cathedrals of Santo Domingo and Puerto Rico and the innumerable frescoes in the earliest Mexican churches; in sculpture — Diego de Robles' group *The Baptism of Christ*, at Quito, is still essentially Gothic in style; in architecture,[43] in poetry. The traditional ballads, the *romances*, as well as the old lyric songs, the *canciones viejas*, often in free rhymed verse, were still living things, and the followers of Cortés and Pizarro, of Pedro de Valdivia and Nuflo de Chaves, improvised new ones on journeys and between battles; the *arte mayor*, the Juan de Mena type of verse, came also with the first settlers, as is shown by the oldest poem on the conquest of Peru, probably written around 1548, and by a few later works. Juan de Castellanos testifies to the displeasure with which the adoption of the Italian *endecasílabos* in Spain was received in New Granada by one of the greatest lovers of literature among the conquerors, Gonzalo Jiménez de Quesada, and by the soldier poet Lorenzo Martín.

The first churches, palaces, and fortresses are in the Isabella style — so named by Bertaux — "the most vivid expression of the national genius of Spain in architecture," which combines the late Gothic with the early Renaissance. Now and then there are even Romanesque reminiscences. The city of Santo Domingo, surrounded by walls like a medieval town until the late nineteenth century, is a museum of the transplanted Isabella style; there may be found direct influences from such typical structures as the New Cathedral of Salamanca, the churches of Santa Cruz and San Juan de los Reyes in Toledo, the palace of Saldañuela and the Casa del Cordón in Burgos. Even later buildings, like the church of Regina Angelorum, follow the pattern of the earlier ones.[44] The *mudéjar*, the style of the Moors who lived among Christians, was occasionally remembered — it appears in one entire building, a church of Santiago de los Caballeros in Hispaniola, ruined by an earthquake in 1524, and in isolated details of many others, from Mexico to Chile. Towards the end of the seventeenth century it enjoyed in the Mexican province of Puebla a belated rebirth and a transmutation into a new form of art, with its decorations of glazed tiles on wall and towers.[45]

Our first architectural structures were adapted to the peculiar circumstances of the surroundings. The danger of attack from Indians in revolt made battlements necessary at times, in churches no less than in palaces. The need for making religious services visible to a multitude produced the open chapels, vast churches without doors at the front.[46] And not infrequently a Spanish building was erected over the partial ruin of an Indian temple or castle — for example, in Cuzco, the convent of Saint Catherine, the palace of the Marquis of San Juan de Buena Vista, the Casa de las Sierpes, and the church of Saint Dominic, in which a portion of the walls of Coricancha, the central Inca temple, still survives. In Mexico, a huge and beautifully carved serpent's head, taken from an Aztec temple, serves as a cornerstone to one of the colonial palaces.

In such buildings the blend of cultures is merely a superposition. A real fusion begins when the native of Mexico or Peru works under European guidance and his old technique modifies the new one he is learning. His situation is similar to that of the Moor who became a vassal of the Christians in Europe and worked for them. The structures, the façades, then reveal a new symmetry, of Indian origin. Lampérez, the Spanish historian of architecture, considers the façade of the church of Saint Lawrence in Potosi as the specimen where the fusion of styles, the *criollismo*, as he calls it, "shows most terribly, if one may say so." And he adds: "The composition is genuine Spanish *plateresque*, and so is every detail. But how Indian their interpretation, with its profusion, its interlacings, its flat modelling, its angularity of design, the darkness of the whole!"[47] The trapezoidal doors and windows, typical of Inca constructions, appear in a number of buildings of the viceroyalty of Peru. There are, besides, Indian motifs — sun, moon, and stars, human figures, fauna and flora in great variety. The zone where the fusion becomes most evident lies in

South America, around Lake Titicaca, including the towns of Puno, Zepita, and Pomata.

In painting, the outstanding examples of fusion are the Mexican codices produced after the Conquest: the old Aztec glyphs are still used, but there is a distinct influence of European realism, especially in the figures of Spaniards.[48] In sculpture, the Indian influence is discernible in the flat modelling and in ornamental details.[49]

The fusion of cultures is equally evident in literature. It is significant that the earliest book we possess printed in the New World should be in two tongues — a Christian doctrine with two texts, one in Spanish and one in Nahuatl, the language of the Aztecs (Mexico, 1539). It is no less significant that the first printed book from the pen of a man born in the New World should be in a native tongue — Friar Juan de Guevara's *Christian Doctrine* in the Huasteco language (Mexico, 1548). The most formidable ethnographical and archaeological work of our sixteenth century was written in three languages, Latin, Spanish, and Nahuatl — the *History of New Spain*, by Friar Bernardino de Sahagún, born in the old kingdom of León. The saintly missionary José de Anchieta, in Brazil, wrote history, prayers, poems, and plays, now in Spanish, now in Portuguese, now in Latin, now in Guarani. Many writers, born on either side of the Atlantic, were bilingual. And a few who wrote only one language semed to think in two — Santa Cruz Pachacuti (who wrote a beggarly Spanish), Blas Valera, Alvarado Tezozómoc, Alba Ixtlilxóchitl, and our first classic, the Inca Garcilaso.

In the drama, this fusion appears most strikingly. Among the Aztecs of Mexico, among the Mayas and Quiches of Yucatan and Guatemala, among the Quechuas of Peru, several types of tragedy and comedy had developed, it seems, from ritual acts — one of them, perhaps, from vegetation rites, if I rightly interpret Garcilaso.[50] The early chroniclers — Santa Cruz Pachacuti, Acosta, Durán, Alba Ixtlilxóchitl, Landa — describe the Indian drama, its theatres, and its technique of scenery and acting. One play, at least, remains, the *Rabinal Achí*, a ritual dance-tragedy of the Quiches. It seems authentic: it is so archaic in form, and so unlike any type of drama in Europe.[51] When the missionaries came, they decided to adapt the medieval religious play to the propagation of the Faith among the Indians and sagaciously combined the European and the native techniques, both in the drama and in the ritual dance. The fusion was deliberately attempted even in music — Garcilaso relates that the *kapellmeister* of the cathedral at Cuzco composed in 1551, for the festivity of Corpus Christi, a hymn based on native music. We do not know whether the practice was continued or whether any consequences might be detected today. The missionaries wrote their plays mostly in Indian languages; the performances were usually given in churches or near them, but also, upon occasion, in vast open spaces with a background of natural rocks and vegetation, to which were added artificial ornaments such as garlands of flowers and stuffed birds. The players were allowed to resort to their Indian stage tricks, such as imitating the lame or the deaf or the ways of animals. There were also Indian and European dances, performed with the plays or in separate ceremonies. This type of drama persisted until the end of the colonial period and is still acted in remote villages, in many places, including the Hispanic Southwest of the United States. It had a varied offspring, in many native languages, in Spanish and Portuguese, and in Latin. Two or three languages may be used in the same play now and then — Latin and Spanish, as in the Jesuit drama in Spain itself, or, say, Spanish, Nahuatl, and Otomi. Such combinations appear, as ornamental incidents, even in the *villancicos* written for great cathedrals by Sor Juana Inés de la Cruz toward the end of the seventeenth century. Or else a mixed *lingua franca* is used. The *mangues* of Nicaragua still perform a comedy-ballet, *El güegüence*, in a mixture of Nahuatl and Spanish.[52] Religious or historical pantomimes and dances too, on such subjects as the Conquest, are still common. Finally, in Peru, during the seventeenth and eighteenth centuries, long secular dramas were written in Quechua, following the Spanish patterns of Lope and Calderón — who, besides, were translated into Indian languages in both North and South America.[53] One of these secular plays, *Ollantay*, a romantic story of love and civil strife, was once supposed to have survived from ancient times prior to the Conquest. Perhaps the songs and a few details, as well as the basis of the story itself, are really old, but the dramatic structure and even the metrical patterns derive from Spanish models. *Ollantay* was performed in 1780 before Túpac Amaru, the last great Inca rebel against the Spanish kings, although, paradoxically enough, Ollantay himself was a rebel against a ruling Inca. It was soon forbidden, and, in consequence, carefully preserved by a faithful few. It has been translated into many languages, from Latin to Czech, and is still a source of inspiration to modern poets and musicians.[54]

3

THE FLOWERING OF THE
COLONIAL WORLD
1600–1800

THE SPANIARDS and the Portuguese who settled in the New World became new men, as we know, through their new experiences. By the end of the sixteenth century, their descendants, a number of them purely European in race, but most of them partly Indian, were men of a new type, "the new autochthonous men," living in a unique environment, where two cultures were in fusion. The Indians, too, at least those who learned to speak the languages of the conquerors, were different from what they had been — life had changed for them as much as for the newcomers. Spain and Portugal laid the main lines of the new social structure and gave it its leading principles. The higher forms of the native culture disappeared, but many of the humbler techniques remained and still remain — in agriculture, in medicine, in cooking, in weaving, in ceramics; even, as we have seen, in literature and architecture and sculpture and painting — grafting themselves upon European forms.

This new society very soon became conscious of its individuality and jealous of its rights. The rivalry between the Spaniards and Portuguese who flocked across the ocean and the men born this side of it, whether *criollos* or *mestizos*, became an open quarrel before the end of the sixteenth century and persisted until the wars of independence. The poet Terrazas complains that Mexico acts as a stepmother towards men who were born there but as a loving mother to men from abroad. Later on, Gregorio de Mattos defines Brazilians as beasts who toil all their lives to support Portuguese rascals, *maganos de Portugal*.[1] An early anonymous sonnet gives vent to the wrath of the new man of the New World against the fortune-seekers from abroad:

> There comes from Spain through the salt sea, to our Mexican abode, a rough man, lacking in resources, ill-nourished and poor. And when he has gathered energy and wealth, others of the same ilk award him in their barbarous councils the two crowns — laurel and oak — of Caesar and Virgil. And another who, when he arrived, sold pins and shoelaces on the streets, is now a count in quality and a Fugger in magnitude;[2] yet he dares speak ill of the country where he acquired money, position and taste. And he was a fisherman in Sanlúcar![3]

Often enough, the grumbler who resents the intrusion of the European or finds fault with his ways was himself born in Europe, only he had come much earlier. Dr. Juan de Cárdenas, a Spanish physician who published in Mexico, in 1591, a book on "The Marvellous Problems and Secrets of the Indies," compares the uncouth manners of many of his compatriots the *chapetones*, the newcomers, with the fastidious refinement of the *criollos*, even of those born and bred in villages. This refined tone was an unsuspected but pervading inheritance from the Aztecs, whose courtesy became so proverbial in Spain itself that the novelist Espinel describes one of his characters as being "polite as a Mexican Indian."

The kings of Spain and Portugal were accustomed (in contradiction of their own legislation) to sending men from Europe to hold important political, administrative, judicial, and ecclesiastical posts. Now and then they appointed men from the colonies, but seldom gave them authority over their own native districts. We find Vértiz, from Yucatan, as viceroy in Buenos Aires, or Friar Domingo de Valderrama, from Quito, as archbishop in Santo Domingo and later in La Paz.[4] *Criollos* and *mestizos* naturally resented this policy; they thought themselves entitled to a measure of self-government, such as they enjoyed at least in the administration of the towns. In retaliation, whenever possible, they blocked the advance of a man of European birth to positions over which they had power of appointment. In the University of Mexico, for instance, a chair would always be given to a Mexican in preference to a Spanish candidate.

By the year 1600, the colonies were already in full activity, especially the two great viceroyalties — Mexico, then called New Spain, extending from Nevada to Yucatan, and Peru, extending from Quito to Potosi. Social wealth was based there on numerous and hard-working Indian populations, but also, there as everywhere else, on the bountifulness of the soil and mines. Not all the countries were developed as yet — thus Argentina and Uruguay had few inhabitants, either Spanish or Indian, but by the middle of the eighteenth century they had become very active in trade. Paraguay had been, up to 1600, the most important section of the River Plate zone; it had already produced eminent men like Hernandarias de Saavedra and his brother the bishop Trejo; the first Jesuit missions had just been founded there (1585). Meanwhile, Santo Domingo, seat of the first short-lived viceroyalty (1509–1526) under Diego Columbus, suffered an economic decline, but maintained its importance and its pride as the political, ecclesiastical, and cultural capital of the eastern part of the Caribbean zone for more than two hundred years, until Cuba and Venezuela rose to prominence. New Granada, the modern Colombia, was already a small autonomous world; so was Chile. Guatemala had developed a character of its own. And in Brazil the Portuguese settlers of the northeast were becoming fabulously rich with their sugar plantations, manned by black labor, while the *bandeirantes* were taking by force the lands of the south.

Bernardo de Valbuena published in 1604 a splendid poem on "The Greatness of Mexico," describing the opulence and refinement of the city, the sumptuousness of the palaces, the beauty of the gardens, where the finest trees and flowers from Europe were planted, the luxury of garments and carriages, the variety of horses — the Mexicans were already famous horsemen, and Cervantes in *Don Quixote* compares them to the Andalusians of Córdoba.[5] Luxurious living and artistic taste were general among the most fortunate members of society, and not there only, but also in colonies that might be called poor, except in natural resources. As early as 1520, the Italian prelate Geraldini remarks on it in Santo Domingo: "How shall I tell of the noble gentlemen, resplendent in purple and silk garments intertwined with gold, since they are innumerable?"[6] It is true that, according to Juan de Castellanos, the city had the agreeable peculiarity that people there could live well and keep their station with no visible means of support — *sin dineros y sin renta*.[7] It was true, indeed, until not very long ago. In Lima, according to Father Bernabé Cobo, towards 1629, there were throngs of people in the main streets and much commercial activity. He speaks of "the vanity in clothes, ornaments and pomp of servants and liveries." The nobility, and many plain citizens, dressed only in silks. There were more than two hundred carriages, adorned with silk and gold. In the houses one found fabrics from Venice, Flanders, or Holland. The poorest people had "jewels of gold or silver" — but there he is probably indulging in exaggeration. In Brazil luxury and good taste were common. According to the Portuguese Jesuit Fernão Cardim, there was more vanity in Recife de Pernambuco, by the year 1584, than in Lisbon.

> Some people [he says] run greatly into debt . . . on account of the excesses and expenses of their way of living. They dress themselves, and their wives and children, in all kinds of velvets, damasks and other silks. The women are very great ladies and not very devout. . . . Some men have as many as three or four horses of great value. At a marriage feast, some of the men were dressed in crimson and some in green velvet, and some in damask and other silks of various colors, and the bridles and saddles of their horses were of the same silks in which they were dressed.

The *Dialogue on the Greatness of Brazil,* of uncertain authorship, written in 1618, gives similar pictures.

The colonial world developed with astonishing rapidity, even if we remember that the settlers transplanted to it all their civilization. This flowering was all the more astonishing, since only about one tenth of the population could speak perfect Spanish or Portuguese. Literature and the arts were fostered by the universities and schools, by the convents, by the political and ecclesiastical authorities. The viceroys tried to live up to the Maecenas tradition. As soon as modern drama became a fashionable entertainment, they built private theatres in their palaces at Mexico City and Lima. A few had *salons* or organized literary academies, such as the *Academia dos Esquecidos* founded by the Count of Sabugosa at Bahia (1724). Three of the viceroys of Peru were poets, the Prince of Esquilache, the Latinist Count of Santisteban del Puerto, and the Marquis of Castell-dos-Ríus. Another viceroy, Amat, was an amateur architect.

The living word held a permanent charm for our colonial society. Our people enjoyed reading poetry aloud, attending plays, listening to sermons and scholastic debates, even to college examinations. And they enjoyed music. We know little about the music of colonial times, but we do know that it was both an aristocratic and a popular diversion. Even the black slaves were taught to play instruments. New dances and songs appeared in the colonies; they were often carried to Spain and had a vogue there. The moralist poet Bartolomé Leonardo de Argensola remonstrates about "the song that comes from the Indies, together with their gold, to make us effeminate." He seems to have already scented the languorous caressing quality of much of our music, as contrasted with the energetic rhythms of Castile or his native Aragon.[8] That music was by no means Indian — there can be no delusion as to that, in spite of many arbitrary surmises;[9] its ancestry was in Europe, but the new environment and the customs soon modified it and gave it a new unmistakable flavor. From around 1580, there are many references in Spanish literature and documents to the dances that were adopted from the Americas: the *gayumba*, which survived in the Antilles until the past century (the name is still applied to a musical instrument there); the *zambapalo*, perhaps related to the modern *zambas*; the *zarandillo*; the *retambo*; the *chaconne*, which crossed the Pyrenees and became a classical form from Lully and Purcell to Rameau and Gluck. The *chaconne* was the most popular of all, and its origin is often mentioned. "It came from the Indies to Seville by mail," says Lope. Cervantes calls it "a swarthy daughter of the Indies." [10] The *són* of the Antilles belongs to that early period and still exists, but did not travel to Europe until recent times, as a rule in confusion with the *rumba*, which originally bore no relation to it. In the eighteenth century, the *guajira* (and the type of song called *guaracha*) was imported from Cuba, as in the nineteenth the *habanera*, preceding the musical flood from all the Americas, north and south, in the twentieth. The Brazilian songs introduced in Portugal, especially the *modinhas*, are said to be part ancestors of the *fado*.[11]

A baroque world, this, of easy wealth and luxury and songs — a world very much in keeping with the baroque period into which Europe was entering after the bloom of the Renaissance. But the two classic Spanish writers born in America, the two highest representatives of this New World in literature, as Menéndez Pelayo calls them, the Inca Garcilaso de la Vega (1539–1616) and Juan Ruiz de Alarcón (*ca.* 1580–1639), were not attracted by the new current of taste. The Inca Garcilaso developed under the light of pure Renaissance ideals; Alarcón was guided by norms of symmetry and unity of tone.

The Inca, as he liked to style himself, was the son of the conqueror Garcilaso de la Vega, a member of the most powerful and numerous family of the nobility in Spain and cousin to the admirable Spanish poet his namesake. The Inca's mother was a granddaughter of Túpac Yupanqui and a cousin of Atahualpa. At the age of twenty-one he left his native land, never to return. In Spain he enlisted in the king's army, and saw fighting in Navarre under the Marquis of Priego, his distant relative, and in Granada, against the Moorish rebels of the Alpujarras, under Prince Don John of Austria (1568). However, his ancestry was a grievous handicap — it seems to have been the cause of his departure from Peru, and was the cause of his lack of advancement in Madrid. His father's conduct during the civil war between the conquerors of Peru was not free from shadows, and probably his Inca blood also made him suspect. After several ineffectual efforts to gain recognition from the court, he retired to Córdoba, the ancient Moorish capital, and devoted his life to literature. In 1598 he was ordained as a deacon.

He was a master of beautiful prose in that age of excellent writing, and his first endeavor (1590) was one of those perfect Renaissance translations in which the original work is rendered with a spirit closely akin to the author's intentions and with a similar flow of words. In this case, the translation has a better style than the original. The book he chose was the masterpiece of Renaissance Platonism, the *Philographia* or *Dialogues on Love* of the Spanish Jew Judah Abravanel, or Leon Hebreo, who wrote it during his exile in Italy. The first version of the *Dialogues* may, indeed, have been written in Spanish, but it was printed only in Italian. They soon became the favorite manual of aesthetics in Italy and Spain, and many who did not read them were influenced by them through Castiglione's *Courtier*. Garcilaso's translation gave back to Spain a book that was essentially her own, although it took its final lustre from the Italian Renaissance. It is a singular coincidence that both the author and the translator were outside the pale of what might be considered strictly and legitimately Spanish, and yet both within the ample range of Spanish culture.

After the *Dialogues* Garcilaso published *La Florida* (1605), a story of Hernando de Soto's expedition to the flowery peninsula. He never visited the land; he may, at most, have seen it from a distance, if on his voyage to Spain he crossed the channel that separates it from Cuba. He was not, therefore, writing a strict historical work, with direct knowledge of the territory involved, differing in this respect from the contemporary chroniclers of Hispanic America — excepting such men as Gómara or Herrera, who worked in Europe with a great mass of documentary material. He took his subject in the spirit of the modern writers who treat history like a piece of imaginative fiction. Soto's adventure was in truth full of picturesque incident, and Florida a garden of tropical spring, its beauty entirely different from the majesty of the Peruvian sierras and high valleys. Garcilaso's book was an innovation and one of the most exciting historical books of the period.

His last and greatest task was the *Royal Commentaries* (1609–1617), in some ways the best of all the works on the early history of the Americas. Its first part is the story of the Inca Empire; the second part, the story of the conquerors. Here again, the historian is a very imaginative historian. Modern criticism, from Prescott to our own day, has cast grave doubts on his accuracy. His picture of the Inca civilization seems too perfect. But a reaction in his favor has set in and is slowly increasing. A point, here and there, may have been embellished, or a displeasing fact silenced; the chronology may be faulty. The bulk of the story, however, is proved true by careful comparison with the earliest sources, both archaeological and historical, which are very numerous. The skepticism of the modern critics was due to prejudice and routine, to their provincial inability to conceive a culture that was neither classical nor Christian. In Europe, as we know, the first reports of the Aztec and Inca civilizations were not even understood — Montaigne, as always, was the exception; but the men who actually saw them did understand. In the eighteenth century an effort at comprehension began, and it went on through the nineteenth;

but it is only today that the conception of the individuality of cultures is becoming an acceptable notion. Furthermore, we begin to discover that mankind has known scores of civilizations now buried under dust, that at many different times and in many different places great cities have been built, great scientific discoveries made, great forms of art created. Many works that were formerly kept in ethnological or archaeological collections now migrate to art museums, and the sculptures from Cambodia or Ur of the Chaldees, from Guatemala or Cuzco, from Easter Island or from Central Africa, now hold their own side by side with the formerly unapproachable statues of Greece and Italy. We are not now ashamed to confess that any civilization may have been, in some of its aspects, as great as ours, if not greater. Why should not the Incas have conceived the ideal of organic peace and imposed it upon backward and reluctant populations, although at the time of the Spanish invasion they were engaged in a dynastic war? Why might they not have had a satisfactory communal economy and a rigorously organized public administration like that of the Aztecs, which Cortés so greatly admired and which was so superior to any system then practiced in the Western world? Were not their roads far superior to any in Europe since the Romans? The optimistic descriptions of Garcilaso, dismissed once as utopian fancies, now seem quite plausible in their essential features. By means of long study and great love he collected a vast store of information, both Indian and Spanish, and one of his best sources was the living word of the men and women of his own family. If he undervalued the earlier aboriginal cultures of Peru, now revealed by archaeological research, just as his censors undervalued the Inca civilization, he may be pardoned because he knew nothing of them. Prescott, the least severe of his old critics, tells us that "he writes from the fulness of his heart and illuminates every topic he touches with a variety and richness of illustration that leave little to be desired by the most importunate curiosity. The difference between reading his *Commentaries* and

the accounts of European writers is the difference that exists between reading a work in the original and in a bald translation.
Garcilaso's writings are an emanation of the Indian mind." He is
the Herodotus of the Incas; he captured and rendered, as no man
from Europe could, the true spirit of their civilization, together
with the feeling of the landscape that encircled it, with "the over-
whelming immanence of the Andes"; he erected to them a monu-
ment not unworthy of their powerful architectural structures.
And, as a historian of the Spanish conquest and the ensuing civil
wars, he has a rival only in Cieza de León, who does not equal
him in artistic form but is his peer in dramatic imagination.[12]

Juan Ruiz de Alarcón had not, so far as we know, any Indian
ancestry; but, like Garcilaso, he grew up in the new society of
Hispanic America, and his work shows, in subtle ways, the influence of his native environment. He left Mexico when he was
about twenty years old (1600); by 1597 he had already finished
his *bachillerato en artes* at the local university and had seen plays
performed on the capital's first public stage. Such a novelty must
have kindled his youthful imagination; Hartzenbusch, one of the
keenest critics of his work, suspects that he may have written two
or three of his plays before he was twenty. He spent eight years
in Spain, studying law at the University of Salamanca and then
practicing it in Seville; then, five years in Mexico again, vainly
trying to obtain a position befitting his expectations as a member
of a distinguished family "who had rendered good services to the
king." Four times he failed to obtain a chair in the school of law
at the university. Like Garcilaso, he suffered from a handicap —
a bodily one in his case. It is likely that, in a society where external appearance counted so much, university men winced at
the prospect of a hunchback member of the faculty in their solemn processions and ceremonies. Alarcón, at last, made a bold
decision — he returned to Spain to demand a post there. After
thirteen years of petitioning, of *pretender*, he obtained a place as

relator supernumerario in the Council of the Indies (1626); his work was such that he did not need to be seen by the public. A few years later (1633) his appointment was made permanent.

While he was a mere aspirant, a *pretendiente*, he probably earned his living by writing plays — not many, for he lacked the copious vein of Lope or Tirso; he wrote only twenty-three. Sometimes they met with success, sometimes they failed. Their success or their failure was a matter of chance, of the occasional mood of the boisterous and outspoken audiences of the times. His competitors in the theatrical trade would at times go so far as to organize hootings and have stink-bombs thrown into the pit. Alarcón — a very sensitive man, of course — must have been very glad to retire from the theatre as soon as he had a fixed and sufficient income. His plays remained there, however, and both because he loved them and because they were already appearing in piratical editions, he published them himself in two volumes (1628–1634), with the same meticulous care with which he wrote them. There are no seventeenth-century editions of Spanish drama that compare with his as to clearness and accuracy. In the short notice that precedes the first volume he shows how, in retrospect, he still writhes under the lash; he addresses the public: "I speak with thee, wild beast. . . . These plays face thee with contempt and without fear, since they no longer run the risk of thy hisses. . . . If they displease thee, it shall give me joy to learn that they are good."

Alarcón is called "the classicist of a romantic school of drama," the school of the Spanish *comedia*. It had been created, a few years before Alarcón discovered it in Mexico, by Lope de Vega and his companions, and was a typical creation of the then budding baroque period. The *comedia* was still moderately baroque in style — the stylistic frenzy begins only with Calderón. But it was clearly baroque in construction; it was essentially a thing of movement, like a complex dance pattern. In his early youth, Alarcón must have been captivated by it; he naturally adopted its form, and a few of his early plays are not only romantic but extravagant. As years went by, he began to feel slightly uncomfortable in the accepted pattern — the construction was too loose for him, the tone too uneven. He did not dare make any structural changes — Cervantes, and lesser men too, failed in the attempt. Lope was too powerful, too brilliant, to be contradicted — the public would not listen. Alarcón, then, contented himself with adapting the triumphant *comedia* to his own tastes, in such a way that the public would hardly notice. He achieved unity of tone, made his plot move smoothly and even slowly, gave it logical sequence, left no loose ends. He even omitted the songs and dances which are so common — and so delightful — in Lope and Tirso. His style is limpid and concise, far more epigrammatic than poetic. His scenes are clear-cut, with very definite time and place — they are never what Mr. Granville Barker calls "person scenes," with subjective time and unstable location, of the kind that is as common in Lope or Tirso as in Shakespeare. But the public probably did notice. A faithful disciple of Lope, Montalván, speaks of Alarcón's "novelty and strangeness" — *strange* being then a term of praise in Spanish, but not without a distinct overtone.

Ferdinand Wolf, the eminent German scholar, remarks that Alarcón seems less Spanish than his contemporaries. Fitzmaurice-Kelly, the English literary historian, describes him as "less national" than they. A witty writer of modern Spain, José Bergamín, depicts him as an intruder in the *comedia*. To me the explanation seems clear: he is not a Spaniard of Spain, he is a colonial, and a colonial from Mexico at that, bred in a society already quite different from that of the mother country. We know that life in Mexico was, for the privileged classes, full of amenities but lacking in movement. Alarcón naturally makes his plays less lively than Lope's or Tirso's. His characters spend more time in their houses than in the street; duels are not inevitable; reserve and prudence are possible. We know that Mexican society was pe-

culiarly courteous; so it has remained, in fact. Alarcón makes his
characters, at times, excessively polite — as he himself was, if we
are to believe Quevedo's gibe calling him a fawner and a fly —
mosca y zalamero. We know that servants, in Mexico, being
mostly Indians, members of a vanquished race, with no great
command of Spanish, did not dare to be as impudently familiar
with their masters as they were in Spain, both in real life and in
comedias. Alarcón openly condemns such familiarity in *The Fa-*
vors of the World and proceeds to make respectful followers out
of the servants in his plays, though they keep their character as
graciosos. But he, poor hunchback, lacks the sense of opulence
and ease of his native land, except on a few occasions, as when
his Don García, in *Truth Made Suspect,* pretends to be a rich
newcomer from the Indies and lies with true baroque zest —
even his language becomes baroque in his first lies. In exchange,
Alarcón has the cold persistence of the Mexican character — fire
below, snow above, like the volcanoes of the country.

Alarcón is not wholly to be explained by his origin, of course.
There is, first of all, his genius. It was a rational, ethical genius.
He might have foreseen his success among the French (had he
known their literature) when Corneille fashioned his *Menteur*
(1643) out of *Truth Made Suspect* — it is a work in which *la*
raison watches every step, and fancy, after enjoying its own wild
flights, gets punished. His ethics are essentially rational. The
virtues he praises most are generally those which might be called
logical, those which show a clear relation of cause and effect —
sincerity, loyalty, gratitude, discretion. He also loves another,
less logical, even reckless, virtue — generosity. His logic and his
morals, after all, are the outcome of a somewhat secluded life,
such as his bodily handicap would compel him to lead, making
him ponder on the fundamental problems of human conduct and
the common tables of values. He is not revolutionary, he is only
insistent — he merely asks men to live in accordance with the
morality they profess. Honor — yes, it was the main principle of

worldly Spanish morality. It should not yield even to a king. But
there was no need to make it aggressive. Why should we attack
all the problems with the sword? When he must choose between
the code of chivalry and the teachings of Christianity, he decides
in favor of Christ — thou shalt not kill. Nobility was a thing of
the soul, not a matter of mere heritage. Still, he has a weakness
for noble blood. And he scorns the cult of riches. In his comedy
No Evil but Brings Some Good — probably his last play, written
for his own pleasure when he had nothing more to fear from un-
ruly audiences — his Don Domingo de Don Blas carries criticism
of social conventions and loyalty to reason to the ultra-rational
extremes of a character out of Bernard Shaw: "let them say"
might be his motto.

A somewhat grey world, this of Alarcón's plays, very unlike the
world of enterprising romantic love, of dance and song and sun-
burnt mirth into which Lope and Tirso carry us. He does not
belong, like them, to the splendid joyous race of Aristophanes and
the Shakespeare of the early comedies. He belongs to another
line, the line of Menander and Terence. He recreates on the modern stage the comedy that makes a study of character and customs, and thereby, through his adapter Corneille, he anticipates
Molière. His is a rare conjunction of reasonable ethical purpose
with a gift for vivid dramatic creation. He has the perfect touch
that allows his logic and his morals to enter into the texture of
his work without ever impairing its artistic balance.[13]

Bernardo de Valbuena (*ca.* 1562–1627) had all the opulence
and brilliancy that Alarcón lacked. Menéndez Pelayo calls him
"the first genuinely American poet." He was, it is true, born in
Spain (the attempt to prove him a native of Mexico is not well
grounded), but when he was a very small child he was brought
to the New World, where his father had already taken up his
residence. He received his education in New Spain and was ordained as a priest; in 1606 he went to Spain in search of advance-

ment and stayed until 1610. The last part of his life he spent in
the Antilles — first in Jamaica, where he held the ecclesiastical
post of abbot and "thought himself enchanted," so great was his
isolation in the all but desert island, then in Santo Domingo, the
largest city of the Caribbean zone at the time, where he stayed
for a rather lengthy period as a visitor unwilling to depart; finally,
in Puerto Rico, where he was appointed bishop. Four of his
works, including a *Cosmography* (in verse, we may wonder?),
were lost during his lifetime, when the city of San Juan in Puerto
Rico was sacked by Dutch pirates (1625); three remain, together
with a few minor pieces, two of which, in prose, are defenses of
poetry, the Letter to Dr. Antonio de Ávila y Cadena and the
Apologetic Compendium. The three important works are the
poem on *The Greatness of Mexico*, the pastoral novel *A Golden
Age in the Forests of Eriphyle*, and the long fantastic epic of
chivalry *Bernardo.*[14]

Unlike Garcilaso and Alarcón, Valbuena is frankly a baroque
artist. He belongs to an age of invention and has inventive genius.
Several types of baroque poetry were then appearing in Spanish.
Góngora's *culteranismo* is the most famous and brilliant of all.
A colorful style was developed by the poets of Antequera and
Granada — Pedro Espinosa, Luis Martín de la Plaza, Pedro Soto
de Rojas — as later, in Seville, by Rioja. And Castile eventually
evolved its own *conceptismo.* In Lope's fluent verse there is a
baroque tinge too — it is fluent but not really simple; it is a traditional Spanish structure with Renaissance ornament. Spanish
America's main contribution to the baroque in literature came
from Valbuena.[15] His style is lavishly ornamental, but its structural lines remain clear, as in the baroque architecture of Mexico.
His *Bernardo*, by means of which he aspired to become the Spanish Ariosto, is comparable, in its magnitude, to the Convent of
Tepozotlan; his *Greatness of Mexico*, to the Sagrario by the side
of the Mexican Cathedral. By an unexpected contrast, the ec-
logues included in his *Golden Age* are written in a simpler style,

though with learned artifice; the names of humble animals and plants and the realistic pictures of common things make them unique in the Spanish literature of the period. As a bucolic poet, it has been said, he stands nearer to Theocritus than to Virgil; he attempted a renewal of the eclogue, and the consequences might have been interesting if the genre had not just then begun to decline.

He is little read nowadays. Pastoral novels and fantastic epics of chivalry now find few readers. Only his *Greatness of Mexico* has been reprinted of late and read, I hope, at least in the city it describes. His *Bernardo* is inordinately long and complex, but it should be read at least as Spenser's *Faerie Queene* is generally read — by taking up the book now and then and going over two or three pages. If the art of making anthologies were more in vogue in Hispanic countries than it is, Valbuena might still be saved for an indifferent posterity that, through carelessness, misses some of the most tender notes, the most brilliant descriptions, and the most beautiful lines to be found in the language — as, for example, when he speaks of "the waves and floods of things" ("las olas y avenidas de las cosas"), or the sorrel horse, "all fire, both in its color and in its energy" ("hecho de fuego en la color y el brío"), or a youth "of glad eyes and fiery glance" ("el doncel de alegres ojos y de vista brava"), or "the sea's shoulders of crystal and ice" ("hombros de cristal y hielo"), or the swan that "vanishes with the soft sound of his song" ("al suave són de su cantar se pierde"), or the sun rising over the still dark sea, "the light trembling over the sombre crystal" ("tiembla la luz sobre el cristal sombrío").[16]

Antonio Vieira (1608–1697), the most eloquent religious orator the Portuguese language has known, came to the New World as a small child, like Valbuena. At the age of six he was brought from Portugal to Brazil, where his father was a resident, and remained there until he was thirty-three. He identified himself entirely with his new country. As a Jesuit priest he devoted himself to the education and defense of the Indians. After years of persistent effort he obtained for them, from the king, the right to live freely under their own native chiefs and under the spiritual guidance of the Jesuits (1655). His apostolic zeal moved him also to preach against black slavery; in his *Sermon on Captives* he unfolds in masterly fashion his emotional and logical arguments. And he preached against the exploitation of the colony by its distant capital. "The cloud," he says, "swells in Brazil and it rains in Portugal. The waters that are squandered there do not come from the abundance of the sea, as in olden times, but from the tears of the unhappy and the sweat of the poor, and I do not know how it is that the constancy and fidelity of these vassals lasts so long." In his attitude, says Afranio Peixoto, Brazil first becomes conscious of itself.[17] But this attitude does not yet mean a desire for independence.

He went to Europe in 1641, a young man of wide experience, with a great name as a missionary and as a preacher. He accompanied Mascarenhas, the delegate from Brazil whose mission was to give Portugal, now freed from the brief dominance of Spain (1580–1640), the assurance that the vast colony would remain united to its original founders. In Lisbon he soon achieved fame and was appointed preacher to the king, João IV (1644). He spent many busy years in Europe, which included several diplomatic commissions (Stefan Zweig calls him a diplomat of genius), a long sojourn in Rome (where he acted as private preacher to the former Queen Christina of Sweden), and even a prosecution and imprisonment by the Portuguese Inquisition (1665–1667). But he did not turn European — twice he returned to Brazil, first in 1652, to spend nine years in missionary work (save for a few months in Lisbon, where he went to plead for the Indians), and then in 1681, when he again engaged in missionary work until old age compelled him to retire. And in Brazil he died, when nearing his ninetieth year.

Vieira's voluminous writings comprise many tomes of sermons and letters. He also wrote a treatise on oratory. As a preacher, he acted according to his own notions as to what a sermon should be, spiritually as well as artistically, and he did not forget to give rules about the voice and gestures. In his style he mixes a complex scholastic method, which he adapts to his own imaginative trains of reason, with a clear and vivid turn of phrase. He is one of the true masters of Portuguese prose, and influences it to this day.[18]

There were at least two women, as we know, a "great lady" and a nun, among the earliest writers and poets born in the colonies. To the seventeenth century belongs Saint Rose of Lima (1586–1617), who found time, in the scarce moments left her between her prayers and mortifications of the body, to write simple and delicate devotional verse. Two mysterious ladies, her contemporaries, Peruvians also, who signed themselves Clarinda and Amarilis, wrote in a far more sophisticated style. Clarinda dedicated to the Andalusian poet Diego Mejía a lengthy *Discourse in Praise of Poetry* in tercets (1608). Amarilis addressed to Lope de Vega, some time before 1621, an Epistle in free stanza form. Both ladies are marvellously versed in the fine intricacies of post-Renaissance poetry; their brilliant work is a typical fruit of the literary culture of the southern viceroyalty. An ill-grounded scepticism tries to deprive them both of their enigmatical glory. I do not find sufficient reasons for assenting.

By the end of the century, a distant and interesting disciple of Saint Theresa appeared in Bogotá, Sor Francisca Josefa de la Concepción (1671–1742), generally called "la Madre Castillo" from her family surname. She wrote good verse and eloquent imaginative prose, in which she related her religious life, like her great model.[19] The women writers were, in fact, many. One of them, the Brazilian Rita Joana de Sousa (1696–1718), wrote a treatise on physics, *Tratado de philosophia natural*, besides *Historical Memoirs*.

None of these women equalled the extraordinary fame or the genius of the Mexican nun, the "tenth Muse," Sor Juana Inés de la Cruz (1651–1695). Her life is a prodigious tale of devotion to knowledge. She was born in a farmhouse, near the two gigantic snow-capped volcanoes Popocatepetl and Iztaccihuatl. When a child of three, she was taught to read on her own initiative, without telling her parents. She began to write verse very early and declares that in her childhood she believed that everybody wrote poetry. When she heard that there were universities and colleges where all the sciences were taught to men, she begged her mother to dress her as a boy so that she might be admitted to attend courses. She was, at least, sent to the city of Mexico, to live in her grandfather's house, where she read all the books in his library — according to her biographer Calleja, that library had served only ornamental purposes before. At fourteen she was already famous for her learning and her poetry no less than for her beauty. The Marchioness of Mancera, the viceroy's wife, invited her to live in the palace as one of her attendant ladies. Once (she was seventeen then) the Marquis invited some forty university professors and dilettanti (*tertulios* they were called, men who enjoyed intellectual conversation) to question her on all sorts of subjects. In this unofficial examination she "defended herself," in the words of the great viceroy, "like a royal galleon surrounded by shallops." But she soon realized her awkward position in the world — being poor, she risked being "persecuted because of her beauty and unhappy because of her keen mind" — *perseguida por hermosa y desgraciada por discreta*. And then how could she satisfy her thirst for knowledge? Marriage was not to be thought of, with the encumbrance of the manifold and endless household duties of a seventeenth-century wife. The cloister was better, both for the soul's salvation and for studious leisure. And so it was necessary to tame, she says, "all the little importunities of my humor, such as the wish to live alone and the wish to have no compulsory occupation to hamper the freedom of my studies, nor the noise of a congregation to disturb the placid silence of my books." In her sixteenth year she entered the Carmelite Order as a novice; the rule proved too rigorous for her, and she returned to the viceregal palace; a year later she chose the Order of Saint Jerome and, after a short novitiate, took her final vows there (1669). Convent life, after all, did not imply any too great seclusion — hardly greater than that of a married lady. Visitors were received at the locutory, and talked to, though not seen. Of Sor Juana Inés it is said that she had to spend hours at the locutory, as it was not seemly that she should retire when the visitor, as often happened, was a distinguished personage.

However, things did not always run smoothly. Her fame might cross the oceans and bring her tributes from all the corners of the Spanish empire, literary dukes and counts in Madrid vying in enthusiasm with priests from Puerto Rico and gentlemen from Lima or Bogotá. But she found many censors at home, who doubted the wisdom of so much learning in a woman. *Mulieres in ecclesia taceant!* They even succeeded once in inducing a mother superior — "a very saintly and very foolish woman" — to forbid her the reading of books. Fortunately, the prohibition lasted only three months.

After her fortieth year, she gave up her usual studies and devoted herself to prayer, penance, and charity. Her country was suffering from many evils — famines, plagues, pirates off the coasts, bloody political disturbances. Sor Juana sold her four thousand books, her scientific and musical instruments, and all the valuable presents she had received, to help the poor. Finally when the plague invaded her convent she strained herself in the nursing of her sick sisters, caught the disease, and died. In her twenty-six years of monastic life, she had twice refused the post of abbess.

In the record of her life, her desire for knowledge and her scientific turn of mind seem even more striking than her literary talent. When Bishop Manuel Fernández de Santa Cruz wrote to

her suggesting that she give more of her time to sacred than to
secular studies, she humbly defended herself by telling the story
of her life and her strange pursuit of learning in spite of all the
hindrances she had met. Persistence was a trait of her character,
as it was with Alarcón. She asserts that women have as much
right to study as men and proposes that girls be taught by learned
women of mature age. She shows — without explicitly saying it
— how versed she is in scripture and theology, and argues that
every kind of knowledge helps every other kind. "Angels are
higher than men because they understand more" —intellectual-
istic angelology! The personal defense she advances is that she
seems unable to stop herself from wishing to know more.[20] When
studying was forbidden her, "I obeyed," she says, "by taking no
book in my hands; but to give up studying altogether does not lie
in my power . . . and so, though I did not study in books, I studied in all the things that God created." During that period of
deprivation, she seems to be always concerned with scientific
problems. Whence come so many individual differences between
people, they being all of one species? The geometrical figure of
any object holds her attention, and she tries to discover its relation to other figures. In a very long room, she remarks how the
parallel lines of the structure seem convergent to the eye, the
result being a pyramidal shape. She observes two girls playing
with a spinning top and decides to find out what sort of curve it
draws while it spins — she sprinkles flour on the floor and discovers that the curve is a spiral. In the kitchen, she remarks on
the properties of sugar or eggs, and adds: "If Aristotle had known
how to cook, he would have written even more than he did."

￫ So far as we know, she left no scientific writings; it may have
been difficult for her to coördinate her spontaneous experimental
observation with the scholastic structure of her book knowledge.
She does not show any acquaintance with either Galileo or Descartes, although they were already known to a few in Mexico.
A philosophical essay on *Moral Equilibrium* had been preserved

in manuscript, but it was lost or stolen during the American invasion of Mexico in 1847. Her treatise on music, *The Snail*, is also
lost.[21] Judging from her references to music in her extant writings, she still accepted the medieval system, whether she had or
had not heard of the sixteenth-century revolution in harmony. We
have proof that Zarlino and later theorists of music were read in
Mexico; but Sor Juana's references show the peculiar tendency to
stagnation that seemed inherent in our theoretical knowledge,
both in Spain and Spanish America, during the seventeenth century — a tendency against which the efforts of a few men were
of little avail.

Her scientific bent, then, which in later times might have led
her to follow the example of a Sonia Kovalevska or a Marie Curie,
found no outlet, and her fame rests, now as in her own times,
upon her poetry. Her autobiographical letter, however, deserves
as much fame as her best poetry. In spite of the many pedantic
quotations with which she felt obliged to adorn it, it is one of the
most refreshing documents in Spanish literature, and one that
may be reread with genuine pleasure. It has the true feminine
ring, even in the rhythmic structure of its sentences, like the prose
of Saint Theresa or of Queen Isabella's letters.[22]

It seems that after she took the veil she hardly ever wrote unless
asked (but she was asked very often); she says so herself, and
singles out as an exception her long poem *First Dream*, of almost
a thousand lines. The preservation of her writings has been
mainly casual. A large portion of what got into print is mere
unimportant *vers de circonstance* that the recipients had kept —
such things as epistles to her patronesses the Marchioness of Mancera and the Countess of Paredes, whom she calls, respectively,
Laura and Lisi, in the Arcadian jargon of the times. Yet she succeeded in writing very good poetry in the *villancicos* she scribbled
off to be acted and sung in religious festivals at the Cathedrals of
Mexico, Puebla, and Oaxaca.

In her earliest verse she shows already a thorough mastery of the three varieties of poetic style then current in Spanish — the fluent form of Lope, the *conceptismo* of Quevedo, the *culteranismo* of Góngora and Calderón.[23] None of her contemporaries, whether in Spain or in the Americas, equals her in technical virtuosity. Considering the circumstances of her life and her capacity for observation and for pure intellectual effort and enjoyment, it might be expected that much of her work would be impersonal in subject — in the manner, say, of Góngora's *Polifemo* and *Soledades*, or Pedro Espinosa's *Fabula de Genil*, or Lope's own *Circe* and *Gatomaquia* — or else that she would write plays. She did write, before entering the convent, two comedies in the manner of Calderón, one of them in partnership with her cousin Juan de Guevara, *Love is the Greatest Labyrinth*; [24] in the only one that is entirely hers, *Complications in a House*,[25] the personal element is easily discernible in the character of the heroine, who makes us think that the author had not yet lost her illusions about the prospects of worldly success for a clever and cultivated girl. Her ecclesiastical plays and playlets, the *autos sacramentales* and the *villancicos*, are testimonies to her religious feelings, especially the beautiful *Divine Narcissus*. The only poems that may be called impersonal are a few rhetorical exercises, mostly in the forms of sonnets on such subjects as Lucretia or Pyramus and Thisbe, a satire (*ovillejos*) on literary fashions under the pretext of drawing the portrait of a lady, and the *First Dream*. This *Dream* is a fine poem in the manner of Góngora's *Soledades*; Karl Vossler calls it a masterpiece.[26] It is, besides, a complex intellectual construction, typical of her mind — a description of night and sleep, during which the mind is purified,[27] rises to the contemplation of the universe, and tries to master its laws. The dawn comes too soon, but, as this was only a first dream, perhaps in a second she might have outlined a poetic cosmology. As Vossler says, starting from the baroque we are approaching the poetry of "enlightenment" and anticipating Goethe and Shelley.[28]

We find her most personal expression in the love poems of her early youth and in the later poems of disillusion and of religious devotion. At times she attains a luminous height of tense emotion, mirrored in the smooth intensity of the verse, in the love poems, as in the sonnet "Tarry, shadow of my elusive treasure" ("Deténte, sombra de mi bien esquivo"), in the *liras* on absence, with the loving soul, at the sight of the beloved, swiftly running to the eyes to come out dissolved in smiles ("el alma que te adora, — de inundación de gozos anegada, — a recibirte con amante prisa — saldrá a los ojos desatada en risa"), or in the *redondillas* on the torment of love, "a frenzy that begins as desire and ends in melancholy" ("devanco — que empieza como deseo — y pára en melancolía"). In the poems of disillusion her cadences are softer and slower — thus in the *romance* "Let us feign that I am happy" ("Finjamos que soy feliz"), in the sonnet on hope as a "perennial ailment" ("Diuturna enfermedad de la esperanza" — in the original the initial adjective throws a nocturnal darkness over the lines),[29] in the sonnet to her own portrait, which she calls "a wary deceit of the senses, in which flattery attempts to defeat old age and oblivion, a useless protection against fate, a foolish and mistaken effort, a corpse, a shadow, dust, nothing" ("cauteloso engaño del sentido, en quien la lisonja ha pretendido triunfar de la vejez y del olvido, es un resguardo inútil para el hado, es una necia diligencia errada, es cadáver, es polvo, es sombra, es nada" — the last line a reminiscence of Góngora).[30] In a superb sonnet to the rose she draws from its brief life the traditional lesson — "thy life deceives and thy death teaches" ("vivendo engañas y muriendo enseñas"); but in another sonnet she approves the rose's life — "happy it is to die while young and fair and not to endure the insult of old age" ("que es fortuna morirte siendo hermosa — y no ver el ultraje de ser vieja"). This is an expression of her persistent, fighting spirit, which led her to write the defiant lines "If my displeasure from my pleasure comes, may heaven give me pleasure even at the cost of displeasure" ("Si de mis mejores gustos — mis disgustos han nacido — gustos al cielo le pido —

aunque me cuesten disgustos") — lines strikingly coincident with a number of folk songs and proverbs in Mexico. Her best known poem is the one in *redondillas* in defense of women, a tissue of antitheses in the manner of the *conceptistas*; it is her thesis that men are irrational in blaming women for their imperfection, since men constantly contrive to make women imperfect. It is not great poetry, but it is a polemical masterpiece.[31]

By the side of the great figures there were innumerable minor men and women. Literature was for them an incredibly fertile field. But it is likely that not more than one-twentieth, or less, of what was actually written ever came to light — the printing plants were sadly insufficient, even in Mexico. In the seventeenth century, Córdoba del Tucuman, in Argentina, was a city of importance, the seat of a bishopric and a university; yet from its literary activity only one work has survived, in manuscript, of course — the miscellaneous volume of Luis de Tejeda (1604–1680), in prose and verse, including his autobiography, which reveals the crowded variety of experiences of a man who had been a frivolous youth, a faithless husband, a soldier, and who finally became a repentant friar. Incidentally he speaks of plays written and performed by himself and his friends. In the city of Santo Domingo, the self-styled "Athens of the New World," many names of native poets, writers, and orators of that century remain, but the only literary survivals are a historical work by the priest Luis Jerónimo de Alcocer, preserved in a handwritten copy,[32] and twelve laudatory poems, both in Latin and in Spanish, which accompany the *Anti-axiomas* (Madrid, 1682) of Fernando Díez Leiva, a physician from Seville. And what happened to the plays acted in the once thriving city of Potosi?

Midway between the great figures and the mass who wrote religious tracts and historical chronicles,[33] we find men of original minds like Friar Gaspar de Villarroel (*ca.* 1587–1665), from Quito, bishop of Santiago de Chile, then of Arequipa, and finally of

Charcas. In his huge work on *The Two Powers*, ecclesiastical and secular (*Los dos cuchillos*, 1656–1657), he makes the customary display of erudition; at the same time he shows himself a master of clear reasoning as well as of vivid description and anecdote. The book contains what is deemed "a theory of the colonial system of Spain." The Chilean captain Francisco Núñez de Pineda Bascuñán (1607–1682), in his *Happy Captivity*, tells how he fell into the hands of the Araucanian Indians against whom he had been fighting and how for seven months (1629) he lived among them, until ransomed, in pleasant comradeship. He has many picturesque tales to tell and many good things to say about the Indians, whose rebellion against the *encomienda* he justifies. It is curious to find him commenting upon his experiences among savages with translations from Latin poets. Juan de Espinosa Medrano (*ca.* 1640–1682), nicknamed "El Lunarejo" and renowned for his sermons, wrote a treatise in defense of Góngora, the *Apologético* (1662); it has been called "a pearl of baroque poetics" because of its smooth logic, its terse style, and its discerning appraisal of beauty. Espinosa was well known also as a dramatist, both in Spanish and in the Quechua of his native Cuzco.[34]

It is often said that the baroque taste, and especially Góngora's influence, cast a dire shadow over the minds of our poets, and even of our prose writers, in the latter half of the seventeenth century. It is true that, as a sort of *reductio ad absurdum* of the baroque, there were plenty of extravagant and useless productions, from the centoes of lines extracted from Góngora or from Virgil down to acrostic sonnets, "labyrinths" with cryptograms, ballads with echoes, poems in eleven languages, and "retrograde poems" in Latin which can be read backward just as well as forward. To blame Góngora for them is an aberration of late misinformed critics — he never fathered such bizarre monsters himself. On the contrary, he encouraged the pursuit of relief and color in images and novelty in the combination of words which gave permanent or occasional distinction to the work of Hernando Domínguez Camargo (1601–1656) in Bogotá, of Jacinto de Evia in Quito, of Matías de Bocanegra in Mexico, of Luis de Tejeda in Argentina. The baroque was replaced in Spain by the "prosaic school" of Gerardo Lobo and other insignificant and justly forgotten men; academic classicism came later from France and Italy. But the colonies were fortunate in upholding the baroque tradition, at least in part, and to its persistence we owe the brilliancy and the refinement of Juan Bautista Aguirre (1725–1786) in Ecuador, and F··iar José Antonio Plancarte (1735–1815), Francisco Ruiz de León, Cayetano Cabrera Quintero (d. 1775), and Joaquín Velázquez de Cárdenas y León (1732–1786) in Mexico.[35] In the early years of the nineteenth century the *Diario de México* still published poems written in *culterano* style.[36]

The classicist school imposed itself very slowly in Hispanic America, far more slowly than in Spain or Portugal. Its influence is seldom evident before the end of the colonial era, and it is best represented by the poets of the wars of independence. In the Spanish colonies, the best classicist poets of the eighteenth century are those who write in Latin — the Mexican Jesuits Diego José Abad (1727–1779) and Francisco Javier Alegre (1729–1788), and the Guatemalan Rafael Landívar (1731–1793). They are counted among the very best modern Latin poets, but, excepting Landívar, are very little read today. Abad's greatest effort was a theological poem, *De Deo* (Cadiz, 1769; enlarged, Cesena, 1780); Alegre's, an excellent but unfortunately unnecessary translation of the *Iliad* into Latin (Bologna, 1776; reprinted with many corrections in Rome, 1788) — he was, besides, a good historian. Landívar owes his success to the subject he chose for his poem in fifteen cantos, *Rusticatio mexicana* (Modena, 1781; enlarged, Bologna, 1782). The *Rusticatio* is a rich panorama of nature and of country life in Mexico and Guatemala. Landívar is, among the poets of the Spanish colonies, the first master of landscape, the first who entirely breaks away from Renaissance conventions and brings out the characteristic features of nature in the New World, in flora and fauna, in fields and mountains, in lakes and waterfalls. His pictures of customs, of industries and games, have a graceful vivacity. And he shows a deep sympathy and understanding for the survivals of Indian culture. His poem is still loved by Mexicans and Guatemalans; several portions of it have been put into Spanish at different times, beginning with Heredia, and two complete translations were published as late as 1924.[37]

Brazil produced, during the eighteenth century, a school of epic poets who wrote on native subjects. A "nativist" feeling, which feeds at the same time on the love of tropical nature and on the defense of the colony against the greed or the indifference of the mother country, may be traced as far back as the early sermons of Father Vieira and Friar Vicente do Salvador's *History of Brazil*, and then through the satires and epigrams of Gregorio de Mattos (1633–1696) and his poems to be sung with the guitar, spiced with Indian and African words; through the pleasant descriptions of fruits — amid much prosaic verse — in *The Island of Maré* of Manoel Botelho de Oliveira (1636–1711), the baroque and bountiful *History of Portuguese America* (1730) of Sebastião da Rocha Pitta (1660–1738), and the picturesque discoveries about nature and man in the *Pilgrim of America* of Nuno Marques Pereira (1652–1728). This "nativism" is one of the distinctive traits of the epic school. It lifts the canto on *The Island of Itaparica* above the rest of the lengthy and heavy *Eustáchidos* of Friar Manoel de Santa María Itaparica (1704– after 1768). The two best poems of the school, the *Uraguay* (Lisbon, 1769) of José Basilio da Gama (1740–1795) and the *Caramurú* (Lisbon, 1781) of Friar José de Santa Rita Durão (1722–1784), depict nature in the tropics and its aboriginal inhabitants with accurate vividness and often with relish for minute detail. Durão still adheres, in his style, to the tradition of Camoëns. Gama is freer and simpler, fresh and spontaneous.

Gama and Durão belonged to a group of poets who lived in the province of Minas Geraes, the *Escola Mineira*. The other important members of the group wrote mostly lyric poetry — Claudio Manoel da Costa (1728–1789), who also wrote the languid epic *Villa Rica* and probably the acidly satirical *Cartas chilenas*, Thomaz Antonio Gonzaga (1744–1810), Ignacio José de Alvarenga Peixoto (1744–1793), and Manoel Ignacio da Silva Alvarenga (1749–1814). Costa was the most accomplished rhetorician, Gonzaga the best poet — he became the most popular love singer in all Portuguese literature. Costa, Gonzaga, Alvarenga Peixoto, and a younger poet, Domingos Vidal Barbosa Lage (1761–1793), took part in the conspiracy of Tiradentes, the *infidencia mineira* of 1789, to make Brazil independent. Gonzaga, Alvarenga Peixoto, and Barbosa Lage were deported to distant colonies — Gonzaga, born in Portugal, died in Mozambique; Alvarenga Peixoto died in Angola; Barbosa Lage in Cape Verde. Costa was found dead in prison. Two tragic romances are connected with the conspiracy — Barbara da Silveira Bueno, the wife of Alvarenga Peixoto, equally renowned as a beauty and as a poetess, died soon after her husband's deportation; Gonzaga, who for years had courted another famous beauty, the Marilia de Dirceu of his dainty Arcadian rhymes, was at last going to marry her when he was arrested. There is nothing very unusual in Gonzaga's implication in the conspiracy, in spite of his Portuguese birth (his father was Brazilian, his mother Portuguese); in that age of rigorous adherence to lofty principles, a votary of freedom would defend it against his own country — years afterwards, the Spaniards Mina and Arenales were to defend the independence of the Spanish colonies against Spain.[38]

From the intellectual point of view, our most distinguished men of the "age of enlightenment" were scientists and scholars of a truly modern type.[39] The type is foreshadowed by the Mexican Carlos de Sigüenza y Góngora (1645–1700) and the Peruvian

Pedro de Peralta Barnuevo (1663–1743). Both were mathematicians. Sigüenza was, besides, a disciple of Descartes and an enemy of the scholastic tradition; he divulged in three different books the most advanced astronomical and physical knowledge of his times, and took part in a hydrographic expedition to the Gulf of Mexico (1693). Peralta distinguished himself as an engineer and made astronomical observations, although he was not free (as Sigüenza was) from astrological superstitions. Literature was their foible, and they wrote very baroque poetry — Peralta went so far as a full epic poem on the founding of Lima (1732) and several plays of middling quality in which he combines Calderón, occasionally, for the first time in Spanish with Corneille and Molière.[40] As the century advanced, the devotees of science became innumerable, and they were generally versed in two or three branches of knowledge — thus, the famous jurist Francisco Javier Gamboa (1717–1794) was also a geologist by avocation; José Ignacio Bartolache (1739–1790), a physician and a mathematician; Antonio León y Gama (1735–1802), mathematician, astronomer, and archaeologist. Very seldom did they attempt any comprehensive theoretical generalizations — the only important example seems to be the essay *On the Influence of Climate on Organic Beings*, by Francisco José de Caldas (1771–1816), who, besides, wrote a prose "worthy of Buffon and Humboldt." They made many useful contributions to descriptive science — astronomical observations that were not practicable in more northern skies, determination of geographical positions and altitude of mountains, land measurements, sounding of seas, maps and charts, classifications of fauna and flora, investigations of industrial and medicinal properties of plants — the discovery of India rubber is one of their achievements — archaeological researches, and studies on native languages. In many cases they had to construct their own instruments, since it was not always a simple matter to procure them from Europe. They published books, pamphlets, and periodicals — among these, the *Diario literario* (1768), which was neither a daily nor mainly literary, the *Gacetas de Literatura* (1788–1795) of Father José Antonio Alzate (1729–1799), and the *Mercurio Volante* (1772) of Bartolache, in Mexico, the *Mercurio Peruano* (1791–1795) in Lima, the *Primicias de la Cultura de Quito* (1791), and the *Semanario de la Nueva Granada* (1808–1811) in Bogotá. They took part in the scientific expeditions sent by the Spanish kings to study the New World. They naturally found fault with the antiquated curricula and methods in universities and colleges; sometimes they succeeded in introducing reforms. They founded, or assisted in founding, a number of institutions which included the School of Mines (1792) and the Botanical Gardens (1788) in Mexico City, the Museum of Natural History and Botanical Gardens at Guatemala (1796), and the Astronomical Observatory in Bogotá, as well as the first public libraries.[41] Their splendid effort was cut short by the wars of independence. But they brought fresh air to the intellectual atmosphere; thanks to them, scholasticism was at last partly replaced by modern philosophy and science.[42]

Not a scientist, but a man of wide learning, the Peruvian Pablo de Olavide (1725–1804) became a striking public figure whose brilliant successes were followed by unjust persecutions. In Lima, at the age of twenty-one, he had already a doctor's degree in law and was a judge of the Real Audiencia when he distinguished himself by his philanthropic energy and his honesty in the reconstruction of the city after the earthquake of 1746. He was accused of mismanagement, however, and went to Spain to clear himself. In Madrid he was given important functions to perform. According to one of his bitter censors he came to embody the spirit of innovation that was characteristic of the period of Charles III. His fertile mind conceived plans of public welfare and he had the ability to carry them out once they were accepted. In philosophy he was a follower of both Rousseau and the *Encyclopédie*; in literature, a classicist. He held one of the first salons of the Parisian pattern in Spain and built a private theatre

for which he translated or adapted French and Italian plays —
among these, Racine's *Phèdre*, Voltaire's *Zaïre*, Regnard's *Le
Joueur*, Maffei's *Merope*, and Favart's comic opera *Ninette à la
cour*. In 1767 he was appointed governor (*intendente*) of Andalusia. He reorganized the University of Seville (1769) in accordance with the principles of "enlightenment" — his was the
first curriculum of a modern type in Spain, and it is said to have
been adopted at Salamanca (1770). His most ambitious undertaking was the winning of Sierra Morena; the empty lands where
bandits used to rove were now peopled by Flemish and German
Catholics. But in 1776 he was brought before the Inquisition
under charges of impiety and in 1778 he was condemned. His
work in Sierra Morena was deliberately destroyed. He fled to
France (1780), where he had many friends; the French Academy
received him in a public session, at which Marmontel greeted
him with a poem. Diderot wrote his eulogy.[43] His reputation was
still great when the Revolution broke out, and the *Convention*
named him an adopted citizen of the Republic and voted him
a civic crown. But no one's luck lasted for long in that whirl-
wind — Olavide was imprisoned in 1794. He then repented of
his philosophical faith, turned devout, wrote his autobiography,
The Gospel Triumphant (*El Evangelio en triunfo*, Valencia,
1798), which obtained great vogue, and put into Spanish verse
the Psalms and many medieval hymns. He managed to go back
to Spain, where he died in obscurity.[44]

A puzzling problem remains: why, if ability and knowledge
were plentiful, did our colonial world produce a much smaller
sum of enduring work than was to be expected? In regard to
science the reasons do not seem difficult to ascertain — the theoretical foundations were less ample than the aptitude and resources for the investigation of natural facts; in Spain and
Portugal, where conditions were similar, science did not go beyond
the point it reached in Hispanic America.[45] But in literature, why

were the colonies only inferior rivals of their European capitals
during the main creative period of Hispanic literature, from 1500
to 1660, from the times of Fernando de Rojas and Gil Vicente to
the times of Gracián and Mello? One of the reasons is that the
colonies, from the point of view of European culture, had a very
scanty population — there were millions of Indians, there were
thousands of African slaves, who spoke little Spanish or Portuguese as yet. The actual number of inhabitants in the two vast
colonial empires was slightly higher than in Spain and Portugal
taken together; only about one tenth, as we know, were of
European origin or had fully adopted European customs.[46] Literature, then, in the European sense, was confined to a far smaller
minority than in Spain or Portugal. Besides, the colonial mind
was cramped by a timidity that compelled it to wait for a signal
from its distant capital as to "how things ought to be done." Prohibitions such as that concerning novels tightened the cramp.[47]
And the limited means for publishing, partly due to the scarcity
of readers, induced a peculiar situation, in which the author was
never sure of reaching a public, or, if his writings circulated in
manuscript, was only sure of a provincial audience. Only now
and then did our writers move with creative freedom, as in the
case of Alarcón or Valbuena or Landívar. At the end of the
colonial era, there was a frank rebellion — as, for instance, in
Espejo — but the effort was spent in polemics, not in creation.

In painting and sculpture, too, the colonies did not rise to the
heights attained by Velázquez and Zurbarán, Berruguete and
Montañés, but at least they were not dragged down by the tragic
collapse of the spiritual energy in the Iberian Peninsula during
the last part of the seventeenth century. Literature in the colonies
partly escaped the effects of the collapse, as may be seen in Sor
Juana Inés de la Cruz, whose presence at such a period "partakes
of the supernatural and miraculous," in the opinion of Menéndez
Pelayo; but after her death only minor figures appear, if we

except the Jesuit poets who wrote in Latin, especially Landívar, the Brazilians Gama and Durão, and a few of the scientists, whose merits are only incidentally literary. Painting and sculpture flourished until the end of the colonial era. The majority of the best artists belong to the seventeenth century — the painters of the Echave and Juárez families together with the Spaniard Arteaga in Mexico, Gregorio Vázquez (1638–1711) in Bogotá, Miguel de Santiago (d. 1673) in Quito, Juan Espinosa de los Monteros in Cuzco, and sculptors like Father Carlos in Ecuador and Alonso de la Paz (1605–1676) in Guatemala. During the eighteenth century the artistic output was greater in the colonies than in Spain and Portugal — the mere number of the works is astounding; and, although the quality is generally lower than before, there were men of exceptional ability — the greatest, no doubt, the Aleijadinho, Antonio Francisco Lisboa (1730–1814), of Brazil, sculptor and architect. Just before the wars of independence, José Luis Rodríguez Alconedo, of Mexico, caught a glimpse of the elegance of Goya, and Francisco Javier Matiz (1774–1851), of Bogotá, was "the best painter of flowers anywhere," in the opinion of Humboldt.[48]

The highest creative gifts were displayed in architecture. After the Conquest, there were towns to be built in the European manner, whether, as in Lima, in hitherto empty spaces, or as in Mexico, gradually replacing the Indian seats of population. From the beginning, this enormous activity was a spur to creation. In 1623, Gil González Dávila says that seventy thousand churches and five hundred convents had already been erected in Hispanic America — at that time, Portugal was still united to Spain.[49] Seventy thousand, of course, is sheer hyperbole, quite easy to detect when we consider that many of the buildings now standing belong to later dates. In Mexico alone, it is said, there are "nine thousand churches of architectural merit" — which sounds less improbable. For a hundred years or more after the Conquest, the architects were European — Spaniards and Portuguese, a few Italians and Flemings. The Indians took part in the work only as subordinates, but, as we know, they were not entirely passive. The styles, at first, followed the trends from Europe — first, the Isabella transition from Gothic to Renaissance, then the *plateresque*, then the severe classicist forms of Herrera and Siloe, and finally the baroque, which lasted for two centuries. The Moorish ornament is applied to details, such as arches, doorways, window-frames and ceilings, and Moorish influence shows in the use of glazed tiles. By the end of the sixteenth century we find among the master builders men born in the New World. At the same time, architectural innovations appear. One of the earliest — besides such traits of Indian influence as the trapezoidal openings — is the transplantation of the spiral column — *la columna salomónica* — in church architecture, from the altar to the façade. This innovation takes place in Quito. Quito, also, seems to be the Hispanic home of the column with *entasis* — which may, or may not, have come there from Asia. And then the baroque becomes the typical style of Hispanic America. It develops and grows when architectural inspiration in Spain runs thin, when royal and private wealth becomes scarce there, while the colonies maintain their opulence or begin to attain it. By 1700 the Spanish American baroque is already ultra-baroque, wrongly called Churrigueresque since Churriguera has only a slight connection with it. It differs, both in essence and externals, from that of Spain. The Spanish Churrigueresque tends to blur structural lines: witness Narcisco Tomé's *Transparente* (1732) in the Toledo Cathedral, the palace of the Marquis of Dos Aguas (1740) in Valencia, and the Royal Chapel of Saint Pascual at Villarreal in the province of Castellon. In the ultra-baroque of Spanish America structural lines are never lost under the amazing profusion of ornament — for example, in the tall gilded altars. As Manuel Toussaint puts it, architecture tends to become sculpture; yet the lines of the architectural composition become obscured only in given portions, not in the whole — as in the churches of Santa María Tonantzintla and

Our Lady of Ocotlán.[50] In one of the varieties of the baroque, the local style of Puebla, a sort of transmigration of the old *mudéjar*, called *talaverano* by Romero de Terreros, the glazed tile is transplanted from the interior of the buildings, or from the domes, to the façades and towers.

The culmination of the baroque in all Spanish America, and signally in Mexico, between 1700 and 1780, produced a great number of buildings in which the magnificence of the structure is matched by the luxury of the ornament. These buildings influenced architectural forms in Spain — several Spanish critics (Juan de la Encina, Francisco de Cossío, Enrique Díez Canedo, Luis Bello) have commented upon this reflux, which is very noticeable in Andalusia. It has been said that, out of the eight masterpieces of the baroque in the world, four are in Mexico — the Sagrario by the side of the Metropolitan Cathedral, the Jesuit Seminar at Tepozotlan, the Convent of Santa Rosa at Queretaro, and the parish church of Santa Prisca at Tasco.

In contrast with Spanish America, which began to diverge from Spain in the earliest times, Brazil never markedly differed from Portugal in its beautiful baroque architecture. In all the remotest corners of the old Portuguese empire, from Rio de Janeiro to Mozambique, from San Salvador de Bahia and Recife de Pernambuco to Goa and Macao, not excluding Madeira or the bewitching Açores, there was a clear unity of style. Only a few minor departures have been noticed, such as the oval towers of Minas Geraes, and ornamental details like pineapples or Indians with feathers.[51]

The baroque was succeeded, after 1780, by the academic classicist style. The change is brilliantly exemplified by the Mexican architect Francisco Eduardo Tresguerras (1745–1833) — of his two most famous works, Santa Rosa at Queretaro and the church of the Carmen — Our Lady of the Garden — in Celaya, the first is typically Mexican baroque, the second is classicist. The Carmen (1802–1807) is, in the explosive terms of Mr. Sacheverell Sitwell, "the last good church ever built." [52]

4

THE DECLARATION OF INTELLECTUAL
INDEPENDENCE
1800–1830

UNDER THE apparent immobility of the colonial system in Hispanic America there was, we know, a latent anarchy. Politically, it was felt in the recurrent plots and uprisings. In the eighteenth century, the last and most important revolts were the insurrection of Túpac Amaru, a descendant of the Incas, in Peru (1780), and the mutiny of the *comuneros* in New Granada (1781). By that time, the independence of the United States had been proclaimed, and new political doctrines were spreading through the Hispanic colonies, mainly through French books which were read with no very great concealment. Montesquieu, Voltaire, and Rousseau were among the most influential authors. Then the French Revolution came. It startled and bewildered the imaginations of the colonists; only a few of them discerned its essential principles. Antonio Nariño (1765–1823), of New Granada, translated into Spanish the *Déclaration des droits de l'homme*, had it secretly printed (1794), and circulated it through South America.

The movement that eventually led to the wars by which the colonies became free nations may be traced back to the years 1781–1782, when the extraordinary pioneer Francisco de Miranda (1750–1816) was already exchanging correspondence with dissatisfied Venezuelan aristocrats. At that time he was a member of the naval expedition sent by Charles III of Spain to help the United States by attacking English possessions; he was one of the victors who entered Pensacola in May, 1781, and New Providence, then the capital of the Bahamas, in May, 1782. After that, severing his ties with Spain, he entered the United States. The spectacle of democracy, both in political institutions and in social customs, was for him a not wholly pleasant surprise but a fruitful lesson. He set down his impressions of the country in his diary. Although he was a man of wide reading, he had no literary ambitions, but the journal he kept — a most amazing record — gives him a unique position in the literature of Spanish America.[1] He is always collecting information that may prove useful later on, and noting every personal idiosyncrasy and every peculiar custom in every country. His comments are brief and pointed; very often, too, quite unpredictable. He coldly remarks on the delirious admiration of the American people for Washington, that "fortunate man" in whom "the achievements of many men in the United States who aimed at independence are now gathered up as to a focus." Washington, in fact, does not seem entirely to fulfill his ideal of greatness — perhaps his ideal was too Latin. He holds no very high opinion of Lafayette — for one thing, he finds the French hero too restless. He likes Yale College, and its debating exercises seem to him a good preparation for public life. Harvard College he believes "better adapted to train clergymen than to mould capable and well-informed citizens." He thinks it "an extraordinary thing" that there should be no chairs of modern languages, and remarks on the bareness of the students' rooms and the frugality of their meals. The prosperity of New England he rightly attributes to the industry of its people and to the encouragement they find in their freedom. But he discovers two flaws in the Constitution of Massachusetts, which he discussed at length with Samuel Adams:

> Why, in a democracy whose basis is Virtue, is there no place assigned to it? on the contrary, all the dignity and powers are given to Property, which is the blight of such a democracy? Another point is the contradiction I noticed be-

tween admitting as one of the rights of mankind the right to worship a Supreme Being in the manner and form in which it may please one, yet afterwards excluding one from office if one did not profess Christianity. Grave solecisms, no doubt.

He made innumerable friends. Stiles, the president of Yale, called him, in the oratorical style of the period, "a learned man and a flaming son of liberty." John Adams said that admiration for him became so "fashionable" in the United States that it was generally believed he "knew more of every campaign, siege, battle and skirmish that had ever occurred in the whole war [of American independence] than any officer of our army or any statesman in our councils." He was deemed "a man of universal knowledge . . . , of great sagacity, an inquisitive mind and an insatiable curiosity." [2] In Europe, many years afterwards, Napoleon called him, according to the Duchess of Abrantès, "a Don Quixote — with this difference, that he is not mad." "That man," he added, "has a sacred fire in his soul."

In the United States his plans for the independence of Spanish America took definite shape. He held long conversations about them with Alexander Hamilton and Henry Knox. Then, in England, whose help he sought, he laid them before Pitt. All Colombia, as he called Spanish America, from the sources of the Mississippi to Cape Horn, was to become one great nation under a constitutional monarch, who was to be called Inca and chosen from among the descendants of the ancient rulers of Peru. Indian institutions were to be revived and adopted, as far as possible, to modern ways. Senators were to be called *caciques*. Many years went by before he received the help he sought. Meanwhile he had travelled through all continental Europe, from Turkey to Sweden, had become a friend of Catherine the Great in Russia and received very useful aid from her (1787), had served as a general of the French Republic and captured Antwerp (1792), and had been unjustly imprisoned in Paris on four occasions — the first, because he had incurred the enmity of Robespierre. At last, in 1806, he led his first unsuccessful expedition to Venezuela. In 1810 he returned there as a recognized leader. His campaign failed once more, and he died a prisoner in Spain.

Miranda disappeared a short time before his plan of independence succeeded. When Napoleon invaded Spain in 1807, the colonies found themselves in a contradictory situation — they did not wish to accept the Napoleonic rule, but there was no Spanish king in Spain; both Charles IV and his heir apparent Ferdinand had abdicated and emigrated. What had become of the sovereignty? The modern theory — modern at least in form — of the sovereignty of the people blended, in the minds of many colonists, with the sole tradition of self-rule they knew, the Spanish tradition of municipal government. Meetings were called in the city halls of the colonial capitals. This new departure was a revolution, and in Buenos Aires (May, 1810) it took that name. The allegiance to the crown was nominally maintained, however, and most of the colonies sent their representatives to the Congress (*Cortes*) that met at Cádiz (September, 1810) to reorganize Spain while it fought the invasion. That famous assembly has no less significance in our intellectual than in our political history. A number of the *diputados* elected by the colonies were men of letters who displayed there unsuspected gifts of eloquence and fought in favor of intellectual freedom and progress. At times they spoke disturbing words, especially the Inca Yupanqui, from Peru, and the incisive orator — the best in the Cortes — José Mejía (1777–1813), from Ecuador. "A people that oppresses another cannot itself be free," said the Inca. And Mejía:

> They say that we ought to reject the idea of revolution. I say that I regret, not that there should be a revolution, but that there has not been one. Such words as *revolution, philosophy* [he means, of course, free philosophical thought], *liberty* and *independence*, all have the same character — those who do not know them see them as birds of evil omen.

But those who have eyes look and judge. I judge and say that it is a pity that there is no revolution in Spain.[3]

In the Spanish colonies the wars of independence began in 1810; the last battles were fought in 1825.[4] Brazil became independent in 1822, with no great struggle.[5] In these movements, many of the leaders — besides Nariño and Miranda — were men who had a philosophical and literary education. Literature played an ancillary role to their political activity; in fact, it had been a herald already, in the writings of such men as Baquíjano and Espejo. Newspapers and pamphlets were essential instruments of their campaigns. The diffusion of new ideas, and the "enlightenment" and education of the people, in opposition to the restricted and old-fashioned culture that had prevailed in colonial times, together with the perfection of individual freedom through the abolition of all forms of slavery and serfdom, were conceived as normal concomitants of national liberty.

Miguel Hidalgo (1753–1811), the curate of Dolores, had translated Molière and perhaps Racine for performance before his Indian flock, whom he had taught to make silk, pottery, and bricks. After he gave the Mexican people the signal to rise (September 15, 1810), he decided to publish a paper, *El Despertador Americano*, December 20, 1810; the editor was another priest, Francisco Severo Maldonado (*ca.* 1770–1832), a sort of spontaneous socialist. Camilo Henríquez (1769–1845), "the Friar of Good Death," was the first man to demand· independence for Chile and made it a subject of sermons, poems, dramas, pamphlets, and articles. He gave his country its first newspaper, *La Aurora de Chile* (1812–1813); its appearance brought forth such enthusiasm that, according to his contemporary Friar Melchor Martínez, "men ran through the streets with the paper in their hands, stopped any friend they met, read and reread its contents, and congratulated themselves on their good fortune, hoping that the ignorance and blindness in which they had lived would disappear and be followed by enlightenment and culture, which would transform Chile into a country of wise men." It is significant that Father Henríquez, in his defense of the freedom of the press, quoted from Milton's *Areopagitica*; toward the end of the eighteenth century our men of letters had begun to read English authors as well as French — such widely divergent thinkers as Tom Paine and Adam Smith were translated or quoted, and, of course, the American statesmen, Washington, Jefferson, Madison, and John Quincy Adams. In Argentina, Mariano Moreno (1778–1811) and Bernardo de Monteagudo (*ca.* 1787–1825) expressed their political conceptions in excellent prose — Moreno had the gift of complex architectural syntax, Monteagudo, of crisp and concise utterance. Simón Bolívar (1783–1830) himself, the most brilliant and original of the liberators, the *Libertador* par excellence, wrote in clear, vivid language. His best pages are probably in his speech before the Congress of Angostura (February 12, 1819), to present the project of a constitution drafted by himself and Zea for the republic of Colombia. His letters contain striking passages, especially the "prophecy" written in Jamaica (September 6, 1815). He even wrote a sort of prose poem on his ascent of Mount Chimborazo.[6] And José Bonifacio de Andrada e Silva (1765–1838), the power behind the throne in the curious process of Brazilian independence, was also the best informed man of letters of his times in the country and, at least in the opinion of Afranio Peixoto, the promoter of literary autonomy.[7]

The desire for intellectual independence is first made explicit by Andrés Bello (1781–1865) in his *Allocution to Poetry*, the first of his two *Silvas americanas*. [8] Bello had gone to England in 1810, together with Bolívar, on behalf of the patriots of Venezuela. His *Allocution* was printed as a sort of editorial program (could any man but a Spanish American have done that?) in the opening pages of a magazine that he and the Colombian Juan García del Río (1794–1856) published in London, in 1823, under the title of *Biblioteca Americana*. Many years later, the Argentine critic and historian of culture Juan María Gutiérrez reproduced the poem as a declaratory introduction in our first great anthology, the *América poética* (Valparaiso, 1846). It begins with an invocation to the muse in six lines of silvery verse, in which the delicate interplay of vowels gives a fresh quality to old pastoral images.[9] He calls on the muse for a "return to nature," inviting her to leave Europe, over-sophisticated Europe, "land of light and misery," "unloved by the Muse's native rusticity," and fly to "the great scene of the world of Columbus," where "earth still wears her primitive dress." Like Emerson in his lecture on *The American Scholar* (1837), he thinks "we have listened too long to the courtly muses of Europe." He proceeds to describe the natural wealth of the New World and the prowess of the liberators, who were still fighting their last campaign. These were new subjects for poetry. The peaceful imperial shadows of Virgil and Horace are his guides in this revolutionary attempt, together with the eighteenth-century writers who make literature out of scientific material — a promising road from which we have unfortunately turned aside. His style has been described as classical, conceived in the Roman mold, with a touch of the native flavor of our soil.

The *Biblioteca Americana* appeared only during 1823. In 1826 Bello and García del Río started another magazine, the *Repertorio Americano*. It lasted until 1827 and contained, like the *Biblioteca*, articles on many subjects, the natural sciences, pure and applied, history and archaeology, politics and economics, education and grammar, art and literature. Like the *Biblioteca*, too, it contained in its opening pages a poem by Bello on *The Agriculture of the Torrid Zone*, the second of his *Silvas americanas*. Here he depicts again, at greater length than in the *Allocution*, the natural wealth of the tropical lands that "circumscribe the wandering course of the loving sun," and sketches a prosperous future for the young nations if they are willing to devote their efforts to the cultivation of the soil. The war of independence being over, he extends a friendly unarmed hand to Spaniards.

His famous descriptions of the plants, both native and imported, that grow in the tropics are a curious blend of realistic detail and classical allusion — cotton "opens in the soft breeze its golden roses and its snowy fleece"; maize is "the haughty chief of the spiked tribe"; cocoa "curdles its almonds in purple urns"; the pineapple "seasons its ambrosia." At times he falls into somewhat cryptic conceits in the old manner of Góngora and Calderón, a relic of his early youthful tastes.[10] As a rule, his verse is more eloquent than poetical, for our present-day tastes at least. We probably need in Hispanic America a critic of the school of T. S. Eliot to make us relish again the virtues of our classicists of the eighteenth and early nineteenth centuries. In any case, if Bello now and then writes prosaic lines, he often attains a very effective concise expression in accordance with the Latin tradition of sententiousness.[11]

Bello did not write much original verse. His was a very original mind, as we shall see, but his habits were those of the scholar rather than of the poet. He was curious about all literature, and translated or imitated many types of poetry, from Plautus and the Nibelungenlied to Byron and Hugo. His translation of Boiardo's *Orlando innamorato* is prized as the best Spanish version of an Italian epic.[12] Occasionally he takes a poem from a foreign language and adapts it to the circumstances of his own life. The most striking example is his *rifacimento* (1843) of Victor Hugo's *La Prière pour tous* (1830). It was no mean critic — Menéndez Pelayo — who said that Bello's poem is more beautiful than Hugo's beautiful poem. I feel that the French poet remains supreme and unsurpassed in the truly inspired first part of *La Prière pour tous*, but that his following nine parts are mostly amplifications. Bello uses only the first four, following a procedure that seems to us strange and difficult to recapture — he does not paraphrase the poem line by line, or even always stanza by stanza; he composes his work with thoughts and images taken from the French and often placed in a different order, adds many new details, with now and then a reference to his own life — such as the mention of his dead child Lola — and ends with two very personal stanzas of his own on his old age and the approach of death. The tone of the poem is entirely changed. Hugo is a father, but a young man, when he summons his daughter to pray for all men, and he has all the lyrical as well as the rhetorical exuberance of youth. His poem is written as evening falls, and we feel it as a brilliant sunset in spring. Bello was past three-score when he thought of reshaping the poem for his own youngest daughter, and as we read it we feel it as a clear but sad autumnal dusk. He has given up the complex Latinized syntax and the at times epigrammatical tendency of his earlier work. His verse has now a slow tempo and a star-like limpidity.[13]

As a scholar, Bello did work of exceptional quality. His education, in his native Caracas, had been unusually ample. He was trained in the classics, in philosophy and in law; to this he added the study of the sciences of nature, improving it through his friendship with Humboldt.[14] In London (1810–1829) he became acquainted with James Mill and Lord Holland, among other men of distinction, and frequented the British Museum. From England he was called to Chile (1829), where he acted as legal adviser to the government on foreign affairs and partly reorganized public education, especially the university over which he presided (1843). He was the principal author of the Chilean Civil Code (1855), one of the earliest in this hemisphere, and wrote one of the first treatises on international law that combined theory with an extensive use of actual treaties and cases (1832). In his *Philosophy of the Understanding* he steers a middle course among the many alluring islands of English thought, now approaching Hume, now Berkeley, now Hamilton, now anticipating John Stuart Mill. In his vast literary researches he acted with originality and daring. He proved the early medieval Latin origin of assonance, which was then conceived of as a unique peculiarity of Spanish poetry, and proved its existence in Old French from poems he had read in manuscripts when not even the *Chanson de Roland* was printed.[15] In his edition and study of the *Poem of the Cid*, begun in London in 1827 and finished in Chile in the year of his death, he undertook, with a great measure of success, the restoration of the twelfth-century text from the fourteenth-century manuscript; he wisely accepted the irregularity of the verse form as evident; he discovered the influence of the French epics; he detected the prose versions of Spanish poems in the historical chronicles and asserted the precedence of the long *cantares de gesta* over the short *romances* or ballads. Finally, in his *Grammar of the Spanish Tongue* (1847) and in his *Principles of Orthology and Metrics* (1835) he established the study of the language and of its verse on a basis of fact which had been obscured latterly by a blind adherence to Latin models, although the grammarians and prosodists of the fifteenth century, Nebrija and Encina, had originally taken the right road. Bello's *Grammar* is still, after nearly a hundred years, the most complete synchronic description of our tongue and one of the best of any modern language.[16]

Bello's friend from Guayaquil, José Joaquín de Olmedo (1780–1847), was the poet who sang in sonorous verse the final battles of our wars of independence, the victories of Junin and Ayacucho. His ode in praise of Bolívar is entitled *The Victory of Junin* (1825); Sucre's greater and final victory at Ayacucho is announced by the spirit of the Inca Huayna Cápac. Even though Olmedo wrote in the classical manner, and visions were still in vogue, the Inca's apparition has given rise to objections. One of them is that the Peruvian emperor hails Bolívar as the liberator of his race. Was the object of Bolívar — they say — the restoration of the Inca Empire, or the establishment of a modern nation whose official language would be Spanish and not Quechua? We know that Bolívar intended no such restoration — except the purely symbolic reconstruction of the Inca temple of Pacha Cámac; but we also know that Miranda had dreamed of something very like it, and a few of the later leaders — the Argentine Belgrano, for instance — still entertained similar projects. It is even more pertinent to remark that the liberation of South America from the Spanish rule was expected to bring not only political independence for the community but also personal freedom of the Indians, many of whom were still under a legally disguised bondage. They formed the majority of the population in most colonies. In Peru they had planned serious revolts at least once in each century. Olmedo himself had spoken against the *mita*, the tribute the Indians had to pay, in his only important speech at the *Cortes* of Cadiz. Mariano Moreno, the leader of the *Revolución de Mayo* (1810) in Buenos Aires, had written his thesis for the degree of Doctor of Laws at the University of Charcas (1802) on the personal service of the natives. San Martín, addressing the Araucanians of Argentina in 1816, told them in order that they might understand his campaign of independence: "I am an Indian too" (which literally he was not). Justice to the Indian was one of the ideals of the movement of independence. The failure, all through the nineteenth century, to make that ideal a reality left the problem to our own times.

Bello did not disapprove of Olmedo's vision; on the contrary, in the *Repertorio Americano* (1826) he praises the Inca's prophecy and the chorus of virgin priestesses of the Sun who invoke the aid of their luminous god. The Indian inhabitant and his traditions, as well as the features of nature in the New World, often named with native words, were ever present in Bello's own *Silvas americanas*, and there is a long passage, in his *Allocution*, on the legend of Huitaca, goddess of waters, and Nenqueteba, child of the Sun, in Bogotá. In short, the Indian had become as important in literature as in politics.[17]

Olmedo's qualities in his *Victory of Junin* were his sense of structure and development — often called Pindaric — his gift of metaphor and description, and the rotund fulness of his verse. He had the *os magna sonaturum*, as shown in the opening onomatopoetic passage on thunder, a reminiscence of Horace's *Caelo tonantem*.[18]

The ode is of unusual length — more than nine hundred lines — but Olmedo wrote very little. His political activities usually deprived him of time for literature.[19] He had, besides, the classical habit of constantly retouching and polishing his poems, with frequent consultation of learned friends. So he wrote a not very large number of unimportant *vers de circonstance* and very few important poems besides *The Victory of Junin*; the superb ode to the victor at Miñarica (1835), the pre-Leopardian ode (1817) to a friend's first-born child ("¿Tanto bien es vivir?"), and a translation of the first three epistles of Pope's *Essay on Man*.[20]

With Bello and Olmedo the conscious effort towards intellectual independence was justified by success. They brought no innovation to verse or to style, except the deft use of Indian words, carefully framed in rigorously pure Spanish. Their descriptions of nature, however, were new — they were definite conquests in our search for expression. New, also, was their giving voice to political and social aims in poetry. Furthermore, in public life they helped to shape the young nations, especially Bello, who played the most prominent part in the reorganization of the cultural life of Chile.

Bello, Olmedo, and Andrés Quintana Roo (1787–1851) in Mexico, and Juan Cruz Varela (1794–1839) in Argentina, among many, were the poets of independence achieved.[21] José María Heredia (1803–1839), of Cuba, was the poet of frustrated independence. Like Domingo Del Monte (1804–1853), the other great literary figure of his generation in Cuba, he was the son of a distinguished migrant family from Santo Domingo, a country that underwent a distressing crisis with the invasions of the insurgent slaves from Haiti and thereby lost many of its men of wealth and culture. Heredia's short life was a procession of misfortunes. His father, José Francisco Heredia (1776-1820), was a very honest and humane judge who became a broken man after years (1811-1818) of fruitless exertions in Venezuela during the revolutionary period and died soon afterwards in Mexico. The son then went to Cuba (1820-1823), joined a conspiracy to make her free, was exiled, spent two years in the United States (1823-1825), and finally took up his residence in Mexico, where he endured many hardships because of the political unrest. He saw his native island again only once, in a visit of a few weeks (1836).

His poetry is a clear reflection of his unfortunate life. He began writing verses in childhood, and his two best poems, *On the Teocalli of Cholula* (1820) and *Niagara* (1824), were written before he came of age. In fact, during his last sickly years he did not often write well. His education had been classical — the poet Francisco Muñoz Del Monte remembers his translating Horace in Santo Domingo before he was ten — and he adhered to the classicist style of the eighteenth century; but his life was similar to that of his contemporaries the romantic poets of Europe, and his poetry, like that of the Spaniard Cienfuegos, although conceived in a classicist frame, is already a premonition of our romanticism, in its emotional outbursts and even, at times, in its carelessness of form. When the long campaigns of continental Spanish America began, Bello and Olmedo were fully grown men, and as such assumed their part and responsibility in it. Their literary work still profits from the leisurely habits of their colonial upbringing — it is carefully planned, developed, polished, and finished. Heredia had neither the peace of mind nor the time to acquire the habits of lucid order and impeccable language. He was a child when the struggle began, and as a child he suffered its consequences. When, a boy still, he tried to help his native island to be a free nation, the attempt failed. Cuba was not to become independent during his lifetime. He is the poet of

INTELLECTUAL INDEPENDENCE   107

failure, of unsuccessful rebellion; at best, the unhappy prophet of freedom, whose stanzas his compatriots repeated during seventy years to spur themselves to effort and sacrifice. Meanwhile, he gladly sang the praises of the heroes of free countries, especially Washington and Bolívar.

As might be expected, Heredia is the most truly lyrical among our poets of those troublous times. He is the first of our long line of poets who sing of absence and exile (a Latin tradition!), of hopes unfulfilled and lost treasures. The love of his native land is a constant desolate passion. The mere caress of a warm breeze from his native climate is enough to evoke a cry, as in his *Return to the South* (1825), one of his most original if least remembered poems.

But, like Bello and Olmedo, he had an objective gift — description. His ode *On the Teocalli of Cholula* depicts the slow fall of evening on the solemn tablelands of Mexico, among the snow-clad peaks, and discourses on the mortality of civilizations and the vanity of human endeavor. His ode on *Niagara* portrays the falls with quick strokes, interspersed with emotional remembrances. The most striking moment comes when, impelled by his nostalgia to evoke the palms of the tropics, he collects himself, thinking they would be out of place by the side of the great falls, whose only fit crown is the wild pines. The verse has a magnificent sonority.[22]

Many novelties are introduced into our literature during this brief period — the desire for independence and innovation grows and spreads. The landscapes of Mexico, after Landívar and before Heredia, appeared in the work of many poets, especially in a few passages of Friar Manuel de Navarrete (1768–1809). This refined provincial poet probably never saw the thronged streets of the capital, but was recognized and proclaimed as leader, *mayoral*, by the metropolitan band of his Arcadian brothers, which included a very able translator of Ovid's *Heroides*,

Anastasio de Ochoa (1783–1833). In contrast, the energetic and uncompromising Friar Servando Teresa de Mier (1765–1827) travelled through many countries and led a political life of perpetual restlessness, during which he developed a peculiar ability to escape from prisons again and again. He had a keen eye for political and social problems, as his writings and speeches show. His memoirs read at times like a novel of roguery. And a real novel of roguery, the last of its kind in Spanish, was written by José Joaquín Fernández de Lizardi (1776–1827), who signed himself "the Mexican Thinker," *El Pensador Mexicano*, taking as his pen-name the title of one of the periodicals he published (1812) for the diffusion of new ideas. His *Itching Parrot* (1816; completed, in four volumes, 1830) is actually the first novel written by a native of Hispanic America and printed this side of the Atlantic.[23] It is a story in the manner of Alemán's *Guzmán de Alfarache* and Espinel's *Marcos de Obregón*; the hero is a rogue, a *pícaro*, who goes through many inglorious adventures, and travels as far as the Philippines. While by its structure it belongs to an old and at that time already extinct school, by its matter it is a realistic picture of Mexican life in all its strata, down to the lowest, where squalor and vice take ghastly shapes. And its moral comments are properly mixed; they are partly quotations from classical wisdom — Aristotle, Horace, Juvenal, or Seneca, translated by the author — and partly reflections suggested by very modern authors, Rousseau in particular.[24] Afterwards Lizardi took Rousseau as his direct model for another of his four novels, *The Little Quixotic Lady and Her Cousin* (1818–1819).[25] His innumerable writings — more than three hundred pamphlets, newspapers, almanacs, plays, novels, and fables — are a rich source from which we may draw a complete knowledge of those complex times in a very complex society.[26]

Mariano Melgar (1791–1815), in Peru, for the first time consistently tried to give utterance in Spanish verse to Indian ways of feeling. He wrote *yaravíes*, in the manner of the native love songs, and fables that were flavored with sly native humor. If he had been a great poet, he might have laid open a mine of incalculable wealth. He did not; nor did José Joaquín Pesado (1801–1861), in Mexico, a sort of lukewarm poet, although far superior to Melgar in his command of language and traditional poetic resources. He was a man of classical culture and approached the Indian themes in a scholarly manner. With the help of a friend's literal translation, he clothed in Spanish verse a number of old Aztec poems. The result, if not great, is at least decorous and pleasing. Pesado's *Las Aztecas* is his best effort, together with his descriptions of nature around Orizaba, in the mild and lovely stretch of land between the torrid coast and the cool plateau of Anahuac.

During this time, satires and fables multiplied. Satirical verse had been plentiful in Hispanic America from the times of the Conquest — the conquerors themselves, and the first settlers, were curiously prone to improvise humorous comments in verse on current happenings, as a compensation for their harsh experiences. Later on, the city of Lima became famous for its wit and has remained so — Caviedes is still remembered as the embodiment of the *ingenio limeño*.[27] But colonial satire usually remained unprinted. Now, in the wars of independence, satire became a political weapon, and as such persisted through the nineteenth century. Two typical satirists were Francisco Acuña de Figueroa (1790–1862), of Uruguay, who wrote nearly fifteen hundred epigrams (besides a tragic poem, *The African Mother*, against slavery), and Antonio José de Irisarri (1786–1868), of Guatemala. Irisarri, however, who led a very active political life in his native country, in Chile and in Colombia, ranks higher as a master of polemical prose. He left an unfinished autobiographical novel, *The Wandering Christian* (1845–1847).

The best of the poets who had the gift of humor was José Batres Montúfar (1809–1844), of Guatemala. Shortly after the end of the colonial era, he detected that country's quaint reposeful charms — a surprising feat, considering the short distance in time, but less surprising if we consider the changes in spirit and in ways of living brought about by the independence. He wrote three short satirical novels in verse, in the manner of La Fontaine and Casti, with a few drops from Byron's *Don Juan*, the *Traditions of Guatemala*. He discovered a field at once picturesque and rich in comedy.

In Cuba, Domingo Del Monte discovered contemporary rural life as a subject for literature and became the father of one of our types of *poesía criollista*.[28] A few years before, in Uruguay and Argentina, Bartolomé Hidalgo (1788–1823) had appeared as the first acknowledged master of *criollismo* in the *gauchesco* dialect.[29] In its spontaneous form, of course, *criollo* poetry had existed from the earliest times. The Spaniards and the Portuguese brought their traditional songs and ballads — a few, like *Delgadina* and *Gerineldo*, the *Pájara Pinta* and *A la limón* (or the "Broken Bridge"), are still sung or recited in town and country. They began, besides, to improvise new ballads and songs. This type of informal, everyday poetry soon became one of the permanent habits of the new men in the New World. Among the peasants in the fields as well as among the humblest laborers of the cities there were always — and still are — poets who improvised with the help of the guitar. They compose narrative ballads, especially in Mexico, where thousands of *corridos* have been recently collected, as *chácaras* have been collected in Brazil. They compose love songs, religious songs, humorous songs, moral homilies, and sceptical discourses in verse. They compete in long poetic tournaments called *porfías* and *contrapuntos*. In countries or regions of large Indian population, the *criollo* verse often becomes *mestizo*: it mixes native with Spanish or Portuguese words. In Cuba, and in Brazil too, there are medleys of African and European words. In the literature of colonial times, echoes of folk songs and parodies of local dialects were heard now and then, as, for example, in the *villancicos* of Sor Juana Inés de la Cruz; this practice also came from Spain and Portugal, from Juan del Encina and Gil Vicente, from Lope and Tirso, Quevedo and Góngora. At last, between 1810 and 1830, we find the first city poets who describe at length the life of the *criollos*. Bartolomé Hidalgo, besides, systematically wrote the *criollo* dialect of Uruguay and the lower provinces of Argentina. His *cielitos* and *díalogos* in the language of the gauchos deal with political questions of the day, and by preference with the independence of the River Plate countries; the brief touches of rural life herald the ample frescoes of *Santos Vega* and *Martín Fierro*. His modest attempt was probably the most revolutionary of all.

5

ROMANTICISM AND ANARCHY
1830–1860

INDEPENDENCE did not bring the long-expected happiness to the peoples of Hispanic America. Most of the countries found their wealth destroyed and their population decimated by the long bloody struggle. And then the latent anarchy of the colonial regime broke loose; civil war and despotism ware alternately dominant, save when a man of high character and energy happened to be the ruler. There were two main exceptions: Brazil, a monarchy, and Chile, an aristocratic republic — both achieved organic peace about 1830. Monarchy was tried in Mexico, with Iturbide, and failed (1822–1823); it was to fail again with Maximilian of Hapsburg (1864–1867). And both the conservative and the liberal organizations of republican government failed again and again, in Mexico as elsewhere. The men too. The good and the bad, the sage and the tyrant, Rivadavia and Rosas, Gómez Farías and Santa Anna, all were eventually ousted from power. A dictator like Dr. Francia in Paraguay, who was still in office at the time of his death, was exceptional.[1]

At last, between 1850 and 1870, stability slowly asserted itself, either because democracy was becoming a reality, as in Argentina, or because a man with a strong hand held power for a long period and kept up a semblance of republican rule while inducing material progress. Only in a few countries, mostly of small territory or sparse population, did the old turbulent conditions persist.[2]

During the fifty restless years between 1820 and 1870, a titanic task was undertaken. The structure of society was changed. Slavery was abolished; as abolitionists, the Spanish-speaking republics were all in advance of the United States and frequently in advance of England (1833).[3] The virtual servitude of the Indians was also abolished by the law — but more than the law was needed to destroy it. The economic system was radically altered, in accordance with the principles of liberalism. And, above all, a comprehensive educational reform was attempted and partly carried out. Popular education, schools for every man and woman, had been one of the ideals of the intellectual leaders in the campaigns for independence; it never ceased to be one of the ideals of the best men in public life. Poverty prevented its becoming a fact, but at least many schools were founded. And in the higher forms of education the scholastic tradition of the colonial era was supplanted by the influence of modern French, English, and German philosophy and by modern science.[4] Finally, our legislation was often at odds with the social facts in our anarchical societies, but in defiance of all sceptical opinions it played a prophetic role and gradually shaped the unwieldy mass of reality. In that, it was in accord with the Roman tradition, which, in the words of Lecky, "instead of being a mere empirical system adjusted to the existing requirements, laid down abstract principles of right to which it endeavored to conform."

With the general decline of wealth, the arts suffered. Hardly a new church was ever built now, and very few public buildings. There was little demand for pictures. Religious painting survived as a modest craft that catered to the needs of devout ladies, or else it sank into folk art, in the guise of votive offerings for the poor to place in humble churches; it still exists as such in countries like Mexico and Peru. The colonial traditions dissolved. In the academies of fine arts that had been established in the late eighteenth century or in the early nineteenth — among them the Academia de San Carlos in Mexico (1783), preceded by a school of engraving (1778), the Escuela de Bellas Artes in Guatemala (1797), the Escola de Bellas Artes in Rio de Janeiro (1815), and the Academia de San Alejandro in Havana (1817) — the classicist style was imported from Spain and France. It proved a sterilizing influence, probably not from any fault of its own but because no use was found for the new secular painting.[5] In Hispanic America, only the portrait, among the polite forms of art, retained originality and character.[6] Sculpture survived, also, as a minor craft, the clients being small churches and pious homes.

Only in imperial Rio de Janeiro were there new sumptuous palaces and gardens, in the French classicist manner. There began, then, the unexampled city planning that soon transfigured the Brazilian capital into a delightful labyrinth of perpetual luminous surprises between the peaks and the waters.[7]

Most unreasonably, it would seem, literature throve during the turmoil of these years. But there were reasons — political, not economic reasons. Literature was not paid; nobody in Hispanic America lived by writing literature; hardly anybody does even now. But it had political uses which the arts did not seem to have — although later in the nineteenth century our rulers discovered that architecture might serve as propaganda, and in the twentieth our paintings are carrying social messages. Literature proved its usefulness in public life during the campaigns for independence. It often took the form of journalism, or oratory, or the political essay; we know that it also took the form of the novel (our first novel, The Itching Parrot, had a social purpose), of the patriotic drama, of the classical ode to be read in public, of the hymn that was set to music. There were special types of political folk songs — the cielitos of Argentina and Uruguay are the best examples. In Cuba and Puerto Rico, where independence had not been obtained, all literature, all culture even, was a kind, at times a very subtle kind, of rebellion.

In the already independent countries, literature in all its forms kept all the public functions it had assumed with the movement of liberation. In the midst of anarchy, the men of letters were all in favor of social justice, or at least in favor of political organization against the forces of disorder. To mention a few salient instances — in Mexico, when Iturbide was crowned as emperor (1822), Francisco Ortega (1793-1849), a classicist and a devout Catholic, prophesied his downfall in a Horatian ode; in Chile, when the eminent statesman Diego Portales was murdered (1837), outraged public sentiment found voice in a solemn elegy written by a lady of distinction, Mercedes Marín de Solar (1804-1866). In Peru, the aristocratic poet and playwright Felipe Pardo (1806-1868) expressed his opinion of democracy in disdainful satire. In the strife of parties in Colombia, her two best poets, Julio Arboleda (1817-1861) and José Eusebio Caro (1817-1853), wrote eloquent political verse. In Brazil, the prophets of the abolition of slavery were Antonio Gonçalves Dias (1823-1864), Antonio de Castro Alves (1847-1871), Luis Nicolau Fagundes Varella (1841-1875), and Tobias Barreto (1839-1889). And the two most important national movements of the century, the *Reforma* of Mexico (1855-1874), and the struggle against Rosas (1837-1852) followed by the organic reconstruction of the country (1853-1880) in Argentina, were carried on with the aid of a huge amount of literature. There were in Mexico, besides the innumerable journalists and orators, the poets: among the *conservadores*, José María Roa Bárcena (1827-1908), who hailed the arrival of Maximilian of Hapsburg (1864), evoking the shades of the old Indian rulers as sponsors to the new emperor, and the bishop Ignacio Montes de Oca (1840-1921), the translator of Pindar and Theocritus, who bewailed the ephemeral empire's misfortunes; among the *liberales*, men of even higher qualities, Ignacio Ramírez (1818-1879), Ignacio Manuel Altamirano (1834-1893), Vicente Riva Palacio (1832-1896), and Guillermo Prieto (1818-1897), the author of a collection of ballads on patriotic subjects that he entitled *Romancero nacional*. And, after the poets, there were the historians, to justify the ways of the heroes to posterity.[8] The political folk song, which during the campaigns of independence had flowered in the touching *coplas* in praise of Morelos, the village priest turned general,[9] now gave forth the red prickly pears of the *Cangrejos*, likening the conservative party to crabs that walk backwards, and the *Mamá Carlota*, pouring sarcasm on the unreal empire and predicting its fall.[10] And when the exiles from Argentina were contriving the destruction of the power of Rosas and all the other *caudillos*, their most potent literary weapons were José Mármol's impetuous verses and his tragic novel *Amalia* (1851), Hilario Ascasubi's songs in gaucho dialect, and Sarmiento's great books, very appropriately reaching their climax in his journal of the military campaign by which Buenos Aires was seized and Rosas deposed (1851–1852).

Our men of letters were then, as a rule, also men of action. A number of them became presidents of republics.[11] Many were cabinet ministers. Most were, at one time or another, members of congresses. Often they suffered exile. Even peaceful Brazil had her exiles, such as José Bonifacio de Andrada e Silva, or, much later, Ruy Barbosa. A few died by violence — Arboleda, for example, shortly after his election as president of Colombia. In Cuba, where the struggle for independence went on at intervals from 1823 to 1898, two poets, Plácido (1809–1844) and Juan Clemente Zenea (1832–1871), were condemned to death by Spanish judges; José Martí died on the field of battle (1895), and after him the young poets Francisco Gonzalo Marín (1863–1897), from Puerto Rico, and Carlos Pío Uhrbach (1872–1897) also perished in the war.

The poets of the campaigns of independence had discovered the public uses of poetry, and even the odes in which Bello proclaimed our aspiration to intellectual self-rule were a manner of political activity. A new generation, after 1830, felt that this proclamation was incomplete, that Bello, Olmedo, Heredia, and Juan Cruz Varela were too European in the forms they adopted to express America. Novelty of subject was not enough — there should also be novelty of form, a form strictly adapted (such was the dream) to the new subjects.

This dream was born, it may easily be surmised, from the contact with European romanticism. In 1825 a young man from Buenos Aires, Esteban Echeverría (1805–1851), went to Paris, where he spent five years in the midst of the romantic insurrection. He discovered romanticism as a spiritual revolution that opened to every national or regional group the road to self-expression, to the full revelation of its soul, in contrast with the cold ultra-rational universality of academic classicism. The *Stimmen der Völker* were to be set free, the *Zeitgeist* commanded; "the spirit of the century leads nations to become emancipated, to enjoy independence, not only political but also philosophical and literary independence," says Echeverría, who knew his Herder and his Mme. de Staël. Romanticism was a battle of the nations, waged on many fronts, from Norway to Russia and from Scotland to Catalonia. Echeverría wished to extend the field of battle to our hemisphere and conceived this purpose as a patriotic duty. When he sailed for Europe he did not think himself a poet, although he must have written a poem or two, like every self-respecting young man of our "good families" at the time. Now he made the decision to study the Spanish literature of the past in order to acquire skill in language and verse. He acquired it, though he never became a true poet — his lines yield only opaque sounds, magic of imagery is lacking in his style. His only merit lies in simplicity and clearness of design. It is a misfortune that he should have chosen verse as his vehicle, but the prejudice in favor of poetry was still too great in Hispanic America. His prose is far better — excellent, in fact — both in his lucid philosophical essays and in the bold realistic descriptions of *The Slaughter-House*, a vigorous piece which he seems to have valued little, since he never printed it. Yet his success as a poet was extraordinary — the success, it is true, of a discoverer rather than that of an artist.

The first poem he published after his return to Buenos Aires was *Elvira, or The Argentine Bride*. The date — 1832 — is significant; *Elvira* precedes by a year the first acknowledged work of the romantic school in Spain, *The Moorish Bastard*, by the Duke of Rivas (1833-1834). Our literary emancipation proved true in regard to Spain; we adopted the new movement without waiting for her signal.[12]

But *Elvira* drew little attention. It had failed of its purpose — Echeverría had only exchanged one European allegiance for another. His poem is a story in the manner of Bürger's ballads, with phantoms and all; it is South American only in its subtitle, *The Argentine Bride.* Two years later he brought out a volume of romantic lyrics, *The Consolations*, with another ballad-like story, *Laida*, and they were more warmly received than *Elvira*. His crowning success came in 1837 with his volume of *Rhymes*, which included a third story in verse, *The Captive Woman*.[13] Here, at last, he fulfilled his promise: *The Captive* conveyed to the reader a faithful semblance of nature and life in Argentina — the "open and immeasurable" pampa, all grass and no trees, with its persistent winds and its elongated clouds, its rains, its droughts, and its fires, its pugnacious howling Indians who had already mastered the horse and the European weapons, and its *criollos* struggling to lead a civilized life, surrounded by the vast emptiness of the land and perturbed by the ever present fear of attack from the savages. Echeverría is the ancestor of the great line of Argentine painters of nature — one of them a master of English prose, W. H. Hudson, the naturalist. The style of *The Captive* was direct, clear, simple; so simple, indeed, that it attained originality, though it did not attain distinction.

1837 was Echeverría's *annus mirabilis.* He was acclaimed as the poet who had revealed the soul of the pampa, its splendor and its tragedy.[14] He was acclaimed also as the leader of the young political idealists with whom he founded the *Asociación de Mayo* (1838) and wrote the *Symbolic Words*, later renamed *Socialist Dogma* — socialism meaning, for them, the desire for social welfare, not the later program of economic reform; in regard to the economic organization of society, they adopted the principles of classical liberalism, then a novelty in Hispanic America. The young idealists were soon persecuted by Rosas and fled one by one; they returned, after fifteen years of exile, to reorganize the country in accordance with their dreams. Echeverría saw the promised land only from a distance — he died a few months before the fall of the tyrant.

He wrote four long poems after *The Captive*, all on Argentine subjects. Usually they are deemed inferior to his earlier work; they are not really very inferior, but they came after it, and the novelty had now worn off. Only a canto in *Avellaneda* found many admirers, because it described a new type of landscape, tropical Tucuman, entirely different from the pampas.

Echeverría found, naturally, many followers. A year after *The Captive*, his friend Juan María Gutiérrez (1809–1878) wrote *The Love of the Gaucho Songster*[15] and afterwards other poems on the gauchos or the pampas; he also wrote poems on Indian subjects (*Liropeya, Caicobé, The Flowers of Lilpu*), not realistically portraying, like Echeverría, the modern fighters of the pampas, but idealizing the less troublesome natives of the past. And Bartolomé Mitre (1821–1906) wrote *Santos Vega* (1838), a short poem, the first about the legendary *payador* who eventually became the favorite subject of gaucho literature.[16]

But neither Gutiérrez nor Mitre owed their fame to their poems. Both were scholars. Gutiérrez is best known as a literary critic and a historian of culture, who conceived and triumphantly carried out the project of the first systematic anthology of Spanish American poetry of the nineteenth century, the *América poética* (Valparaiso, 1846); he also wrote at length on the colonial poets and printed or reprinted some of their works. Mitre was, with Vicente Fidel López (1815–1903), one of the two master historians of Argentina. He made history, too, as the ruler (1862–1868) who started the country along the road of modern progress, as a moulder of opinion in his great daily *La Nación* (since 1870), and finally, during his long old age, as a democratic patriarch.[17]

The typical romantic poet of Argentina, typical in his qualities and in his defects, was José Mármol (1817–1871), who won his reputation by means of his explosive invectives against Rosas. In his campaign against tyranny he seemed driven by the faith that "the poet who divests the tyrant of his usurped glory is a godlike genius who avenges the outraged dignity of history," in the words of a contemporary of his.[18] He had a true lyric gift and a vivid perception of nature — land, sea, and skies. But he lacked patience, and all his poems are careless impromptus, now brilliant, now dull. A born poet, as Echeverría was not, he never wrote a perfect poem. His nearest approach to that ideal is the *Hymn to the River Plate*. For the most part, in reading him we have to content ourselves with a beautiful stanza or line, here and there, as when he describes the tropical landscape in Rio de Janeiro or when he speaks of the "brotherhood of tears" ("fraternidad de lágrimas") addressing the Countess Walewski.[19]

The exiles from Argentina during the tyranny of Rosas (1837–1852) carried the romantic movement to Uruguay and to Chile, where they fought a brief noisy battle (1842) with the classicist disciples of Andrés Bello. The Argentines were supported by a number of young Chileans, especially by José Victorino Lastarria (1817–1888), whose address before the Literary Society of Santiago, in May, 1842, is said to be the origin of the controversy. Lastarria had spoken of the need of "literary emancipation," declared that literature should be "the authentic expression of national character," and, although he cautiously avoided the word *romanticism*, quoted Victor Hugo and praised the literature of France, at last free from "rigorous and petty rules." The contending parties soon came to an agreement. Bello himself proved that he was not unaware of the qualities of the new poetry by publishing his own adaptations from Hugo (he had already given to the stage — 1839 — a translation of Dumas's *Thérèse*), and in his inaugural address as Rector of the new University of Chile (September, 1843) finally settled the dispute in masterly fashion, recognizing "freedom in everything" as essential to creative art, although never renouncing the Platonic norm of "ideal beauty." [20]

Elsewhere in Spanish America the movement began independently, but later than in Argentina.[21] As a rule it came from France. France had become for us the main source or else the channel of modern culture, even before the wars of our independence, and so she remained until the twentieth century; German and English ideas came to us mainly through France. Now and then there was direct contact with English literature, as in the case of Caro and Arboleda in Colombia. Besides, the ties with Spain had never been really broken, and, when her own romanticism came to full flower, Larra, Espronceda, and Zorrilla found many followers among our young writers.

Contrasting with the Spanish-speaking countries in their relation to Spain, Brazil lagged behind Portugal, where the romantic movement began, with Almeida Garret, before 1830. Attempts have been made to date the beginnings of Brazilian romanticism as far back as José Bonifacio de Andrada e Silva's *Poems*, printed in Bordeaux in 1825, or José Domingos Gonçalves de Magalhães' *Poems* printed in Rio de Janeiro, 1832; but these were men of classic training who felt the attraction of romanticism and read Scott or Byron or Lamartine, like the Cuban Heredia. They were not revolutionists. Gonçalves de Magalhães (1811–1882), being younger than José Bonifacio, came much nearer to romanticism, and his *Poetic Sighs*, printed in Paris in 1836,[22] contained enough novelty to move a respected contemporary writer, Torres Homem, to declare that they "opened a new era in Brazilian poetry." In 1839, however, Gonçalves de Magalhães still called himself an eclectic: "I do not accept the rigor of the classicists nor the carelessness of the romanticists. . . . I make due concessions to both."

The first full-fledged romantic of Brazil, and by far the best Brazilian poet of the period, is Antonio Gonçalves Dias (1823–1864), whose *First Songs* appeared in 1846.

His poetry was simple and fresh; without any apparent effort he gave voice to a wide variety of feeling and emotion. In him, more than in any other of our poets, the program of romanticism is fulfilled in regard to the central problem of giving artistic expression to our life. His *Song of Exile* — he said exile, but it was merely absence — is a song of exalted, feverish love of his native land (like the songs, a few years later, of Casimiro de Abreu, 1837–1860). And he founded the "Indianist" literature in Brazil with his *Y-Juca-Pyrama*, his *Song of the Tamoyo*, and his *Tymbiras*, a long poem he planned in sixteen cantos, but of which he wrote only four (1848). He brought to it, not only his gifts of imagination and his passion for the beauties of nature, but also the fruit of his ethnological and linguistic studies, which he pursued all through his life. In 1857 he published a *Dictionary of Tupi* and in 1860 he joined, as ethnographer, an official expedition sent by Pedro II to study the north of Brazil. He also took pleasure in proving his skill in traditional Portuguese by writing the *Sextilhas de Frei Antão* in fifteenth-century language. So much importance was attached to Guarani that José de Alencar said in 1865, in a letter attached to his novel *Iracema*: "Knowledge of the Indian tongue is the best criterion for judging of the national character in our literature." The "Indianist" question, of course, was hotly debated. But several poets followed the example of Gonçalves Dias; among them, very significantly, his elders Gonçalves de Magalhães in *The Confederation of the Tamoyos* (1856) and Manoel de Araujo Porto Alegre (1806–1879) in *Colombo* (1866), an enormous poem, saved from oblivion by a few finc descriptions.[23]

Our romantic movement began in poetry, and then spread to the drama and the novel. Our first romantic play shows the influence of Victor Hugo — *Don Pedro de Castilla*, by Francisco Javier Foxá (1816–*ca.* 1865), born in Santo Domingo. It was written in Cuba during 1836, a year after the appearance of the first fully romantic tragedy in Madrid, the *Don Álvaro* of Rivas, and performed in Havana in 1838, with great applause. There was even a public coronation of the author, following the custom of the early Italian Renaissance. A verse translation of Hugo's *Hernani*, by Agustín Zárraga y Heredia, had already been published in Havana, 1836. It is unfortunate that the drama should have declined into gradual eclipse at this very time in Spanish America. Only in Lima did a school of comedy maintain the tradition of the colonial theatre. The plays of Felipe Pardo and Manuel Ascensio Segura (1805–1871) are still partly eighteenth-century in manner, but they have genuine and delightful local color. In Brazil, too, where the theatre enjoyed a brief period of activity after 1838, Luis Carlos Martins Penna (1815–1848) gave amusing pictures of everyday life. And Spanish America gave to Spain two of the best dramatists of her romantic period, Ventura de la Vega (1807–1865), born in Buenos Aires, and Gertrudis Gómez de Avellaneda (1814–1873), born in Camagüey. Vega is a case of complete transplantation. He was taken to Europe, much against his will, when only eleven years old, never returned to Argentina, and seldom mentioned it in his writings.[24] La Avellaneda was already a young poetess when she left Cuba (1836),[25] never lost connection with it even in the midst of her resounding triumphs, and returned there in her prime to be crowned as a native glory (1860). It is a coincidence that neither Vega nor La Avellaneda were fully romantic in their plays — they always tempered romantic fire with classic logic. The life of La Avellaneda, however, was restlessly romantic — twice forsaken by faithless lovers (one the handsomest fop in Madrid, the other a poet who was at the same time a political leader — García Tassara), twice married to distinguished men who seem to have given her a few years of peaceful happiness, acclaimed in her heyday by her admirers, even by the sceptical Juan Valera, as the greatest woman poet that ever lived, but at the time of her death forgotten and penniless. Her magnificent poems, as might be expected, are now playful and joyful (*Los Reales Sitios*, a graceful account of a feast offered by the Queen of Spain in Aranjuez), now tragically passionate; in the end, she finds consolation in devotional verse. She found time also for classicist exercises on impersonal subjects — her sonnet to Washington, for instance, is written in the most majestic seventeenth-century manner.[26]

Even in the historical novel, a literary type so closely related to the romantic movement, Spanish America did not wait for Spain's example. *Jicoténcal*, a story based on the conquest of Mexico, was published in Philadelphia, 1826; the anonymous author was probably a Mexican.[27] In fact, the beginnings of romanticism in Spanish America might be dated from its appearance, were it not a solitary work that attracted little notice and had no sequel or influence. Not until after 1845 were many novels written — on historical as well as on contemporary subjects and in the manner of Walter Scott, or Victor Hugo, or Eugène Sue. In Mexico a whole school of novelists appeared, after Manuel Payno's *The Devil's Scarf-Pin* (1845), and it was supported by the publishing houses that managed to thrive in the midst of political turmoil, to the extent of issuing a Bible in several volumes and an excellent encyclopedia.[28] The novels of this period are generally weak in structure, but often they excel in the depiction of customs, one of the typical features of our literature at that time. As a genre by itself, the *cuadro de costumbres* had a long vogue in countries such as Venezuela, Colombia, Peru, and Chile. It is one of our most genuine expressions, especially in the Chilean Jotabeche (José Joaquín Vallejo, 1811–1858); in the Venezuelan Daniel Mendoza (1823–1867), who created a magnificent specimen of the peasant visiting the town, Palmarote; and in the Colombians José Caicedo Rojas (1816–1898), and José Manuel Marroquín

(1827–1908), who displayed a racy originality in *Yerbabuena*, the story of his own country-place, and in *El moro* (1897), the autobiography of a horse.[29] The *cuadro de costumbres* was a criticism of social life, often with an avowed public purpose, the correction of antiquated and injurious habits. It was related to political literature, to the writings of men who wished to remodel society and the state — such men as the Mexicans of the *Reforma* movement; the Argentines who fought and drove away the *caudillos*; the Venezuelans Antonio Leocadio Guzmán (1800–1884) and Fermín Toro (1807–1865), whose description of a small town, a *parroquia*, in a speech made in 1858, might be mistaken for a page from a *costumbrista*; and the Chilean Francisco Bilbao (1823–1865), whose violent pamphlet on the structure of Chilean society (*Sociabilidad chilena*, 1844) burst with a crash upon the mental drowse of the privileged families and the smug narrowness of the reigning politicians (Bilbao, of course, came too soon; his only possible choice, after the scandal, was exile). In Peru, the first clash between the old and the new social and political ways took the shape of *cuadros de costumbres*, and comedies too, in the hands of Pardo and Segura. In Argentina, Juan Bautista Alberdi (1810–1884), the future mentor of the constitutional legislators of 1853, the future preacher against *The Crime of War* (1870), began his public career as the first *costumbrista* of the country (and, curiously enough, also as a musician). The *costumbrista* frankly becomes a political writer and a sociologist in Echeverría's *The Slaughter-House* and in Sarmiento's portraits of human types in the pampas, the *rastreador*, the *baquiano*, the *gaucho malo*, and the *cantor*, in his *Facundo*.

The most interesting novels of the period were written in Brazil. Joaquim Manoel de Macedo (1820–1882) gives pleasant transcriptions from aspects of everyday life and portraits of human types, like his famous "little brunette," *moreninha* (1844), and "blond young man," *moço louro* (1845). More ambitious than Macedo, José de Alencar (1829–1877) essayed the archaeological and historical novel on Indian and colonial subjects, and succeeded especially well in *O guarany* (1856) and *Iracema* (1865) by his narrative skill, his unusual powers of description, and the sober beauty of his style. His characters were conceived in the romantic manner of, say, Scott, and the simpler they are the better. He also essayed the social novel, as in *O gaucho* (1870).[30]

The romantic movement took on a character of its own in Hispanic America. First of all, in breaking away from the classicist set of rules, our romantics really tried to cast off all rules.[31] Not that they always clearly realized it. In Europe itself it was not always clearly understood that the romantic revolution implied the assumption that no rules were possible in literature, that poetic creation was in its essence free, since the only limitations it was bound to respect arose from the nature of language — and in more recent movements, in which romanticism is carried to its ultimate consequences, from Mallarmé to Gertrude Stein and the surrealists, the attempt is made to transcend even such limitations. Our poets merely believed they had given up the "imitation of models" — no more reminiscences of Virgil and Horace, of Garcilaso and Luis de Léon — and that their field of subjects had been enlarged, as well as their vocabulary and their repertory of metrical forms. But they had, moreover, adopted a new emotional manner of composition and development instead of the supposedly rational technique of the classicists. And they were convinced, as Ion was convinced by Socrates, that inspiration was their sole guide. That, unfortunately, led to the loss of two excellent habits of our classicists — to obey the normal usages of language and to learn all that should reasonably be known about the subject with which they were going to deal. Carelessness became a fashion, and the poet felt entitled to any "poetic license" he pleased — he would twist his words to suit his scansion or his rhymes, and would not inquire whether the gazelle had wings or whether Leonidas died at Thermopylae or at Plataea. Anarchy was as frequent in literature as in public life, and political unrest, through its influence on private affairs, was another cause of haste and carelessness. Inspiration was expected to sanctify everything. Many of our innumerable poets acted as if they thought, like Rimbaud in later years, that their mental lawlessness was sacred ("J'ai fini par trouver sacré le désordre de mon esprit"). How could any line of a true poet fail to be perfect? There were exceptions, naturally: Gonçalves Dias in Brazil, for example, the Colombians, ever careful of the proprieties of language — Caro, Arboleda, Gutiérrez González — and a few of the Venezuelans, Yepes, Escobar, Calcaño, Pardo, and Gutiérrez Coll.[32] Then the poets who were still partly classicists, like La Avellaneda, with her unfailing mastery, or Baralt, or Ignacio Ramírez.

Romanticism was in Europe the literature of rebellion — rebellion against political oppression and in favor of freedom, whether embodied in Marco Botzaris or in Toussaint Louverture; occasionally too, rebellion against society itself. Afterwards, political and social problems ceased to be poetic subjects; the poet chose to live in isolation, in his private world of imagination and emotion. Not that he gave his assent to the existing order; on the contrary, he became an exile, like Baudelaire's albatross.

Our romantics, in Hispanic America, now and then spoke as though they were exiles; but that was merely playing the sedulous ape to their European masters. They often were exiles in fact, political exiles — which meant exactly the opposite of exiles from society, since it proved what part they played in communal and public life. And their writing, as we know, often became a form of public service. In that they were nearer to the earlier than to the later romantics of Europe, nearer to Wordsworth or Shelley, or to Byron as the champion of Greece, nearer to Victor Hugo, who kept through the years his faith in the prophetic role of the poet — and partly for that reason exerted a powerful influence in Hispanic America. Never were they rebels, in spite of a few stray echoes from Byron or from the Spaniard Espronceda; [33] they were closely tied to the soil and the family and the traditional ways, and never became insurgently individualistic. Only in Brazil do we find, toward the middle of the century, an epidemic of *mal du siècle*; the infection spread from the poems (*Lira dos vinte annos*, 1851) of Manoel Antonio Alvares de Azevedo (1831–1852) and reached Laurindo Rabello (1826–1864), Luis José Junqueira Freire (1832–1855), the monk who felt compelled to leave the cloister, and, in later years, Fagundes Varella.

In sharp contrast with Europe's literature of free passion at odds with society, Hispanic America produced a large quantity of domestic poetry. Much of it seems now slightly ridiculous; when the mediocre poets bore us, their tears may seem indeed idle tears, but it should be remembered that their sufferings were real — seldom have men suffered so much, for so long, as they did in most of the countries of Hispanic America during the anarchical romantic years. At times "the tear changes to a pearl," as in the *Canto fúnebre* of the Venezuelan José Antonio Maitín (1804–1874) on the death of his wife, or, in later years, in the *Return to My Native Land*, by another Venezuelan, Juan Antonio Pérez Bonalde (1846–1892), or in *The Return to the Forest*, by the Cuban poetess Luisa Pérez de Zambrana (1837–1923).

With the spread of "enlightenment," religious faith vanished from many minds or reduced itself to a vague theism. In political controversy, such of our writers as belonged to liberal parties attacked the influence of the Church, especially in Mexico; they seldom discussed religion,[34] and it is only incidentally that they spoke of their beliefs. Occasionally, a poet who was also a student of science would rise to a Lucretian inspiration when discoursing on change as the only permanent feature of the universe and on the human spirit as a mere momentary flame that disappears like the body. Thus Ignacio Ramírez ("Mother Nature, when I was born I had no hopes and no fears; I return to thy bosom without fears and without hope") and, in a later generation, Manuel Acuña

(1849–1873).[35] Among the poets who kept the traditional faith a few were also philosophical, especially José Eusebio Caro and Gertrudis Gómez de Avellaneda; the majority wrote religious verse that was merely devotional or narrative. But, on the whole, romantic poetry, in Hispanic America as in Europe, made no systematic effort to adapt itself to the new scientific and philosophical interpretations of the universe. The poets of the eighteenth century wrote as if they still conceived of the world in the shape of Greek and Roman myths; but a few attempted to introduce in their work the modern conceptions of the world — Pope, Chénier, Goethe (very different poets, as we see), and, in Spanish, Quintana, Bello, Olmedo (at least as translator of Pope), and in later times Heredia. The romantics rid themselves of classical mythology as the frame of their universe: the sun is no longer a god, nor are trees and brooks inhabited by nymphs; the ancient myths they use as myths — Prometheus, or Hyperion, or Endymion. But at the same time, as a duty of their new cult of imagination and emotion, they give up the attempt to lodge their poetry in a world built with the materials of modern science. Professor Whitehead explains their attitude as a refusal to accept the mechanistic explanation of the universe; but they seldom tried, like Wordsworth, to assert a wider faith. In this, as in other ways, nineteenth-century poetry lived in a none too splendid isolation.

The description of nature, which began with the classicists, was now for our romantics a duty to be religiously fulfilled. It was a dogma that our landscapes surpassed all others in beauty. Our poets and writers attempted and practically achieved a literary conquest of nature in every aspect — our interminable mountain ranges, the high tablelands with their clear sharp outlines, thin air, and quiet light, the tropical forests, the deserts, the sea-like plains, the sea-like rivers, and the loud-sounding sea itself.

A truly original poet, Gregorio Gutiérrez González (1826–1872), combined the descriptions of nature with the description of customs in his poem entitled *Memoir on the Cultivation of*

Maize in Antioquia (1868). It has been called the Georgics of Colombia. But the poet was not moved to write by any classical example; his work was the outcome of a happy chance. When invited to join a learned society, in which it was an entrance requirement to present a more or less scientific report, he decided to do it in verse, taking as his subject the rural labors of his mountainous native province. He wrote with charming simplicity and clearness that often rose to vigor or gracefulness.

The cult of the past was not so prolific in Hispanic America as in Europe at this period. Biblical or Greek or Roman subjects were seldom touched. The Middle Ages — crusaders, troubadours, single combats, tournaments — and the beginnings of the modern era, with its arbitrary kings as painted by Schiller and Hugo, appear frequently in our dramas, but very seldom in our novels.[36] Our three colonial centuries, which we had begun to conceive of as our Dark Ages, appear also in plays and in fiction.[37] Of our own past, the event usually chosen is naturally the Conquest — as in Arboleda's unfinished *Gonzalo de Oyón*, a brilliant effort in the already moribund form of the epic, with vivid pictures of mountains and rivers, warriors and horses, battles and excursions and disputes. The Indian is rarely presented in his own unadulterated past — *The Tymbiras* of Gonçalves Dias, Alencar's *Ubirajara*, and Plácido's ballad *Jicoténcal* are outstanding exceptions. The formidable subjects offered by the empires of the Incas and the Aztecs were left untouched or else they yielded meagre results in the hands of men who showed more industry than talent; most writers were discouraged by the need for archaeological studies. As a rule they chose to draw the Indian when he faced the European conquerors, the moment when, by means of contrast, he might be drawn with fewer lines; it was also his most pathetic moment.[38]

The main lines of our romantic movement may be most clearly discerned in poetry, plays, and fiction; its best embodiment, however, is not a poet but a prose writer who never essayed either the drama or the novel, Domingo Faustino Sarmiento (1811–1888).[39] He had the full impetus of romanticism, its imaginative energy and passionate rush of language, together with a vivid sense of fact and a swift flow of thought. With all these gifts, he had no desire to be a mere writer; he thought only of service, to his own Argentina, to Chile, where he lived in exile for many years, to all Hispanic America. Education was his earliest passion, education for himself and for everybody. In childhood and early youth he strove to acquire knowledge, struggling against poverty in his old-fashioned mountainous province of San Juan, and succeeded in obtaining the type of education he needed, according to his way of thinking. He plodded through Latin, which interested him little but taught him, he says, a simple mechanism that proved of great help in the acquisition of French and English; he read all he could find in philosophy, history, political theory, and pedagogy; as he could not help reading everything that lay around, he also read the Bible and many books on religion, including Paley's *Evidences*. When only fourteen years old, he knew enough mathematics to learn the elements of surveying while helping the French engineer Barreau. He felt the usual nineteenth-century reverence for natural science, but there was not very much that he could learn of it in the parts where he lived. At fifteen he began to teach (the three R's, of course), by the side of his uncle the priest José de Oro, whom he helped to build a school and to rebuild a country church that had been struck by lightning. But he was not precocious in his literary career. After many changes of place and trade, he began to write when he was already in his twenty-eighth year, and then his motive was political. He started a paper in San Juan, *El Zonda* (1839), to fight for progress. In the then normal run of things, he was exiled and went to Chile. There he caught the eye of a statesman of large views, Manuel Montt (1809–1880), who did not fear to trust this self-made teacher and asked him to organize the first normal school of

Hispanic America in 1842.[40] At that time he was already writing in the leading newspapers of the country and taking part in the literary controversy between classicists and romanticists. In the same year he founded the first daily of Santiago, characteristically named *El Progreso*.

From then on, and during the rest of his life, he was usually engaged in two or three different tasks at the same time. In 1845 he undertook his systematic study of despotism in Argentina, choosing as his subject the life of Aldao, the friar turned military chief, and immediately afterwards he published *Facundo*, a life of the ferocious *caudillo* of La Rioja — thereby earning from Alberdi, in a moment of anger, the title of "Plutarch of the bandits." A description of Argentina preceded this biography of Facundo Quiroga, a sort of essay in human geography in which he tried to ascertain the causes of the social disease of the country, tyranny engendered by anarchy; at the end there was a study of the political situation, proving the inevitability of the fall of Rosas and the whole *caudillo* system, to be succeeded by organic reconstruction. It was a startling prophecy that came true a few years later. This powerful book is the masterwork of the period. It has obsessed many readers whose permanent preoccupation is the sources and remedies of the ills of Hispanic America.[41]

Three years (1845–1848) spent in Europe and the United States studying new developments in education yielded two new books, one on schools for the people (*De la educación popular*, 1849), the other on his travels (*Viajes*, 1849).[42] In 1843, as a reply to foul attacks from the partisans of the *caudillos*, he had written a pamphlet (*Mi defensa*); upon his return to Chile he enlarged it into *Provincial Memories* (*Recuerdos de provincia*, 1850), a book that contains his autobiography as well as forceful or picturèsque or tender descriptions of the common life in his native province and splendid portraits like that of Domingo de Oro.

In the last months of 1851 he joined General Urquiza in the march from Entre Ríos to fight Rosas in Buenos Aires, as the official gazetteer of the campaign; he was present at the battle of Caseros (February 3, 1852), in which the dictator was finally routed, and recorded his experiences in a very original book (*Campaña en el Ejército Grande*, 1852). The goal had been reached, it would seem. But Sarmiento fled from Urquiza, in whom he still found the traits of the *caudillo*, and returned to Chile. Eventually he went back to Buenos Aires (1855) to start on his long career as the greatest nation builder that any country in Hispanic America has known. That career included many campaigns in the press and in Congress, two years as governor in San Juan (1862–1864), three as minister to the United States (1865–1868), and six as president of the republic (1868–1874). The prodigious list of his achievements comprises hundreds of schools and libraries, astronomical observatories, zoological and botanical gardens, parks, roads, railways, ships, telegraph lines, immigration, even new cities. He took part in every contention in which the issues were freedom and justice, and, best of all, the regeneration of the people through education. The war of three countries — Brazil, Uruguay, and Argentina — against Paraguay came to an end while he was president, and his government was asked to make its territorial demands. The immortal reply was given by Mariano Varela as minister of foreign affairs — "Victory gives no rights."

Sarmiento lived always pen in hand, and wrote as much after his return from exile as before — newspaper articles, speeches, official messages and reports, text-books, lives of men who interested him, Lincoln, or the naturalist Muñiz, or his own son who died in the Paraguayan war (*Dominguito*, 1886), and finally a vast sociological work that he never finished, *Conflict and Harmony of Races in the Americas* (1883).

To his early period belong his three best books, *Facundo*, *Recuerdos de provincia*, and *Viajes*. They are solidly built; he wrote them in haste, but conceived their structure complete and harmonious from the start. Fact and theory in them go hand in hand.

Every fact he notes — and there are many — is always, explicitly or implicitly, placed in relation to an ample and coherent body of ideas. Anything that holds his attention immediately spurs him to thought. But his grasp is not merely intellectual; it is also imaginative. He has the gift of description — his ten-line picture of Rio de Janeiro is a classical example. No less classical is his picture of the pampas of Argentina in the first pages of *Facundo* (after the Introduction), with its crowning thrill — the automatic movements of the gauchos in the midst of the plain, looking first toward the desert south, then at the ears of their horses, if there was the least whisper of wind through the grass, fearing that the sound might be the distant cry of approaching savages ready to murder and pillage. When he wrote these stirring pages, Sarmiento knew the pampas only by hearsay.

At times his thought embodied itself in images — Dr. Francia, the tyrant of Paraguay, "dead from the quiet weariness of sitting motionless, crushing under his feet a submissive people" ("muerto de la quieta fatiga de estar inmóvil pisando un pueblo sumiso"); or the ignorant traveler who understands nothing of the marvels of modern invention shown to him, "Anacharsis who insults the statue by merely looking at it with his Scythian eye"; or our Latin traditions, summed up in a sentence, "We belong to the Roman empire"; or the habits of the gauchos, whom he describes as living in a "leathern age," hides being used by them, not only to make shoes, hats, clothing, saddles, beds, chairs, tables, and carpets, but even to cover houses and to build boats.

He had a strange mastery of language. There were many legends about him while he lived, and one of them has survived — that of his slipshod writing. It came from his earliest censors. As he began his literary career when romanticism was new and judgments were still governed, knowingly or unknowingly, by classicist assumptions, he was condemned in the name of the eighteenth century. But, after a hundred years, his best writings show him as a master. He is unequal, no doubt. Both as a man in public office and as a journalist, he wrote many pages that he did not expect to live more than a day; but we have preserved them all. He is hasty, as a man who usually wrote for immediate publication; hasty, too, because his ideas came with such tumultuous impulse that at times he forgot to join them with the proper links; his style is often elliptical. "A careful style," he said in 1842, "can only exist as the flower of a complete and well-developed civilization." But he was not careless in the manner of the mediocre, and never wrote journalese, not even in his unsigned newspaper articles. His style was racy and could rise to brilliancy without effort. He could be a master of the apt word, which might be a single adverb, as when he spoke of "the road that leads only to wealth" ("el camino que sólo conduce a la riqueza"). He was accused of using too many Gallicisms, a plague that infected Spanish during the eighteenth and nineteenth centuries; in fact he made use of few, and those he employed, as a rule, deliberately, believing that the impoverished Spanish of his day wanted enrichment. On the contrary, his language was richly idiomatic, a quality he derived from the traditional speech of his native province, then, as now, free from the international winds that blow over Buenos Aires. "My Spanish," he said once, "is somewhat colonial."

The books that Sarmiento wrote after his return to Argentina in 1855 do not equal, as literature, the books written before. He was even more pressed than before by his many activities, and he was now a builder, straining himself in "the effort of every minute" that would yield "the prodigy of the year" and no longer a critical fighter whose eyes try to pierce through appearances to reach the core of social reality.[43] But he still penned many fine pages, such as his speech on the Argentine flag, at the unveiling of Belgrano's statue (1873). Not long before his death, he wrote in a few sentences his autobiography, a fit conclusion for such a life:

> Starting from the slope of the snowy Andes [he says], I have ascended all the minor summits of my native land. A

few words describe a long life. I leave behind me a lasting trail in education. I waged war against barbarism in the name of healthy and practicable ideals; being called to carry out my program, I was unable to fulfill all my promises, but I advanced beyond what had been done until then in this part of the Americas. Like the silkworm, I have built my coarse cocoon; I shall not grow into a butterfly, but I can see that my thread is of use to those that come after me. I was born in poverty and grew up amid many struggles; I attempted all that I conceived as good, and success crowned my perseverance. I have visited all the civilized lands of the earth; have been favored by the esteem of great men; have written some good pages among many indifferent ones; never tried to amass a fortune, which would have been a heavy load in my incessant war; and expect a good death in the body, since in public life my end is what I wished it to be: I have improved the intellectual condition of many; I leave my country prosperous and at peace, so that all may enjoy the banquet of life, in which I took part only by stealth.[44]

6

THE PERIOD OF ORGANIZATION
1860–1890

THE RESTLESS PERIOD in Hispanic America after the campaigns for independence was at the same time, we know, a period of complete transformation. The structure of society was changed, with new political institutions and new customs; education was remodeled in accordance with nineteenth-century ideals. Then, between 1850 and 1870, a period of organization began. The social innovations were by now permanent. There were no longer any classes after the old European manner (we know that even during the colonial era they were never rigid); there were only divisions according to power, or wealth, or upbringing. The republican institutions persisted, in name at least, and their forms were either actually or nominally respected. In education, after a variety of philosophical influences which supplanted the scholastic tradition of the colonial era, French and English positivism became dominant, signally in Brazil, Mexico, Argentina, and Chile.[1] The great national movements of Argentina and Mexico came to fruition. In Argentina, after Rosas was deposed (1852), the country was organized in all its activities by an intelligentsia whose members had been living in exile for the greater part of fifteen years; after ten years more of effort and discussion, a constitutional era opened in 1862. The source of the new Constitution, voted in 1853, was the work of a man of letters, the *Bases* of Alberdi. The first president (1862–1868) of the federated republic was another man of letters, Mitre. The second (1868–1874) and the third (1874–1880) were also men of letters, Sarmiento and Avellaneda. They were the best rulers of the country, together with Rivadavia, the prolific pioneer.[2] Under them with organic peace finally assured, civil liberties guaranteed, and schools established in great number, a flood of European immigration swept over the well-nigh empty land, which under the direction of the *criollos* soon became wealthy and prosperous. The neighboring Uruguay, though less peaceful, profited by the example of Argentina and the influx of population.

In Mexico, the movement of political innovation, adequately called *la Reforma*, took on legal shape in the liberal Constitution of 1857. It aroused a powerful opposition that eventually brought about the reappearance of monarchy, yet the republican government never considered itself defeated — it persisted, at times over a thin fringe of territory; when Maximilian of Hapsburg was executed (1867), after due process of law, in retaliation for his own decree against "rebels," [3] and the *conservadores* finally disappeared from the political field, Juárez set himself to the task of reconstruction, with the help of faithful liberals — among them the writers and poets Prieto, Ramírez, Altamirano, and Riva Palacio. Prieto, the poet of the *Romancero nacional*, was once the minister of finance, and introduced in his department the practice of double-entry bookkeeping. After the death of Juárez (1872), his successor Sebastián Lerdo de Tejada, a brilliant orator, carried the program of liberal reform to further lengths. Then came Porfirio Díaz, and during his long, peaceful, but undemocratic reign (1876–1911)[4] the country frankly took the road of material progress that the efforts of Juárez and Lerdo had opened.

In Chile, the conservative aristocratic governments of the era of Portales and Montt (1831–1861), which had given the country its stable organization, were succeeded by liberal administrations (1861–1891); the rulers, however, still came from traditional families.

Brazil, under the benevolent and active rule of the Emperor Pedro II (1825–1891), a scholar and a true believer in liberty, enjoyed peace and progress. Then in 1889 the monarchy peacefully gave way to the republican form of government.[5]

Two political tragedies cast a gloomy shadow over this period: the war of Brazil, Uruguay, and Argentina against Paraguay (1864–1869) and the war between Chile and Peru (1879–1881). Literature, as might be expected in Hispanic America, took part in the struggles. Its finest utterances came from the Argentine poets, especially Carlos Guido Spano (1827–1918) and Ricardo Gutiérrez (1836–1896), who bewailed the fate of Paraguay.

Sarmiento's government itself had declared, as we know: "Victory gives no rights." The *Nenia* of Guido Spano is a lament of a Paraguayan girl over the destruction of her native land. *La victoria*, of Gutiérrez, declares why he refuses to sing a paean of triumph: "I do not sing the death of my brother." The attitude of these poets is similar to that of a few great American writers during the war against Mexico in 1847. But in Argentina the feeling of pity for the vanquished spread to very wide circles. Even unknown versifiers wrote poignant elegies that were sung to languid music. "A great thing," said a later poet, Arturo Capdevila, "to see a nation saddened by victory."

During this fruitful period of social and political reconstruction there was no revolution, nor much deliberate innovation, in the arts or in literature. The romantic program was still in force. If we except Brazil, no country had as yet enough wealth to undertake any architectural work on a large scale. In the smaller cities — Guayaquil or San José de Costa Rica — houses were still built in the traditional way inherited from colonial times; in ancient Santo Domingo, for example, it is difficult to tell at first sight whether a private residence belongs to 1570 or to 1870. The larger cities, Mexico or Buenos Aires or Santiago de Chile, began to adopt the anarchic nineteenth-century European fashion of reproducing and even mixing the most diverse styles and periods.[6] There was little demand for pictures, yet the academies of art grew and multiplied. We have from those years many good and occasionally excellent portraits, a number of accurate landscapes and picturesque street scenes, a few historical canvases.[7] The most original and racy work we owe to cartoonists in newspapers, especially José María Villasana in Mexico and Pancho Fierro (1803–1879) in Peru. At a humbler social level, a sort of city folk art flourished in the drawings of José Guadalupe Posada (1851–1913), of Mexico, for ballads and stories printed in leaflets and pamphlets.[8] Sculpture was now for the most part imported; it was the rule to assign public monuments to European artists, a rule that persisted until the beginning of the twentieth century — Rodin's statue of Sarmiento, in Buenos Aires, bears the date 1910. Miguel Noreña's majestic figure of Cuauhtémoc (1889) in the Mexican capital is one of the few exceptions; on its pedestal, besides, there is a very interesting graft of Aztec motifs upon a European structure, deliberately repeating the process that had spontaneously occurred when European architecture was first transplanted to the New World. Even religious sculpture now came from abroad — machine-made, alas! Only the poorest churches persisted in giving employment to local talent.

In music, the colonial traditions had not been interrupted as in the plastic arts. Palestrina and Victoria, Bach and Haydn, were still heard in churches. Opera was a frequent entertainment in cities. Symphonic orchestras, which made their first appearance in the eighteenth century, were slowly developing.[9] And the conservatories grew and multiplied like the academies of art. Composers essayed the most ambitious types of music, the symphony, the quartet, the sonata, the opera, the cantata, the mass — as the churches kept their organists and choirmasters, sacred music outlived religious painting.[10]

Among these composers the best known is the Brazilian Carlos Gomes (1836–1896), whose opera *Il guarany*, written in the manner of Verdi and produced at the Scala of Milan in 1870 (Verdi himself, very appropriately, being present), is one of the best scores of the Italian school during the transitional years of *Don Carlos* and *Aida*, Boito's *Mefistofele* and Ponchielli's *La Gioconda*; at the same time it is prized as a national classic in Brazil because of its Indian tunes and its subject, drawn from Alencar's novel.[11]

Carlos Gomes was not, of course, the only nativist composer. Musical nationalism had already appeared in Europe as a late offshoot of romanticism, and its most typical method was still the exploitation of folk songs and dances. In Hispanic America we undertook a similar task, exploiting the Indian tunes (not always of untarnished authenticity), or the local types of song and dance that the *criollos* had developed from European models, or the tunes and rhythms of the transplanted Africans.[12]

The invention of songs and dances among the *criollos* began, we know, soon after the Conquest; we may feel certain that it never suffered any interruption thereafter and it was permanently nourished by the influx of European models. All the models quickly suffered a sea-change; after a few years they had begot new forms which differed greatly from their originals. The European sources were, naturally, Spain and Portugal, then Italy and France; then during the nineteenth century we received and eagerly accepted Germanic and Slavic dances, the waltz, the schottische, the polka, the mazurka, the *varsovienne*, the *cracovienne*. New types sprang from them, such as the "tropical waltz" of the Caribbean zone, the "pasillo" of Colombia, the "Paraguayan polka," the "ranchera" of Argentina.[13] The finest fruit of the harvest was the habanera. Around the year 1800 the *contredanse* arrived from France in Cuba and became extremely popular. Many *contradanzas* were composed in Havana and their name was shortened to *danza*. By 1840 it had become a new thing, with a distinctive rhythm of its own, no longer that of its ancestor.[14] Under the name of *danza* or habanera it invaded all, Hispanic America and finally Europe. Perhaps no man did as much for its diffusion as Sebastián Iradier, a Basque who lived in Cuba and died around 1865; he is remembered as the author (or was he merely the transcriber?) of *La paloma* and of the habanera adopted by Bizet in *Carmen*. Although this Cuban invention was not transmuted into a classic form, like our *chaconne*, at least it engaged the attention of Gade and Saint-Saëns, Chabrier and Ravel. In Hispanic America it was a favorite form of composers of "light music," such as the delightful Juan Morel Campos (1857–1896), of Puerto Rico, who had an exquisite gift of melody. The most learned composers also wrote habaneras — for example, Ignacio Cervantes (1847–1905) and José White (1836–1918) in Cuba, Felipe Villanueva (1863–1893) and Ernesto Elórduy (1853–1912) in Mexico, and Enrique Price (1819–1863) in Colombia.[15]

In literature, romanticism had by now become a tradition in Hispanic America, as in Spain and Portugal. It pursued its appointed tasks — the conquest of the landscape, the reconstruction of the past, the description of customs. The poets retained the imagery, the vocabulary, and the verse forms of Echeverría's generation. Now and then they seemed to long for diversity. A few took up the study of the masters of the "golden centuries" of Spanish and Portuguese literature, or at least went back, in part, to eighteenth-century forms, such as the free ode or *silva*, frequently used by Meléndez, Quintana, and Gallego, Bello, Olmedo, and Heredia, but discarded by the romantics.[16] And not only the poets did so, but also the prose-writers, such as Ricardo Palma and Juan Montalvo. In Spain, Bécquer simplified his verse, divesting it of the ornaments in vogue; his poignant song had the purity of a nude body; it was "the song that loaded poets reach at last." Although it perplexed readers who felt that poetry without ornament was unpoetical, many of the young followed his example in Spanish America, far more than in Spain itself.[17]

The poets who wrote in Portuguese — the Brazilians — were less timid in their search for novelty. They learned of the change from romanticism to *Parnasse* in France and partly adopted the Parnassian technique, while remaining romantics at heart, especially in their persistent melancholy, their *saudade*. One of them, ˙Antonio Gonçalves Crespo (1847–1883), was a "transplanted" poet, who lived most of his life in Portugal; the others remained in Brazil — Joaquim Maria Machado de Assis (1839–1908), better known as the novelist of imperial Rio de Janeiro, Luis Guimarães (1847–1898), and Theophilo Dias (1857–1889). At the same time, romanticism in its undiluted form persisted among the *condoreiros*, so named from their habit of exploiting the condor, the huge vulture of the Andes, in metaphors or as a continental symbol (Tobias Barreto, 1839–1889; Antonio de Castro Alves, 1847–1871).[18] In this they resembled the Argentine poet Olegario Víctor Andrade (1839–1882), whose best known ode is the solemn and sonorous *Nest of Condors* (1877), written on the occasion of the repatriation of the remains of San Martín, the national hero of the campaigns of independence, who, like most of our early heroes, had died in exile.

A group of poets achieved original expression in dealing with the rural life of the *criollos*, especially in the River Plate countries. This *poesía criollista*, we know, began its full life with Bartolomé Hidalgo and Domingo Del Monte, during the campaigns for independence or shortly afterwards. Del Monte found a large following in Cuba, Santo Domingo, and Puerto Rico; Hidalgo, who belongs to Uruguay and Argentina, was the ancestor of the family of the *gauchescos*.[19] Then, in the first romantic generation, the leading *criollistas* were Guillermo Prieto (1818–1897) in Mexico and the Argentine Hilario Ascasubi (1807–1875). Their political and literary careers were very similar: they both lived many years; they both took part in the long struggles through which their countries emerged from anarchy into organization; they suffered persecution and exile, but were able, in their maturity, to enjoy the fruits of victory. With no great mastery of form, but with a quick grasp of popular feeling, they wrote political poems that were sung in army camps and country stores. When their countries were finally at peace, they wrote, or rather completed and polished, their longest works. Prieto's ballads, in his *Street Muse*, paint the motley world of the poor in Mexico — scenery, human types, costumes, feasts, and fights — and sing its loves and griefs with peculiar tenderness.[20] Ascasubi's lengthy poem *Santos Vega* (1850–1872) is written in the name of the *payador* who, according to his legend, disputed a poetic tournament with the Devil. The old singer is made to tell, in gaucho dialect, the story of two brothers, *Los mellizos de la flor*, in the eighteenth century; in addition, the poem is an encyclopedia of old gaucho life.[21]

To a later generation belong the two best *gauchesco* poets, Estanislao del Campo (1834–1880), the author of *Fausto* (1866), and José Hernández (1834–1886), the author of *Martín Fierro* (1872–1879). Estanislao del Campo began his career as a *gauchesco* by writing political satires in the manner of Ascasubi. He also wrote undistinguished verse in normal Spanish. *Fausto* is his single achievement. A gaucho, nicknamed "El Pollo" — the Chick — tells his chum the story of Dr. Faustus and how he came to know it. He had seen the Devil! A few days before, in Buenos Aires, he noticed many people going towards the Teatro Colón, went in with the crowd and witnessed a performance of Gounod's opera. He believed, of course, that the episodes of the drama were actually happening before his eyes. Critics who adopt a limited notion of what is "real" have objected to the poet's fancy. Whether the Pollo's adventure seems likely or not, the story is magnificently told. It is as clear and simple as the tales written or rewritten by Tolstoy for *muzhiks*; the talk of the two gauchos is excellent and their comments very apposite — for instance, on Siebel, the ridiculous character Gounod's librettists added to the plot; the descriptions of nature in South America — justified by the pretext that the Pollo is glib of tongue — are always delightful, especially the well-known picture of the sea at sunrise, now unavoidable in anthologies. A graceful imagination and a delicate humor are permanent qualities of this poet.[22]

In contrast, the main qualities of José Hernández are an abrupt strength, a dry humor, and a devotion to naked truth. He was a true master of his craft. Estanislao del Campo had proved that the country dialect of the River Plate lands could be used like a refined woodwind instrument; José Hernández made it sound like powerful brass.

Hernández loved the political fray, and threw himself into it, even as a soldier, like his forerunners Hidalgo and Ascasubi. He also fought many journalistic battles, and never feared to back the losing side, if the cause seemed to him just. His *Martín Fierro* is a plea and a criticism of public life. The gauchos, he thought, were unfairly treated by the government; in the name of order and progress, and under the belief that they were lawless and lazy vagabonds and their shiftless freedom the main source of political anarchy and economic backwardness, many of them were enrolled by force in the army and sent to fight wild Indians on the frontier. The country was reorganized and developed without them — against them, we might say. The consequence, for them, has been called "an ethnic shipwreck." [23] The European immigration which then began to flood the country cut asunder the body of the population, the unity bred by three centuries of living together. The most fortunate class of *criollos*, the men of property and education, who lived mostly in the cities, reaped the benefits of the new situation, which was the crown of their own efforts. But the hapless country folk who were used to living on horseback and feeding on wild cattle, with nothing to hinder them in their perpetual roaming, were suddenly confined to narrow paths by the barbed wire of the *estancias* where the wealthy *criollos* fenced in their cows and the *chacras* where the industrious immigrants grew their vegetables. The government offered to the gauchos its schools and a few other advantages; it had no plan that might entice them to compete with the ambitious newcomer from Europe. A number of them patiently submitted and became peons in the *estancias* — growing vegetables they deemed below manly dignity; many were caught by conscription. And the government did not bother to be very scrupulous in its recruiting methods.

Hernández makes his Martín Fierro a good gaucho, who worked

every day; probably there were a number like him. The poem is written as an autobiography: the hero, a *payador*, tells his own story in verse. He describes (canto II) a sort of golden age of the gauchos, who were happy in their toil. Like the Westerner in Robinson Jeffers' poem, he thought the life of men who ride horses a good life. Then he is drafted by compulsion as if he were an idler and had no family to support, merely because they find him improvising poetry in a tavern; he is taken away from his family, his horses, and his cows. In the army the officers treat him harshly (he had never known any master), they give him little food (food had never been a problem for him) and no pay (although he was entitled to it by law); finally, he has to face the merciless savages. After years of such misery, he deserts the army, becomes an outlaw and falls into the worst habits of the *gauchos matreros* — drinks, gambles, gets into brawls and even kills two men. He is free, but always fleeing from persecution. At last he decides to join the Indians. Even so, on going away, when he looked at the last villages of the whites, two big tears ran down his cheeks.

In 1872 the story ended there. Seven years later, both Hernández and his hero were willing to come back and accept the new customs of the country. The poet wrote the second part of *Martín Fierro*, "The Return." Things had improved in the meantime, of course. Conscription was no longer as arbitrary as it had been. Fierro had lost everything, his family and his little property; he now succeeds in finding his two sons, young men now, and begins life again.

Martín Fierro made its way to the very people in whose defense it was written. Printed in thin pamphlets that sold for a few pennies, it ran into many editions, and was read aloud in country taverns. Many of its lines have become proverbs; at the same time, Hernández had taken many proverbs from the mouth of the people and now it is not easy to tell whether a particular line existed as a proverb before he wrote or became a proverb afterwards. Men of letters wrote to the author applauding his work; it is doubtful that any one of them thought of it as "literature," just as, about that very time, learned musicians in the United States would have thought that Stephen Foster's songs were excellent in their way, but not "music," that is, not the sort of thing heard at concerts. Only after more than twenty years was there a voice that unequivocally declared *Martín Fierro* great literature: it was the voice of Unamuno in Spain (1894). Then Menéndez Pelayo (1895) praised the *gauchesco* poems as "the most original works of South American literature." Finally, Leopoldo Lugones, in Argentina, proclaimed in a series of lectures (1913) that *Martín Fierro* was the national epic. His proclamation, a belated echo of the nostalgia of the epic that afflicted the romantics, aroused a heated discussion in the pages of *Nosotros*, then the chief literary review of Buenos Aires. The discussions were inconclusive, as they could not help being, but *Martín Fierro*, whether epical or not, is now for every Argentine a truly national poem.[24]

Among the poets of Argentina who wrote on rural subjects in standard Spanish, Rafael Obligado (1851–1920) is the most distinguished. One of his several Argentine legends obtained a wide diffusion, *Santos Vega* (1877–1885), probably because of its subject, around which so much had been written already; it is also the best of his series. In it he displays a rare originality of imagery, which is surprisingly absent from the rest of his works.

The cities now had their novelists — José Tomás de Cuéllar (1830–1894) in Mexico, Cirilo Villaverde (1812–1894) in Havana, Alberto Blest Gana (1830–1920) in Santiago de Chile, Manoel Antonio de Almeida (1830–1861), Machado de Assis, and later Aluizio de Azevedo (1857–1913) and Raul Pompeia (1863–1895) in Rio de Janeiro. The novelists were often ahead of the poets in their search for innovation, and advanced from romanticism to realism. In many cases they did it spontaneously and drew from the well of tradition. The sketches of customs, the innumerable *cuadros de costumbres*, served as a bridge between romanticism and realism. Cuéllar's twenty-four novels collected under the title of *The Magic Lantern* (1889–1892) were enlarged sketches rather than novels. But Blest Gana, a genuine novelist, was also a conscious realist who learned from French masters — as far back as 1860 he had read, not only the already famous Balzac, but also the still obscure Stendhal, from whom he quotes. Balzac he adopted as his model, and yet his first important books, like *Martín Rivas* (1862), seem closer to the Spanish realists of the late nineteenth century, such as Galdós, than to Balzac. That is to say, he resembles less the French authors he had read and striven to imitate than the Spaniards he had not read and could not have read, since their books were yet unwritten — Galdós's *La Fontana de Oro*, the first novel of the new realistic era in Spain, was not published until 1871. As it happened with romanticism in poetry, modern realism in the novel made its appearance in Spanish America earlier than in Spain.[25]

In Brazil, the realistic novel began even earlier than in the neighboring Spanish-speaking countries. Almeida, in his only story, *Memoirs of a Sergeant* (1854–1855), showed himself already a follower of Balzac. The true artist of the novel was Machado de Assis, a creator of characters, gifted with a singular deftness of psychological detail, a refined sense of humor, and a limpid style. His stories do not try to include too much; he often prefers the restriction of focus imposed by the autobiographical form, which in his hands becomes, at times, "a desperate monologue." A few exact touches suffice for the social background. He has been rightly called the novelist of the reign of Pedro II; after the abdication of the emperor his novels reflected the social changes that came with the republic. When he began to write, "the girls used to love the wrong men and had to be married to the right"; afterwards, they were freer in their choice of husbands. But he made no effort to be Brazilian by means of local color — "There is," he said, "a way of feeling and seeing which gives the intimate note of one's own country, apart from the external face of things." [26]

Of the two typical forms of the romantic novel, one, the truculent and somber, gradually vanished, while the other, the idyllic, remained and bore its ripest fruit in the *María* (1867) of the Colombian Jorge Isaacs (1837–1895) — a perfect story in its way, with its delicate intensity of feeling, which just escapes sentimentality, its exquisite landscapes, which have endeared the Cauca valley to readers, and the purity of its prose.[27]

The romance of the colonial past did not again engage the talents of a poet like José Batres Montúfar in the early part of the century, but a delightful prose-writer now made it his, the Peruvian Ricardo Palma (1833–1919). It was for him, as for Batres, a humorous romance, especially in the period of the viceroy Amat and his mistress the lovely, capricious Perricholi, the period known to European readers through Mérimée's *Carrosse du Saint Sacrement* and to American readers through Mr. Thornton Wilder's *Bridge of San Luis Rey*. Lima, we know, is and always was famous as a city of wits, where life is pleasant and gossip entertaining. Palma is the chronicler of Lima. Out of the archives of the viceroyalty he extracted any fact that lent itself to humorous treatment and told it in one of the miniatures which he called *Peruvian Traditions* (1860–1906). He was steeped in the proverbial lore of Spanish tradition and in the inexhaustible verbal humor of Cervantes and Quevedo. Many have followed in his footsteps; he still outdistances them all.[28]

While the romantics looked upon the colonial past as our Middle Ages, they looked upon the Indian past as our Antiquity; the Indian cult was now at its highest point. The four outstanding works it produced were two novels, the *Cumandá* (1871) of Juan León Mera (1832–1894) and the *Enriquillo* (1879–1882) of Manuel de Jesús Galván (1834–1910), the poems of José Joaquín Pérez (1845–1900) entitled *Indian Fantasies* (1877) — one of them a brilliant though fanciful theogony, the *Choral Song* [Areito] *of the Virgins of Marien* — and the lengthy poem *Tabaré* (1886) of Juan Zorrilla de San Martín (1857–1931).[29] As often happens, the last of the series was the best. It was also the last important poem of great length published in Spanish America, and yet it attracted innumerable readers in a time when they were usually bored by the old epic. But Ercilla's *Araucana* and Valbuena's *Bernardo*, as well as Arboleda's *Gonzalo de Oyón*, were in octaves with complex rhyme schemes that put a constant though unconscious strain on attention; while in *Tabaré* the simplest assonance binds the lines together and demands little effort from the reader. This device was a lucky choice. But the simplicity is coupled with a rich variety of musical nuances, which includes the use of the leitmotif. The poet, furthermore, had the gifts of pathos, narrative and descriptive skill, and a fertility in the invention of imagery that was free from the now hackneyed ornament of many of our romantics. *Tabaré* is one of the most original works in our literature.[30]

It does not seem mere chance that some of the best novels and poems on Indian subjects should come from countries like Uruguay and the Antilles, where the natives had already disappeared, partly from ill treatment, partly through mixture with the Europeans and their descendants. The living Indian was not deemed poetical. He is the hero, however, of a unique book, *Excursion to the Ranqueles* (1870), by the Argentine Lucio Victorio Mansilla (1837–1913). It is comparable only to the colonial *Happy Captivity* of Pineda Bascuñán. The author was a military chief whom Sarmiento sent to the province of Cordoba to induce the tribe of the Ranqueles to give up the land they occupied and move elsewhere in order to allow a railroad to be built there. Naturally, the Ranqueles were averse to moving, and it took a long time and much effort to convince them. Meanwhile, Colonel Mansilla was able to observe them day by day and write letters to a friend describing their customs, tempers, and beliefs. He was an unusual man, with a wide variety of experience; a nephew of Rosas, he became a friend and admirer of Sarmiento, whom he was glad to serve; he travelled and read much, knew the most sophisticated society of Paris, in the *côté de Guermantes* (Proust actually met him), as well as the habits of the gauchos and the Indians, and suffered from none of the limitations of his countrymen for whom the native was only a dangerous savage. His book contains a marvellous wealth of detail and his fund of wisdom and humor seems inexhaustible.[31]

The most typical men of letters, in this period, were those whom we may call fighters and builders, heirs of Bello and Heredia, of Sarmiento and Mitre, men for whom literature was often a part of their public service, in accordance with what was by now one of our traditions — Ruy Barbosa (1849–1923) in Brazil, Juan Montalvo (1832–1889) in Ecuador, Manuel González Prada (1848–1918) in Peru, Justo Sierra (1848–1912) in Mexico, Enrique José Varona (1849–1933) in Cuba, and Eugenio María Hostos (1839–1903) in Puerto Rico. Their disciples and admirers have called them apostles, and they devoted a truly apostolic zeal to the defense of freedom and the diffusion of truth. They were often persecuted by the enemies of "sweetness and light," but they were supported by the faith of their many followers. And their writings enriched Hispanic literature with new types of prose.[32]

Ruy Barbosa was, first of all, a statesman, but as such his main resource was the spoken or the written word. He wanted politics to be articulate and in the open air; the prejudice — then a budding prejudice — against public men who are also men of letters, he says, tends to make politics "a sort of stuttering divinity, short-sighted and nearly deaf, inimical to the color and bustle of life: a combination of the sterility of the steppes and the taciturnity of the landscapes of Java, where birds do not sing." Mere politics he really despised: "All the evil that may be said of it falls far short of the reality," he declared in his speech of welcome to Anatole France upon his arrival in South America (1909). As a twice defeated candidate for the presidency of the republic, who had met with "the resistance of mud," he knew whereof he spoke. He was willing to put up with all the ferocity and pettiness of the struggle for power only because he had to serve Brazil. As a mere youth (1869) he had joined the campaign of the abolitionists and for twenty years fought memorable battles — one of them his funeral oration on José Bonifacio de Andrada e Silva the younger (1827–1886), in which his invective acquires tragic force when he speaks of "the great national crime" that makes all classes "the slaves of slavery." At last complete abolition was proclaimed by the imperial government, in the midst of a delirious exultation of the multitudes (May, 1888), and then the empire itself vanished (November, 1889). Ruy Barbosa was now one of the acknowledged leaders of public life. Although the republic proved incapable of entrusting him with its highest official mandate, it gradually came to regard him as the national mentor. He had brought to the service of his country an ample volume of thought and knowledge and a rare lucidity of vision. As a writer, too, he had exceptional gifts: abundance together with clearness, eloquence together with precision, which made him a master of memorable sayings.[33]

Juan Montalvo's single form of political activity was polemics — conditions in his native Ecuador never allowed him to play the part of a builder. The butt of his invectives, for nearly ten years, first in Quito, then from his place of exile, was the somber tyranny of Gabriel García Moreno (1821–1875), who instituted in the country a sort of ruthless theocracy.[34] When a group of young men, who had learned from their reading of Plutarch to admire Brutus, slew the despot, Montalvo uttered his famous boast: "My pen killed him!" But the new rulers were not to his liking, nor could they well be; he returned to the fray, staying until his friends, fearing his life might be in danger, compelled him to set up his residence in Europe. There he gave himself entirely to literature, except when he had to defend himself against charges of heterodoxy. He was a normal Christian, but the partisans of

García Moreno had never pardoned him, and the Archbishop of Quito declared one of his literary essays heretical.

His polemical writings were not conceived as tracts on any new doctrines; he was not a very original or daring thinker; he merely repeated old, simple, and clear principles — justice, honesty, tolerance. The value of those writings, today, is mainly historical. They are remembered, also, by lovers of style.

Montalvo was an extraordinary master of language. He knew all the wealth of words and turns of phrase that Spanish can offer to an assiduous reader of the books written in the "golden centuries"; he could, at will, feign any style of the past, and partly succeeded once with the style of Cervantes. But his peculiar vivacity marks him as a modern man and a man from South America. He had, besides wealth of vocabulary and syntax, an infallible sense of rhythm and a great, but less infallible, command of color and light. He might be described as a Landor or a Thomas De Quincey with the liveliness of a Shaw or a Chesterton. In his disputations he appears as a fighter who is also an artificer: a kind of Benvenuto Cellini, with a difference — that he is a good man and reveres virtue.

He survives mainly as a sort of novelist, in his *Chapters that Cervantes Forgot* (posthumous), and as an essayist, in his *Seven Treatises* (1882) and his *Geometría moral* (posthumous). The *Chapters* were begun as a satire in which the enemies of Montalvo appeared as enemies of Don Quixote; later on he effaced the allusions, and the book remains as more or less the parody of a novel. In his essays, it is not the ideas that matter — his thoughts always sound obvious and occasionally shallow, and they are given at random, somewhat in the manner of Emerson (his model was, of course, Montaigne) — but the imaginative part: the brief stories, the dialogues, the brief orations, such as the praise of water and the praise of Indian corn, or the defense of classical antiquity and especially of Roman virtue, the innumerable descriptions — of women, of fruits, or horses, or dishes, or gardens, or battles — and such feats of virtuosity in historical painting as the cave of Numa Pompilius or the tributes exacted from the Moorish king Galafre.[35]

Very similar to Montalvo in his public life, Manuel González Prada was never allowed to build. He fought a long battle, and the young of Peru are still fighting in his name, with the hope that eventually they may be able to build. Born into the most traditional society of South America (member of a traditional family himself), Gonzáles Prada rebelled against its polished narrowness, its essential backwardness and injustice. He denounced the rulers of the country and the system they represented; he probed into the social structure and found the causes of corruption in the colonial survivals, the moral sluggishness of the ruling classes, and the subjection of the Indians, then as now the majority of the population. As time passed, the situation did not improve; on the contrary, feudal exploitation was reinforced by capitalistic methods. González Prada's first campaigns (1886) were strictly political; his last were mainly social. Social justice, economic sufficiency, and education for the masses were his demands. His defense of the native is the first since the Hispanic American nations won their independence that assumes a systematic form and becomes a program. The recent literature of protest against the oppression of the Indian, a modern version of the long campaign of the sixteenth century, begins with him, both in prose and in verse — witness his *Peruvian Ballads*, especially *El mitayo*.[36]

As a writer, González Prada was a master of a concise, forceful, lucid, and luminous style. A rebel in letters, as in politics, he rid himself of the involved syntax and cumbrous paragraphs that passed for style in academic circles, especially in Spain, and sought brevity and clearness, attaining a sort of mathematical elegance. Never awed by reputations, no matter how entrenched in common opinion, in literary criticism he showed himself as keen and incisive as in his social polemics. He often wrote poetry, and made innumerable experiments in types of verse and stanza, inventing them himself or else adopting Greek or oriental or medieval or Renaissance patterns, such as the *pantum* or the *gazelle* or the Alcaic strophe or the Spenserian. No other poet has undertaken such a variety of experiments in Spanish. The most persistent note in his poems is a mild bitterness, a disillusioned view of the world and human life; while now and then scepticism gives way to righteous indignation.[37]

Eugenio María Hostos, unlike Montalvo and González Prada, was able to build, but, like them, was unable to see the fulfillment of the ideal he most loved. From early youth he dreamed of the independence of his native island, Puerto Rico; [38] not as a tiny nation by itself, but as a member of a confederacy of the Antilles, together with Cuba and Santo Domingo. Since both Cuba and Puerto Rico were still under the rule of Spain, he gave much of his time during more than thirty years (1868–1899) to the cause of their liberation. When, at last, Cuba obtained her freedom (1898), there was only a change of masters for his own Puerto Rico. He never recovered from the blow of this disaster.[39] Meanwhile, he had really built, in education, for future times. In Santo Domingo (1879–1888), where he settled with the hope of winning supporters for his project of a confederacy, he founded the first normal school of the country, giving it a curriculum of which science was the nucleus and establishing pedagogical methods that were in advance of his time. Since poverty prevented the immediate expansion of elementary schools, which were the main need of the country, Hostos resolved to form teachers, hoping that the few would teach the many. Eventually this hope was fulfilled, and the influence of his school was enormous; it changed the intellectual atmosphere. In Chile likewise (1889–1899), he contributed many ideas to the advancement of public education. Then, in his last years (1900–1903), in Santo Domingo again, he reorganized the whole educational system there.

Both his political and his pedagogical campaigns were carried on with the help of a large amount of writing. His first book, *The Pilgrimage of Bayoán* (1863), is a political novel. His best, *Social Ethics* (1888), was planned as a school text. His most brilliant pages are probably contained in the addresses he read when the first groups of normal teachers received their degrees in Santo Domingo, the first group of men (1884) and the first group of women (1887). Antonio Caso, the Mexican philosopher, calls the 1884 address "the master work of ethical thought in Hispanic America."

As a thinker, Hostos is essentially ethical; at the same time, he is a rationalist, with a deep faith in the power of reason to ascertain truth. "Give me truth," he says, "and I shall give you the world. Without truth, you will destroy the world, while I, with truth, with truth alone, shall rebuild the world as many times as you may have shattered it. And I should give you not only the world of matter, but also the world that the human mind perpetually builds above the natural world." He compels himself to believe that harmony (i.e., ethical conduct) and truth (mainly as knowledge) are the ultimate goals of human endeavor; he even thinks that the contemplation of the heavens impresses the law of order on our minds; but he ponders on "the eternity of efforts spent in the simple aim of making rational the only inhabitant of the earth who is endowed with reason," and the vast spectacle of conflict in individual and social life is for him a perpetual distress; only by a constant heroic effort does he maintain his metaphysical optimism, his mystic faith in reason and in "the constructive power of virtue." Despite his early and solid classical education (or because of it?), he developed a Platonic distrust of all literature that seemed to be in conflict with ethics. Fortunately, unlike Bernard Shaw, he discovered a moral lesson in Shakespeare and wrote a superb essay on *Hamlet* (1872), a psychological and moral analysis of all the characters in the play. In fact, whatever his distrust of literature, he was a born writer, with a powerful imagination — shown, for example, in the description of the peasant woman who mistakes his school for a church, kneels before it, prays, crosses herself, "and thus consecrates the temple." And another gift, the gift of eloquence, is shown on every page, even in letters jotted down in haste, in hardly legible script.[40]

Enrique José Varona, philosopher and statesman, began his political life by working for the independence of Cuba; when the island was free, he reorganized public education along modern lines, from the kindergarten to the university, sweeping aside the backward system that the Spaniards maintained until 1898 and multiplying the number of schools by four; besides, he often expressed in the press his opinions on many public questions. Never a "practical politician," he was yet elected vice-president in 1913, since his name would confer prestige on the administration; but he did not cease to publish his opinions, even in disagreement with the government or with the party that voted for him. After 1917 he severed all his political ties and acted as a national mentor, like Ruy Barbosa in Brazil (though, unlike the eminent Brazilian, he did not always receive due respect from the governments). He drew nearer, as the years passed, to the political and social ideals of the young; nothing new surprised or alarmed him, not socialism, of course, nor feminism.

In Cuba, since the times of Heredia, Domingo Del Monte, the sociologist José Antonio Saco and the philosopher José de la Luz y Caballero (1800–1862), literature, and culture in general, had been a form of rebellion against Spain's domination. Literature, of course, was usually insurgent. Philosophy too. What the official institutions were still teaching, during the nineteenth century, was a dilution of scholasticism; the Cubans, then, set themselves to study and spread modern thought: first Félix Varela, then Luz Caballero, the Socratic awakener of minds, and finally Varona were the leaders of the philosophical opposition. Varona belonged to a generation of men of exceptional talent and learning — Manuel Sanguily, Enrique Piñeyro (1839–1911), Esteban Borrero Echeverría (1849–1906), Rafael Montoro (1852–1933), and Rafael María Merchán (1844–1905) were the most brilliant of the group. Their organs were the *Revista de Cuba* (1877–1884), edited by José Antonio Cortina (1852–1884), and the *Revista Cubana* (1885–1895), edited by Varona. *Hojas Literarias* (1893–1894) was the purely personal organ of Sanguily, like Benedetto Croce's *Critica* in twentieth-century Italy.[41] Varona was still a young man when he became a philosophical leader by means of his lectures (1880–1882), afterwards published as treatises (1880–1888), on logic, psychology, and morals, conceived along the lines of positivism as taught by John Stuart Mill, Herbert Spencer, and Alexander Bain, but not without original views, as shown by his pages on imagination, on attention, on the consciousness of personality. In his early youth, however, literature had been his first devotion — poetry, criticism, even philology. At nineteen he published a commentary on one of Horace's odes; in his twenties he still wrote articles on archaisms in the rural Spanish of Cuba and on iotacism in the pronunciation of classical Greek. Like Hostos, he might have developed into a great philosophical critic of literature — his lecture on Cervantes (1882) was a true novelty in Spanish criticism; he was one of the first to discover the equation Don Quixote = Cervantes and to draw the parallel between the life of the author and the life of his hero; one of the first, also, to perceive that the novel of Cervantes (like the plays of Shakespeare's maturity, one may add) is the mirror of a great historical crisis.

Gradually, after his fortieth year, Varona began to write more and more briefly; his articles, even his lectures, were shorter; in the end he often preferred to write aphorisms — sparks, he called them (*Con el eslabón*). What he had to say, he felt, did not need many words and certainly no embellishments; his thought was always clear, his style concise, pure, and terse. His articles were marvels of condensation — a fine example is his comment on Oscar Wilde's trial viewed as a retaliation (*Un desquite*, 1895).

The only lengthy book he composed after 1890 was his new treatise on psychology (1905–1908), a masterly work, entirely different from the earlier; his philosophical point of view had changed and was no longer attached to positivism. However, he did not trouble to rewrite his old treatise on morals, although his views on human conduct changed far more than his views on the mechanism of the mind. He had grown sceptical: "Men," he said, "have invented logic, and yet there is nothing as illogical as men, unless it be nature." He liked to repeat Puck's words: "What fools these mortals be!" But scepticism did not lead him to ataraxia — like Santayana, he maintained his "animal faith," and in his case it led to the service of his fellow beings; the more sceptical he grew in his philosophical thought, the more he threw himself into public life. This seeming paradox was frequently remarked upon, by his political opponents in particular. At last, he felt compelled to explain himself publicly, and in 1911 he spoke out, in the Ateneo of Havana, on the matter of his scepticism, declaring that whatever his doubts, from the point of view of pure reason, about universal principles, practical reason showed him the path of duty. "Action saves." [42]

Another life spent in service was that of Justo Sierra. Public education was his passion. He established schools, like Sarmiento and Varona; in 1910 he reëstablished the University of Mexico, which the liberals of the eighteen-thirties had sundered into separate professional schools. Like Varona, he was called a sceptic, but only because he never attached himself to any creed or doctrine, not even to positivism, so much in vogue when he was young. In 1908, in his speech honoring the memory of Gabino Barreda (1818–1881), the philosopher who introduced positivism into Mexican public education (1867), he drew a vivid picture of the crisis of thought in our times, "the earthquake under the great theories of science," making geometry itself a debatable problem, and concluded that "the flag of science is not a flag of peace." At bottom he was an enthusiast, a lover, as one of his admirers calls him, in the sense in which Walter Pater called Plato a lover. As with Varona, his early devotion had been to literature — poetry, short stories, travel, criticism; like Varona again, and like Hostos, he might have become a great critic, and he at least wrote one of the best essays of literary appreciation in Spanish — his preface to the poems of Gutiérrez Nájera, comparable in quality to Varona's essay on Cervantes and Hostos' essay on *Hamlet*, or, in Spain, to the best pages of Menéndez Pelayo. But the love of his native land drove him to history, conceived as the philosophical interpretation of human effort through the ages based upon a solid foundation of historical and archaeological data, and so his main achievements were the two books in which he told the story of Mexico: one, written for school children, but equally stirring and illuminating for grown-ups; the other, a synthesis of "the political evolution" of the country since Cortés set foot upon its soil, with a prefatory description of the Indian civilizations before the Conquest. It ends with the régime of Porfirio Díaz; Sierra was a member of his government, as secretary of education, but did not hide the truth: the political life of the country had been stifled in the interests of peace and prosperity. This powerful book should hold in the esteem of the Mexicans the place that Sarmiento's *Facundo* holds for the Argentines.

When Justo Sierra died, Mexico paid him a most eloquent tribute of love and admiration, in which all men and women took part, all who knew what his life had meant. His funeral was, according to one who witnessed it, one of the highest and purest moments in the spiritual life of the country.[43]

7

PURE LITERATURE
1890–1920

INDEPENDENCE was followed in Hispanic America by a period of anarchy, followed by a period of organization; after 1870, we began to reap the fruits of stability; by 1890 there was prosperity. In Argentina and Uruguay, prosperity reached many levels of society; in countries like Brazil, Chile, or Mexico, it reached only the dominant classes; elsewhere, with a more imperfect organization, and anarchy still lurking in corners or occasionally bursting into civil war, the economic advancement, if not very marked, was none the less in evidence.

Prosperity, brought about by peace and the application of the principles of economic liberalism, had a distinct effect on intellectual life. A division of labor began. Men of the intellectual professions now tried to restrict themselves to their chosen task and gave up politics — the lawyers, as usual, less and later than the others. The helm of the state passed into the hands of mere politicians; nothing was gained by it, quite the contrary. The men of letters — literature not being really a profession, but an avocation — became journalists or teachers or both. Many still went to the universities to study law, but few practiced it. Some obtained diplomatic or consular posts; the custom is maintained to this day, and it includes women now, such as the Chileans Gabriela Mistral and Marta Brunet, the Cuban Flora Díaz Parrado, and the Colombian Laura Victoria.

In Cuba and Puerto Rico, under the rule of Spain, the economic development was exactly parallel to that of the free nations of Hispanic America. But men of letters still took part in public life

— usually, as we know, to demand the freedom of the two islands. The revolution of 1895, through which Cuba became independent, was mainly due to the efforts of José Martí (1853–1895), the last of the great men of letters in Hispanic America who were at the same time political leaders.

When the Ten Years' War began in Cuba (1868), Martí was only fifteen, and yet he undertook to publish, with the help of his beloved teacher the poet Mendive, a political journal under the title of *La Patria Libre* (1869).[1] It may have escaped the eye of the Spanish authorities. But soon afterwards he was put in prison for opinions expressed in a private letter and was finally sentenced to hard labor in chains; after six months of suffering, which permanently affected his health, his sentence was commuted to deportation to Spain. There he published his first pamphlet, *Political Imprisonment in Cuba* (1871), and studied at the universities of Madrid and Saragossa, where he finally took two degrees, one in "philosophy and letters," one in law. After four years he left Europe (1875). After a few more years of wandering through Mexico and Guatemala, a brief stay in Cuba (1878–79), where the Ten Years' War had just ended in failure for the patriots, confirmed him in his resolution to devote his life to redeeming the island from a bondage that showed no signs of ever becoming tolerable. His too outspoken speeches and his secret plans forced him to leave the island. In 1881 he settled in New York, where he earned his living as a journalist,[2] and in fourteen years of constant effort, of eloquence and patience, succeeded in organizing the new revolution of Cuba. He knew nothing of the art of war, but persuaded two great soldiers, Máximo Gómez and Antonio Maceo, to take command of the military campaign; when the time came to go to the front, he went among the first. "A people," he said, "does not willingly let itself be served by a man who preaches the need of dying and is not among the first to face danger." He was also one of the first to fall in battle. His life, says Federico de Onís, is one of the purest in the history of mankind.

Excepting most of his poems and a few prose works of his youth, Martí wrote nothing that was not intended to promote the liberation of Cuba or else to earn his living. His work is thus journalism; but journalism raised to an artistic level that has never been equalled in Spanish, nor probably in any other language. When as still a youth he began to write, he already had a style, although it cannot be said of him, as of Ruskin, that he wrote as well at eighteen as at forty. His style developed and matured slowly; it attained its fulness when he was nearly thirty, and from then on no insignificant line flowed from his pen, whether in a bit of journalistic news or in a private letter. From his youth onward he was a dazzling orator, in both impromptu and written speeches, but seldom did the oratorical manner creep into his articles. His knowledge of the Spanish literature of the past was very ample, and one of his favorite authors seems to have been Saint Theresa, who fashioned a subtle form of expression for her mystical experiences out of her colloquial everyday speech, so typically feminine in construction that we seem to hear the intonation of her voice; he must have been also an attentive reader of the seventeenth-century *conceptistas*, Quevedo, Mello, and Gracián, as well as of writers less prone to baroque complications, like Saavedra Fajardo. The two extremes coincide: the spontaneous, the "natural" writer, Saint Theresa, is as great a mistress of innovation and complexity as the writers whose main stylistic concern was a pithy conciseness. Among the modern writers of Spanish America, Martí certainly read Hostos and Montalvo, to whose spiritual family he belongs. Hostos's essay on *Plácido*, compared with a page of Martí in his youthful maturity, is like a painting of Tintoretto that foreshadows El Greco.

The style he achieved was entirely new to the language. He follows no single rhythmical pattern, but constantly varies it; as to vocabulary, he shuns pedantic words, except when they are strictly, technically necessary and therefore lose their pedantic air, yet he is very free in choice, ranging from Latinisms like *pervadir*

— "to pervade," not used then in Spanish, and seldom since — to rustic Indian words; his syntax is full of unexpected but racy constructions, such as the use of the ethical dative; he combines words — and meanings — in many unfamiliar ways. The effect is a constantly varied interplay of light and color. In style, as well as in what lies beyond style and becomes expression, his power of invention was inexhaustible.

The main bulk of his work in prose is in the publications he edited, such as *Patria* (1892–1895), the organ of the campaign for Cuban independence, and *La Edad de Oro* (1889), a magazine for children, written as from a child's mind — something no one else has so well succeeded in doing in Spanish (witness, in particular, the stories *Mischievous Nené* and *The Black Doll*, or the poem *The Little Rose-Colored Shoes*); then, there is the series of long *crónicas* for newspapers and reviews in Mexico and South America, especially for *La Nación* of Buenos Aires (1882–1890). A *crónica* was a comment of events of the day; when sent from a foreign country, it was expected to cover all sorts of happenings — a political campaign and a scientific discovery, a railway wreck and an art exhibition, a financial crisis and a new play or book, the murder of Jesse James and the erection of the Brooklyn Bridge. This form of literary journalism did not exist before the seventies and is now out of fashion. Shallow it would be, very often, if the author was shallow. But Martí was unusually well fitted to cope with difficult subjects — besides his legal and literary studies, he had given himself a special training in science as editor of a Spanish version of *The Scientific American* and in the appreciation of art by assiduous visits, taking copious notes, to the Prado and the Louvre. Among his *crónicas* we find unforgettable pages on the life of Grant, from his birth in the shingled cabin to his hearse drawn by twenty-four black horses, on the poetry of Walt Whitman and the celebration of his seventieth birthday, on the first exhibition of French impressionist paintings in New York. No less plentiful and even more significant are his writings on

Hispanic America, "Our America," according to the expression he coined in a famous article (1891); he paid equal attention to the humblest events that might denote originality in our life or progress in our civilization and to the gravest problems, such as the condition of the Indians. Cruelty and greed and dishonesty and the impulse to move backwards did not escape his eye, yet he preserved his courage, his tenderness, his faith in "Our America," and his faith in man and the universe, his faith, as he would say, in "music and reason."

In poetry he was an innovator, as much as in prose. With him, Spanish verse definitely gave up the now stale ornaments of romanticism and became again a fresh and living thing. He achieves intensity through simplicity in his *Simple Verses* (1891) and brilliancy with delicacy in *Ismaelillo* (1882).[3]

Martí had no intention of starting a literary revolution, being much too busy with his plans of political insurrection, but 1882, the date of publication of *Ismaelillo*, is generally adopted as the initial date of a new trend in our poetry, afterwards known under the colorless title of *modernista*. The first work of this new movement appeared exactly fifty years after the first of our romanticism. Echeverría's *Elvira* preceded by a year the earliest romantic work in Spain; now Martí's *Ismaelillo* preceded by more than sixteen years the beginnings of *modernismo* in Spain. Not only did Spanish America now show itself independent of Spain in literature: it was a Spanish American, Rubén Darío, who carried the message of the new movement to the mother country (1899), as his critic Rodó had prophesied. And again, as in 1832, the European influences that brought forth the change came from France or through France;[4] but the movement went far beyond its origins and became typically Spanish American in character.

The transition from romanticism to *modernismo* began with writers like González Prada and Zorrilla de San Martín.[5] Then, Othón, Díaz Mirón, and Icaza in Mexico, Almafuerte in Argentina, and Deligne in Santo Domingo, men who wrote poetry of a high quality, partly belong to the new movement.[6] The general consensus recognizes Martí, Casal, Gutiérrez Nájera, Silva, and Darío as the leaders. All five were born in countries that lie north of the equator: Julián del Casal (1863–1893), like Martí, in Cuba; Manuel Gutiérrez Nájera (1859–1895) in Mexico; José Asunción Silva (1865–1896) in Colombia; Rubén Darío (1867–1916) in Nicaragua. Martí was the only one who took part in politics; Casal, Gutiérrez Nájera, and Darío earned their living as journalists; Silva's family had a fortune which he eventually lost. Darío held diplomatic or consular posts at irregular periods; Silva entered the diplomatic service for a brief time.

Casal was a mournful romantic poet and at the same time a word painter in the manner of the *Parnasse*. His sadness sprang from the roots of his being, from his sickly body, his unhappy life, deprived of most of the joys of youth, and his forebodings of early death. He aspired to become a consistent pessimist, read and quoted Leopardi, but never really believed this world a vale of tears, except for himself. In one of his sonnets he pictures the pomp of a holiday, when houses are hung with violet-colored banners, and yet he can feel only "an infinite longing to weep all alone"; in another poem, *Pages of Life*, he gazes at "all that joyfully exists" by his side and asks God: "Why hast Thou made my soul so sad?" The visible aspects of the world charmed him; in them he found his only escape. For description he seldom chose a landscape or scene of Cuba (a striking exception is a sonnet on a stormy day, with the wind howling over the rocks by the sea); distance seemed necessary to his vision, and he sought his subjects either in antiquity (*Helena*, or *Hercules and the Stymphalids*, or *The Road to Damascus* — his most richly colored poem, purely pictorial, without the least allusion to Saul's conversion) or in lands far off, like Japan (*Kakemono, Surimono*). He was the first to introduce into Hispanic America the Japanese subjects then so much in fashion in France. Even Spain — the only European country he visited — seemed to him picturesque because he could look at it as an exotic country, through the eyes of a Gautier or a Mérimée. However, he did not hold himself aloof from the problems of his native island, and drew, in prose, acid pictures of political life under the rule of the unscrupulous men sent there by the Spanish government.[7]

Silva too was a mournful romantic. His posthumous fame — posthumous outside Colombia at least — he owes to a *Nocturne*, a tragic elegy, romantic in feeling, but revolutionary in subject, style, and metre. It gave a *frisson nouveau* to thousands of readers. Unlike Casal, Silva developed into a consistent pessimist, with a touch of sarcastic cynicism in his *Bitter Drops*, but his pessimism did not go very deep. He lived in despair because he saw his world crumbling around him and — darkened by many deaths among those nearest him, his future uncertain with economic disaster and hard, unsuccessful work — he often sought refuge in the happy memories of his childhood.[8]

Equally romantic, at bottom, was Gutiérrez Nájera, and his sadness equally tragic; in expression he was less vehement than Casal or Silva, except in a very few poems, such as *Afterwards*. Usually he spoke of his sorrows in a soft murmur, and his despair gave way to a resigned philosophy of life, which he condensed into the mellow quatrains of *Pax animae*. There is an autumnal tinge in his melancholy, which accords with the constant autumnal climate of the high tablelands of Mexico. He is the most Mexican of poets — a Mexican of the valley of Anahuac, in which the capital city lies — as Casal is one of the most Cuban in his love of vivid color. His poetry is also pictorial, especially in the *Brief Odes*, full of Greek and Latin reminiscences. In *Pax animae*, a few landscapes in miniature serve as a frame for his meditation. And in *Non omnis moriar*, in which he takes leave of life at thirty-four, he develops with classical perfection the image of the dying warrior.[9]

There are two periods in this literary movement: the first runs from 1882 to 1896; the second from 1896 until it gradually merges, after 1920, into a new period with newer tendencies. Martí, Casal, Gutiérrez Nájera, and Silva died between 1893 and 1896; Darío,· then, remains alone as undisputed chief for twenty years. Meanwhile, a second group joins him: in Argentina, where he took up his residence between 1893 and 1898, Leopoldo Díaz (b. 1862), Enrique Larreta (b. 1875), and Leopoldo Lugones (1874–1938); in Uruguay, José Enrique Rodó (1871–1917), Carlos Reyles (1868–1938), Horacio Quiroga (1879–1937), and Julio Herrera y Reissig (1875–1910); in Bolivia, Ricardo Jaimes Freyre (1868–1933); in Chile, Manuel Magallanes Moure (1878–1924) and Carlos Pezoa Velis (1879–1908); in Peru, José Santos Chocano (1875–1934); in Colombia, Baldomero Sanín Cano (b. 1860) and Guillermo Valencia (1873–1943); in Venezuela, Manuel Díaz Rodríguez (1868–1927), Rufino Blanco Fombona (1874–1944); in Mexico, Luis Gonzaga Urbina (1868–1934), José Juan Tablada (1871–1945), Enrique González Martínez (b. 1871), Amado Nervo (1870–1919).[10] These writers, for the most part, did not go into politics — Valencia is the only one who may be called fairly successful in that line, although as the presidential candidate of the conservative party he was defeated twice; Blanco Fombona knew alternatives of success, prison, and exile; Sanín Cano and Rodó appeared only for a while in public life; Lugones and Chocano failed in it.[11]

The new movement now reached all countries, north and south of the equator; between 1896 and 1900, its center lay south, in Buenos Aires and Montevideo. In the two groups, before and after 1896, the poets predominated in number, but the movement affected prose as well as poetry. Several of the poets, besides Martí, were also excellent prose-writers: Gutiérrez Nájera, Darío, Lugones, Valencia, Blanco Fombona, Urbina, and Nervo. Larreta, Rodó, Reyles, Quiroga, Sanín Cano, and Díaz Rodríguez have written only or mostly prose. Together with the Spaniards who appeared about the fateful year 1898 or shortly afterwards, the Spanish Americans have given the language its best poetry since the "golden centuries." Literary Spanish, both in verse and in prose, acquired a new youth, and this miracle, which began in "Our America," was prolonged and completed in Spain by Unamuno, Valle Inclán, Azorín, Juan Ramón Jiménez, Antonio Machado, and finally José Ortega y Gasset.

After 1896, when he published *Prosas profanas* (*Lay Hymns*) in Buenos Aires, and still more after 1905, when he published *Songs of Life and Hope* in Madrid, Rubén Darío was hailed as the greatest poet in the language since the death of Quevedo. Around 1920 the inevitable reaction against his glory set in. Whatever the final appraisal of his work may be, his influence has been as long and far-reaching as that of Garcilaso or Lope, Góngora, Calderón, or Bécquer. Of any poem written in Spanish it can be told with certainty whether it was written before or after him. His admirers were fascinated by his colorful imagery, his wealth of literary allusion, his verbal felicity, and the boundless variety, flexibility, and rhythmical skill of his verse, in which he surpasses any other poet in the language and becomes a peer of Swinburne in English. His detractors feel annoyed by his preciosity, by his excessive love of the external world — in which he is akin to Góngora — and find him wanting in rich intimacy like that of Garcilaso or Bécquer and in philosophical depth similar to that of Luis de León or Quevedo. His emotional life, it may be granted, is indeed narrow, and during his youthful years seemed shallow; but later, in a few of the *Songs of Life and Hope* and in the *Poem of Autumn*, he reached the intensity of despair. These poems, at least, leave no doubt about his greatness. He had given to the language its most joyful poetry, equal to that of Góngora's youth; in his maturity, he gave it its most bitter poetry, comparable to that of Quevedo's old age. There are two immortal moments in his work: one, the glad discovery of the beauty of "the world's unwithered countenance" and the primrose path of youthful pleasure; another, the sad discovery of the fragility of love and the emptiness of success, the vanity of life and the terror of death.[12]

Our poetry underwent at this time a total change, in subjects, style, vocabulary, and verse forms. The young rebels adopted a severely aesthetic attitude towards their art and were resolved to write pure poetry — if not in the sense of the Abbé Brémond's formula, at least in the sense of poetry freed from the impurities of everyday life which romantic verse so often carried in suspension. They laughed at the "explicit poets," as Santayana calls them. Our romantics, when in love, addressed a particular woman and named her — the Julia whom Gutiérrez González married, the Rosario who drove Acuña to suicide — or spoke of her under a thin disguise — the María of Isaacs' novel. But love poetry now wore a vaguely impersonal air; it was kindled with no romantic fire and often resembled the "carpe diem" poems of the Renaissance. The new poets bewailed their sorrows with a heartier sincerity than they showed in their loves; a deep sadness, a mournful loneliness, runs through the elegies of Gutiérrez Nájera, Casal, and Silva. Darío, in his youth, was full of the joy of living; after his thirty-fifth year he insistently ponders on life and death, tries to react again and again, but in the end falls under the ever-growing shadow of his disillusion and his fears. His best volume, *Songs of Life and Hope* (1905), opens with a lyrical autobiography in which he asserts his faith that "all's right with the world," and ends on one of the gloomiest notes ever sounded by any poet — "We know not whither we go nor whence we come." [13] When these poets refer to actual events in their lives, they are not explicit; only through outside information do we discover, for instance, that *Pages of Life*, by Casal, refers to his talks with Darío; *The Poet asks about Stella*, by Darío, to his dead young wife; *Afterwards*, by Gutiérrez Nájera, to the death of his father; the famous *Nocturne* that begins "Una noche . . . ," by Silva, to the death of his sister Elvira. We may never unveil the meaning of Casal's "dagger that shone in the dark." Romantic emotion was not dead ("whoever *is*, is a romantic," says Darío), but they chose to express it in the manner of the French symbolists, as when Mallarmé wrote, on the birth of his daughter, the cryptic *Don du poème*. In later years, Lugones and González Martínez ventured so far as to address poems to their wives and inscribe volumes to them; the inscriptions are in Latin. Let it be added that the poets who appeared after 1896 were far less sorrowful and pessimistic than Gutiérrez Nájera, Casal, Silva, and the mature Darío; they also told far less about themselves. In short, they were less romantic than the first foes of romanticism.

The example of the French *Parnasse* pointed to impersonal descriptive or narrative poetry as a safe road to artistic purity; it pointed, also, to all lands and all times as harvest fields. Casal, we know, took his subjects from Greece, the Orient, even the Far East. Jaimes Freyre drew from Scandinavian myths the material for his *Barbarian Castaly* (1899); Valencia, from early Christian legends the material for his *St. Anthony and the Centaur* and his *Palemon the Stylite*. The native subjects, which both the classicists and the romantics thought essential to our literary independence, were now mostly in abeyance. There is a tropical landscape by Silva, two or three by Casal; Gutiérrez Nájera, without naming Mexico, conveys a faithful image of that country's landscape in the high lands and its nuances of light, color, and temperature. But Darío, in the defiant preface to *Prosas profanas*, declared that he disliked the period and places in which he lived, and that "if there is anything poetical in the Americas, it is in the old things, in Palenque and Utatlan, in the legendary Indian, in the refined and sensual Inca, in the great Moctezuma of the golden throne." "The rest," he added, "is yours, democratic Walt Whitman." *Prosas profanas* is a revelry of luxury drawn from all the points of the compass (witness the poem *Divagación*), with Versailles as the meridian. The poetry contained in the volume is often superb; but the settings and trappings have aged — palaces, lilies, swans, peacocks, ivory, pearls. Darío and his followers have been accused of excessive addiction to Old World traditions and fashions. But all their foreign paraphernalia were really a disguise. Under the mask, what we see is the reappearance of wealth and luxury in Hispanic America, with the prosperity of the eighteen-eighties and nineties. A comparison with our romantics makes it clear. When our romantic poets described a palace or a princess, they tried to suggest majesty and luxury by means of feeble nouns and vague, generic adjectives. They had little actual experience, or none, of what they attempted to depict, while the colonial poets, even the last of them, the classicists who witnessed the wars of independence, had known that experience in full. The countries of Hispanic America — Brazil excepted — had been impoverished by the campaigns of liberation and the ensuing civil wars; only when the romantic poets depict nature, as they know it, is there variety and precision in their images. Now Casal and Gutiérrez Nájera and Darío had not merely read about wealth and luxury: they had seen it. Versailles was a symbolic name for the new life of the now prosperous cities of Hispanic America.

But Darío seldom complied with his own rules. In *Prosas profanas* there were already two poems on Buenos Aires ("regal Buenos Aires," he calls it) and the countryside around it, and in one of them he even introduces "the last gaucho." Step by step, the landscape of the Americas, their legends and their history, reappeared in his work, and, of course, in that of many more poets. Chocano's volume of poems *Alma América* (1906) represents the full return of the native subjects in Spanish American poetry. While this process was going on, however, a number of very interesting and original minor poets, who were really independent of the main current of their times, had maintained the tradition of *criollo* subjects — Aquileo Echeverría, Francisco Lazo Martí, Arturo Pellerano Castro, *El Viejo Pancho*.[14]

The traditional tie between our public life and our literature dissolved with the social transformation and division of labor. Martí, of course, was the great exception; in that he stood nearer to the generation that preceded him than to his own. Gutiérrez Nájera was the first poet to announce that he would have nothing to do with politics — when asked to sing the praises of Hidalgo, the priest liberator of Mexico, he wrote a reverent ode in which he declared himself incapable of "brandishing the high sword of song"; years afterwards, when asked to honor the heroine popularly called *la Corregidora*, he complied by describing the flowers that pay their tribute to her statue. Casal seldom broke the rule of abstention, except in prose. Silva broke it once — only once — in the presence of the statue of Bolívar when he visited Caracas. Darío, in his early youth, was not averse to romantic politics in verse (witness his poem to Columbus); then, during the period of *Prosas profanas* — the most typical book of poems, and the most influential, that the movement produced — he deemed politics unpoetical, and so did his innumerable followers; but after he arrived in Spain, late in 1898, and the young poets of the old country acclaimed him as their master, a new emotion arose in him, a new sort of patriotism, based on the spiritual unity of the Hispanic peoples, and it flowered in A *Salutation from the Optimist* (1902). Then came his challenge *To Roosevelt*, after the seizure of the Isthmus of Panama (1903), the elegy on the death of Mitre (1906), the poems on his native country in the *Voyage of Nicaragua* (1909), and the opulent *Canto a la Argentina* on the centenary of its independence (1910). It might have been feared that our masters of preciosity were no longer capable of "loving a woman, hating a tyrant, or brooding over the mystery of the world," that they might have shut themselves into their ivory tower forever. But Darío's reversion to the great themes of our public life set an example to the younger men, and certain of them followed it — Lugones with his *Odas seculares* (1910) and Valencia with his ode to his native city of Popayan. There was, however, no return to what we might call fighting literature; we shall have to wait until Chocano writes his *¿Quién sabe?* (1913) before seeing poetry again become a weapon.

With the subjects, the style, too, naturally changed. The very words were new. In Spanish, after the verbal opulence of the baroque seventeenth century, the classicist reform of the eighteenth impoverished the language of poetry. In the nineteenth, romanticism made many additions, unfortunately not as many as in French. Now the *modernistas* gave up soft classicist words like *ledo* (from Latin *laetus*) and strenuous romantic words like *bravío* or *fatídico*; but they put to use a very extensive vocabulary — as, for instance, the vocabulary of luxury, the names of gems, metals, cloths, furs, birds, flowers. In contrast, they simplified syntax. Inversion, except such forms of it as were usual in actual speech, they suppressed, and all "poetic license" too, which was the resource of the lazy. They fought against romantic carelessness. Their grammar was impeccable. They were justly accused of using Gallicisms, but they always did it deliberately and judiciously.

In verse forms the wealth of innovation was extraordinary, and most of it due to Darío. Spanish poetry had never had in circulation, at any given time, more than a few types of verse, such as the *endecasílabo*, imported from Italy, and the national *octosílabo*, during the "golden centuries" and even later (any other forms being used only occasionally), although the last classicists and then the romantics, during the late eighteenth and the nineteenth centuries, went so far as to handle five or six types of verse, and a few invented new types, which were not successful. Now, with the *modernistas*, all the known verse forms were used, new ones essayed, and a few of the old ones renewed by changes of stress or of cesura. The stanza forms became infinite in their variety. Darío even attempted free verse, with *Heraldos* (in *Prosas profanas*), but recoiled afterwards with surprising timidity. That conquest remained for the generation of 1920 to achieve. He went back, however, especially in his *Canto a la Argentina,* to the short fluctuating line of the twelfth and thirteenth centuries, of the *Razón de amor* and the *Elena y María.* Lugones, in his *Lunario sentimental* (1909), and later Chocano, wrote a sort of free verse — free as to the number of syllables in the line — but with regular rhyme. Silva invented, in his *Nocturne,* a new type of verse, consisting of a four-syllable foot which might be freely repeated from two up to six times; in order to break the monotony that might have ensued, he introduced now and then a two-syllable foot. Darío adopted the principle, generally preferring a three-syllable foot, and applied it with martial rigidity in his *Triumphal March* and with elasticity in his *Salutation to Leonardo.* He also — like a few other poets before and after him — essayed the hexameter, in his *Salutation from the Optimist* (1902) and *Salutation to the Eagle* (1907), but adopted no definite system, effecting merely a vague resemblance of rhythm:

> ¡Inclitas razas ubérrimas, sangre de Hispania fecunda!
> Espíritus fraternos, luminosas almas, salve . . .[15]

While the *modernista* movement began and grew in Spanish America, a similar one began and developed, independently, in Brazilian poetry. It was less sudden and less revolutionary. It had been prepared, before 1880, by the first *parnasianos* — Luis Guimarães, Machado de Assis, and Theophilo Dias — who paved the way for Raimundo Correa (1860–1911), Alberto de Oliveira (1857–1937), Olavo Bilac (1865–1918), Bernardino Lopes (1859–1916), and João de Cruz e Sousa (1862–1898). Correa published in 1877 his *First Dreams,* in which the new manner is not yet clearly defined, and then in 1883 his *Symphonies* — whose title immediately evokes Théophile Gautier's *Symphonie en blanc*

majeur — which also influenced the poets of Spanish America
(witness Gutiérrez Nájera's *All in White*, Darío's *Symphony in
Grey Major*, and Balbino Dávalos' superb translation). Alberto
de Oliveira's *Romantic Songs*, of 1878, still avowing his early
affiliation, was followed by his pictorial sketches *Meridionais* in
1884. Lopes published his *Cromos* in 1881. Olavo Bilac's first book
of *Poems* appeared in 1884. In the beginning, these poets devoted their efforts to the search for pictorial expression and a
jewel-like polish of style. In the first decade of the century, the
trend changed from Parnassianism to symbolism, under the influence of Verlaine, with Cruz e Sousa's *Broqueis*, in verse, and
Missal, in prose, both of 1893.

Raimundo Correa has been defined as "a landscape painter,
exquisitely impressionistic, who reflects, with delightful feeling,
the shadows and the light of Brazil." He was, they say, a timid
man, quietly and sadly living his secluded inner life. Under his
love of nature lies a pessimism devoid of all illusions. All is
suffering ("dolor é tudo"), and God is cruel — such were his final
conclusions about life. Alberto de Oliveira, after acquiring fame
with typically Parnassian sonnets (it was the fashion to call him
"aristocratic," a word much in vogue at the time in Brazil as well
as in Spanish America), little by little gave up ornamental form
and verbal pyrotechnics and sought a classical simplicity which
he triumphantly achieved. He describes "vast and sombre
stretches of forest," says Ronald de Carvalho, "where trees centuries old spread their heavy foliage, full of parasitic plants and
birds' nests; the valleys covered with tremulous reeds, where birds
and butterflies swarm; the sleepy lakes, spotted with aquatic
plants; the impetuous rivers, carrying, in their winter floods, thick
knotty tree-trunks; the nights, heavy with stars; the mountains
with their luxuriant vegetation." As he developed, Oliveira became more and more subjective; the change is shown, for instance,
in the well-known sonnet in which he speaks to the noisy forest
and says: "If you and I cry at the same time, we shall not under-

stand each other." Olavo Bilac is probably the most typically Brazilian of the group and was rewarded with the greatest popularity. A true son of the tropics, he links a spontaneous magnificence to a perfect grace and harmony. The brilliancy of his descriptions and his love songs has a touch of delightful voluptuousness; but a vague nostalgia — which never became pessimism — pervades his joy of living. In Bernardino Lopes and João de Cruz e Sousa we do not often find the formal perfection of Correa, Oliveira, and Bilac. Lopes draws landscapes and scenes of rural life — modest houses, domestic tasks, field labors — with vivid color and many delicate touches of character — he resembles the *criollo* poets of Spanish-speaking countries. Cruz e Sousa attained, in his best moments, a bitter depth and a sorrowful intensity.[16]

In prose, the *modernistas* of Spanish America cast off the slow and involved solemnity of academic discourse, which had invaded many fields besides oratory, and the forced old-fashioned humor of the storytellers. They adopted a simple, brief type of paragraph; in this they had been preceded by men like Varona and González Prada. They lost raciness, no doubt, and eloquence, but they acquired a new elegance, not before known to the language, a fine freedom of movement, and a delicate skill in nuances of rhythm. As usual, Martí was the exception: he was both racy and eloquent, without falling into the mechanical ways of the recent past. But the majority of the new writers had neither relish for eloquence nor any need of it, since they played no part in public life. The best of them acquired the art of imaginative prose, which Walter Pater deemed typical of the late nineteenth century. In Gutiérrez Nájera we find an admirable variety of style, ranging from ornamental frescoes, with a brilliancy similar to that of his pictorial poems, to neat miniatures, drawn with many precise lines, an art in which he preceded Azorín by many years. Darío, in the short stories and sketches of *Azul* (1888), set a pattern of frivolous elegance, now out of fashion, the more so because it

was so much admired and copied in its day. He achieved a more
sober and yet colorful style in his later *crónicas*, especially in the
group collected under the title *Tierras solares* (1904). The
Guatemalan Enrique Gómez Carrillo (1873–1927), whose *crónicas*
from Paris were read in all Hispanic America for over thirty
years, gave also a practical example of simple and graceful prose.
Rodó, universally acclaimed as the greatest prose-writer of the
second group of *modernistas*, proved himself a master of all the
new graces and subtleties in his long essay on Darío's *Prosas
profanas* (1899); later on he went back to the long paragraph
as best fitted — he thought — to the sort of lay preaching he used
in *Ariel* (1900) and in *Motives of Proteus* (1909), but enriched it
with color and nuance. Oratory was at this time seldom raised to
the strictly artistic plane on which it had moved in the past, with
Ignacio Ramírez, Justo Sierra, Hostos, or finally Martí. As exceptions we may recall Guillermo Valencia and the Mexican Jesús
Urueta (1868–1920).

Judging by the display of imagination and technical perfection
in the poetry of the *modernistas*, we might have expected a
parallel flowering in fiction. Yet most of their prose, and as a
rule the best of it, took the form of essays, *crónicas*, articles and
books of travel, and literary criticism. A large part of the writings
of Martí, as we know, and of Gutiérrez Nájera and Darío as well,
consists of *crónicas*. A travel sketch by Díaz Rodríguez, for example, would be as carefully wrought as a poem. Criticism, of
course, was of extraordinary importance for the movement, by
way of defense and explanation against the attacks of the re-
actionaries and the inertia of the public. Darío's book *Los raros*
(1896), first published in the shape of separate articles in *La
Nación* of Buenos Aires, was a brave attempt to acquaint the
unwilling reader with the names of a few European masters and
a number of minor figures whose fame has proved ephemeral;
to the Europeans he added Poe and Martí. Rodó's persuasive

and beautifully written essay on Darío probably won many
readers to their side. Yet, as late as 1907 Díaz Rodríguez was
still writing his contentious *Road to Perfection* and Gómez Carrillo conducting a symposium on *modernismo* in *El Nuevo Mercurio*, the literary review he edited in Paris. Sanín Cano, in Bogotá, was among the first critics to put his wisdom and his learning
at the service of the cause of modernity; then he grew from a literary critic into a critic of public life, both local and international,
whose analysis of modern society is radical and ruthless. Rodó,
too, developed from a literary critic into a moralist. His *Ariel*
(1900), a discourse in six parts, addressed "to the youth of America" — "our America" — preaches fundamental truths, however
obvious they may seem, because there is always a new generation
growing up and "the seed of a word spoken at the right moment
may beget immortal fruit." He stressed the need of protecting
the wholeness of the human personality against the encroachments
of specialization or any other manner of narrowness; the lesson
of Greece, with its full humanity, as contrasted with Phoenicia
or Carthage; the faith in the democratic way of life, which, if
rightly understood, acts as a safeguard to spiritual freedom. The
words of *Ariel* were spoken at the right moment. The prodigious
development of the United States, followed by the astoundingly
easy victory of 1898 over a nation that still nominally counted as
a world power, found innumerable admirers in the countries to
the south. There was a budding *Nordomania*. Admiration leads
to imitation, and a number of the admirers of success dreamed of·
a South America entirely given over to "practical" pursuits, in
accordance with their short-sighted interpretation of the example
set by the American democracy. Rodó admonished them against
the injudicious aping of a civilization that seemed to him a magnificent torso, not a finished statue, and warned us all of the
danger that our recent prosperity might lead only to a Phoenician
future. *Ariel* was widely read and discussed, for many years, from
Mexico and the Antilles to Argentina and Chile, and *Arielismo*

replaced *Nordomania*, at least among many of the young. Then Rodó published *Motives of Proteus* (1909), a very lengthy book, made up of connected essays and parables on the development of human personality; its leading motif is the unbounded possibilities of renewal in the human spirit. Its philosophical basis is a sort of ethics of renewal, quite in keeping with the then new doctrine of "creative evolution" of Henri Bergson. Rodó's later essays on Bolívar and Montalvo, included in his book of essays *El mirador de Próspero* (1913), are the outcome of studies on the history and the problems of Hispanic America. In the *Montalvo* he shows himself, although the younger generation does not seem to have discovered it, a forerunner of the recent literary movement that takes the sufferings of the Indians as its main subject, and, accordingly, of that vast portion of our literature which deals with the problems of today. Until 1914 he kept his optimistic faith in the effort of mankind towards light and truth, preaching enthusiasm and hope, "the gifts of youth"; then the European war shook his faith, and in Florence (1916) he fancied a dialogue between Michelangelo's David and Cellini's Perseus in which these two embodiments of full and harmonious humanity ponder on the causes of the conflict and conclude that man has unmade himself.[17]

A Brazilian essayist, Eduardo Prado (1860–1901), preceded Rodó as a critic of American democracy, but only from the political point of view.[18] His contemporary the scholarly historian Manoel de Oliveira Lima (1867–1928), on the contrary, was very active in fostering the mutual understanding between North and South America.[19] Of much higher literary importance was Euclides de Cunha (1866–1909), the author of *Os sertões* (1902), in the opinion of many the greatest book as yet written in Brazil. In several ways it resembles Sarmiento's *Facundo*; it is a tragic story, taken as a case to illustrate the social and political problems of the country, and preceded by a sort of essay in human geography. The story is not that of a *caudillo*, a military and political chief, as in Sarmiento; it is the story of a delirious rural mystic, Antonio Conselheiro, around whom a fanatic multitude gathered and settled down in the *sertão*, that vast and peculiar geographical zone in the interior of Brazil. Their anomalous community eventually became rebellious, and the republican government sent four successive military expeditions to subdue them; the first three were defeated, but the fourth wiped out the settlement.[20] The somber story is powerfully and brilliantly told; no less powerful and brilliant is the description of the *sertões* and the human types they produce, although the science on which it rests has grown partly obsolete.[21]

Our philosophical outlook was at this point undergoing a change. Positivism was still dominant at the end of the nineteenth century: José Ingenieros (1877–1925), of Argentina, was its last and most popular representative; Alejandro Deústua (b. 1849) in Peru, Farías Brito (1862–1917) in Brazil, Alejandro Korn (1860–1936) in Argentina, and Carlos Vaz Ferreira (b. 1873) in Uruguay acted as the pioneers of new ways of thought. Korn and Vaz Ferreira are very original thinkers and masters of philosophical prose.[22]

In fiction, the preferences of the *modernistas* rallied to a type of short story poetically conceived and developed. Such were the stories written by Martí for the children who read *La Edad de Oro*, the stories written by Casal, by Gutiérrez Nájera (the best example is his haunting fantasy on Rip van Winkle), by Darío in *Azul* (a book that also contained prose poems in the manner of Baudelaire), by Díaz Rodríguez (*Cuentos de color*, 1898 — there is a different dominant color in each story), by Urbina, by Nervo, and by Lugones (particularly *The Rain of Fire* and *The Horses of Abdera*). This poetical manner of conceiving and developing was also adopted, though less frequently, in novels. A famous specimen is Larreta's *Glory of Don Ramiro* (1908), a story laid in the Spain of Philip II.[23]

Two currents, poetical fancy and realism, met and clashed or mixed in fiction. The realistic novel, which began in Hispanic America with Blest Gana and Almeida as far back as the eighteen-fifties, had been slowly growing, and in the eighteen-eighties received the influence of French naturalism — the first book of the Argentine Eugenio Cambaceres (1843–1890), *Potpourri*, is dated 1882, the very year of publication of *Ismaelillo*, the first book of poetry of the *modernista* movement. Cambaceres, although read by many, lacked the stature necessary to become the master of a school. In Brazil, the beginnings of naturalism are usually dated from the publication of *The Mulatto* (1881), by Aluizio de Azevedo, a far better writer than Cambaceres, with a great variety of resources in description. Azevedo was a realist rather than a strict naturalist according to the notion of Zola, and at times he even went back to the romantic habits of his early youth. Julio Ribeiro (1845–1890), with *Flesh* (1888), came nearer to the French master's theory and practice.[24] But the majority of our novelists instinctively clung to our traditional and spontaneous realism, already apparent in Lizardi's *Itching Parrot* in 1816. The most refined writers, like Reyles and Díaz Rodríguez, arrived at a compromise between the two conflicting currents — there is realism in the description of the outward aspects of life, but the life of their characters is confined and self-centered. There is a gap between the individual lives and the life of the cities where they are placed, a lack of what might be called social density. The style is always carefully polished.[25] There were, besides, less exacting writers who contented themselves with realism in a workaday prose, like most of the Spanish novelists of the same period. The best of these writers is Roberto José Payró (1867–1928), of Argentina, a master of the satirical portraiture of social types, such as his Laucha, a twentieth-century *pícaro*, an itinerant rogue; in his *Pago Chico* — not a novel, but a series of sketches — he draws a finely ironical picture of Main Street in South America.[26]

While the novel was growing and multiplying, the drama en-

joyed in the city of Buenos Aires a flourishing period at the beginning of the present century. Our drama, as is well known, began
as a religious festival shortly after the Conquest, and as such it
survives still in remote places; then the lay drama became, at the
end of the sixteenth century, one of the principal amusements in
the larger towns. It declined after the winning of independence,
during the anarchical years of the first half of the nineteenth century, and for a long time all our cities, still very much given to
theatre-going, had to content themselves with the performances of
dramatic companies from Spain or Portugal. Our own theatre
was reduced, as a rule, to short comedies — little *zarzuelas*, with
music, or *sainetes*; the more ambitious plays written by our men
of letters were performed now and then — with little fervor, when
not with thinly disguised hostility — by the European companies.
But then South America was to witness a new and original rebirth of the drama — and in the humblest cradle imaginable, the
circus. In 1884, a circus manager of Buenos Aires, José Podestá,
decided to present a pantomime about the life of the outlaws, the
gauchos malos, adapted by the novelist Eduardo Gutiérrez from
his own story *Juan Moreira*. The pit allowed great freedom of
movement: the actors could appear on horseback, cavort and
gallop; dances and songs were introduced. Then, in 1886, in the
small town of Chivilcoy, Podestá added words to the pantomime.
The show was very successful, as might be expected, considering
its subject and its public, and many more plays were staged, all
about country life: *Martín Fierro, Santos Vega, Juan Cuello,
Julián Jiménez, Pastor Luna, Zorzal,* and *Tranquera*. By the beginning of the twentieth century there was in existence a flourishing folk drama, presented either in circuses or in theatres, in
Argentina and Uruguay, by several companies of the Podestá
family. They now performed, besides their old rude plays born
of the pantomime, plays by men of letters like Martiniano Leguizamón and the Uruguayan Elías Regules.[27] In the year 1901 the
Podestás invaded the central theatrical district of Buenos Aires,

and four of the new plays they performed between February, 1902, and August, 1903, obtained great success. Very soon many young men of letters in the city were writing plays and, as a rule, seeing them performed. This enthusiasm lasted some twelve or fifteen years. Then gradually the theatre became commercial, and much of the best talent withdrew from it, until at present its highest level is maintained by experimental playhouses like the Teatro del Pueblo. During the early years of the century its outstanding figure was the Uruguayan Florencio Sánchez (1875–1910), who has left us a masterpiece, his powerful and somber rural tragedy *Down the Hill* (1905).[28]

8

PROBLEMS OF TODAY
1920–1940

WITH political stability, under a real or a feigned democratic form, and economic development, in most of the nations of Hispanic America, there came, as we know, a division of labor through which men of letters were no longer leaders in public life as well. They now wrote "pure literature" — such, for a time at least, was their purpose and their ideal. The ivory tower became a familiar symbol. Their vain attempt at "splendid isolation" was intended as a vengeance upon the supposed inattention of the much-abused bourgeoisie. At bottom, there was dissatisfaction — they felt they were no longer important in the public eye; but they were not justified in their complaints. Our writers have never lacked readers — if our reading public is not bigger, the fault lies in the illiteracy and poverty of a large part of our population; our poets, indeed, have much wider audiences, proportionally, than the poets of any other countries of Western culture.[1] Eventually, they came down from their uncomfortable ivory tower to the market place, at least from time to time, to deal with questions of public interest.

Our literature, since then, has run in two channels — one in which purely artistic ends are in view; another in which the ends in view are social.

Between the last group of the *modernistas*, the group of Lugones, Valencia, Chocano, and the first group of the *vanguardia* in the twentieth century, the group of Borges and Neruda, there came a transitional generation, born between 1880 and 1896, which gradually drew away from the ideals and the practices of their forerunners.[2] The new generation, born after 1896, broke away from them altogether.

The influence of the poets and writers of the eighteen-eighties and nineties was favorable to the study of literary form, as against the carelessness of the romantics; in the normal run of things, it often led to preciosity, both in style and in subjects. Then, as might be expected, there were signs of restlessness, and protests against the literature of palaces, lakes, peacocks, and swans. "Wring the neck of the deceitful swan," was the cry, "the wise owl is a better counsellor." These portentous words appeared in a sonnet (1910) of González Martínez, for whom poetry is, above all, contemplation or "emotion recollected in tranquillity."[3] Amado Nervo, who had begun as a follower of all the aristocratic and exotic fashions of 1896, now became a sort of lay preacher of Christian love and prayer with a touch of Buddhist mysticism. Another group of poets decided, somewhat after the manner of Wordsworth, to strip their verse of ornament, adopting "a selection of language really used by men" and carrying the simplification of style to extremes that surprised their readers — who, however, soon accustomed themselves to it, as well as to the new themes: events of everyday life, memories, travels, roads, villages. The most typical of these poets were Fernández Moreno, Luis Carlos López, and the Brazilian Mario Pederneiras (1868–1915).

The impersonal attitude which had tended to suppress or repress personal feeling was attacked from another side by a new sort of exalted romanticism, represented by poets like Miguel Angel Osorio, Arturo Capdevila, Carlos Sabat Ercasty, and especially by a distinguished group of women of Uruguay (María Eugenia Vaz Ferreira, Delmira Agustini, Juana de Ibarbourou), Argentina (Alfonsina Storni), Chile (Gabriela Mistral), and Brazil (Gilka Machado). It is perhaps significant that, with a very few exceptions, women were absent from the copious literary movement of the eighties and nineties; it was probably too impersonal for them.[4] When at last they came into it, as a group, they came as rebels. In their own way, they were all rebellious. They did not openly reject the traditional restrictions of feminine life in the countries of Hispanic culture — they merely ignored them at the time of writing. They laid their souls bare and spoke frankly of love and passion, of joy when it came to them, but more often of disillusion and thwarted lives. The greatest of them, Gabriela Mistral, has already outgrown the stage of youthful disenchantment and become a voice of counsel and pity, through her love of children, of mothers, of the poor, of the peasant, of the Indian and the Negro, of all the part of mankind that suffers. Her work, both in prose and in verse, is one of the noblest of our times.[5]

In this generation which I have called transitional our writers gradually came back to their old habit of taking part in political affairs. If not all the writers, at least many more took part now than in the two preceding groups of the *modernistas*. But now they knew it was unlikely that they should be chosen as leaders; their main function was the discussion and diffusion of political doctrines, not infrequently examining and explaining their philosophical foundations. Thus, in Argentina, Ricardo Rojas began in 1909 to preach a new and ampler form of patriotism which should have as its aim a spiritual development.[6] Then in 1918 a movement of "university reform" swept the country; its program demanded a renewal of the intellectual content of higher education and a living connection between the universities and the people.[7] In Mexico, the political revolution of 1910 was preceded by a purely intellectual movement that began around 1907 in the Sociedad de Conferencias, later called the Ateneo de México (1909–1914). The members of this youthful group were as much interested in the problems of literature and philosophy as in the social and political problems of the country. Their most important public activity, besides their lectures, was the organization of a center of cultural diffusion, the first of its kind in the country, called Universidad Popular de México (1912–1920). They attacked positivism, the official philosophy of the last twenty years of the regime of Porfirio Díaz; two members of the group, Acevedo and Mariscal, started the new interest, now grown to such huge proportions, in the Mexican architecture of colonial times. Afterwards the Mexican revolution was to have a vast literature of its own, culminating in *The Under Dogs* of Mariano Azuela and *The Eagle and the Serpent* of Martín Luis Guzmán, a member of the Ateneo.[8] In Peru, after the literary movement of the review *Colónida* in 1915, edited by Abraham Valdelomar, came the "Reforma Universitaria," following the example of Argentina, in 1919, and then the political movement of the APRA (Allianza Popular Revolucionaria Americana), under the leadership of Víctor Raúl Haya de la Torre (b. 1895), a political thinker with a sound philosophical education and a lucid style.[9] A typical feature of this Peruvian movement was the establishment of a chain of Universidades Populares named "González Prada" in homage to its great forerunner. Later on, in Puerto Rico, the great party leaders were men of letters — Pedro Albizu Campos and Juan Antonio Corretjer, of the Partido Nacionalista organized in 1922, and Luis Muñoz Marín, founder of the very recent Partido Popular Democrático. In Brazil, the literary movement of 1922 was, according to one of its leaders, Mario de Andrade, the premonition of the coming revolutionary attitude concerning the social problems of the country. And the story of a well-known periodical, the *Repertorio Americano* edited by Joaquín García Monge in San José de Costa Rica, is very significant: it began in 1920 as a literary publication and has gradually developed into a tribune of the social and political problems of all Hispanic America. The men of letters who take part in our public life are seldom members of any administration; they belong to the opposition, and are far more frequently in prison than in power — when not in exile, whether forced or voluntary. Even if the party to which they adhere takes hold of power, they are often ahead of it in their views. A party with a political philosophy, as T. S. Eliot says, is a revolutionary party; in our case we may say a man instead of a party.[10]

In the purely literary field, another line of innovation consisted in carrying to an extreme certain tendencies inherent in the literature of the eighties and nineties. Preciosity changed into complexity, in which unexpected associations of images — or of mere words — became normal. The change may be traced to Lugones, who by 1898 had already become the "extreme left" of the movement, with his sequence of sonnets *The Twelve Delights*, later included in his book *The Sunsets of the Garden* (1905). There is a similarity, in this change, to the transition from the style of the Renaissance to the baroque. Lugones did not stop there: like Stravinsky and Picasso, he changed his manner every few years. The baroque tendency grew with Julio Herrera y Reissig, whose imagery soon became startling, even delirious at times; its full bloom was reached in *The Ecstasies of the Mountain*. In a different way, the poems of Enrique Banchs, or José María Eguren, or Alfonso Reyes, became esoteric, not in each separate image, but in the remote sources and allusions of their poems.[11] Still another type of baroque poetry, in which complexity and novelty of imagery blend with a fond tenderness of common daily things, appeared with Ramón López Velarde, who partrayed the picturesque life of old-fashioned towns in central Mexico and finally drew a brief synthesis of the country in *Suave patria*.[12]

By 1920 a new movement was launched, in which Spain and Spanish America went hand in hand — not, as in the romantic period, with both starting at the same time but separately, and each going along its own road afterwards, nor, as in the period from 1882 to 1900, with the New World preceding the Old. As usual, there were foreign influences, from France and elsewhere.[13]

A similar movement began in Brazil in 1922; it is usually dated from the "week of modern art," devoted to exhibitions of painting and sculpture, concerts, readings, and lectures, in the city of São Paulo. The leaders were the poets Mario de Andrade (1893–1945) and Manuel Bandeira (b. 1886). They were supported not only by very young writers and artists, but also by some of their own age who were already well known, like Ronald de Carvalho, Guilherme de Almeida, Alvaro Moreyra, and even by the veteran Graça Aranha.

The name first given to this movement in Spain was *ultraísmo*: the new writers proposed not only to go beyond — *ultra* — everything that had been done before, but even beyond the mere facts of reality as commonly interpreted by the literature of the past. The recent past was, naturally, the most detested; anyone who accepted its outworn interpretations was nicknamed, with a word taken from the Italian futurists, *passatista*, a partisan of the past, a *laudator temporis acti*. Even the reshaping of reality was not enough for some — they proposed the creation of a new "realm of being" from which the poet and the artist should draw their material, and they called themselves *creacionistas* (the word comes, it seems, from one of the leaders of the movement, the Chilean Vicente Huidobro).[14] The general result was a cryptic form of expression, a web of complex metaphors, a persistently elliptical passage from one image to another. One of the most refined poets, Mariano Brull, went so far as to invent — only as a pastime, it must be said — the *jitanjáfora*, a poem without words, a mere succession of syllables without meaning, which derived all its charm solely from the combination of sounds.[15]

This search for new expression, whatever the value of the work it begot, was a fruitful experiment. The metaphysical claims of the pioneers were not upheld. Even the name of the movement was changed to a vague general term, *vanguardia* ("the vanguard"). The name became popular. In Brazil, however, the name adopted for the local movement was *modernismo*, already applied in Spanish America to that of the eighteen-eighties and nineties; the most revolutionary of the Brazilian revolutionists, in search of the most thunderstriking name they could contrive, called themselves *anthropophagists*.

Gains that last to this day, after twenty years, are a daring use of metaphor, a great variety of image association, and a free and living syntax. Free verse, as was to be expected, also came into vogue. It has not become, as many supposed, and as for a time seemed probable, the only acceptable type of verse, but it is still a normal vehicle of expression for poets as different from one another as the Argentine Jorge Luis Borges, the Chilean Pablo Neruda, the Colombian Rafael Maya, the Ecuadorian Jorge Carrera Andrade, the Guatemalan Luis Cardoza y Aragón, the Dominican Héctor Incháustegui Cabral, the Brazilians Jorge de Lima, Carlos Drummond de Andrade, and Cecilia Meirelles. Not many years after the vogue of free verse began, a number of poets set themselves to revive such rigid classical forms as the sonnet, Dante's tercet, the *espinela* of Calderón and Zorrilla, and the *lira* of Friar Luis de León and Saint John of the Cross. At times they adopted, also, a classical lucidity of expression, but quite often the old forms contain bold metaphors of the most modern type.

To take an example from a book of poems recently published, the first of a brilliant poetess from Uruguay, Sara de Ibáñez:

> Diré a mi nube blanda:
> Can de mi pensamiento, vuelve al río.
> Tus espumas desanda.
> Muérete en el rocío,
> en el oro, en la sangre y en el frío.[16]

The literature of the pioneers of this movement aspired to an even greater "purity" than that of the eighties and nineties. Their poetry, if their wishes had been fulfilled, would have been the purest of all, free from all the dross of nature, from the dregs of reality.[17] But even among the pioneers there were a few who never gave up the clear reference to immediate facts, who — for instance — persisted in loving and describing their native land, and, as in the case of Borges and his followers in Argentina, depicted the poor suburbs of large cities, with forgotten streets that end in limitless plains, with humble houses and rose-colored grocery stores, or the habits of men who tame horses and tend cows.

Paradoxically enough, some of the innovators condemned all our preceding literature because, according to them, it was too European in manner and lacked the flavor of the soil. The title of their organ in Buenos Aires, around 1925, was *Martín Fierro*, the name of the gaucho of Hernández's poem, one of the few works of the past that were excepted from condemnation. In that review there were poems on native subjects side by side with what might be called "abstract poetry" and might have been written in Mars as well as in South America. This quarrel was not new; the search for an artistic expression that should be our own, and not subservient to Europe, had begun, we know, as early as 1823, when Bello proclaimed our literary independence in the first of his *Silvas americanas*; it was renewed in 1832 by Echeverría and his fellow romantics; it reappeared with Martí, and Rodó, and even Darío, in spite of his forswearing for a short while all American subjects as unpoetical. That campaign in Buenos Aires was a sign of the times. In most of the countries of Spanish America, literature had largely "gone native" already, after the signal given by Darío's *Voyage to Nicaragua*, Chocano's *Alma América*, and Lugones' *Secular odes*.[18] And from Brazilian poetry the native landscapes, at least, had never been absent.

Meanwhile, another typical quarrel was going on. The writers of the eighties and nineties had not met with any opposition to their ideals. Their readers enjoyed their pictures of palaces and gardens because they themselves were enjoying the novelty of their own prosperous and luxurious cities. But the charm of such a novelty wears off, and soon there was, on the one hand, weariness and disappointment in the midst of splendor, and on the other hand, as we have seen, the rediscovery of social and national problems as subjects for literature. Now the writers and poets of the "vanguard" movement, when true to the tenets of their creed of "pure literature," placed themselves at a far greater distance from social and political questions than their predecessors. They were first attacked by a group of socialist writers who were, as far as literary form went, *passatisti*, behind the times, in the opinion of their opponents. In the city of Buenos Aires, there was around 1925 a quarrel between two streets: the Calle de Florida, the thoroughfare of luxury trades and art exhibitions, and the Calle de Boedo, where a hard-working middle class lived. In the city of Mexico another quarrel broke out at about the same time, and there it included painting as well as literature. As often happens, the most radical in their political and social points of view were not "advanced" in their notions of art and literature, and vice versa. But this simple and easy cleavage lasted only a short time. A part of the group of literary innovators became interested in social problems, and most of the socialists learned the technique of the new literature. Today, the poet whose influence is the widest in all Hispanic America, Pablo Neruda (b. 1904), is a bold innovator from both the social and the literary point of view.[19]

At the bottom of this quarrel was the well-known question, which soon came to the front: art for art's sake or art at the service of great human ideals? Or, if art for art's sake seems too futile a purpose, and too easy to discredit, art as self-expression or art as service? The question, indeed, lacks meaning outside a complex urban civilization. In any society that may, by comparison, be called simple — that of the early Greeks, or that of the French or the Spaniards in the eleventh and twelfth centuries — most art sets forth the common religious and heroic ideals. Even in Athenian civilization, Gilbert Murray contends, the ideal of the poet or the artist was service — glory was mainly recognition of service, not mere applause to genius. In Rome, Virgil and Horace sing as prophets of imperial greatness. In modern times, however, it is easy to distinguish between the poet who is or seems interested only in his own creation and the poet who writes with a more than individual purpose: between Shakespeare and Milton, Góngora and Quevedo, Keats and Shelley, Musset and Hugo, Poe and Whitman. The comparison only proves the possibility of both. The quarrel, then, narrows itself to whether — as would happen if either faction had its way — no artist or writer is to be allowed to introduce social and political questions in his work or whether every artist and writer is to be compelled to introduce them. Both compulsions are abhorrent to the modern mind, accustomed as it is to its romantic freedom. Human genius has a way of working miracles under the tyranny of a petty prince of the Renaissance or of a publisher in a city of our own day. Let us hope that in the future it may be free from any compulsion.

A large part of the significant literature of Hispanic America today presents social problems, or at least describes social situations that contain the germs of problems. The novel is, normally, the form in which such aspects of society most frequently appear in modern times. In our literature they began to appear as soon as our novelists moved from romanticism toward realism. Realism, as it was understood in the nineteenth century, with its chronicles of unhappy life, mostly among the poor, naturally led to a type of problem novel, just as the psychological drama of the same period led to the problem play.

Canaan (1902), by the Brazilian Graça Aranha (1868–1931), is the most significant among our earliest problem novels of this century. It partakes of the nature of the essay, like later novels of Wells or Thomas Mann's *The Magic Mountain*. The distant model is Goethe's *Wilhelm Meister*. Aranha's *Canaan* contains very vivid descriptions of tropical natures and human types. Some of the characters discuss Brazil, its past, present, and future. At that time, racial theories emanating from European sources, dressed in what looked like a scientific garb, received serious consideration in Hispanic America. Now our attitude is changed.[20] A realistic survey of the actual situation of the many races that mingle in Hispanic America has given us a simple and clear conviction: that no "racial problems" need exist in any community unless it wishes to create them. Brazil is, among all the Hispanic countries, the one in which the coexistence of many different racial strains has best been solved in practice. But in *Canaan* the main problem discussed is not that of coexistence; it is the question of racial aptitude. Very appropriately, in the dialogues of the novel the extreme view of European superiority is maintained by a German. The author, after letting his characters express themselves to the full, does not allow himself to be overcome by any pessimistic views of the future of Brazil.[21] Forty years have elapsed since he wrote his novel, and his hopes seem justified. No better testimony could be adduced than Rudyard Kipling's unexpected tribute to Brazilian civilization, written toward the end of his life.[22]

Our "racial problems" have been gradually reduced by habit and common sense to their cultural and economic grounds. The Indians, we know, have preserved a large part of their old cultures, in fusion with the meager portion of European civilization they have received. The Negroes, too, brought much of their tribal African cultures. In both cases we were accustomed to look upon such survivals as problems; we believed that our social development would be imperfect until the Indian and the Negro were thoroughly "Europeanized," until they had adopted the techniques and the habits that the industrial revolution compelled Europe and the United States to adopt. We know better now. The mere survivals, as such, imply no danger — quite to the contrary, they add color and zest to a social life that might become too drab and monotonous; in many cases, besides, they save the native from the factory or the plantation.[23] All hindrances to our progress come from the insufficiency of the education and economic opportunities offered to the masses.

In literature, Indian subjects, old and new, are treated in many countries in Spanish or Portuguese, or in native languages.[24] And a poetry on Negro life — *poesía negra*, as it is called — appeared in Puerto Rico and Cuba around 1925. It enjoyed an immense vogue and produced very beautiful verse in the works of Nicolás Guillén (b. 1904), Emilio Ballagas (b. 1908), Luis Palés Matos, and a few more. On the whole, these poets do not dwell on the black man's sufferings; they prefer to speak of his African traditions, to describe his loves and pleasures, to imitate the rhythms of his speech and his dances.[25] Agustín Acosta (b. 1887) has not written *poesía negra*, but we may connect with it his long and original poem on the sugar cane industry, *La Zafra* (1926).

There is, of course, the age-old question of the exploitation of the Indians, who make up the majority of our proletariat in the fields, the mines, or the factories in such countries as Mexico, Guatemala, Ecuador, Peru, and Bolivia. The writers who apply themselves to the social problems of the Indian present him, therefore, as a proletarian, and incidentally avail themselves of the picturesque aspects of his manner of living. Their campaign is a part of the endeavor to redeem him from his old servitude and raise him to the status of a real citizen, an endeavor that is partly successful in Mexico while in the other countries it is all but limited to the pages of writers and poets and to the platforms of political parties bent on social reform, parties which so far have never come into power.

After the few recurring pleas in favor of the Indian in our literature throughout the nineteenth century, from the writers who took part in the movement of independence to González Prada and Clorinda Matto de Turner, to Martí and Rodó, the systematic Indianist movement began, both in politics and in literature, with the Mexican Revolution of 1910. Its first significant literary page

was the poem ¿Quién sabe? of the Peruvian Chocano, written in
1913 while he accompanied the revolutionary army:

> Indio que labras con fatiga
> tierras que de otros dueños son:
> ¿ignoras tú que deben tuyas
> ser, por tu sangre y tu sudor?
> ¿ignoras tú que audaz codicia,
> siglos atrás, te las quitó?
> ¿ignoras tú que eres el amo?

The Indian replies "Perhaps! Who knows!", and his reply becomes the refrain of the poem:

> ¡Quién sabe, señor! [26]

In later years, Indianist poetry grew in connection with the
insurgent social literature — for example, the poems of César
Vallejo, Carrera Andrade, and the Venezuelan Jacinto Fombona
Pachano.[27]

Most of the literature concerning the Indian took the shape of
fiction. The most famous novel of this type, and one of the earliest, is *The Under Dogs* (1916) of the Mexican Mariano Azuela
(b. 1873). It is developed as a succession of brief, sharp sketches,
written in a crisp, concise style, and presents the Indians as the
victims of the civil wars — they are drafted by either one or the
other of the contending factions and do not know what cause they
die for.[28]

The problem, in *The Under Dogs*, is the military exploitation
of the Indian. His virtual servitude, from all points of view, especially his economic servitude, is mainly or partly the subject of
many more novels and short stories. The best-known authors are
the Peruvians Vallejo, Falcón, and Alegría, the Ecuadorians Jorge
Icaza, Fernando Chaves, and Enrique Gil Gilbert, the Bolivian
Alcides Arguedas, and the Mexican Gregorio López y Fuentes.[29]

The most brilliant group of novelists who present social problems, especially since 1930, is the Brazilian — Rachel de Queiroz,

Graciliano Ramos, Jorge Amado, José Lins do Rego, Lucio Cardoso, Marques Rebelo, and Érico Verissimo. Their task is not limited to the description of how Indians or Negroes live and suffer; it is a vast picture of the toil of men in Brazil, how they work and love and play and die on the coffee, cocoa, and cotton plantations, on the cattle ranches, in the sugar mills, in the mines, in docks and ships, in city slums.[30] Incidentally, both in Brazil and in Spanish America the writers of fiction describe the full regional variety of all the countries down to the remotest parts — even Tierra del Fuego and the Straits of Magellan, the Orcades and the Chiloe islands.

The problems of Hispanic America are not all merely problems of relations between human beings. There is the struggle with nature, the effort to master it. The pioneer in the attempt to describe man's fight with the jungle was Horacio Quiroga. In his powerful and harrowing stories man is often defeated by the jungle or the desert. Man's foes, which he knew so well from actual experience, attract him so much that at times he transfers his attention from man to the animals. He has written fine tales of serpents. José Eustasio Rivera, a younger writer, who died a few years after the publication of his only novel, *The Vortex* (1924), takes his principal characters across the South American jungle from Colombia to Brazil in search of rubber. Their trip becomes an Odyssey in which all the places visited belong to the kingdom of Hades. In its most striking episode, the travellers are compelled to throw themselves into a marsh and stay in it for twelve hours, surrounded by frightened rodents and serpents, while a huge army of red ants, *tambochas*, goes by, devouring everything that is sufficiently soft, stripping every plant of its leaves and every animal of its flesh.[31]

Another novelist, Rómulo Gallegos, records a similar struggle against barbaric nature in the novel to which he gave the symbolic title of *Doña Bárbara* (1929). Not only nature is barbaric in the prairies of Venezuela — man is also made barbaric by it, and the protagonist is a typical instance. But hope is easier to conceive in the prairies than in the jungle, and in his next novel, *Chanticleer* (1934), the author appears more hopeful of man's victory over his dumb enemies and over his own excesses.[32]

A very different literature deals with the plains, the pampas of Argentina and Uruguay, now entirely subdued and reshaped by man. To understand the change they have undergone, we must go back to the pages of Sarmiento in his *Facundo* and W. H. Hudson in his autobiographical book *Far Away and Long Ago* and his descriptions of *The Naturalist in La Plata*. The pampas had no trees, except on the banks of rivers; only grass, six or eight feet high. The horses and the cows brought by the conquerors bred freely in the plains and became wild; a hundred years ago there were many thousands of them. Men — the gauchos — became as wild as they, though they kept their European garments. Taming the pampa and the gaucho was the seemingly Utopian plan of the men of 1852; it was fulfilled in a surprisingly short time, even though it strewed many victims along its road, like Martín Fierro. Now the best emblem of the modern pampa is that admirable invention, the Argentine and Uruguayan *estancia*, the vast estate in which as many as two million trees may have been planted by man.

The novel of the modern pampa is Ricardo Güiraldes' *Don Segundo Sombra* (1926). The new gaucho is no longer the lord of the plains; he works for the owners of *estancias*. But he keeps his old love of freedom and often prefers, to a stable life, a continual wandering from place to place, breaking rough colts or driving cowherds across the roads. Don Segundo Sombra travels in this manner across the province of Buenos Aires; the boy Fabio, fascinated by his calm strength and his infallible skill, follows him as his pupil. Nothing happens, except the incidents usual in such a life, painted by Güiraldes, in spite of all its roughness, with the delicate brush of a poetical imagination that never fails him.

At the end, when Fabio unexpectedly inherits a fortune, Don Segundo stays in his *estancia* a short while, but at last his rambling instinct calls him away.[33]

The rural novel and the social novel of the proletariat in the towns or in the fields now outshine in Hispanic America the other types of fiction — for instance, the novel of the large city, conceived in the manner of Balzac or Tolstoy, or (among Hispanic novelists in Europe) Pérez Galdós and Eça de Queiroz. But many forms are attempted, with various degrees of success.[34] The psychological novelist is often also essentially an essayist, like the Argentine Eduardo Mallea, whose most widely read and influential book is not one of his several intense portraits of solitary souls in conflict but his long interpretative essay, *Story of the Passion of an Argentine* (1937).[35]

As early as the sixteenth century, we know, probably within fifty years of the Conquest, Hispanic America began to create a music of its own. It was not based on Indian music, nor even, as far as we can ascertain, influenced by it. It was European music, which, transported across the ocean, became a new thing; when heard again in Europe, it sounded different, as we learn from Bartolomé de Argensola; the new men of the New World, in the new society they had established, so unlike any other that had existed before, transformed the music they brought with them, or received, into something as rich and strange as the *chaconne* proved to be. Since then, the countries of Hispanic America have never ceased to produce new types of song and dance. Besides, music was taught there, privately, or in schools and universities, as one of the essential subjects, one of the seven liberal arts, and taught to all social classes and races. Operas had already been composed and performed in Mexico and Peru in the early years of the eighteenth century. A recent discovery in Venezuela of a large collection of old manuscript scores seems to prove, according to its enthusiastic discoverers, that music in Hispanic America during the colonial period reached as high a degree of excellence as architecture. We know that the European masters of three centuries were studied in most of our countries — Palestrina and Victoria, Bach and Haydn, Gluck and Mozart.[36] In contrast to what happened in painting and sculpture, the official (and the private) teaching does not seem to have had any pernicious effect on music during the nineteenth century. It is true that in Europe, while the official teaching of painting and sculpture degenerated into a frigid academicism, nothing so deadly happened to music. Hispanic America produced, during the last hundred years, a number of distinguished composers such as Carlos Gomes, Felipe Villanueva, Ignacio Cervantes, and Julián Aguirre, and interpreters of international fame like Teresa Carreño and José White. Probably its distinctive contribution was in that type of popular music which lies half-way between the classical forms and the folk tunes — the waltz *Over the Waves*, of the Mexican Juventino Rosas, which still enjoys as great a vogue as that of the Viennese waltzes on which it is modelled; the *danzas* of the Puerto Rican Juan Morel Campos; the habanera *Tú*, of the Cuban Eduardo Sánchez de Fuentes; or, more recently, the best tangos of Argentina and Uruguay, the Cuban Ernesto Lecuona's songs and dances, the Chilean Osmán Pérez Freire's *Ay ay ay*; to which we may add because of its wide diffusion, although written in a strictly cultivated idiom by a learned musician, the Mexican Manuel M. Ponce's *Estrellita*.[37]

Today there is a vast musical activity in all Hispanic America, and the names of a few of our composers have already crossed our frontiers — above all the names of Carlos Chávez, embodying both the energy and the reserve of his native Mexico, and Heitor Vila-Lobos, a true revelation of Brazil, through his splendid originality and his deft use of Brazil's colorful treasures from three folk traditions. Our best musicians — such as Juan José Castro, of Argentina, Silvestre Revueltas, of Mexico, Humberto Allende and Domingo Santa Cruz, of Chile, Alejandro García Caturla and

Amadeo Roldán, of Cuba, Burle Marx, Camargo Guarnieri, Lorenzo Fernandes, and Francisco Mignone, of Brazil, besides Chávez and Vila-Lobos — study the traditions of their native countries and distill the finest essence of the local idiom into a musical language that is perforce international. With the changes required by individual talent and local environment, we might apply to them the words of Virgil Thomson about Revueltas: "his music is both racy and distinguished." It does not "make any pretense of going native. He wrote Mexican music that sounds like Spanish Mexico, and he wrote it in the best Parisian syntax." But "it would never be mistaken for French music." [38]

Yet, while "nativism" is seldom wholly absent, there are many degrees of it. Our composers may be classed, according to William Berrien, in three groups: "those who prefer to write in a 'European' idiom and in forms now consecrated and universally employed" (Juan José Castro, for example; but he is not averse to the transmutation of native material); "those who seek to employ at least the spirit of the popular Latin American musical heritage in an effort to achieve an original and authentic idiom — comparatively independent of the European tradition, especially in its 'academic' aspects" (Vila-Lobos and Chávez, for instance); and "those more 'austere' experimentalists whose music reflects little their environment and racial background" (Santa Cruz and the Argentine Juan Carlos Paz).

Finally, painting is the art through which Hispanic America has at last proved to the modern world its creative aptitude. Our "new painting" is not old, except in the tradition that partly inspires it; it began in Mexico as recently as 1921, yet its apparition is already treated as an historic international event. In 1921, after fourteen years spent in Europe, Diego Rivera returned to the capital of his native country and was invited to decorate the National University with mural paintings. His masterly technique proved equal to this — for him — new undertaking, since he had acquired through long study, ranging from Giotto to Cubism, a wide variety of resources. Upon his arrival in Mexico, he directed his attention towards the study of Indian architecture and sculpture and Mexican folk art, from the votive pictures in humble churches to the drawings in satirical journals and in pamphlets containing ballads. When the Mexican government invited other artists besides Rivera to paint the walls of the University, and then of several other public buildings, a new personality soon revealed itself — José Clemente Orozco. Painting became a national passion, and even country children were taught to paint, with astonishing results. Since then, many artists have appeared and developed.

"By 1925," so it is explained in the Foreword of the Museum of Modern Art to the catalogue of the exhibition of Twenty Centuries of Mexican Art held in New York in 1940, "rumors of the Mexican Renaissance began to reach the United States, and within a decade Mexican mural painting had become the most important foreign influence upon the art of this country." The Mexican influence did not extend only to the United States — all our hemisphere caught fire from it. All the countries with Indian traditions followed the example of Mexico, which became a land of pilgrimage for artists from all the Americas. A brilliant group of painters appeared in Central America, Ecuador, Peru, Bolivia, and Brazil. In fact, the modern movement in Brazil had already begun independently by 1922, before any news of the Mexican activities had reached South America. Argentina and Uruguay confined their imitation of Mexico to a growing and even feverish artistic activity, especially after the first exhibitions of Emilio Pettoruti (1924); but their painters have attained a high degree of technical accomplishment and are gradually producing a typical art, though without recourse to any of the picturesque elements that abound in the life that surrounds them — a difficult feat. The most conscientious artists who seek an authentic expression of their own in Argentina or Uruguay seldom paint the Indian, or the gaucho, now a thing of the past, or the Negro, also a thing of the past there; only the Uruguayan Pedro Figari (1861–1938) painted from memory delightful scenes of gaucho and Negro life of a hundred years ago, together with no less delightful landscapes in which he caught the long shapes of the clouds in the pampas and the delicate play of light and color there.[39]

Many of the painters, principally in Mexico, but elsewhere too, strive to relate their art to the social movements and aspirations of their countries. Their work is thus, at the same time, a singular artistic achievement and, through their love of the past and the present of Hispanic America, a unique aid to its effort towards a greater freedom and a better civilization.

NOTES

NOTES TO CHAPTER 1

1. This and the subsequent quotations are taken from Mr. Cecil Jane's translation of *The Voyages of Christopher Columbus* (London, 1930). I have slightly retouched them, trying to reproduce the peculiarities of the Spanish original, for which I have made use of Cesare de Lollis' edition in the *Raccolta di documenti e studi pubblicati dalla R. Commissione Colombiana* . . . (Rome, 1892). I am indebted to Professor Samuel Eliot Morison, of Harvard University, for many useful indications concerning the translation and regret that I am unable to make use of his own, which is still in the preparatory stage. Cf. his article "Texts and Translations of the Journal of Columbus' First Voyage," in The Hispanic American Historical Review, XIX (1939), 235–261. On how Columbus handled Spanish, cf. Don Ramón Menéndez Pidal's essay, "Cómo hablaba Colón," in the *Revista Cubana* of Havana, XIV (1940), 5–18, later reprinted in his book *La lengua de Cristóbal Colón* . . . *y otros estudios* . . . Buenos Aires, 1942).

2. In Santo Domingo there is still a popular belief, among the peasants, that one may find in the woods of the island wild women with inverted feet, as described by Pliny. They are called by the Indian name of *ciguapas*.

3. Professor Samuel Eliot Morison, in his exciting biography of Columbus, *Admiral of the Ocean Sea* (Boston, 1942), published after these lectures were delivered, says that the Discoverer "had a Hellenic sense of wonder, combined with an artist's appreciation of natural beauty."

4. I quote from the translation by Professor George Tyler Northup, *Letter to Piero Soderini* (*The Four Voyages*) (Princeton, 1916). The passages I have transcribed are from the *First Voyage*.

5. The Decades *De Orbe Novo* of Peter Martyr were published 1511–1516–1520–1530. The mention of the new stars appears in Decade I, book 9, printed 1511 (probably written 1504). Geraldini's *Itinerarium ad regiones sub aequinoctiali plaga constitutas* was written in 1520 and published in Rome, 1631. Gonzalo Fernández de Oviedo's *Historia general y natural de las Indias* was probably begun around 1520; it was published, in part, 1535–1557, and complete in four volumes, Madrid, 1851–1855 (see III, 360). Fracastoro's poem *Syphilis sive Morbus gallicus* appeared in Verona, 1530: see book II, lines 19–20 and 35–36. Étienne de la Boétie's Epistle was written about 1550; Mellin de Saint-Gelais's sonnet, about 1558. Camoëns' *Os Lusiadas* was published in 1572: see canto V. Ercilla's thirty-seventh canto of *La*

Araucana, to which the line quoted above belongs, was printed in 1589; the first parts of Castellanos' *Elegías,* also in 1589 (see *Primera Parte, Elegía* I, canto II). Bernardo de Valbuena refers to the new stars in his poem on "the greatness of Mexico," *La grandeza mexicana,* and in his *Canción* to the Duke of Lemos, both published in 1604, and many times in his long epic *El Bernardo,* published in 1624: see cantos IV (three times), XVI, and XIX.

In later times, the new stars have reappeared in José Maria de Hérédia's well-known sonnet *Les Conquérants* (1868) and in Rubén Darío's *Canto a la Argentina* (1910).

6. Decade I, book I. I quote from the translation of Francis Augustus MacNutt (New York, 1912).

7. Decade I, book III.

8 Decade III, book VII.

9. Decade I, book II.

10. Decade I, book III. In the translation by Richard Eden (1555) this passage reads. "For it is certain that among them the lande is as common as sonne and water, and that Mine and Thine (the seedes of all mischiefe) have no place with them. They are content with so little, that in so large a countrey they have rather superfluitie than scarcenesse: so that . . . they seeme to live in the golden worlde without toyle, living in open gardens, not intrenched with ditches, divided with hedges, or defended with walles; they deale truely one with another without lawes, without booke, and without judges: they take him for an evill and mischievous man, which taketh pleasure in dooing hurt to other."

11. Lewis Mumford, *The Story of Utopias* (New York, 1922): see p 57.

12. Thus in Gregory Martin's translation from the Latin Vulgate, in the Rhenish Bible, 1609. Las Casas, when speaking about the sermons of Montesinos, quotes from the Vulgate: *Repetam scientiam meam a principio. . . . Et probabo esse sine mendatio.* It seems likely that Father Montesinos was playing with the sound of the Latin verb-form *repetam,* similar to the Spanish *repetir* "to repeat," and disregarding its actual meaning, as in Martin's translation. The King James Bible says: "I will fetch my knowledge from afarre. . . . For truely my words shall not be false."

On Friar Pedro de Córdoba and Friar Antón de Montesinos, see Las Casas, *Historia de las Indias,* book II, chapter 54, and book III, chapters 3–12, 17–19, 33–35, 81–87, and 94–95. It is not clear, be it said in passing, whether Montesinos preached his sermons in 1510 or in 1511. Cf., besides, José María Chacón y Calvo, "Cartas censorias de la conquista," in the *Revista Cubana,* October–December, 1937; he quotes from a letter of Friar Pedro, written about 1517: the Indians of the Antilles are "so mild, so obedient, so good, that I think one might found with them a Church almost as excellent as the primitive one."

13. In Salamanca, Friar Francisco de Vitoria lived in the Dominican Convent of Saint Stephen, the original home of Friar Pedro de Córdoba, Friar Antón de Montesinos, and their companions in missionary work Friar Domingo de Mendoza, Friar Domingo de Betanzos, and Friar Tomás de Berlanga.

14. Vives shrewdly remarked that the distinction between just and unjust wars is a trap used by warmongers to their own advantage. It is a pity that he did not write (or at least it has not come down to us) the treatise he promised in defense of the Indians.

15. Marcelino Menéndez y Pelayo, "Algunas consideraciones sobre Francisco de Vitoria y los orígenes del derecho de gentes" (1889), in his *Ensayos de crítica filosófica*. On Vitoria, cf. also Eduardo de Hinojosa, *Estudios sobre la historia del derecho español* (Madrid, 1903); Ernest Nys, "Les publicistes espagnols du XVI⁰ siècle et les droits des Indiens," in his *Études de droit international et de droit politique* (Brussels and Paris, 1896); Luis G. Alonso Getino, *El Maestro Fr. Francisco de Vitoria y el renacimiento filosófico-teológico del siglo XVI* (Madrid, 1914); James Brown Scott, *The Spanish Origin of International Law* (Oxford, 1934) — on the front page of the book, Professor Scott quotes Dr. Johnson as reported by Boswell: "I love the University of Salamancha; for when the Spaniards were in doubt as to the lawfulness of their conquering America, the University of Salamancha gave it as their opinion that it was not lawful"; Silvio Zavala, *Las institutiones jurídicas en la conquista de América* (Madrid, 1935); finally, the *Anuario de la Asociación Francisco de Vitoria*, begun in 1929.

16. Dr. Chacón y Calvo, in his essay on "Cartas censorias de la conquista," already mentioned, says he has collected as many as two hundred letters which contain very severe criticisms of the conquerors: a number of them are from government officials.

17. A comparison of the Spaniards with the English in their relations with the Indians, both in thought and in action, may be found in Professor Herbert Ingram Priestley's *The Coming of the White Man* (New York, 1929) — see chapter v.

18. Cf. Geoffroy Atkinson, *The Extraordinary Voyage in French Literature before 1700* (New York, 1920), *The Extraordinary Voyage in French Literature from 1700 to 1720* (Paris, 1922), and *Les Relations de voyages du XVII⁰ siècle et l'évolution des idées* (Paris, n. d. [1924]); Philip Babcock Gove, *The Imaginary Voyage in Prose Fiction: a History of its Criticism and a Guide for its Study* (New York, 1941).

19. Francisco López de Gómara, for instance, in his *Hispania victrix* (1552), ventured so far as to say that the monuments of the Aztecs and the Incas were superior to those of the Egyptians; he did not, of course, mention the Greeks or the Romans.

20. A case in point: Friar Jerónimo Román published in Madrid, 1575, his *Repúblicas de Indias*, a survey of the religions, legislation, and forms of government of the Americas before Columbus. He often praises the Indians and their legal wisdom. Only a few copies of the book have survived, and they all have been mutilated by the Inquisition.

A stranger case: in the *auto* of Micael de Carvajal and Luis Hurtado de Toledo, *Las cortes de la muerte*, printed 1557, scene xix is a dialogue between two Indians, Saint Augustine, Saint Dominic, Saint Francis of Assisi, the Devil, the Flesh, and Death; the Indians complain about the treatment they suffer at the hands of Spaniards, and the saints agree that their complaints are justified. Micael de Carvajal had lived in Santo Domingo and may have come under the influence of the Dominican friars; but we do not know whether he or Hurtado de Toledo wrote that scene. At any rate, it seems to have passed unnoticed.

21. The Brazilians were in great favor in France, and the Court attended a festival of dances and religious ceremonies, in Rouen, in which Indians and disguised Frenchmen took part. Cf. Ferdinand Denis, *Une Fête brésilienne célébrée à Rouen en 1550* (Paris, 1850). This entertainment preceeded by nearly two centuries Rameau's opera-ballet *Les Indes galantes* (1735); according to Mr. Lincoln Kirstein, it is "not only a perfect example of the . . . semi-political opera-ballet but also of the geographical mode of a Europe newly aware of our globe's size" (*Dance*, New York, 1935; reprinted under the title *The Book of the Dance*, 1942, see p. 204).

22. I quote Florio's translation of Montaigne, from the Oxford collection of *The World's Classics*.

23. They may be followed at length in M. Gilbert Chinard's well-known book on *L'Amérique et le rêve exotique dans la littérature française au XVII? et au XVIII? siècle* (Paris, 1913). His earlier book, *L'Exotisme dans la littérature française au XVI? siècle* (Paris, 1911), practically ends with Montaigne. Mr. Bissell's *The American Indian in English Literature of the Eighteenth Century* (New Haven, 1925) and Mr. Hoxie Neal Fairchild's *The Noble Savage* (New York, 1928) describe similar but less important developments in English. Cf. also Albert Keiser, *The Indian in American Literature* (New York, 1933). A few facts may be added from H. F. C. Ten Kate's article "The Indian in Literature," in *Annual Report . . . of the Smithsonian Institution* (Washington, 1922). I have not come across any study

NOTES TO CHAPTER 2 211

of the Indian in German Literature. Of course, Kotzebue's *Die Sonnenjungfrau* (1791) and *Die Spanier in Peru* or *Rollas Tod* (1796), which Sheridan adapted in English as *Pizarro* (1799), were famous in their times.

24. Cf. Professor Arthur Oncken Lovejoy's keen analysis of "The Supposed Primitivism of Rousseau's 'Discourse on Inequality'," in *Modern Philology*, XXI (1923), 165–186. On the connection between Rousseau's theories and his knowledge of American Indians, cf. M. Chinard's *L'Amérique et le rêve exotique*, already mentioned, and Senhor Afonso Arinos de Mello Franco's *O indio brasileiro e a Revolução Francesa* (Rio de Janeiro, 1937).

25. G. Elliot Smith, *In the Beginning* (London, 1937; Thinkers' Library edition), pp. 22–23. Of course, the majority of the Indian tribes of the New World were not primitive: most had at least a rudimentary culture; but a few are mentioned as examples of Natural Men (G. E. Smith, pp. 20–21).

26. Cf. my book *Para la historia de los indigenismos* (Buenos Aires, 1938), a preparatory study towards a Dictionary of Spanish words of Indian origin, planned by the Instituto de Filología of the University of Buenos Aires.

27. Cf. "El enigma del aje," in my book *Para la historia de los indigenismos.*

28. Clarence Henry Haring, *Trade and Navigation between Spain and the Indies* (Cambridge: Harvard University Press, 1918); see preface. Cf. also Earl Jefferson Hamilton, *American Treasure and the Price Revolution in Spain, 1501–1650* (Cambridge: Harvard University Press, 1934). Montesquieu's essay on *Les Richesses de l'Espagne* should not be forgotten. In the eighteenth century, the gold from Brazil was still, according to Werner Sombart, one of the main factors of the industrial revolution in Europe.

29. *Journal* of Columbus, February 21, 1493.

30. Thomas Skelton, *Spanish Parrot*, 1525.

NOTES TO CHAPTER 2

1. A masterly description of how colonial society was organized appears in Justo Sierra's *Evolución política del pueblo mexicano* (Mexico, 1940; first edition, 1900–1902; there is a poor English translation, 1900–1902).

On colonial Brazil: Pedro Calmon, *Historia social do Brasil*, I, *O espirito da sociedade colonial* (São Paulo, 1937); Gilberto Freyre, *Casa-grande e senzala* (Rio de Janeiro, 1934).

2. The Spaniards were at times allowed to enslave Indians who

made war on them, but as a rule the consent was soon withdrawn, until it was abolished by the king at the end of the seventeenth century.

Cf. José Antonio Saco, *Historia de la esclavitud de los indios en el Nuevo Mundo* (Havana, 1883); Henry Charles Lea, "The Indian Policy of Spain," in the *Yale Review*, VIII, 119–155; Ricardo Levene, *Introducción a la historia del derecho indiano* (Buenos Aires, 1924); José Maria Ots Capdequí, *Instituciones sociales de la América española en el período colonial* (La Plata, 1934) — see chapter iii; Lewis Hanke, *The First Social Experiments in America* (Cambridge: Harvard University Press, 1935).

3. The first legal prescriptions (there is one dated 1518) about the education of the Indians concern the Antilles. Later on we find schools and colleges especially established for Indians alone admitting them together with the *mestizos* (of mixed race) and the *criollos* (of pure European descent): for instance, in Mexico alone the School of San Francisco, founded by Friar Pedro de Gante (1523), the College of Santiago Tlaltelolco, founded by Zumárraga (1536), the College of San Juan de Letrán, founded by the viceroy Antonio de Mendoza, the College of San Gregorio (1573), or, in Peru, the College of Caciques.

4. Cf. Justino Fernández and Edmundo O'Gorman, *Santo Tomás Moro y la Utopía en la Nueva España* (Mexico, 1937); Silvio Zavala, *La "Utopía" de Tomás Moro en la Nueva España* (Mexico, 1937) and *Ideario de Vasco de Quiroga* (Mexico, 1941); and Benjamin Jarnés, *Don Vasco de Quiroga, obispo de Utopía* (Mexico, 1941).

5. Cf. Otto Mass, *San Francisco Solano*, originally in German, English translation by Marion A. Habig (Paterson, New Jersey, 1942).

6. Cf. *A Spiritual Conquest: The Jesuit Reductions in Paraguay, 1610–1767* (published by Marygrove College, of Detroit, and printed at Westminster, Maryland, 1942).

7. Ronald de Carvalho, *Pequena historia da literatura brasileira* (Rio de Janeiro, 1919) — see chapter iii; Pedro Calmon, *Historia social do Brasil* (São Paulo, 1935) — see chapter vi; Gilberto Freyre, *Casa-grande e senzala* (Rio de Janeiro, 1933) — see chapter ii. Similar testimonies may be found in the writings of Joaquim Nabuco and Eduardo Prado. Father Serafim Leite is engaged in a monumental *Historia da Companhia de Jesus no Brazil;* the first two volumes have appeared in Lisbon, 1938.

8. Avendaño, *Thesaurus Indicus* (Antwerp, 1668); Antonio Vieira, *Sermão dos cativos* (see next chapter); Ribeiro Rocha, *O Ethiope resgatado, empenhado, sustentado, corregido, instruido e libertado* (Lisbon, 1758). In Spain, besides Domingo de Soto: Bartolomé Frías de Albornoz, *Arte de contratar* (Madrid, 1573); Alfonso de Sandoval, *De instauranda Aetiopum salute* (Madrid, 1647). On slavery in Spain, cf. article by William E. Wilson, in the *Hispanic Review*, VII (1939), 171–174.

9. It is common to draw a contrast between colonial life in Hispanic America and in the thirteen English colonies that became the United States — a contrast between aristocracy and democracy. That is, of course, a superficial view. Most of the English colonies, it is well known now, began with a more or less aristocratic organization (cf. Samuel Eliot Morison and Henry Steele Commager, *The Growth of the American Republic*, New York, 1937, especially the beginning of chapter iii, and Vernon Louis Parrington, *Main Currents of American Thought*, New York, 1926); but there was a continuous development towards democracy, both social and political. In Hispanic America there was also a gradual movement towards social equality, but no political development — democracy, after independence, had to be imposed by law.

10. Cf. Ángel Rosenblat, "El desarrollo de la población indígena de América," in *Tierra Firme* (Madrid), 1935, nos. 1 to 3; soon to be published in book form, with many additions and corrections, in Buenos Aires. On the disappearance of European classes in the New World, cf. Edward John Payne, *History of the New World called America* (Oxford, 1892), I, 60.

11. This flux and reflux had its effect on language: it was probably one of the causes of the acceleration of that great change which Spanish underwent in the sixteenth century, especially in its phonetic aspect.

12. On the presence of foreigners, cf. C. H. Haring, *Trade and Navigation between Spain and the Indies*, already mentioned, part I, chapter v, and Germán Arciniegas, *Los alemanes en la conquista de América* (Buenos Aires, 1941).

The Inquisition was kept busy by accusations against Jews as late as the end of the seventeenth century: cf. José Toribio Medina's book *La primitiva Inquisición americana (1493–1569)* (Santiago de Chile, 1914), and his Histories of the Inquisition in Lima (1887), in Chile (1890), in Cartagena de Indias (1899), in the River Plate provinces (1899), and in Mexico (1905). It had to deal also, during the sixteenth century, with followers of Erasmus: cf. my article "Erasmistas en el Nuevo Mundo," in *La Nación* (Buenos Aires), December 8, 1935, and M. Marcel Bataillon's masterly work *Erasme et l'Espagne* (Paris, 1937) — pp. 580, 674, 770, 852, and 854. With Protestants too: Gil González Dávila in his *Teatro eclesiástico de la primitiva Iglesia de las Indias Occidentales* (Madrid, 1649–1655) tells us that three hundred Bibles in a Protestant translation (evidently the splendid work of Casiodoro de Reina, reshaped by Cipriano de Valera) were burned in the city of Santo Domingo between 1600 and 1604.

13. On Jewish infiltration: Solidonio Leite filho, *Os Judéus no Brazil* (Rio de Janeiro, 1923); *Los judíos en el siglo XVI* [en México], a collection of documents published by the Archivo General de la

Nación (Mexico, 1932); Julio Jiménez Rueda, *Moisén* (Mexico, 1934); Marie Syrkin, "Jews in Mexico," in *Jewish Frontier*, August–September, 1940.

14. James Bryce, in his book on *South America* (London, 1911), remarks: "In the case of the Spaniards and the Portuguese, religion, as soon as the Indians had been baptized, made race differences seem insignificant"; Gilberto Freyre comments: especially in the case of the Portuguese.

In Lima, however, the Church at times made discriminations, yielding to local snobbery.

15. It is artificial to draw a sharp line of distinction between the *criollo* as a pure descendant of Europeans and the *mestizo* as a man of mixed ancestry. A *criollo* as a rule was a member of the higher social groups, even if he had Indian blood — which perhaps was not very noticeable after the sixteenth century, because the groups to which he belonged constantly intermarried with newcomers from Europe. The *mestizos* constituted a sort of budding middle class. The harshest friction did not occur between *criollos* and *mestizos*, but between both groups and the Europeans, especially on account of the preference accorded them for official posts, in violation of the law. A *locus classicus* about this problem of the preterition of the *criollos* in public life is to be found in Juan de Solórzano Pereira's *Política Indiana* (1648). A later one is José de Baquíjano's *Elogio* addressed to the viceroy Jáuregui in Peru (1781). The word *criollo*, by the way, is not early; it probably does not appear until the end of the sixteenth century.

16. Cf. J. M. Ots Capdequí, *Instituciones sociales*, already mentioned, chapter v.

17. A partial list of Indian or *mestizo* writers and artists in the colonial period includes, among the men of letters, in Peru, the Inca Garcilaso, Blas Valera, Tito Cusi Yupanqui, Juan de Santa Cruz Pachacuti, Felipe Huaman Poma de Ayala, Cristóbal de Molina "of Cuzco," Juan de Espinosa Medrano, Calixto Bustamante Carlos Inca (if he was really the author who signs Concolorcorvo), and Mariano Melgar; in Mexico, Pedro Gutiérrez de Santa Clara (his mother is said to have been a Cuban Indian), Alba Ixtlilxóchitl, Alvarado Tezozómoc, Muñoz Chimalpahin, Diego Muñoz Camargo, Pablo Nazareo, Juan Bautista Pomar, An Nakuk Pech, and Gaspar Antonio Xiu (or Herrera); in Guatemala, Friar Diego de Reinoso or Diego de la Anunciación (who is said to have written down the *Popol Vuh* between 1534 and 1539) and Francisco Hernández Arana Xahilá, Francisco Díaz Gebuta Quej; in New Granada (what is now Colombia), Bishop Lucas Fernández de Piedrahita and Friar Alonso de Zamora; in Ecuador, Francisco Eugenio de Santa Cruz Espejo; in what is now

Bolivia, Vicente Pazós Kanki, José Domingo Choquehuanca; in Paraguay and Argentina, Ruy Díaz de Guzmán; and in Paraguay, Nicolás Yapuguay.

Among the sculptors, in Mexico, Luis de la Cerda, Pedro Patiño Ixtolinque; in Quito, José Olmos (nicknamed Pampite), Francisco Tipan, Gabriel Guillachamin, José Díaz, Manuel Chilli (nicknamed Caspicara), and Gaspar Zangurima (nicknamed Llauqui); in Peru, Juan Tomás, Melchor Huaman, Francisco Tito Yupanqui, Juan Huaican, Marcos Rengifo, Baltasar Gavilán, and José Condori; in Argentina, José "el Indio," Juan "el Indio," Hermenegildo de Eguívar.

Among the painters, in Mexico, Marcos or Andrés de Aquino (whose original Indian name was Cípac), Juan de la Cruz, and Crespo, "El Crespillo," all three mentioned by Bernal Díaz del Castillo in his *History of the Mexican Conquest*, chapter 209 (according to F. B. del Paso y Troncoso, Aquino painted the miraculous image of Our Lady of Guadalupe, but according to Joaquín García Icazbalceta it probably was not painted until the seventeenth century), Juan de Arrué or de Rúa, Miguel de Mendoza, and Miguel Cabrera; in Peru, Juan Zapata Inga, Simón Inca, Bartolomé de Figueroa, Diego Quispe Tito, and José Uscamaita; in Quito, Friar Pedro Bedón, Miguel de Santiago, his daughter Isabel and his nephew Nicolás Javier de Goríbar, and Brother Domingo; and in Paraguay, J. M. Kabiyú.

A few more names of Mexican painters are mentioned by Manuel Toussaint, *La pintura en México durante el siglo XVI* (Mexico, 1936).

Music was usually performed, but not so frequently composed, by men and women of humble birth, Indians and Negroes.

18. Vicente Fidel López, *Historia de la República Argentina* (Buenos Aires, 1883–1893) — see vol. I, chapter 26; Bartolomé Mitre, *Historia de Belgrano y de la independencia argentina* (fourth edition, enlarged, Buenos Aires, 1887) — see vol. I, Introduction.

19. Rufino José Cuervo, preface to the seventh edition of his *Apuntaciones críticas sobre el lenguaje bogotano* (Bogotá, 1939). This preface had already been published as a separate book, *El castellano en América* (Bogotá, 1935).

In regard to the evolution of Spanish in this hemisphere, cf. Amado Alonso, "Primeros problemas históricos del castellano en América," in *II° Congreso Internacional de Historia de América*, third volume (Buenos Aires, 1938), and the *Biblioteca de Dialectología Hispanoamericana*, published by the Instituto de Filología at Buenos Aires since 1930. Our ways of speaking naturally vary with the locality; there is no unity of "American Spanish" to be opposed to the "Spanish of Spain," where local variations are far greater still. The Spanish of the Americas does not derive from Andalusia, as a number of writers have carelessly assumed. As far back as 1901 (in the *Bulletin His-*

panique, III, 41–42) 'Cuervo disproved the assumption and maintained that our population came from "all the Iberian Peninsula," Portugal included. I have collected data that support Cuervo's assertion in my book *Sobre el problema del andalucismo en América* (Buenos Aires: Instituto de Filología, 1932).

On the characteristics of the Portuguese spoken in Brazil, which naturally diverges from that of the mother country, cf. Antenor Nascentes, *O idioma nacional*, in 5 vols. (Rio de Janeiro, 1926–1935), and Jacques Raimundo, *A lingua portuguesa no Brasil* (Rio de Janeiro, 1941).

20. On the adoption of Indian and African customs by the Portuguese in Brazil, cf. Pedro Calmon, *Historia da civilisacão brasileira* (Rio de Janeiro, 1933), chapter iii, and especially Gilberto Freyre's excellent sociological study *Casa-grande e senzala* (both hold, like Ortega, that the European settlers became new men in the Americas from the beginning). On Cuba: Fernando Ortiz, *Los negros esclavos* (Havana, 1916).

21. A commendable attempt at a panorama of that society is made in *Colonial Hispanic America*, a collective work edited by Professor Alva Curtis Wilgus (Washington, 1936); it contains a very extensive critical bibliography. Another useful collective work, *Concerning Latin American Culture*, edited by Professor Charles Carroll Griffin (New York, 1940), is ampler in scope (it reaches down to the twentieth century) but makes no pretension to completeness.

22. It might be argued that at least the universities were aristocratic, because people with Negro blood were not supposed to attend them; but this rule, like many others, was persistently violated, even in proud and exclusive Lima. Even after its enforcement had been insisted upon (*reales cédulas* of 1752 and 1768), an exception was made in favor of the brilliant physician José Manuel Valdés, who was eventually appointed professor at the University (1811) and elected as a member of the Royal Medical Academy of Madrid (1815). Valdés was a *zambo*, with both African and Indian blood. Cf. J. A. de Lavalle, *El Doctor Don José Manuel Valdés* (Lima, 1866), and Fernando Romero, "José Manuel Valdés, gran mulato del Perú," in *Revista Bimestre Cubana*, XLIII (1939), 178–209.

Indians and *mestizos* had, of course, free access to the universities; for instance, a number of them, students at the College of San Juan de Letrán in Mexico, were regularly made to attend classes in the University. I have found it stated that they were excluded in Peru, but it does not seem probable. Juan de Espinosa Medrano, for one, was a graduate of the University of Cuzco.

In Panama, the University of San Javier was founded (1749) by a mulatto priest, Dr. Francisco Javier de Luna y Victoria, afterwards appointed bishop of Trujillo, in Peru (1759).

The Portuguese, as usual, were less prejudiced than the Spaniards, and their laws specified that no racial strain should be counted as an obstacle to any "office, honor or dignity" (cf. *Anais da Biblioteca Nacional*, of Rio de Janeiro, XXXVII, 85).

23. See above, note 3.

24. San Marcos, in Lima, is at present the oldest university with a continuous history in the Western hemisphere. Those of Santo Domingo and Mexico suffered long interruptions in the nineteenth century; their modern descendants are really new creations. The total number of universities in Hispanic America during the colonial period seems to have been twenty-six. Professor John Tate Lanning, in his article "The Transplantation of the Scholastic University," in *University of Miami Hispanic-American Studies*, vol. I, 1939, gives them as twenty-three. He does not mention Santiago de la Paz; this, and not Santo Tomás de Aquino, is the college which is said not to have begun to function *as* a university until 1558 or 1559 (see pp. 7 and 12 of his article). Cf. also, his book *Academic Culture in the Spanish Colonies* (New York, 1940). We are still in need of an extensive history of all the colonial universities, although we have a number of books on individual institutions and also on colonial education in several countries, taken separately. *Mexico: a Century of Educational Thought*, by Miss Irma Wilson (New York, 1941), contains a preliminary chapter on "Education in New Spain" (pp. 15–53).

25. Concerning the history of printing in Hispanic America, cf. José Toribio Medina's exhaustive books *La imprenta en México (1539–1821)*, 8 vols. (Santiago de Chile, 1907–1912), and *La imprenta en Lima (1584–1824)*, 4 vols. (Santiago de Chile, 1904–1907), and his shorter works on Santiago de Chile (1891), the Missions of Paraguay and Argentina, Cordoba, Buenos Aires, and Montevideo (1892), Oaxaca, Quito, Caracas, and many other cities (1904), Puebla, in Mexico (1908), Guatemala (1910); Joaquín García Icazbalceta, *Bibliografía mexicana del siglo XVI* (Mexico, 1886) — "one of the most perfect and excellent works of its kind in any nation," says Menéndez Pelayo; Vicente de Paul Andrade, *Ensayo bibliográfico mexicano del siglo XVII* (Mexico, 1899); Nicolás León, *Bibliografía mexicana del siglo XVIII*, 5 vols. (Mexico, 1902–1908) — the three works mentioned last contain reprints; Juan María Gutiérrez, *Bibliografía de la primera imprenta en Buenos Aires* (Buenos Aires, 1866), and José Torre Revello, *El libro, la imprenta y el periodismo en América durante la dominación española* (Buenos Aires, 1940); M. Cadwalader Hole, "The Early Latin-American Press," in the *Bulletin of the Pan American Union*, LX (1926), 323–352.

26. The modern stage is, of course, a creation of Italy, but modern drama had to wait, for its full development, until permanent public

theatres were opened in the three leading capitals of sixteenth-century Europe. Cf. John Addington Symonds, *Renaissance in Italy*, chapter xi of the book on "Italian Literature."

27. Cf. my essay "El Teatro en la América española durante la época colonial," in the *Cuadernos de Cultura Teatral*, vol. III (Buenos Aires, 1936). Concerning the great number of dramatic performances in Mexico before the erection of the first permanent theatre, cf. José Rojas Garcidueñas, *El teatro de Nueva España en el siglo XVI* (Mexico, 1935), Amado Alonso, "Biografía de Fernán González de Eslava," in *Revista de Filología Hispánica* (Buenos Aires), II (1940), 213–321 (especially pp. 248–250), and Harvey Leroy Johnson, *An Edition of "Triunfo de los Santos" with a consideration of Jesuit school-plays in Mexico during the sixteenth century* (Philadelphia, 1941). On Lima: Guillermo Lohmann Villena, *Historia del arte dramático en Lima durante el virreinato*, vol. I (Lima, 1941).

28. Cf. my essay mentioned in the previous note, and Enrique de Olavarría y Ferrari, *Reseña histórica del teatro en México* (Mexico, 1895).

29. Cf. F. Pierce, "Hojeda's 'La Cristíada'," in the *Bulletin of Spanish Studies* (Liverpool), XVII (1940), 203–218.

30. Bento Teixeira was formerly supposed to have been born in Brazil; it seems now he was born in Oporto. Pero de Magalhães Gandavo, the Portuguese Latinist and grammarian, who wrote the first book on the great colony of Portugal, the *Tratado da terra do Brazil* and *Historia da provincia de Santa Cruz* (1576), does not seem to have visited the land he described.

31. Cf. Edgar Prestage, *D. Francisco Manuel de Mello* (Oxford: Hispanic Society of America, 1922).

32. On Luis de Carvajal, cf. Pablo Martínez del Río, *Alumbrado* (Mexico, 1937); on Bejarano, my book *La Cultura y las letras coloniales en Santo Domingo* (Buenos Aires, 1936) — see pages 66–67, 79–80, 89–90 — and my article "Erasmistas en el Nuevo Mundo," already mentioned. On Alonso Henríquez de Guzmán, cf. Leslie Byrd Simpson, "A Precursor of the Picaresque Novel in Spain," in *Hispania*, January, 1934.

33. Cf. Robert C. Smith, Jr., "The Brazilian Landscapes of Frans Post," in *The Art Quarterly*, I (1938), 239–268, and "Brazilian Art," in the collective volume *Concerning Latin American Culture*; Thomas Thomsen, *Albert Eckhout . . . und Moritz der Brasilianer* (Copenhagen, 1937). On the first European painters in Mexico, cf. Manuel Toussaint, *La pintura en México durante el siglo XVI*. Their training was Spanish, Italian, or Flemish; quite often a single artist shows a combination of the three. The only extensive work, so far, that covers all countries is Miguel Solá's *Historia del arte hispanoamericano* (Bar-

celona, 1935); it embraces painting, sculpture, and architecture, but does not go beyond the colonial period.

34. Who, if anyone, should properly be called the architect of the Cathedral of Mexico is a well nigh insoluble problem. It has now been proved (cf. Manuel Toussaint, "La Catedral de México," in *Anales del Instituto de Investigaciones Estéticas*, no. 3, 1939, pp. 5-19) that Claudio de Arciniega made the original project and then Juan Miguel de Agüero worked on it; but modifications were made on the advice of Alonso Pérez de Castañeda and Juan Gómez de Mora, both in Spain. It does not seem possible, as yet, to determine the extent and quality of such modifications. Concerning the Puebla Cathedral, it is known that Francisco Becerra was appointed master builder in 1575; but it seems that both Pérez de Castañeda and Gómez de Mora are connected with it.

35. "Ni la maldad, el robo y la injusticia . . . — entrada en esta parte habían hallado — ni la ley natural inficionado." — It has been noticed (cf. Aída Cometta Manzoni, *El indio en la poesía de la América española*, Buenos Aires, 1939) that, with perhaps two exceptions, the authors of epic poems on the Conquest present the Indian under a favorable light. Ercilla, no doubt, set the example. Cf. John Van Horne, "The Attitude toward the Enemy in Sixteenth-Century Spanish Narrative Poetry," in *The Romanic Review* (1925). Incidentally, it should be said that Ercilla has been unnecessarily accused of not describing Chile. Landscapes were not usual in the epic tradition he followed, but his few touches of nature are clear and exact — not artificial scenery, as in his more Arcadian disciple the Chilean Oña. And he was not afraid to use Indian words like *maíz*, *cacique*, *arcabuco*, *caimán*, *piragua*, *curaca*. At the same time, he yields to fashion in the use of classical mythology.

36. The most important names of this literature of transplanted Europeans are, after Columbus (*ca.* 1451-1506), Vespucci (1451-1512), and Francesco Antonio Pigafetta (1491-1534), Martín Fernández de Enciso, Bartolomé de Las Casas (1474-1566), Gonzalo Fernández de Oviedo (1478-1557), Juan de Castellanos (1522-1607), Hernán Cortés (1485-1547), Bernal Díaz del Castillo (1496-1584), Alonso de Zorita (1512-*ca.* 1586), Friar Toribio de Benavente or "Motolinía" (died 1568, in old age), Friar Bernardino de Sahagún (*ca.* 1500-1590), Francisco Cervantes de Salazar (*ca.* 1514-1575), Friar Jerónimo de Mendieta (1525-1604), Friar Diego Durán (born before 1538, in Seville, not in Mexico, but perhaps of an Indian mother), the Jesuit José de Acosta, the admirable naturalist (1539-1600), Friar Juan de Torquemada (*ca.* 1563-1624), Friar Diego de Landa (1524-1579), Gonzalo Jiménez de Quesada (ca. 1499-1579), Álvar Núñez Cabeza de Vaca (1507-1559), Pascual de Andagoya, Friar Pedro de Aguado

(d. after 1589), Friar Pedro Simón (1574–ca. 1630), Father Bernabé Cobo (1582–1657), Pedro Sarmiento de Gamboa (ca. 1530–1592), Friar Antonio de Remesal, Friar Alonso de Espinosa (on this writer, the first ethnographer of the Canary Islands, cf. my book *La cultura y las letras coloniales en Santo Domingo*, pp. 92–93 and 97–99), Francisco de Jerez (1504–1539), Alonso Henríquez de Guzmán, Pedro de Cieza de León (1518–1560), Agustín de Zárate (d. after 1560), Pedro Pizarro (ca. 1514–1571), Juan Polo de Ondegardo, Diego Fernández "el Palentino," Pedro Sancho de Hoz (d. 1547), Juan de Betanzos (d. 1576), Fernando de Montesinos (1593–1655), Cristóbal de Molina "of Santiago" (1494–1578), Miguel Cabello de Balboa, Rodrigo de Carvajal y Robles, Álvaro Alonso Barba, Alonso de Ercilla (1533–1594), Alonso González de Nájera, Cristóbal de Acuña (1597–1675?), Toribio de Ortiguera, Pedro Fernández de Quirós (1565–1615), Friar Reginaldo de Lizárraga (1545–1615), Alonso de Góngora Marmolejo (1536–1575), Pedro Mariño de Lobera (1536–1595), Friar Diego de Rosales (1633–1677), Friar Diego de Hojeda (ca. 1570–1615), Friar Francisco Ximenes (1666–ca. 1722), the Count of La Granja (1636–1717); in Brazil, Pero Lopes de Sousa, the Jesuits José de Anchieta (1530–1597) and Manoel de Nóbrega (d. 1570), Bento Teixeira Pinto (1545–ca. 1619), Father Fernão Cardim (1540–1625), Gabriel Soares de Sousa (1540–1591).

Another group of writers may be considered merely as visitors; the bulk of their work is not related to the Americas, though they may refer, and even devote many pages, to them: Micael de Carvajal, Gutierre de Cetina (ca. 1518–ca. 1554), Friar Alonso de Cabrera (ca. 1549–1606), Eugenio de Salazar (ca. 1530–1602), Juan de la Cueva (1543–1610), Diego Mejía (ca. 1565–ca. 1620), Pedro de Liévana, Lorenzo de Cepeda (d. 1580), Mateo Rosas de Oquendo, Enrique Garcés, Luis de Ribera, Mateo Alemán (1547–after 1614), Tirso de Molina (1584–1648), Luis de Belmonte (ca. 1580–ca. 1650), the viceroys of Peru Prince of Esquilache (1581–1658), Count of Santisteban del Puerto, and Marquis of Castell-dos-Ríus; the bishop Juan de Palafox (1600–1659), Francisco Manoel de Mello (1608–1666), and the viceroy of Brazil Vasco Fernandes, Count of Sabugosa.

Cf. Bernard Moses, *Spanish Colonial Literature in South America* (New York, 1922); Marcelino Menéndez y Pelayo, *Historia de la poesía hispanoamericana* (Madrid, 1911–1913); Carlos González Peña, *Historia de la literatura mexicana* (Mexico City, 1928); Domingo Amunátegui Solar, *Bosquejo histórico de la literatura chilena: Período Colonial* (Santiago de Chile, 1918); José Toribio Medina, *Historia de la literatura colonial de Chile* (Santiago de Chile, 1878); Luis Alberto Sánchez, *Los poetas de la colonia* (in Peru), first volume of an unfinished *Historia de la literatura peruana* (Lima, 1921); José de la Riva Agüero,

La historia en el Perú (Lima, 1910); F. B. Steck, "Early Mexican Literature (1522–1572)," in *Hispanic American Essays: A Memorial to James Alexander Robertson* (Chapel Hill: University of North Carolina, 1942); John Van Horne, "Motolinía as a Man of Letters," in *Philological Quarterly*, XXI (1942), 47–53; R. B. Cunninghame-Graham, *Bernal Díaz del Castillo*.

Las Casas, Oviedo, Cieza de León, Acosta, and Zárate were translated into English in the sixteenth and seventeenth centuries. Part of the writings of Bernal Díaz del Castillo, Álvar Nuñez Cabeza de Vaca, Andagoya, Pedro Simón, Pedro Sarmiento de Gamboa, Espinosa, Jerez, Henríquez de Guzmán, Cieza de León, Polo de Ondegardo, Pedro Sancho, Landa, Acuña, and Fernández de Quirós have appeared in English, generally translated and edited by Sir Clements Markham, in the publications of the Hakluyt Society. Mr. Archibald MacLeish's poem *Conquistador* (New York, 1942) is derived from Bernal Díaz. Cf. Moses, *Spanish Colonial Literature*, Appendix, and Hayward Keniston's *List of Works for the Study of Hispanic-American History* (New York, 1920).

37. Cf. Bernardo de Valbuena, *Siglo de oro*, Spanish Academy edition (Madrid, 1821), p. 133.

38. It has been proved by recent researches, especially those of Professor Irving A. Leonard (see, for example, *Romances of Chivalry in the Indies*, Berkeley, California, 1933), that novels were shipped from Spain to Spanish America in great numbers and openly sold here by booksellers. It is unlikely that this flourishing trade should have been contraband, and therefore it seems that the royal decrees of 1531 and 1543 against the circulation of "feigned stories" in the New World were no longer in force around 1600 (cf., however, A. E. Serrano Redonnet, on a synod in Argentina in 1597, *Revista de Filología Hispánica*, December, 1940). But somehow the prohibition stood, in practice, against the printing of such stories in the colonies, and, if we except a religious pastoral, *Los sirgueros de la Virgen*, by Francisco Bramón (Mexico City, 1620), no novel was printed in Spanish America during three centuries. As soon as the Cortes of Cadiz granted the freedom of the press to all the Spanish empire (1810), the first novel on a lay subject appeared in Mexico, Fernández de Lizardi's *Itching Parrot* (*El Periquillo Sarniento*, 1816).

Valbuena's *Golden Age* was printed in Madrid, 1608; Jacobo de Villaurrutia's translation (through the French) of Frances Sheridan's *Memoirs of Miss Sidney Bidulph* in Alcalá de Henares, 1792. Cf. my article "Apuntaciones sobre la novela en América," in *Humanidades* (La Plata), XV (1927), 133–146.

The only novel written in colonial Brazil, *The Adventures of Diophanes*, by Teresa Margarita da Silva, in the manner of Fénelon's *Télé-*

maque, was printed in Lisbon, 1752. The first novels printed in Brazil were *Jeronimo Corte Real* (Rio de Janeiro, 1839), by João Manoel Pereira da Silva (1817–1898), and *The Fisherman's Son* (Rio de Janeiro, 1843), by Antonio Gonçalves Teixeira e Sousa (1812–1861).

39. In Lima there was a poet who wrote French verse — a whim, evidently, since French was not then a fashionable literary language for Hispanic people.

40. After this lecture was delivered, the best work of Pedro de Oña, the historical poem *The Golden Vase* (*El vasauro*), has at last come to light complete (Santiago de Chile, 1941). It compels us to a revaluation of the poet.

41.   Y sé que por mí sola padeciera
             y a mí sola me hubiera redimido
             si sola en este mundo me criara.

On Doña Leonor, cf. James C. Bardin, "Three Literary Ladies in Spain's American Colonies," I, in the *Bulletin of the Pan American Union,* December, 1940 (the other two ladies are Amarilis and Sor Juana Inés de la Cruz, on both of whom see next chapter).

42. Two of these historians may be read in English: Luis Jerónimo de Oré, *The Martyrs of Florida (1513–1616),* translated by M. Geiger, and Cristóbal de Molina "of Cuzco," "An Account of the Fables and Rites of the Incas," in *Narratives and Rites of the Incas,* translated and edited by Sir Clements Robert Markham (London: Hakluyt Society, 1873).

43. Cf. Manuel Toussaint, *Supervivencias góticas en la arquitectura mexicana del siglo XVI* (Madrid, 1935).

44. Cf. Mario J. Buschiazzo, *Los monumentos coloniales de Santo Domingo* (Buenos Aires, 1940). I may remark, in passing, that it seems doubtful that the church of Regina Angelorum should be of such late date as 1722; the convent existed already in the sixteenth century, and in 1568 it numbered about one hundred nuns (the poetess Leonor de Ovando was one of them); perhaps the church was rebuilt.

45. Cf. Manuel Toussaint, "Arte mudéjar en América," in the magazine *Kollasuyo,* of La Paz, no. 11, November, 1939. Another type of Moorish influence is visible in the Royal Chapel of Cholula, in Mexico, which follows the plan of a mosque, with seven naves and two rows of chapels, hundreds of columns and many domes.

46. Cf. Manuel Toussaint, *Iglesias de México,* vol. VI (Mexico, 1927); Rafael García Granados, "Capillas de indios en Nueva España," in *Archivo Español de Arte y Arqueología* (Madrid), April, 1935; Mario J. Buschiazzo, *Las "capillas abiertas" para indios* (Buenos Aires, 1939). An "open chapel" was recently identified by Professor George Kubler in San Ildefonso, New Mexico.

47. Vicente Lampérez y Romea, *La arquitectura hispano-americana*

en las épocas de colonización y los virreinatos (Madrid, 1922). Quoted in Solá's *Historia del arte hispano-americano*, p. 183; see also pp. 32, 39, 43, 82, 103, 135, 145, 146, 179, 181–184, 197–199, 200, 203, 210–211, 213, 218–219, 221, 279, 283–284, 297, 302.

A brief account, in English, of this fusion of styles is Mario J. Buschiazzo's lecture published in the *Bulletin of the Pan American Union*, April, 1941. Two extensive books on the subject are Ángel Guido's *Fusión hispano-indígena en la arquitectura colonial* (Rosario, 1925), and Martín S. Noel's *Teoría estética de la arquitectura virreinal* (Buenos Aires, 1932).

48. Cf. Manuel Toussaint, *La pintura en México durante el siglo XVI*, pp. 8 and 29–36, and Federico Gómez de Orozco, "La decoración en los manuscritos hispano-mexicanos primitivos," in *Anales del Instituto de Investigaciones Estéticas*, of Mexico, II, nọ 3 (1939), 48–52.

This fusion was possible, of course, only where the Indians before the Conquest had a great art tradition of their own, i.e., in Mexico and Guatemala, or in the territory governed or influenced by the Incas. Nothing similar appears, for instance, in the Antilles, or in Brazil under the Portuguese. Brazil remains purely European during three centuries, save for a few late innovations.

49. Cf. José Moreno Villa, *La escultura colonial mexicana* (Mexico, 1942). He gives the name of *tequitqui* ("vassal" in Náhuatl like *mudéjar* in Arabic) to the peculiar style produced by the fusion of the European and the Indian techniques, especially in stone reliefs and in altars.

50. Inca Garcilaso, *Comentarios reales*, book II, chapter 27.

51. It was published by the Abbé Brasseur de Bourbourg in his *Collection de documents dans les langues indigènes*, vol. II (Paris, 1862).

52. *El güegüence* was published, with a translation into English, by Daniel Garrison Brinton (Philadelphia, 1883).

53. Even Racine's *Phèdre* was translated into Quechua, by Pedro Zegarra (d. 1839) at the end of the colonial era.

On the development of this type of drama, cf. my essay "El teatro de la América española durante la época colonial."

Six of the early short plays have been published in the original Indian languages, with Spanish translations, by the Mexican scholar Francisco B. del Paso y Troncoso, between 1890 and 1907. The earliest known *Coloquio* in Spanish, attributed to Cristóbal Gutiérrez de Luna, but perhaps by another hand, has been published, with an English translation, by Carlos E. Castañeda, in *Preliminary Studies of The Texas Catholic Historical Society* (Austin), vol. III, nọ 1 (1936), under the title "The First American Play." *Los pastores*, a Mexican play of the Nativity, has been translated into English by M. R. Cole (Boston, 1907). See also " 'Los comanches,' a Spanish Heroic Play of

1780," critical edition by Professor A. M. Espinosa, in the *Bulletin of the University of New Mexico*, 1907; Arthur L. Campa, "Spanish Religious Folk-Theatre in the Southwest," in the *Bulletin of the University of New Mexico*, 1934, numbers 1 and 2; Josephine Nigli, *Mexican Folk Plays* (Chapel Hill: University of North Carolina, 1938); and, in addition, articles by Mary Austin, in the *Theatre Arts Monthly*, August, 1929, and August, 1933, and by Dorothy Herschfeld in the same magazine, December, 1928; and John Eugene Englekirk, "Notes on the Repertoire of the New-Mexican Spanish Folk Theater," in the *Southern Folklore Society*, December, 1940. J. H. Cornyn's article "An Aztec Drama," in *Books Abroad*, July, 1934, deals with a mystery play on the Day of Judgement acted in 1535.

54. There are several editions of the Quechua text of *Ollantay*, beginning with J. J. von Tschudi's in his work *Das Kechuasprache* (Vienna, 1853). The play has been translated into Spanish, English, French, German, Czech, and Latin; it has also been set to music. The best English translations are those of Sir Clements Markham (*Ollanta*, London, 1871; new version, in his book *The Incas of Peru*, London, 1910). There are many studies of the *Ollantay* problem. The latest is that of Don Ricardo Rojas, *Un titán de los Andes* (Buenos Aires, 1939), offshoot of his own original tragedy on the subject of the old Quechua play (*Ollántay*, Buenos Aires, 1939). In English there is a careful essay by Elijah Clarence Hills, "The Quechua Drama 'Ollanta'," in *The Romanic Review*, 1914, reprinted in his book *Hispanic Studies* (Stanford University, 1929).

NOTES TO CHAPTER 3

1. On the critical attitude that seems to have prevailed during the last half of the sixteenth century in the colonies, cf. Julio Caillet-Bois, "El teatro en la Asunción a mediados del siglo XVI," in *Revista de Filología Hispánica* (Buenos Aires), vol. III, 1941.

2. Fugger, the German bankers of the sixteenth century. They were the bankers of Charles V. In Spain their name was popularly changed to Fúcar. On their connection with the New World, cf. Germán Arciniegas, *Los alemanes en la conquista de América* (Buenos Aires, 1941; English translation, New York, 1943).

3.   Viene de España por el mar salobre
                 a nuestro mexicano domicilio
                 un hombre tosco, sin algún auxilio,
                 de salud falto y de dinero pobre.
                     Y luego que caudal y ánimo cobre
                 le aplican, en su bárbaro concilio,

otros como él, de César y Virgilio
las dos coronas de laurel y robre.
Y el otro, que agujetas y alfileres
vendía por las calles, ya es un conde
en calidad, y en cantidad un Fúcar.
Y abomina después el lugar donde
adquirió estimación, gusto y haberes:
¡y tiraba la jábega en Sanlúcar!

4. It has been computed (C. Parra Pérez, *El régimen español en Venezuela*, Madrid, 1932) that from the time of the first appointments after the Discovery down to 1811 there were 702 bishops and archbishops born in Europe to 278 born in the Americas; viceroys, 166 to 4; governors ("capitanes generales"), 558 to 14.

5. One of the first books written in Mexico is the treatise on horsemanship, *Tractado de la caballería de la jineta y de la brida*, by a conqueror's son, Juan Suárez de Peralta, printed in Spain in 1580.

6. "Quid referam, nobiles Equites vestibus purpureis, sericis, auro intertexto claros, qui innumeri sunt?" — In his *Itinerarium ad regiones sub aequinoctiali plaga constitutas*, posthumously printed in Rome, 1631.

7.   Hay una natural magnificencia,
de gente forastera conocida,
pues allí sin dineros y sin renta
en el punto que trajo se sustenta.

On that "cradle of the Americas," cf. Vicente Llorens Castillo, "Vida cultural de Santo Domingo en el siglo XVI," in the *Revista Cubana* (Havana), XV (1941), 176-205, besides my own book *La cultura y las letras coloniales en Santo Domingo*.

8.   Haz que en sus aposentos no consienta [tu hijo]
un paje disoluto, ni allí suene
canción de las que el vulgo vil frecuenta;
canción que de Indias con el oro viene,
como él a afeminarnos y a perdernos,
y con lasciva cláusula entretiene.
Satire *Contra los vicios de la corte*.

9. The study of real Indian music in Hispanic America begins in the twentieth century, especially with Raoul and Marguerite d'Harcourt, *La Musique des Incas et ses survivances* (Paris, 1925). The folk music of people who speak Spanish or Portuguese bears little relation to it. Most of that folk music bears no relation, either, to African forms. In Cuba, Eduardo Sánchez de Fuentes distinguishes "white" music, such as the *habanera*, and music with Negro influence, such as the *rumba* and the *clave* (cf. *El folklore en la música cubana*, Havana, 1923; *Influencia de los ritmos africanos en nuestro cancionero*, Havana.

1927; and *La canción cubana*, Havana, 1930). Brazilians also distinguish between "white," "Negro," and "Indian" music — the "white" including, for instance, the *gaúcho* music of Rio Grande do Sul. In the sixteenth and seventeenth centuries there were also Negro dances, whether real or faked, in vogue in Spain — such were the *guineo*, the *zarambeque*, and perhaps the *cumbé*. We do not know whence that music was taken to Spain — whether from Africa itself, which seems unlikely, or from the African slaves in the Americas.

10. Many passages from Cervantes, Lope de Vega, and other writers, concerning the vogue of dances from the Americas in Spain, have been gathered by Emilio Cotarelo y Mori in the Introduction to his collections of *Entremeses, loas, bailes, jácaras y mojigangas*, vol. I (Madrid, 1911). According to the Andalusian poet Mateo Rosas de Oquendo, in Lima, around 1590, they were dancing, among other things, the *chaconne*, the *Puerto Rico* (evidently American), and the *valona* (there are still *valonas* in Mexico).

11. Very little attention had been paid, until recent years, to the higher forms of music in colonial Hispanic America. Schools of music were established as early as the sixteenth century, and music was taught in the universities also, as a part of the old quadrivium. It is known that the norms adopted, in gradual and overlapping succession, were the polyphonic forms of Palestrina and Victoria, the counterpoint of Corelli and Bach, the sonata and suites of Haydn and Mozart, besides the Italian opera and the Spanish *zarzuela* and *tonadilla*. Beethoven was known in the early years of the nineteenth century, as may be inferred from a reference in a poem of the Mexican botanist Juan José Lejarza (1785–1824). It is interesting to remark that organs were built in several countries, and pianos, toward the end of the colonial era, in Mexico.

The works of many composers of Brazil, Venezuela, New Granada, Peru, Chile, and Mexico have been preserved in manuscript. Most of it is church music. Father Manuel Zumaya, of Mexico, composed the first opera, *Rodrigo* (1708), and later *Parténope* (1711). Another opera, *Perseo*, with a libretto by the viceroy Castell-dos-Ríus, was performed at Lima in 1709. Italian and French opera seems to arrive in the eighteenth century — e.g., Grétry, in Havana, 1790. In regard to the composers of Venezuela (Juan Manuel Olivares, who organized a concert orchestra in 1750, Father Pedro Palacios Sojo, José Francisco Velázquez, José Ángel Lamas, Cayetano Carreño, Lino Gallardo — called "the Haydn of Caracas" — and Atanasio Bello), enthusiastic critics maintain that their merit equals that of the great colonial architects — a bold assertion!

Cf. Renato Almeida, *Historia da musica brasileira* (Rio de Janeiro, 1926); Vincenzo Cernicchiaro, *Storia della musica del Brasile* (Milan,

1926); Ramón de la Plaza, *Ensayo sobre el arte en Venezuela* (Caracas, 1883); José Antonio Calcaño, *Contribución al estudio de la música en Venezuela* (Caracas, 1939); Andrés Martínez Montoya, *Reseña histórica sobre la música en Colombia* (Bogotá, 1932); Miguel Galindo, *Historia de la música mexicana*, vol. I (Colima, 1933); Gabriel Saldívar, *Historia de la música en Mexico* (Mexico, 1934); Eugenio Pereira Salas, *Los orígenes del arte musical en Chile* (Santiago de Chile, 1941); Flérida de Nolasco, *La música en Santo Domingo* (Ciudad Trujillo, 1939), and the *Boletín Latinoamericano de Música*, edited at Montevideo by Francisco Curt Lange since 1935.

The literature on folk music is very extensive; it refers mostly to nineteenth- and twentieth-century forms. Cf. Eleanor Hague, *Latin American Music, Past and Present*, with bibliography (Santa Ana, California, 1934).

12. The *Royal Commentaries* were translated into English by Sir Paul Rycaut (London, 1688). The first part (on the Incas) was translated again by Sir Clements Markham (London, 1869). On the author, cf. Julia Fitzmaurice-Kelly, *El Inca Garcilaso de la Vega*, in English (Oxford: The Hispanic Society of America, 1921). In Spanish, José de la Riva Agüero, *Elogio del Inca Garcilaso de la Vega* (Lima, 1916), later reprinted as a preface to a collection of *Páginas escogidas* of the Inca (Paris, 1938); Luis Alberto Sánchez, *Garcilaso Inca de la Vega* (Santiago de Chile, 1939).

13. Only one play by Alarcón has been translated into English, *La verdad sospechosa*, under the title "The Truth Suspected," by J. del Toro and R. V. Finney, in the Boston magazine *Poet Lore*, XXXVIII (1927), 475–530. In the eighteenth century a distant reflection of this play is found in Steele's *The Lying Lover* (1703), an adaptation from Corneille's *Le Menteur*. On Alarcón, besides the histories of Spanish literature, cf. Dorothy Schons, "The Mexican Background of Alarcón" in *Publications of the Modern Language Association*, LVII (1942), 89–104; S. Griswold Morley, *Studies in Spanish Dramatic Versification of the "Siglo de Oro": Alarcón and Moreto* (Berkeley: University of California, 1918); J. B. Segall, *Corneille and the Spanish Drama* (New York, 1902); and S. M. Waxman, "Chapters on Magic in Spanish Literature," in *Revue Hispanique*, XXXVIII (1916), see pages 351–352, 360–362, 382–383, 400–409, 417, 458–461; also, the prefaces of Caroline Brown Bourland to her edition of *Las paredes oyen*, Spanish text (Boston–New York, 1914), reviewed by Frank Otis Reed in *Modern Language Notes*, XXXI (1916), 95–104 and 169–178; of Arthur L. Owen to his edition of *La verdad sospechosa*, Spanish text (Boston–New York, 1928); and of Frank Otis Reed and Frances Eberling to their edition of *La prueba de las promesas*, Spanish text (New York, 1928).

In Spanish: Juan Eugenio Hartzenbusch, preface to the volume of *Comedias* of Alarcón in the Biblioteca de Autores Españoles (Madrid, 1852); Alfonso Reyes, preface to his edition of *La verdad sospechosa* and *Las paredes oyen* (Madrid, 1918); Julio Jiménez Rueda, *Juan Ruiz de Alarcón y su tiempo* (Mexico, 1939); Antonio Castro Leal, *Juan Ruiz de Alarcón* (Mexico, 1943); and my own lecture *Juan Ruiz de Alarcón* (Mexico City, 1914), reprinted in my *Seis ensayos en busca de nuestra expresión* (Buenos Aires, 1928).

A number of writers feel needless scruples about including Alarcón in the history of Mexican literature because they must also include him in the history of literature in Spain. But Henry James — who was older, when he settled in England, than Alarcón when he finally settled in Spain — must appear in the history of American as well as English literature. At the same time, Bernardo de Valbuena, who probably did not spend in Europe more than seven out of the sixty-five years of his life, is usually included in Spanish literature, as Antonio Vieira is in the literature of Portugal.

There are many more writers in Hispanic America who have spent long years in Europe, without breaking their ties with their native land. Even W. H. Hudson, in spite of his use of a language not his own, must be at least mentioned in the history of Argentine literature.

14. The Spanish titles of the works of Valbuena are: *Compendio apologético en alabanza de la poesía*; *La grandeza mexicana*; *Siglo de oro en las selvas de Erifile*; *El Bernardo, o La victoria de Roncesvalles.*

15. However, in his *Golden Age* Valbuena owes a slight debt to Góngora — in the *romance* and the two sonnets of the third eclogue and in the sonnet "Mientras que por la limpia y tersa frente" of the sixth eclogue.

16. On Valbuena, cf. John Van Horne, *"El Bernardo" of Bernardo de Balbuena* (Urbana: University of Illinois, 1927) — the poet generally, though not always, signed *Balbuena*; the right etymological form is *Valbuena*; Joseph G. Fucilla, "Glosses on Bernardo de Balbuena's 'El Bernardo'," in *Modern Language Notes*, January 1934. Professor Van Horne has also published a book, *Bernardo de Balbuena* (Guadalajara, Mexico, 1940), in Spanish.

17. This attitude is discovered still earlier in Friar Vicente do Salvador, born in Brazil (1564–ca. 1639). His *History of Brazil* was finished in 1627. According to Pedro Calmon, "its purpose, its composition and its style make this book one of the jewels of the early literature of the Americas; it is no less admirable in its prophetic feeling about the country."

18. Vieira began, but never finished, a curious work entitled *A History of the Future*, in which he intended to describe the coming greatness of Portugal. He had a strange fondness for prophecies. A humor-

ous book on the *Art of Stealing* proving the universality of theft, from kings down to common bandits, has been attributed to him, as well as to four other writers. A sermon by Vieira, *Dust Thou Art*, was translated into English by the Rev. W. Anderson (London, 1882).

19. Cf. Thomas Walsh, "A South American Mystic" (with translations), in *The Catholic World*, November 1925.

20. However, in an undated poem — perhaps a late one — she shows discouragement: "If life is so short, what is the good of knowing so much?" ("si es para vivir tan poco — ¿de qué sirve saber tanto?").

21. Sor Juana is said to have written music for *villancicos*. There were many women who composed music in colonial times — e.g., the Marchioness of Vivanco, in Mexico; we have a minuet by her, dated 1804.

22. "Sabe el Señor, y lo sabe en el mundo quien solo lo debió saber, lo que intenté en orden a esconder mi nombre, y que no me lo permitió, diciendo que era tentación: y sí sería" ("The Lord knows, and in the world it is known by him who alone should have known it, what I intended to do in order to hide my name, and how he did not allow it, saying that it was a temptation of the devil: and so it may have been"). — "Sucedía así que él [el pelo] crecía, y yo no sabía lo propuesto, porque el pelo crecía aprisa, y yo aprendía despacio, y con efecto lo cortaba, en pena de la rudeza; que no me parecía razón que estuviese vestida de cabellos cabeza que estaba tan desnuda de noticias, que era más apetecible adorno" ("It so happened that it [her hair] grew, and I had not learned what I proposed to learn, because it grew quickly and I learned slowly, and in fact I cut it, as a punishment for my stupidity; for it did not seem right that my head should be adorned with hair when it was so devoid of knowledge, which was a more desirable ornament") — "En esto sí confieso que ha sido inexplicable mi trabajo; y así, no puedo decir lo que con envidia oigo a otros, que no les ha costado afán el saber: dichosos ellos" ("In this [in studying] I declare that my effort has been greater than I could explain; and so I cannot say what I enviously hear from others, that learning has cost them no pains: happy they!").

23. Cf. Eunice Joiner Gates, "Reminiscences of Góngora in the Works of Sor Juana Inés de la Cruz," in *Publications of the Modern Language Association*, LIV (1939), 1041-1058. Dorothy Schons, "The Influence of Góngora on Mexican Literature during the Seventeenth Century," in *Hispanic Review*, VII (1939), 23-24, shows that his domination was not as formidable as had been thought. Miss Schons has made very valuable researches concerning the life, works and renown of Sor Juana: see, for instance, "Some Obscure Points in the Life of Sor Juana Inés de la Cruz," in *Modern Philology*, XXIV (1926), 141-162. Cf., also, Lucile K. Delano, "The Influence of Lope

de Vega upon Sor Juana Inés de la Cruz," in *Hispania*, XIII (1930), 79–94.

24. In Spanish, *Amor es más laberinto*.

25. In Spanish, *Los empeños de una casa*.

26. Professor Vossler has translated it into German verse: *Die Welt im Traum* (Berlin, 1941). He speaks at length about the poem, besides, in his *Poesie der Einsamkeit in Spanien* (Munich, 1935), I, pp. 152–153, and in his essay *Die "zehnte Muse von Mexico"* (Munich, 1934).

27. How delightfully contrary to modern psychoanalysis! But this was a favorite notion of hers, and in her autobiography she speaks of dreams in which she solves intellectual problems.

28. There is an interesting coincidence between the first lines of the *Sueño:*

> Piramidal, funesta, de la Tierra
> nacida, sombra, al cielo encaminaba
> de vanos obeliscos punta altiva. . . .

and a passage of the fourth act of Shelley's *Prometheus Unbound*, in which the Earth says:

> I spin beneath my pyramid of night. . . .

The geometric shape of which they speak is not a pyramid, of course, but a cone.

29. She wrote another sonnet, in a more *culterano* style, on hope, calling it "green rapture, golden frenzy" ("verde embeleso . . . , frenesí dorado"). Professor Vossler has translated into German the sonnet "Diuturna enfermedad. . . ."

30. And yet it is said that she painted her own portrait, from which all the later ones derive. The oldest in date is now at the Art Museum in Philadelphia, though — I am told — kept in storage. Two other portraits were painted in the eighteenth century, one by the famous Indian artist Miguel Cabrera (now at the Museo Nacional of Mexico City), the other by Andrés de Isla in 1772 (now at the Museo Provincial of Toledo). In all of them she appears a very beautiful woman.

31. There are English translations of a few of Sor Juana's poems: see *Library of the World's Best Literature*, vol. XVII; Thomas Walsh's *Hispanic Anthology* (New York, 1920); Alice Stone Blackwell's *Some Spanish-American Poets* (New York, 1929; reprinted at Philadelphia, 1937); Edna Worthley Underwood's *Anthology of Mexican poets* (New York, 1932); the Hispanic Society of America's *Translations from Hispanic poets* (New York, 1938); Muna Lee's article "A Charming Mexican Lady," in *The American Mercury*, January 1925. Cf., also, Professor G. W. Umphrey's article on Sor Juana in the quarterly *Fantasy*, published at Pittsburgh, first quarter of 1942; Elizabeth Wallace,

Sor Juana Inéz de la Cruz: poetisa de corte y convento (*Vidas Mexicanas*, vol. xiii; Mexico City: Ediciones Xochitl, 1944).

32. The *Relación sumaria* of Canon Alcocer has now been published by Don Emilio Rodríguez Demorizi in the *Boletín del Archivo General de la Nación*, of Ciudad Trujillo, January–April, 1942, numbers 20–21, pp. 31–103.

33. The colonial historians have been read, mainly as sources, and their works printed or reprinted; now and then they have been appraised as writers — for instance, Bartolomé Martines Vela (1645–1702), Friar Antonio de la Calancha, born in Charcas (1584–1654), Juan Rodríguez Freile (1566–1638), and Bishop Lucas Fernández de Piedrahita (1624–1688), both of New Granada, Friar Juan de Barrenechea y Albis, of Chile, whose *Restauración de la Imperial*, written in 1693, and published only in part so far, reads more like a baroque novel than a historical narrative, Pedro Agustín Morell de Santa Cruz (1694–1768), born in Hispaniola, Bishop of Havana, dearly loved by his flock for his heroic attitude during the English invasion of the city (1762), the Jesuit Juan de Velasco (1727–1792), of Quito, the Peruvian Friar Juan Meléndez, and also Peralta Barnuevo (of whom more later), the Chileans Alonso de Ovalle (d. 1650), Diego de Rosales (1603–1677), Miguel de Olivares (1674–1788), and Vicente Carvallo y Goyeneche (1740–1816), the Mexicans Matías de la Mota Padilla (1688–1776), Mariano Veitia (1718–*ca.* 1779), and Andrés Cavo (1739–*ca.* 1795), the Brazilians Friar Vicente do Salvador (see note 17 of this chapter) and Sebastião da Rocha Pitta (of whom more later). Cf. Charles Edward Chapman, "Essay on Authorities," pp. 347–385 of his book *Colonial Hispanic America* (New York, 1933). But the works of the religious writers are difficult to obtain and hardly ever read today. We know very little about their merits. The Chilean Jesuit Manuel Lacunza (1731–1801) is an exception — his prophetic work *The Coming of the Messiah in Glory and Majesty* found many readers; there is an English translation of it. A valiant attempt to clear the fog that surrounds the authors of religious books and sermons is made, for Peru, by Father Rubén Vargas Ugarte, in *La elocuencia sagrada en el Peru* (Lima, 1942), and, for Colombia, by Don Antonio Gómez Restrepo in his *Historia de la literatura colombiana* (two volumes, dealing with the colonial era, have been published already).

34. In Quechua he wrote at least one play, a Biblical drama, *The Prodigal Son*. Another play in Quechua, *The Wealthiest Poor Man*, has been attributed to him, but according to a manuscript it is the work of Gabriel Centeno de Osma, who lived a century before Espinosa; the University of San Marcos published it, with a Spanish translation, in Lima, 1938.

35. Only two sonnets of Velázquez remain. One describes a "crim-

son star," a carnation that the lady Gerarda held between her lips, thus creating a colorful confusion ("Estrella de carmín, que a ser llegaste – lisonja del abril en que naciste"). In the other sonnet he speaks of Belisa's mirror, that had fallen and broken into fragments – "a Cyclops of glass whose luck it was to become an Argos to look at her with a thousand eyes" ("Ciclope antes de vidrio, en mejor suerte – se hizo Argos de cristal para mirarte").

36. Not a *culterano* poet, like Góngora's followers, but one leaning rather toward the opposite type of baroque style, the *conceptista*, was the author of the most famous sonnet that has been written in Spanish, "No me mueve, mi Dios, para quererte. . . ." It is well known that this exciting and puzzling sonnet has been irresponsibly attributed to saints and sinners, from Theresa to Lope. It seems now that it may have been written in Mexico, since the earliest manuscript in which it is found is a book by the Augustinian Friar Miguel de Guevara. Cf. A. M. Carreño, *Fray Miguel de Guevara* (Mexico, 1915).

37. The authors of these translations are Father Federico Escobedo (in verse) and Don Ignacio Loureda (in prose).

38. On Gama and other Brazilian writers, cf. Aubrey Fitz-Gerald Bell, *Portuguese Literature* (Oxford, 1922), pp. 270 ff.; also David Miller Driver, *The Indian in Brazilian Literature* (New York, 1942). A Brazilian who became famous in Portugal during the eighteenth century was Antonio José de Lisboa (1705–1739), "the Brazilian Jew." He gave many comedies to the stage in Lisbon and was called "the Portuguese-American Molière." Finally he was prosecuted by the Inquisition as a false convert, sentenced to death, and burned at the stake. Another case of "transplantation," with better luck, was that of the moralist and architect Matias Aires (1705–before 1770).

39. Cf. the collective work *Latin America and the Enlightenment*, edited by Professor Arthur P. Whitaker (New York, 1942).

40. Cf. Irving A. Leonard, *Don Carlos de Sigüenza y Góngora, a Mexican Savant of the Seventeenth Century* (Berkeley: University of California, 1929); "A Great Savant of Colonial Peru," in *Philological Quarterly*, XII (1933), 54–72; and "An Early Peruvian Adaptation of Corneille's 'Rodogune,'" in *Hispanic Review*, V (1937), 172–176. Professor Leonard has published a complete edition of Peralta Barnuevo's *Obras dramáticas*, with introduction and notes in Spanish (Santiago de Chile, 1937).

41. Humboldt said in 1802 that "no city in the Western Hemisphere, the United States not excepted, contains such large and solid scientific institutions as the Mexican capital." On the whole, scientific culture in the most important cities of Hispanic America was in advance of that of the English-speaking cities until our movement of independence began. And Humboldt tells us that the Mexicans considered themselves more advanced in science than the Spaniards.

42. The leaders of this activity in science and scholarship were, in Mexico, the mathematician, astronomer, and architect, already mentioned as a poet, Joaquín Velázquez de Cárdenas y León (sometimes called Velázquez de León; but this is also the name of a nineteenth-century scientist, 1803–1882), Gamboa, Bartolache, León y Gama, Alzate (all mentioned above), the mathematician Agustín Rotea (d. 1788), the naturalists José Mariano Mociño (ca. 1750–1821), author of the monumental *Flora mexicana*, Luis Montaña (1755–1820), Father Pablo de La Llave (1773–1833), Juan José Lejarza (1785–1824), and Juan José de Oteiza (1777–1810), the archaeologists Márquez and F. Javier Clavijero (1731–1787), whose *Ancient History of Mexico*, published in Italian (Cesena, 1780–1781), rapidly became a classic, the geographer José Antonio Villaseñor, the Cartesian philosophers Guevara and Díaz Gamarra (1745–1783), the bibliographers Father Juan José de Eguiara (1706–1763), and Canon José Mariano Beristáin de Souza (1756–1817); in Central America, José Cecilio del Valle (see next chapter), the physicist Friar José Antonio de Liendo Goicoechea (1735–1814), the anatomist José Flórez (1758–1814); in Cuba, the philosophers Father José Agustín Caballero (1762–1835) and Father Félix Varela (1788–1853) and the economist Francisco de Arango y Parreño (1765–1837); in Santo Domingo, the geographer Father Antonio Sánchez Valverde (1729–1790) — to a later period belongs the naturalist Manuel de Monteverde (1793–1871), but, like the eminent zoologist of Cuba, Felipe Poey (1799–1891), and the historian José Antonio Saco (1797–1879), he is still the product of colonial education; in Venezuela, the philosopher Baltasar Marrero and the jurist Miguel José Sanz; in New Granada, the astronomer-naturalist Caldas mentioned above, the naturalists Francisco Antonio Zea (1770–1822), who helped Bolívar in drawing the Constitution of Angostura (1819), Francisco Ulloa, José Tadeo Lozano (1771–1816), and Florentino Vega, the archaeologist José Domingo Duquesne; in Ecuador, the geographers Pedro Vicente Maldonado (1704–1748), who worked with the members of the French-Spanish scientific expedition of 1736, Antonio de Alcedo (1735–1812) who compiled the *Diccionario geográfico-histórico de las Indias Occidentales o América* (Madrid, 1786–1789; English translation by G. A. Thompson, London, 1812–1815), and Juan Pío Montúfar, Marquis of Selva Alegre, a Maecenas to learned men, the naturalists Mariano Villalobos and Pedro Francisco Dávila, Francisco Eugenio de Santa Cruz Espejo (1747–1795), a physician of encyclopedic knowledge, whose manuscript dialogues *A New Lucian or Awakener of Minds* (*Nuevo Luciano o Despertador de ingenios*), in 1779, ran from hand to hand and impressed many readers as a severe but just criticism of the antiquated system of most Spanish universities and colleges (he also wrote literary criticism and translated Longinus); in Peru, the prolific writer, astronomer, and naturalist José Eusebio Llano de Zapata, the naturalists Gabriel Moreno, Father Francisco

González Laguna, Hipólito Ruiz, and Hipólito Unanue (1755–1833), memorable for his essay on the climate of Lima (*Observaciones sobre el clima de Lima*, 1808), the economist José de Baquíjano y Carrillo, the physicist Toribio Rodríguez de Mendoza (1750–1825), the physician José Manuel Valdés (1767–1843); in Chile, Manuel de Salas (1755–1841), the geographers and naturalists Juan Ignacio de Molina (1740–1829; there is a translation by R. Alsop of his *Geographical, Natural and Civil History of Chili*, Middletown, Connecticut, 1808) and Felipe Gómez de Vidaurre (1740–1818); in Argentina, the naturalist Father Gaspar Juárez (1731–1804), Juan Baltasar Maziel (1727–1788), and Dean Gregorio Funes (1749–1829); in Paraguay, the jurist Pedro Vicente Cañete; in Uruguay, the geographer and naturalist Dámaso Larrañaga (1771–1846); in Brazil, the physicist Father Bartolomeu Lourenço de Gusmão, "the flying priest," *o padre voador*, who is said to have invented the aerostatic balloon (1708) before the Montgolfiers (1783), the naturalists Friar Conceicão Velloso (1742–1811) and Alexandre Ferreira (1765–1815), the geographers Francisco de Lacerda (1750–1798), who explored the Amazon River and Portuguese Africa, and Manoel Ayres do Casal, the lexicographer Antonio de Moraes e Silva (1756–1824), Father Francisco Luis dos Santos Leal (1740–1820), who published a history of philosophy (Lisbon, 1788), José Bonifacio de Andrada e Silva, geologist and mineralogist (on whom see next chapter). A number of Spaniards took part in this scientific movement — the most distinguished were the naturalist José Celestino Mutis (1732–1808), Martín de Sessé (d. 1809), and Juan del Castillo (d. 1793), after whom the india-rubber plant was named *Castilloa*, the chemist Elhúyar and the mineralogist Andrés del Río (already mentioned in the text). Among the Jesuits who lived in Hispanic America there were also learned men from nearly every country of Europe. Cf. Moll, *Aesculapius in Latin America* (1944).

43. Cf. Diderot's *Oeuvres* (Paris, 1875), VI, 467–472.

44. There is not, as yet, a full biography of Olavide. Marcelino Menéndez y Pelayo speaks of him at length, but from the point of view of a not very tolerant Catholic, in his *Historia de los heterodoxos españoles* and in his *Historia de la poesía hispanoamericana*.

45. After 1540, at least. But before 1540 the colonies were too new to count.

46. On the population of Hispanic America at different periods of the colonial era, see Dr. Rosenblat's work, already mentioned, *El desarrollo de la población indígena de América*.

47. See note 38 to Chapter II.

48. Miguel Solá's *Historia del arte hispano-americano* (Barcelona, 1935), which includes architecture and artistic crafts, is the first attempt at a complete survey of the field. It does not go beyond the

colonial era and does not include Brazil – on which cf. Laudelino Freire, *Galeria historica dos pintores do Brasil* (Rio de Janeiro, 1914); A. Morales de los Ríos, *Resumo monographico da evolução da arquitectura do Brasil* (Rio de Janeiro, 1923); Annibal Mattos, *Arte colonial brasileira*, 2 vols. (Bello Horizonte, 1936–1937); Carlos Rubens, *Pequena historia das artes plasticas no Brasil* (São Paulo, 1941), Philip L. Goodwin, *Brazil Builds* (New York, 1943); and Robert Chester Smith, Jr., articles in the collective work *Concerning Latin America* (New York, 1940), in *Estudos brasileiros*, of Rio de Janeiro, IV (1940), 419–429, and in *The Art Quarterly*, especially XX (1938), 110–159.

During the last thirty years a vast literature has appeared in relation to the arts of the several countries, and it is rapidly growing, with no mean contribution from scholars in the United States (see bibliography at the end of this volume). The oldest writings on the subject are Miguel Luis Amunátegui's article about art in Chile (1869) and José Bernardo Couto's *Diálogo sobre la historia de la pintura en México* (1872).

49. Gil González Dávila, *Teatro de las grandezas de la villa de Madrid* (Madrid, 1623).

50. Cf. Manuel Toussaint's pithy syntheses in *Twenty Centuries of Mexican Art* (New York: Museum of Modern Art, 1940), and *II Congreso Internacional de Historia de America*, vol. I (Buenos Aires, 1938).

51. Cf. articles by R. C. Smith, Jr., already mentioned in note 48 of this chapter.

52. Cf. Sacheverell Sitwell, *Southern Baroque Art* (London, 1926), and *Spanish Baroque Art* (London, 1931).

NOTES TO CHAPTER 4

1. Miranda preserved also an immense collection of documents. The story of how the journal and the documents – sixty-three volumes in all – were lost for over a century and then recovered (in England, by Professor Robertson) is a fitting posthumous crown to his fantastic career. Cf. William Spence Robertson, Introduction to *The Diary of Francisco de Miranda, Tour of the United States, 1783–1784* (New York, 1928); also his *Life of Miranda* (Chapel Hill: University of North Carolina, 1929), a scholarly work. The government of Venezuela is publishing the *Archivo de Miranda* at Caracas.

2. John Adams, *Works* (Boston, 1856), X, 134–158. On Miranda's visit to New England, cf. S. E. Morison and H. S. Commager, *The Growth of the American Republic* (2nd ed., New York, 1937), I, 193–194.

3. Session of December 10, 1810.

4. The meetings in the city halls (*cabildos* or *ayuntamientos*) began as early as 1808. Acts of war began in 1810, but the allegiance to Spain was not yet broken. Independence was declared, first in Venezuela (July 5, 1811), then in New Granada (July 13, 1813), in Paraguay (October 12, 1813), in Mexico (November 6, 1813), in Argentina, under the inspiration of San Martín, the great silent leader (July 9, 1816), in Chile (November 12, 1817), in Ecuador (October 9, 1820), in Peru (July 28, 1821), in Central America (September 15, 1821), and in Santo Domingo (November 30, 1821). The last battles were fought in South America on Peruvian territory — Junín, won by Bolívar (August 6, 1824), and Ayacucho, won by Sucre against fourteen royalist generals (December 9, 1824). After a few unimportant encounters in Upper Peru, the modern Bolivia, Sucre declared that the war was over in South America (April 3, 1825). In Mexico fighting ceased in 1821 (September 15). There was no fighting in Central America or in Santo Domingo. Only the islands of Cuba and Puerto Rico remained under Spanish rule, until 1898. Haiti, the former Saint-Domingue, became independent of France in 1804; it does not concern us here.

5. Unsuccessful projects of independence were as common in Brazil as in the Spanish colonies during the colonial era. A great conspiracy, the *conjuração mineira*, was discovered in 1789; its leader, Tiradentes, was executed (1792), and his companions imprisoned or deported to Africa. Napoleon's army invaded Portugal in 1807, and the reigning family, following the advice of England, moved to South America. They brought to Brazil its first public printing plant. A second conspiracy, a real "nativist" revolution led by priests and members of masonic lodges in Pernambuco, was put down in 1817. King João VI returned to Portugal in 1821; during the next year, his son Pedro, who had remained as regent, on being called back decided to stay (*Eu fico* — "I remain," January 9, 1822), declared independence (September 7, 1822) and became constitutional emperor of Brazil (October 1822). He resigned in 1831, returned to Lisbon (where he reigned as Pedro IV until his death in 1834), and was succeeded by his son Pedro II (deposed in 1889 by a republican movement).

6. We need a systematic study of the political thought of all our leaders of independence. The influence of European thinkers has received some attention; the important thing to investigate, however, is not so much what our leaders read but what they did with the ideas they absorbed. The Hispanic traditions, plus the philosophy of enlightenment and the currents of "American federalism, French jacobinism, British realism and constitutional monarchism," converging in Hispanic America, produced such a variety of projects and laws that our

lands became "the most extensive political laboratory the world has ever known" (Belaúnde). The field is partially covered by Bernard Moses, *The Intellectual Background of the Revolution in South America* (New York, 1926) and Víctor Andrés Belaúnde, *Bolívar and the Political Thought of the Spanish-American Revolution* (Baltimore, 1938). Belaúnde distinguishes six stages in Bolívar's thought. On Argentina alone, cf. José Ingenieros, *La evolución de las ideas en la Argentina*, vol. I (Buenos Aires, 1918), and Alejandro Korn, *Influencias filosóficas en la evolución nacional*, in the third volume of his *Obras* (La Plata, 1940). Cf., also, Jefferson Rea Spell, *Rousseau in the Spanish World* (Austin, Texas, 1938).

7. About the men of letters who were implicated in the conspiracy of Minas Geraes in 1789, see Chapter III.

8. "The proper study of the men of America is America," said a contemporary of Bello, born in Honduras, the apostolic José Cecilio del Valle (1780–1834), who drew the declaration of political independence of Central America (1821) and wrote fine descriptions of nature in a sort of personal encyclopedia. Toward the end of 1823, the Argentine poet Juan Cruz Varela published in Buenos Aires a series of articles on the subject of national literature.

In the United States, Noah Webster had declared in 1783 that "America must be as independent in *literature* as in *politics*." During the nineteenth century, Emerson and Channing found it necessary to insist on this question. Oliver Wendell Holmes called Emerson's address *The American Scholar* (1837) "our intellectual Declaration of Independence." Channing, in his essay *On National Literature* (1823), said: "It were better to have no literature than form ourselves unresistingly on a foreign one."

9.   Divina Poesía,
            tú de la soledad habitadora,
            a consultar tus cantos enseñada
            con el silencio de la selva umbría,
            tú a quien la verde gruta fué morada
            y el eco de los montes compañía. . . .

"Divine Poesy, thou dweller of the solitude, taught to heed for thy song the counsel of the shady forest's silence, thou for whom the green cave was an abode and the echo of the mountains a companion."

10. "El algodón despliega al aura leve — las rosas de oro y el vellón de nieve. . . . El maíz, jefe altanero — de la espigada tribu. . . . El cacao — cuaja en urnas de púrpura su almendra. . . . El ananás sazona su ambrosía. . . ."

Describing the source of cochineal scarlet, he becomes frankly baroque — "In thy cactus a living crimson swarms that shames the murex

of Tyre" ("Bulle carmín viviente en tus nopales — que afrenta fuera al
múrice de Tiro").

11. "Tantos héroes contó como soldados" (It counted as many
heroes as soldiers). — "Virtud no le faltó, sino fortuna" (Not virtue
failed it, but fortune). — "La pompa augusta del solemne día" (The
august pomp of the solemn day). — "Y al delito espuela — es antes el
ejemplo que el deseo" (And there example, rather than lust, acts as a
spur to sin). — "No así trató la triunfadora Roma — las artes de la paz
y de la guerra" (Not thus did triumphant Rome deal with the arts of
peace and war). — "La oscuridad de su infructuosa pompa" (The
darkness of the [forest's] fruitless pomp). — "Sólo cenizas . . . burla
del viento" (Only ashes, scorn of the wind). — "Ya la primera flor
desvuelve el seno, — bella a la vista, alegre a la esperanza" (The early
flower, lovely to the eye and gay to hope). — "La libertad, más dulce
que el imperio" (Freedom, sweeter than imperial power).— "Y no basta
la hoz a las espigas" (And the sickle proves unequal to the spikes).

12. Another poet of this generation, José Antonio Miralla (1790–
1825), of Argentina, made a superb translation of Gray's *Elegy*, line by
line — a feat of literal exactness, considering the usual difference between Spanish and English as to length of words.

13. "Brota del seno de la azul esfera — uno tras otro fúlgido dia-
mante" (Out of the depth of the blue sphere comes one after another
gleaming diamond). — "El hombre, tras la cuita y la faena — quiere
descanso y oración y paz" (Man, after the labor and pain of the day,
asks for rest and prayer and peace). — "¡Oh dulce devoción, que reza
y ríe!" (Sweet devotion, at once laughing and praying!). — "Piedad,
Señor, al hombre que criaste: — eres justicia, eres bondad: ¡perdón!"
(Pity, O Lord, the man Thou hast created. Thou art justice, Thou art
goodness: forgive!).

14. Alexander von Humboldt's expedition to Cuba, South America,
and Mexico (1799–1804) and his monumental work, written with the
help of his fellow-traveller Aimé Bonpland, *Voyage aux régions équinoxiales du Nouveau Continent*, 30 vols. (Paris, 1807–1834), had the
value of a new revelation of the New World that influenced the leaders
of the movement of independence as well as the men of letters.

15. The *Chanson de Roland* was not printed until 1837; the *Roman
de Berthe* had already been printed in 1832. Bello published his article "Sobre el origen de la rima asonante" in the *Repertorio Americano*,
1827.

16. On Bello, cf. Elijah Clarence Hills, *The Odes of Bello, Olmedo
and Heredia*, texts in Spanish, introduction and notes in English (New
York: The Hispanic Society of America, 1920). In Spanish there are
two extensive books on Bello, one by Miguel Luis Amunátegui (*Don
Andrés Bello*, Santiago de Chile, 1882), the other by Eugenio Orrego

Vicuña (*Don Andrés Bello*, Santiago de Chile, 1935). The best critical studies of his work are those of Miguel Antonio Caro, preface to a volume of his *Poesías* (Madrid, 1881), and Marcelino Menéndez y Pelayo in the first volume of the *Historia de la poesía hispanoamericana*.

17. The success of Chateaubriand's *Atala* (1800) — which was really the last work of a series as to subject, but the first to treat it in the romantic manner — gave new impetus to Indian themes in literature, especially in Hispanic America. Olmedo's *Canción india* is an adaptation, in Spanish verse, of a prose passage from *Atala*. Heredia and Plácido (1809–1844) also wrote poems derived from Chateaubriand's novel.

18. "El trueno horrendo que en fragor revienta — y sordo retumbando se dilata — por la inflamada esfera — al Dios annuncia que en el cielo impera" (The horrific thunder that bursts in a roar and deeply rumbling rolls through the fiery sphere announces the God who reigns in the heavens).

19. Olmedo represented the district of Guayaquil in the *Cortes* of Cadiz (1810–1814), presided over the *Junta* that declared the province of Quito free from Spanish rule in 1820, and was a member of the assembly that gave a constitution to Peru in 1823. He was always in the forefront of public life, especially after Ecuador detached itself from Colombia and became an independent republic (1830); he was once vice president, once the president of a provisional government (1845), and once a defeated candidate for president of the constitutional government (1845).

20. The best critical estimate of Olmedo's poetry is that of Menéndez Pelayo in his *Historia de la poesía hispanoamericana*, if we except his unjust condemnation of the Inca's apparition.

21. A significant trait of the odes and hymns written during the campaigns for independence is that they speak of Spanish America as a unit — e.g., in Argentina, Vicente López y Planes, Esteban de Luca, and Juan Ramón Rojas. With the birth of the new nations, the literature written in favor of their independence gained in popular esteem; the literature written in favor of the royalist cause was doomed to oblivion. This royalist literature was, on the whole, much inferior to that of the insurgents. But not always — a forgotten Spanish poet, who was born in Granada, lived in Mexico, and became a governor of the Californias, Ramón Roca (d. 1820), had the gift of resounding verse (cf. *Antología del Centenario*, edited by Luis Gonzaga Urbina, Nicolás Rangel, and the present writer, Mexico City, 1910, pp. ccxvi–ccxxiv and 1002–1003). On the connection between literature and the movement for independence in the River Plate countries, cf. Carlos Ibarguren, *Las sociedades literarias y la revolución argentina (1800–1825)* (Buenos Aires, 1938).

22. "Ni otra corona que el agreste pino — a tu terrible majestad conviene" (No other crown than the savage pine is fit for thy fearful majesty). When I noticed, in 1919, that there were no pines by the side of Niagara Falls, I asked Professor Elijah Clarence Hills, who had studied Heredia, to inquire what had happened to the trees the poet had seen — I entertained no doubt that he had. Professor Hills found that in the 1840's a lumber company had acquired the rights to exploit the forests around the falls and so the pines were cut down. When, later on, a park was built there, the embellishers evidently had no notion of the original aspect of the place. Professor Hills's articles on Heredia are included in his *Hispanic Studies*.

About the time when Heredia visited the falls, and for a few years afterwards, they were a favorite subject with American poets — John Gardner Calkins Brainard, John Neal, Mrs. Sigourney. Chateaubriand, it is well known, describes them in *Atala*. Several poets from Spanish America after Heredia have written on them — signally Gertrudis Gómez de Avellaneda (see next chapter), the Colombian Rafael Pombo (1833–1912), and the Venezuelan Juan Antonio Pérez Bonalde (1846–1892). One of the great falls of South America, the Tequendama, is the subject of several poems of Colombian poets, of whom the best known is that of Agripina Montes del Valle (1844–1915). I do not know of any good poem on the falls of Iguazú.

Heredia's poem on Niagara was anonymously translated into English and published under the sponsorship of William Cullen Bryant. Bryant himself translated Heredia's ode on a storm. Cf. Hills's *Hispanic Studies*.

23. Cf. note 38 of Chapter II.

24. The novel is entitled in Spanish *El Periquillo Sarniento*; the name of the hero (Pedro Sarmiento) is disfigured to make it mean *Itching Parrot*. It has been admirably translated into English (in abridgement) by Katherine Anne Porter (New York, 1942).

25. The Spanish title is *La quijotita y su prima*.

26. Cf. Jefferson Rea Spell, *The Life and Works of José Joaquín Fernández de Lizardi* (Philadelphia, 1931), and his articles in the *Romanic Review*, XVII (1926), 338–348, in the *Hispanic American Historical Review*, VII (1927), 104–123 and 490–507, and in *Hispania*, May, 1925; May, 1928; and February, 1931.

27. Juan del Valle Caviedes (*floruit* 1683–1691). It has recently been discovered that he was born in Andalusia, not in Peru. Whatever his place of birth, he developed into a typical Limeño — to many, in fact, the most typical of all. Cf. Guillermo Lohmann Villena, "Dos documentos inéditos sobre don Juan del Valle y Caviedes," in *Revista Histórica* (Lima), XI, 277–283.

28. He was, however, a better prose-writer than poet, a very

scholarly critic, and one of the editors of the renowned *Revista Bi-mestre Cubana* (1831–1834), the best literary magazine, at that time, in any Spanish-speaking country, Spain included.

29. Cf. Madaline Wallis Nichols, *The Gaucho: Cattle-Hunter, Cavalryman, Ideal of Romance* (Durham: Duke University, 1942).

NOTES TO CHAPTER 5

1. On Dr. Francia, cf. Carlyle's well known essay and Edward Lucas White's book *El Supremo* (New York, 1919). This taciturn tyrant and successfully absolute isolationist had been, paradoxically enough, a reader of Rousseau and the *Encyclopédie.*

2. It is often remarked that the approach to democracy increases in Hispanic America in proportion to the number of inhabitants of pure European stock. A journalistic sociology blames the Indians and the Negroes for our political failures. In good logic, the blame should be laid on the Europeans and their descendants who for centuries have kept the Indians and the Negroes in servitude and ignorance, denying them the practice of political rights. Wherever the formerly subject groups obtain a minimum of civic and economic justice, the political improvement becomes evident. And it should be remembered that the European immigration which came in the nineteenth century to countries like Argentina and Uruguay came with the explicit condition that it was to enjoy full political and economic freedom.

3. In Mexico, Hidalgo proclaimed the abolition of slavery when he started the war of independence in September 1810; a presidential decree of Guerrero made it effective in 1829, excepting Texas, then a part of the Mexican nation — the exception being due to pressure from the South of the United States. In 1823, Central America, then a federation, decreed abolition. In "la gran Colombia" it was declared in Bolívar's Constitution of 1819 (it had been first proclaimed by him, in the midst of war, in July, 1815). The three republics that emerged from his confederation confirmed it later — the new Colombia (the former New Granada), in 1851; Ecuador, in 1853; Venezuela, in 1854. Bolívar declared it also for Bolivia in his Constitution of 1826. In Chile, it came during the war of independence, in 1811 (it was completed by the Constitution of 1823); in Argentina, since 1812 — gradual emancipation, which became complete by means of later constitutional precepts (the present Constitution was voted in 1853); in Uruguay, in 1842; in Peru, in 1854.

In Cuba and Puerto Rico, under the rule of Spain, slavery lasted much longer; it was suppressed, at last, in 1872 for Puerto Rico and in 1880 for Cuba. In Haiti, the former Saint-Domingue, on the western side of Hispaniola, it had been abolished by the French Revolution, after four years of unjustifiable hesitation, in 1793; but that French-speaking country does not come within the scope of this book. In Santo Domingo, the Spanish-speaking eastern side of Hispaniola, it disappeared in 1822.

The Brazilian Empire also remained behind. As early as 1823, José Bonifacio de Andrada e Silva, "the patriarch of independence," introduced in the assembly that voted the first Constitution a project for a gradual liberation of slaves, together with a plan to educate the Indians and make black slavery unnecessary. Abolition, however, did not come until 1888; it had been preceded by the suppression of the slave traffic in 1831, really enforced in 1850, and the freedom of the slaves' newborn in 1871. The day when total abolition was proclaimed (May 13, 1888) was a day of extraordinary public rejoicing.

4. There are many books on the history of education in the several countries of Hispanic America. In English, Irma Wilson, *Mexico: a Century of Educational Thought*, already mentioned. In Spanish Juan María Gutiérrez's *Origen y desarrollo de la enseñanza pública superior en Buenos Aires* (1868) is now a classic. Among the more recent works, the *Historia de la enseñanza en Chile*, by Amanda Labarca Hubertson (Santiago de Chile, 1939), is an excellent example.

5. The last great painter of the French classicist school, who after following the strict discipline of Ingres was carried away by Delacroix's romantic *fougue*, Théodore Chassériau (1818–1856), was born in Santo Domingo, under the Spanish rule, and from the maternal side seems to have inherited Indian blood.

6. On nineteenth-century painters see the brief references in the next chapter.

7. Rio de Janeiro is the subject of many brilliant pages in the writings of foreign visitors — in English, Rudyard Kipling, in *Brazilian Sketches*; Philip Guedalla, in *Argentine Tango*; Waldo Frank, in *America Hispana*; in Spanish, Sarmiento, in his *Viajes*.

8. In Mexico, men of two generations took part in the long struggle. Prieto and Ramírez belonged to the first group of romantics; Altamirano and Riva Palacio to the second. On Ramírez, cf. Irma Wilson, *Mexico: a Century of Educational Thought*, pp. 196–208; on Altamirano, pp. 209–211 and 267–269.

9. Por un cabo doy dos reales,
    por un sargento un doblón;
    ¡por mi general Morelos
    doy todo mi corazón!

10. The *Cangrejos* and the *Mamá Carlota* may be called folk songs because they were sung even by the entirely illiterate, but they were not the work of humble unknown poets. Prieto wrote *Cangrejos*; Riva Palacio is said to have written the *Mamá Carlota*.

11. A partial list of writers who have been presidents of Spanish American republics (most of them in the nineteenth century; very few in the twentieth): in Argentina, in 1827, Vicente López y Planes (1783–1856), the author of the national anthem; in 1862–1868, Bartolomé Mitre (1821–1906); 1868–1874, Domingo Faustino Sarmiento (1811–1888); 1874–1880, Nicolás Avellaneda (1837–1885); in Paraguay, 1905–1906, Cecilio Báez (b. 1862); 1910 and 1920–1921, Manuel Gondra (b. 1872); in Uruguay, 1830–1835 and 1839–1845, Bernardo Prudencio Berro (1803–1868); 1890–1894, Julio Herrera y Obes (1842–1912); in Bolivia, 1872–1874, Adolfo Ballivián (1831–1874); in Ecuador, 1830–1835 and 1839–1845, Juan José Flores (1800–1864); 1835–1839, Vicente Rocafuerte (1783–1847); 1845, José Joaquín de Olmedo (1780–1847); 1861–1865 and 1869–1875, Gabriel García Moreno (1821–1875); 1888–1892, Antonio Flores Jijón (1833–18..); 1892–1895, Luis Cordero (1833–1912); 1916–1920, Alfredo Baquerizo Moreno (b. 1859); in Colombia, a true *république de professeurs*, 1857–1861, Mariano Ospina (1805–1885); 1874–1876, Santiago Pérez (1830–1900); 1880–1888, Rafael Núñez (1825–1894); 1892–1898, Miguel Antonio Caro (1843–1909); 1898 and 1900–1904, José Manuel Marroquín (1827–1908); 1918–1922, Marco Fidel Suárez (1855–1927); in Santo Domingo, 1876, Ulises Francisco Espaillat (1823–1878); 1880–1882, Fernando Arturo de Meriño (1833–1907); 1884–1885, Francisco Gregorio Billini (1844–1898); 1916, Francisco Henríquez y Carvajal (1859–1935); in Honduras, 1876–1883, Marco Aurelio Soto (1846–1908). From this list are excluded the purely political writers, like Francisco I. Madero (1873–1913) in Mexico (1911–1913); the journalists, like José Batlle Ordóñez (1854–1930) in Uruguay (1903–1907 and 1911–1915); the orators, like Sebastián Lerdo de Tejada (1827–1889) in Mexico (1872–1876), or Epitacio Pessoa in Brazil (1918–1922) or Mariano Baptista (1832–1907) in Bolivia (1890–1894); and the university professors who wrote only on their special subjects, like José Vicente Concha in Colombia (1914–1918). If any think that these men of letters have failed in politics, let it be remembered, among other significant facts, that modern Argentina was organized, one might even say created, under Mitre, Sarmiento, and Avellaneda; that Colombia has always been one of the honestly democratic republics; that the administrations of Espaillat and Billini in Santo Domingo are always mentioned among the most exemplary that country has known.

12. I compare the two official dates, so to speak, for the beginnings of the romantic school in Spanish. There had been, of course, "pre-romantic" poems in Spain, and in Spanish America also. In the drama, too, and in the novel, the dates run very close; in both cases Spanish America acted in complete independence of Spain. Cf. E. Allison Peers, *A History of the Romantic Movement in Spain* (Cambridge,

England, 1940). "Until 1833," he says, "the Revolt is no more than an undercurrent in an outwardly placid neo-classic river." Cf. also Enrique Piñeyro, *El romanticismo en España* (Paris, 1904), English translation by E. Allison Peers (Liverpool, 1934), and I. L. McClelland, *The Origins of the Romantic Movement in Spain* (1700 to 1800) (Liverpool, 1937).

13. The Spanish titles of Echeverría's poems are: *Elvira* or *La novia del Plata*, *Los consuelos*, *Rimas*, and *La cautiva*. The story in prose, *The Slaughter-House*, is in Spanish *El Matadero*, of which there is an English translation by Ángel Flores in *The New Mexican Quarterly Review*, separately reprinted in New Haven, 1942.

14. Even in Spain — his *Rimas* ran into two editions there.

15. In Spanish, *Los amores del payador*.

16. The best known works on Santos Vega, all bearing his name as title, are the long poem in savory country dialect by Hilario Ascasubi (1807–1875), the shorter, brilliant poem in standard Spanish (1877–1885) by Rafael Obligado (1851–1920), the novel (1881) by Eduardo Gutiérrez (1853–1890), and the play by Juan C. Nosiglia (1894) derived from the novel and acted in circus rings by the Podestá companies. Cf. Robert Lehmann-Nitsche, *Folklore argentino: Santos Vega* (Buenos Aires, 1917).

17. History was one of the favorite forms of writing in Hispanic America during the colonial era and it persisted as such after independence. The leading historians are: in Mexico, Lucas Alamán (1792–1853), Lorenzo de Zavala (1788–1836), José María Luis Mora (1794–1850), José Fernando Ramírez (1804–1871), Manuel Orozco y Berra (1816–1881), Joaquín García Icazbalceta (1825–1894), and Justo Sierra (1848–1912); in Cuba, José Antonio Saco (1797–1879); in Venezuela, Rafael María Baralt (1810–1860), Juan Vicente González (1811–1866), Felipe Larrazábal (1817–1873), Arístides Rojas (1826–1894), Eduardo Blanco (1840–1912), and José Gil Fortoul (1862–1943); in Colombia, José Manuel Restrepo (1782–1863), Joaquín Posada Gutiérrez (1797–1881), José Manuel Groot (1800–1878), Joaquín Acosta (1800–1852), and Ernesto Restrepo Tirado (b. 1862); in Ecuador, Pedro Moncayo (1804–1888), Pedro Fermín Cevallos (1812–1893), and Bishop Federico González Suárez (1844–1917); in Bolivia, Gabriel René Moreno (1834–1908); in Chile, Miguel Luis Amunátegui (1828–1888), Diego Barros Arana (1830–1907), Benjamín Vicuña Mackenna (1831–1886), Vicente Pérez Rosales (1807–1886), Ramón Sotomayor Valdés (1830–1903), and Domingo Amunátegui Solar (b. 1860); in Uruguay, Andrés Lamas (1820–1891), Francisco Bauzá (1849–1899), and Carlos María Ramírez (1848–1898); in Brazil, Francisco Adolfo de Varnhagen (1816–1878), Alexandro Mello de Moraes (1816–1882), João Capistrano de Abreu (1853–1927), and João Ribeiro (1860–1934).

Paul Groussac (1848–1929), born in France, but a resident of Argentina for sixty years, and equally at home, as a writer, in French and in Spanish, was a master of critical method and applied it to South American history. Cf. A. Curtis Wilgus, *Histories and Historians of Hispanic America* (New York, 1937; revised edition, 1942).

18. Félix María Del Monte (1819–1899), of Santo Domingo:

Que el poeta que . . .
arranca al monstruo la usurpada gloria
es un genio, es un dios, que de la historia
la profanada dignidad vengó.

19. Cf. Stuart Cuthbertson, *The Poetry of José Mármol* (University of Colorado Series, 1935). Professor Cuthbertson is an enthusiastic admirer of Mármol, whom he calls "the foremost lyric romanticist of the Argentine." His researches show, in opposition to Menéndez Pelayo's opinion, that the influences received by Mármol were "far more cosmopolitan than Spanish" and that "he derives more from Echeverría than from any other single source." There is an English translation by M. J. Serrano of Mármol's novel *Amalia* (New York, 1919).

20. Cf. Lastarria, *Recuerdos literarios*, first part (Santiago de Chile, 1878). On literary emancipation, see especially pp. 68–70, 92–137, 182–184, 203, 222, and 225–234 of the 1885 edition. He is not always fair to Bello. Cf. also José Enrique Rodó, "Juan María Gutiérrez y su epoca," the best study of a literary period in Spanish America (in his book *El mirador de Próspero*, Montevideo, 1913).

21. In Mexico, the earliest romantic poet Fernando Calderón (1809–1845) published his first volume of poems in 1828; it contains only vague premonitions of romanticism. He did not fully enter into the romantic movement until a few years later.

In Venezuela, the first romantics seem to be Fermín Toro (1807–1865) and Juan Vicente González, already mentioned among the historians (note 17 of this chapter). Maitín, the best of the Venezuelan romantic poets, was still writing classical tragedies in 1836; shortly afterwards he turned toward romanticism. González wrote about the need of a "national literature."

22. In Portuguese, *Suspiros poeticos e saudades*.

23. On the romantic movement in Brazil, cf. Isaac Goldberg, *Brazilian Literature* (New York, 1922); on the "Indianists," Driver, *The Indian in Brazilian Literature*, already mentioned. On "Indianist" poetry in the Spanish speaking countries, Aída Cometta Manzoni, *El indio en la poesía de América española* (Buenos Aires, 1939). — The first "Indianist" poem of Gonçalves Dias was a short dialogue, *O indio*, published in Pitões, Portugal, 1844; he omitted it in his later collections of *Cantos*. His *Primeiros cantos* (1846) contained the *Poesías americanas*, eleven of which treat Indian subjects — *I-Juca-Pyrama* and the *Cancão do Tamoyo* belong to this group.

24. Vega's most famous comedy, *The Man of the World* (*El hombre de mundo*, 1845), was often privately acted in Madrid, before it was given to the public, and the leading lady in one of the performances was Eugenia de Montijo, the future Empress of the French. I have not been able to ascertain whether Eugenia acted together with Vega himself, who was said to be a perfect actor. On Vega, cf. John Kenneth Leslie, *Ventura de la Vega and the Spanish Theatre 1820–1865* (Princeton University, 1940).

Vega belongs to Spanish literature entirely. Gertrudis Gómez de Avellaneda, like Juan Ruiz de Alarcón, belongs to Europe and to the New World at the same time. There are a few more cases like hers among her contemporaries: the Venezuelan Rafael María Baralt, already mentioned as a historian (note 17), and José Heriberto García de Quevedo (1819–1871) are the best known. On the other hand, Antonio Ros de Olano (1802–1887), born in Venezuela, Fermín de la Puente y Apezechea (1821–1875), born in Mexico, and Antonio Goncalves Crespo (1847–1883), born in Brazil, were taken to Europe in their childhood, like Vega. Before this period, Mexico gave to Spain the classicist playwright Manuel Eduardo de Gorostiza (1789–1851), who wrote in Europe his best comedies (1818–1833); when he returned to his native country he made only adaptations of foreign plays, such as Lessing's *Emilia Galotti*. There are later cases of transplantation, with change of language, besides W. H. Hudson: José Maria de Hérédia (1842–1905), the poet of *Les Trophées*, born in Cuba like his cousin and namesake "el cantor del Niágara" (besides his French poems he also wrote a few in Spanish — three sonnets on the centenary of his cousin), and three poets born in Uruguay, Jules Laforgue (1860–1887), the Comte de Lautréamont (Isidore Ducasse, 1846–1870), and Jules Supervielle; all belong to French literature. The composer Reynaldo Hahn (b. 1874) and the pianist Teresa Carreño (1853–1917) are Venezuelans by birth (cf. Marta Malinowski, *Teresa Carreño*, New Haven, 1940).

We may add that many Spanish American writers have lived in Spain or in France or in both countries for very long periods, feeling entirely at home there, yet never renouncing their allegiance to their native lands — for instance, Gonçalves de Magalhães, Felipe Pardo, Hilario Ascasubi, Alberto Blest Gana, Juan Montalvo, Manuel González Prada, Rufino José Cuervo, Enrique Piñeyro, Carlos María Ocantos, Francisco A. de Icaza, Rubén Darío, Enrique Gómez Carrillo, Luis Bonafoux, Enrique Larreta, Carlos Reyles, Amado Nervo, Luis G. Urbina, Carlos Pereyra and his wife María Enriqueta, Rufino Blanco Fombona, Alfonso Reyes, Francisco and Ventura García Calderón, Martín Luis Guzmán, and Teresa de la Parra. Only one, so far as I know, Gonzalo Zaldumbide, has complained about his divided allegiance — *las vicisitudes del descastamiento*. The identity of language and traditions sufficiently explains the fact in regard to Spain and Portugal. And France, since the beginning of the nineteenth century, has been for us a spiritual home and the source of most of our information about European culture. Henry Adams says, in his biography of George Cabot Lodge, that "the illusion of ease and horizon seldom lasts long in Paris. A few days completely dispel it. . . . To an American, the processes and machinery of a French education are hard to apply in his home work." The very opposite should be said about Spanish Americans — Paris is, above all cities, the best suited to our intellectual and artistic leanings. "At best," Henry Adams goes on saying, "the atmosphere of Paris in December lacks gaiety except for Parisians or such as have made themselves by time and temperament more or less Parisian." It is difficult to conceive of a Hispanic American for whom, in normal times, the atmosphere of Paris in December or in any other month, even in summer, would lack gaiety or stimulus. The fall of Paris in 1940 was a personal tragedy for many thousands of Hispanic Americans.

Cf. Richard Eugene Bailey, *French Culture in Mexico in the Nineteenth Century* (Paris, 1936); Gilberto Freyre, *Un engenheiro francês no Brasil* [Louis Léger Vauthier] (Rio de Janeiro, 1940).

25. One of the best poems of La Avellaneda, *Al partir*, was written on leaving Cuba. Cf. Edith L. Kelly, "The Centennial of a Great Sonnet," with an English translation, in *Hispania*, XIX (1936), 337–344.

26. On La Avellaneda, cf. Edwin Bucher Williams, *The Life and Works of Gertrudis Gómez de Avellaneda* (Philadelphia, 1924); Enrique Piñeyro, *The Romantics of Spain*; Edith L. Kelly, "The Metamorphosis of a Poet," in the *Bulletin of the Pan American Union*, LXXI (1937), 546–552. In Spanish, cf. Juan Valera, an article in *Revista de España*, 1869, reprinted in his *Disertaciones y juicios literarios*, and M. Menéndez y Pelayo, *Historia de la poesía hispanoamericana*.

27. All circumstances point to that conclusion. It is highly improbable that the author should have been born in Spain; his criticism of the conquistadors is too harsh, even for a liberal Spaniard. And there is a sort of Indian patriotism in the novel. Cf. J. Lloyd Read, *The Mexican Historical Novel, 1826-1910* (New York, 1939). The first historical novel written by a Spaniard is *Ramiro, Conde de Lucena*, by Rafael Húmara (Paris, 1828). Another Spaniard, Telesforo Trueba y Cosío, wrote in English and published in London three historical novels, *The Castilian* (1829), *Gómez Arias* (1830), and *The Romance of the History of Spain* (1830). We must leave out of account, of course, early works, such as the *Guerras civiles de Granada* (1595-1604?), by Ginés Pérez de Hita, which were not deliberately conceived as historical novels.

28. There is a paradox in the prosperity of the Mexican publishing

houses between 1830 and 1880, the period that saw the war with the United States, the civil war of the *Reforma*, the French intervention, the brief empire of Maximilian, and the final triumph of the liberal republican government of Juárez. The ten-volume encyclopedia published by the firm of Rafael was entitled *Diccionario universal de historia y geografía* (1853–1856); the articles it contained on Mexican subjects were written by the most distinguished scholars of the country (including García Icazbalceta, José Fernando Ramírez, Lucas Alaman, José Bernardo Couto, José Joaquín Pesado, Guillermo Prieto, Manuel Payno, and Count José Gómez de la Cortina) and are still valuable. The first attempt at a classification of the native languages of Mexico, by Manuel Orozco y Berra, appeared there only forty years after Bopp's similar effort in the Indo-European field.

29. The leading *costumbristas*, besides those mentioned above, are the Peruvians Felipe Pardo, Manuel Ascensio Segura, both already mentioned as dramatists, and Abelardo Gamarra (1857–1924); the Colombians Juan de Dios Restrepo, who signed himself Emiro Kastos (1825–1894), José David Guarín (1830–1890), José María Vergara y Vergara (1831–1872), and José Joaquín Borda (1835–1878); the Mexicans Juan Bautista Morales (1788–1856), who published *El Gallo pitagórico* in 1844–45, and *Micrós* (Ángel de Campo, 1868–1908); the Venezuelans Daniel Mendoza (1823–1867), Francisco de Sales Pérez (1836–1926), and Nicanor Bolet Peraza (1838–1906). The authors of memoirs often coïncide with the *costumbristas* — for example Guillermo Prieto in Mexico and the historian Pérez Rosales in Chile. Cf. Jefferson Rea Spell, "The 'costumbrista' movement in Mexico," in *Publications of the Modern Language Association*, March, 1935.

30. On Alencar and the Brazilian novel, cf. Goldberg, *Brazilian Literature*, and Driver, *The Indian in Brazilian Literature*. On "Indianist" novels in Spanish-speaking countries, Concha Meléndez, *La novela indianista en Hispanoamérica* (1832–1889) (Madrid, 1934).

31. Treatises on literary rules, first called in the Aristotelian manner, "retórica y poética" (prose including many more types of literature than those encompassed by Greek rhetoric), then "preceptiva literaria," and finally, with shamefaced falsity, "teoría literaria," continued to be written in Hispanic America (as in Spain) until this century. Long after schools and colleges in most countries of Europe and in the United States had ceased to teach the subject and had changed it to a course in composition (even though the name of *rhetoric* survived here and there), it was maintained in Hispanic America.

32. José Ramón Yepes (1822–1881), Eloy Escobar (1824–1889), José Antonio Calcaño (1827–1897), Francisco Guaicaipuro Pardo (1829–1882), Jacinto Gutiérrez Coll (1836–1901).

33. In the Chilean Guillermo Matta (1829–1899), for instance, or in the Venezuelan Heraclio Martín de la Guardia (1829–1908).

34. Among the inevitable exceptions: Ignacio Ramírez and Francisco Bilbao. In Peru, the priest Francisco de Paula Vigil (1792–1875) attacked the Church of Rome as a monopoly in religion and wished to establish a national church.

35. The poem in tercets *Por los muertos*, of Ramírez, ends in this quatrain:

Madre Naturaleza, ya no hay flores
por do mi paso vacilante avanza;
nací sin esperanza ni temores:
vuelvo a ti sin temores ni esperanza.

Acuña's best-known philosophical poem is *Ante un cadáver*, also in tercets. Its ending proclaims the law of the conservation of matter, but rather incongruously compares matter with glory:

La materia, inmortal como la gloria,
cambia de formas pero nunca muere.

The influence of Schopenhauer is visible in the Ecuadorean Numa Pompilio Llona (1832–1907).

36. Examples in the drama: *Don Pedro de Castilla* (1836), *El templario* (1838), and *Enrique VIII* (1839), by Foxá; *El Conde Alarcos*, by the Cuban José Jacinto Milanés (1814–1863); *El torneo* (1839), *Ana Bolena*, and *Hermán* or *La vuelta del cruzado*, by the Mexican Fernando Calderón (1809–1845); *El cruzado* (1851) and *El templario* (1855), by the Peruvian Manuel Nicolás Corpancho (1830–1863); *El cruzado*, by the Argentine Mármol; *Juana de Nápoles* (1850), by the Chilean Salvador Sanfuentes (1817–1860); *Miguel de Cervantes* (1849), by the Colombian José Caicedo Rojas (1816–1898); *Roberto d'Evreux* (1856), *Bernardo de Palissy* (1857), and *Camoens* (1868), by the Puerto Rican Alejandro Tapia (1827–1882); *Los horrores del triunfo* (1887), by the Puerto Rican Salvador Brau (1842–1913); *Jacobo Molay* (1851) and *El castillo de Berkeley* (1856), by the Colombian Santiago Pérez (1830–1900); *Rienzi*, by the Venezuelan Eloy Escobar; *Leonor de Mendonça* (1847) and *Beatriz de Cenci* (1847), by the Brazilian Luis Carlos Martins Penna (1815–1848).

Munio Alfonso (1844), *El príncipe de Viana* (1844), *Egilona* (1845), and *Recaredo* (1850), by La Avellaneda, *Don Fernando el de Antequera*, by Ventura de la Vega, and *Isabel de Médicis*, by García de Quevedo, were written in Spain.

There were also, but rarely, dramas on subjects drawn from classical antiquity: *Coriolano* (1849) and *Lucrecia* (1849), by the Colombian Manuel María Madiedo (1815–1888).

In Spain, Ventura de la Vega wrote *La muerte de César*. La Avellaneda wrote two splendid Biblical tragedies, *Saúl* (1849) and *Baltasar* (1858).

In the novel, foreign subjects were rare. The most curious exceptions are two novels by the Puerto Rican Francisco Mariano Quiñones (1830–1908), *Nadir Shah* (1875) and *La magofonía* (1875) — the scene is laid in Persia.

37. In the drama: *El privado del virrey* (1841) and *Muñoz visitador de México* (1838), by the Mexican Ignacio Rodríguez Galván (1816–1842); *El oidor* (1865), by the Colombian Germán Gutiérrez de Piñeres (1816–1872); *El corsario negro*, by the Colombian Lázaro María Pérez (1824–1892); *Blanca de Silva* (1879), by the Peruvian Carolina Freyre de Jaimes (d. 1916); *La cruz del Morro* (1862), by the Puerto Rican Bibiana Benítez (1783–1875); *Alfredo el sevillano* (1856), by the Peruvian Luis Benjamín Cisneros (1837–1904); *La hija del rey* (1876) and *El Conde de Peñalva*, by the Mexican José Peón Contreras (1843–1908); *O jesuita* (1875), by the Brazilian Alencar; *Gonzaga ou A Revolução de Minas* (1867), by the Brazilian Castro Alves.

In the novel: *Don Álvaro*, by the Colombian José Caicedo Rojas; *La novia del hereje*, by the Argentine Vicente Fidel López; *La hija del Adelantado* (1866), and *El visitador*, by the Guatemalan José Milla (1822–1882); *El oidor*, by the Colombian José Antonio de Plaza (1809–1854); *El oidor de Santa Fe*, by the Colombian José Joaquín Ortiz (1814–1892); *Cofresí* (1876), by the Puerto Rican Tapia; *Mariana Belzunce*, by the Peruvian José Antonio Lavalle (1833–1893); *El Inquisidor Mayor* (1852), by the Chilean Manuel Bilbao (1827–1895).

We know that the colonial background was first used in the humorous narrative poems of José Batres Montúfar, who was still, in the main, a classicist. A few more works of this type, partly humorous and partly dramatic, were written by the great Bello (*El proscrito*, which did not go beyond the first five cantos); by his Chilean disciple Salvador Sanfuentes (*El campanario*, 1842, and *El bandido*); by the Guatemalans José Milla (*Don Bonifacio*, 1862; cf. article by John L. Martin, in *Hispania*, XXIV (1941), 281–284) and Salvador Barrutia (a continuation of Batres' own *El reloj*, 1881); by the Peruvian Carlos Augusto Salaverry, 1831–1890 (*Abel, el pescador americano*, 1857).

The real master of colonial subjects (in prose), the Peruvian Ricardo Palma, belongs to the next literary period.

38. The best examples are, besides the poems of Gonçalves Dias, the novels of Alencar, Arboleda's *Gonzalo de Oyón*, and the ballad *Jicotencal* by the Cuban Plácido (Gabriel de la Concepción Valdés, 1809–1844), the brief lines *En boca del último Inca*, by José Eusebio Caro, Rodríguez Galván's poem *Profecía de Guatimoc*, and La Avellaneda's novel *Guatimozín* (1846); in later years, the novels *Cumandá* (1871), by Juan León Mera (1832–1894), of Ecuador, and *Enriquillo* (1879–1882), by Manuel de Jesús Galván (1834–1910), of Santo Domingo, and the poems *Fantasías indígenas* (1877), by José Joaquín

Pérez, of Santo Domingo (1845–1900), and *Tabaré* (1886), by Juan Zorrilla de San Martín, of Uruguay (1857–1931).

There are no dramas of very great merit on the conflict between the Indian and his Spanish conquerors, but many plays on such themes were written; these date from the last years of the colonial era, beginning with *Siripo* (1789), by the Argentine Manuel de Lavardén (1754–1809). This conflict, naturally, was often exploited during the campaigns for independence and then during the romantic period.

Cf. Concha Meléndez, *La novela indianista en Hispanoamerica*; Aída Cometta Manzoni, *El indio en la poesía de. América española* (it includes the drama when written in verse); Driver, *The Indian in Brazilian Literature*.

39. Unlike most of our men of letters, Sarmiento never published a poem. It is known that he wrote at least one (1858) and sent it, asking for advice, to his contemporary Alberdi, who was only a year older than he but had the advantages of living in Buenos Aires and of having begun to make a name for himself in literature. We do not know Alberdi's reply; it must have been unfavorable, since Sarmiento does not seem ever to have tried his hand at verse again and occasionally displayed a more or less Platonic contempt for it, thus inciting Mitre to write his defense of poetry (1858).

40. In the same year, a system of normal schools was planned in Colombia by Dámaso Zapata.

41. *Facundo*, or *Civilización y barbarie*, was translated into English by Mrs. Horace Mann, under the title of *Life in the Argentine Republic in the Days of the Tyrants*, or *Civilization and Barbarism* (London, 1868). Mrs. Mann added a biographical sketch of Sarmiento.

42. Madaline Wallis Nichols, "A United States Tour by Sarmiento in 1847," in *Hispanic American Historical Review*, XVI (1936), 19–212 (with many quotations), reprinted, with two other essays, one of them entitled "Sarmiento on Our Sixties," in the volume *Sarmiento: a Chronicle of Inter-American Friendship* (Washington, 1941). Also, Percy Alvin Martin, *Sarmiento and New England* (it deals with his visits to the United States in 1847 and in 1865–1868 and his correspondence with New Englanders).

When Sarmiento undertook his first trip to Europe and the United States, one of his purposes was to discover, through the study of Spain, the causes of the political and cultural diseases of Argentina (he was very censorious of the Spaniard's faults, but very Spanish at heart, as Unamuno often remarked) and to discover in the United States the method of making a democracy succeed. He always kept his faith, but was never blind to social peculiarities that made democracy imperfect.

He was a warm friend of Mrs. Horace Mann, and a very extensive correspondence between them has been published. He also met Emerson, Longfellow, Ticknor, and President Hill of Harvard, where he spent two days. In 1868 the University of Michigan granted him an honorary doctor's degree.

43. Sarmiento's most ambitious work, *Conflicto y armonías de las razas en América* (1883), was first planned as a development of the ideas contained in *Facundo*. It did not become that. When he wrote *Facundo* he clearly perceived and described the influences of geography and history upon the social and political life of Argentina — such facts as the vastness of the country and the sparseness of the population, or the multitude of cattle and horses that made food and travel practically gratuitous. In the later work he wished to explain the history of Hispanic America from the point of view of race. But race explains nothing. And the method he adopted was an encumbrance for him — he read the latest books on ethnology and sociology, quoted authorities, gathered colonial documents. Evidently the process wearied him, for the book was never finished, and even in the part he gave to the press the plan is not clearly discernible. In short, he succeeded in *Facundo* because he sought his explanation in culture, as the term is now understood in ethnology and sociology; he failed in his last book because he sought his explanation in race.

44. Many books on Sarmiento have been written in Spanish. The most important are by José Bernardo Suárez (1863), José María Zuviría (1889), Manuel Antonio Ponce (1890), José Guillermo Guerra (1893), Augusto Belin Sarmiento (1905), Leopoldo Lugones (1911), Enrique Richard Lavalle (1911), Carlos Octavio Bunge (1926), Armando Donoso (1927), Alberto Palcos (1929), Aníbal Ponce (1932), Porfirio Fariña Núñez (1934), Juan Rómulo Fernández (1938), Bernardo González Arrili (1938), Emeterio S. Santovenia (1940), and Ricardo Rojas (1945). Important articles and speeches, or extensive references in books, by Charles de Mazade, in *Revue des Deux Mondes*, November, 1846, and by Juan Bautista Alberdi, Nicolás Avellaneda, Aristóbulo del Valle, Carlos Pellegrini, Diego Barros Arana, Lucio Victorio Mansilla, Santiago Estrada, Pedro Goyena, Miguel Cané, Martín García Mérou, Paul Groussac, Joaquín V. González, David Peña, Ernesto Quesada, Agustín Álvarez, José Ingenieros, Raúl A. Orgaz, and Rafael Alberto Arrieta. Very few studies have been made of his literary work alone; cf. Carlos María Onetti, *Cuatro clases sobre Sarmiento escritor* (Tucumán, 1939); Roberto Fernando Giusti, "Sarmiento, escritor," in the review *Cursos y Conferencias* (Buenos Aires), October–November, 1938, and Juan Pablo Echagüe, *Sarmiento, crítico teatral* (Buenos Aires, 1925).

NOTES TO CHAPTER 6

1. On philosophy in Hispanic America, cf. Francisco García Calderón, book V of his work *Les démocraties latines de l'Amérique* (Paris, 1912) — translated into English as *Latin America: its Rise and Progress* — and his report *Les courants philosophiques dans l'Amérique latine* presented to the International Congress of Philosophy that met at Heidelberg in 1908; Salomón Carrillo Ramírez, "La evolución filosófica en la América hispana," in *Revista de las Españas*, 1935; Aníbal Sánchez Reulet, "Panorama de las ideas filosóficas en Hispanoamérica," in *Tierra Firme* (Madrid), 1936 (and my review in *Sur* (Buenos Aires), September, 1936). On individual countries: in Cuba, José Zacarías González del Valle, *De la filosofía en La Habana* (1839); José Manuel Mestre, *De la filosofía en La Habana* (1862); Manuel de la Cruz (1861-1896), first chapter of his *Reseña histórica del movimiento literario en Cuba* (1890), included in the third volume of his *Obras* (Madrid, 1924); Medardo Vitier, *Las ideas en Cuba* (Havana, 1938), and his studies on Enrique José Varona. In Mexico: Agustín Rivera (1824-1916), *La filosofía en la Nueva España* (1885); Emeterio Valverde Téllez, *Apuntaciones históricas sobre la filosofía en México* (1896); Leopoldo Zea, *El positivismo en México* (1943); Samuel Ramos, *Historia del pensamiento filosófico en México* (1943). In Peru, a few pages of Francisco García Calderón in his book *Le Pérou contemporain* (Paris, 1907). In Argentina, the essays of Alejandro Korn and José Ingenieros mentioned in Chapter IV, note 6; Coriolano Alberini, *Die deutsche Philosophie in Argentinien* (Berlin, 1930); Francisco Romero, Ángel Vassallo, and Luis Aznar, *Alejandro Korn* (Buenos Aires, 1940). In Colombia: Cayetano Betancur, "La filosofía en Colombia," in *Anales de la Universidad de Antioquia*, November, 1933, pp. 15-77. In Brazil, Silvio Romero (1851-1914), *A filosofia no Brasil* (Porto Alegre, 1878); Clovis Bevilaqua, *A filosofia positiva do Brasil*; Leonel Franca, *Noções de historia da filosofia*; Guillermo Francovich, *Filosofos brasileiros* (Rio de Janeiro, 1939).

2. On Mitre and Sarmiento, see Chapter V. Nicolás Avellaneda (1837-1885), orator and essayist, wrote many essays on historical and literary subjects, besides his books and articles on public questions.

Bernardino Rivadavia (1780-1845), as minister of the government of the province of Buenos Aires (1821-1826) and afterwards as president of the first and short-lived Argentine Republic (February, 1826-July, 1827), founded many important institutions, including the University of Buenos Aires (August, 1821) and the Sociedad de Beneficencia (1822), which flourished under the virtual leadership of

Mariquita Sánchez (María Sánchez de Mendeville, 1786–1868), the hostess of the most famed *salon* in the city. He also established a number of schools for women. After Rivadavia's retirement, the Republic broke again into "the United Provinces" until 1853.

3. After 1867 there were no further European attempts at new domination of New World territories. Spain, who maintained her rule in Cuba and Puerto Rico until 1898, reannexed Santo Domingo in 1861, but relinquished her acquisition in 1865. Her attacks on the Pacific coast and islands of South America (1863–1866) were effectively repelled by both Chile and Peru. France invaded Mexico (1862) and helped Maximilian (1864) to ascend his ephemeral throne; then the French army left the country (1865) and the throne vanished (1867).

4. Although Manuel González was president of Mexico from 1880 to 1884, his administration is usually counted as a part of the "era porfiriana," since he became president with the agreement that after his term expired Porfirio Díaz was to be reëlected.

5. The above statements about progress must be understood with a qualification: progress meant prosperity for the upper class and for a growing middle class; the poor remained as poor as ever.

6. Gothic reappeared after 1840. The exact date is not known, since there has been very little research, as yet, on Hispanic American architecture during the nineteenth century (cf., however, Adolfo Morales de los Ríos filho, *Grandjean de Montigny* [a French architect] *e a evolucão da arte brasileira*, Rio de Janeiro, 1941, and Philip L. Goodwin, *Brazil Builds*, New York, 1943).

The most curious example of our new Gothic is probably the parochial church of San Miguel de Allende, in central Mexico, rebuilt by a local architect, Zeferino Gutiérrez. The beautiful church of Gloria, in Rio de Janeiro, was built in 1842 by Julio Frederico Koeller and Philippe Garçon Riviére.

7. Representative painters of the period were, in Mexico, José María Estrada, Hermenegildo Bustos (1832–1907), Santiago Rebull (1829–1902), José María Velasco (1840–1912), and Félix Parra (1845–1919); in Venezuela, Antonio José Carranza, Carmelo Fernández (d. 1877), Martín Tovar (1828–1902), Cristóbal Rojas, and Arturo Michelena (1863–1898); in Colombia, José María Espinosa, Luis García Heria, and Ramón Torres Méndez; in Peru, Ignacio Moreno (1817–1876), Francisco Lasso (d. *ca.* 1868), Daniel Hernández (1856–1932), and, partly in this period and partly later, Carlos Baca-Flor (1869–1941), who painted a well-known portrait of John Pierpont Morgan the elder and other residents of Fifth Avenue; in Chile, Manuel Antonio Caro (1835–1903), Pedro Lira (1845–1912), Alfredo Valenzuela Puelma (1856–1908), Cosme San Martín, Juan Francisco González, and Tomás Somerscales, who lived in London and is often classed as an English

painter; in Argentina, Carlos Morel (1813–1894), who really belongs to earlier years, since he became insane and ceased to paint in 1838, Prilidiano Paz Pueyrredón (1823–1870), and Eduardo Sívori (1847–1918), with whom a new period begins; in Uruguay, Juan Manuel Blanes (1830–1901); in Brazil, Victor Meireles (1832–1903), Zeferino da Costa (1840–1915), and Pedro Americo de Figueiredo (1843–1905). The best seem to be the Mexican Velasco, the Argentine Pueyrredón, and the Uruguayan Blanes. Cf. Lincoln Kirstein, *The Latin-American Collection of the Museum of Modern Art* (New York, 1943).

8. Posada was also a cartoonist and worked for *El Ahuizote, El Hijo del Ahuizote,* and other satirical periodicals. Cf. the magazine *Art and Life,* published in Mexico City, 1938–1939, and especially articles on "The Political Caricature in Mexico" by Manuel Toussaint, on "Mexican Lithographic Tradition" by Francisco Díaz de León, and on "The Art of Engraving in Mexico" by Alfonso Toro; Manuel Toussaint's book *La litografía en México* (Mexico, 1934); Frances Toor, *José Guadalupe Posada,* with a preface by Diego Rivera (Mexico, 1933); Angélica Palma, *Pancho Fierro* (Lima, 1935). For a later period Bernardo G. Barros' *La caricatura contemporánea* (Madrid, n. d.; *ca.* 1918).

9. The earliest orchestra seems to be that of Caracas, organized around 1750. Another one was founded in Guatemala around 1800, under the Spaniard Father José María de Santa Eulalia. In the nineteenth century we know of the orchestras organized in Bogotá, 1846, and in Mexico, 1857. The first programs were not purely symphonic; they contained excerpts from popular operas and even much lighter things. It seems that the earliest periodical exclusively devoted to music was the *Lira Granadina,* of Bogotá, 1836, edited by Eugenio Salas (1823–1853).

10. Among the composers of religious music may be mentioned, in Colombia, José Joaquín Guarín (1825–1854), José María Ponce de León (1846–1882), who wrote a Biblical opera, *Ester,* produced at Bogotá, 1874, Diego Fallon (1834–1905), who was also a good poet, and Julio Quevedo Arvelo (1829–1897). As late as 1892, Father José Guadalupe Velázquez (1856–1920) founded a School of Sacred Music at Queretaro, in Mexico. José de Jesús Ravelo, in Santo Domingo, is still composing oratorios.

11. Two of the operas of Carlos Gomes were written to libretti in Portuguese, *A noite do castello,* produced in Rio de Janeiro, 1861, and *Joanna de Flandes,* in Rio, 1863; the rest had Italian libretti — *Il guarany* (1870), *Fosca* (Milan, 1872 or 1873), *Salvator Rosa* (Milan, 1874; a great success), *Maria Tudor* (Milan, 1879), and *Lo schiavo,* with a Brazilian subject, said to be the best of his works (Rio, 1889). He composed also a vocal-symphonic poem, *Colombo* (1892), and two reviews with texts in Milanese dialect, produced at Milan, *Se sa minga*

(1867) and *Nella luna* (1868). There were several Hispanic American composers, besides Carlos Gomes, whose operas were produced in Europe during the nineteenth century: the Cuban Gaspar Villate (1851–1891), author of *Zilia*, sung in Paris, 1877, by Tamberlick and Elena Sanz, *La czarine*, produced at The Hague, 1888, *Richelieu*, and *Baldassarre*; the Mexican Melesio Morales (1838–1909), author of *Ildegonda*, produced at Florence, around 1868, *Romeo y Julieta* (Mexico, 1863), *Gino Corsini* (Mexico, 1877), and *Cleopatra* (Mexico, 1891).

12. Examples of this nativist music: the *Sinfonía sobre temas colombianos*, by José María Ponce de León, already mentioned as a religious composer (note 10); the *Variaciones sobre el tema del jarabe mexicano* (1841), by José Antonio Gómez; the "Danza tlaxcalteca," in the opera *Guatimotzín* (1871), and *Vals jarabe*, by the Mexican Aniceto Ortega (1823–1875); *Ecos de México*, a potpourri of Mexican folk tunes, by Julio Ituarte (1845– ––); *Rapsodias cubanas*, by José Manuel Jiménez (1855–19–).

Cf. Otto Mayer-Serra, *Panorama de la música mexicana* (Mexico, 1941), and articles by different authors in the *Boletín Latinoamericano de Música*, since 1935, besides the works mentioned in note 11, Chapter III.

13. Cf. Carlos Vega, *Danzas y canciones argentinas* (Buenos Aires, 1936), and *Panorama de la música popular argentina* (Buenos Aires, 1944).

14. The final form of the habanera is said to be due to Manuel Saumell (1817–1870). On the music of the Antilles, cf. Eduardo Sánchez de Fuentes, *El folklore en la música cubana* (Havana, 1923), *Influencia de los ritmos africanos en nuestro cancionero* (Havana, 1927), and *La canción cubana* (Havana, 1930) — all contain musical examples — and my own lecture "Música popular de América," in the collective volume *Conferencias*, vol. I (La Plata: Colegio de la Universidad Nacional de La Plata, 1930).

15. One of the first musicians to pay attention to the songs and dances of Hispanic America was the once famous pianist and composer Louis Moreau Gottschalk (1829–1862), born in New Orleans; he visited Cuba, Peru, Chile, Argentina, and Brazil, where he died. A number of his fantasies and transcriptions of tropical airs, such as the *Cocoyé*, were noted down and published by the Cuban composer Nicolás Ruiz Espadero (1833–1890).

16. Olegario Víctor Andrade (1839–1882), of Argentina; Julio Zaldumbide (1833–1887), of Ecuador; Salomé Ureña de Henríquez (1850–1897), of Santo Domingo; Miguel Antonio Caro (1843–1909), of Colombia; Joaquín Arcadio Pagaza (1839–1918), of Mexico. Pagaza translated Virgil, Horace, and the modern Guatemalan Latinist Landí-

NOTES TO CHAPTER 6

var; Caro made many versions of short poems from classical and modern languages, and the best Spanish versions of the *Aeneid* and the *Georgics*; he also wrote a Latin grammar in collaboration with Rufino José Cuervo (1844–1911). Bello and Cuervo were the greatest grammarians of Spanish in the nineteenth century; Cuervo, besides, developed from a grammarian into a philologist. His *Apuntaciones críticas sobre el lenguaje bogotano* (Bogotá, 1867–1872) — they grew and improved in every new edition until the posthumous sixth (Paris, 1914) — his copious notes to Bello's *Gramática de la lengua castellana,* and his *Diccionario de construcción y régimen de la lengua castellana* (letters *A* to *D,* Paris, 1886–1893; the rest still remains unpublished) are classical works.

At the beginning of the nineteenth century, our writers were still good Latinists and proved it in their translations or at least in the reminiscences of classical literature in their writings: Bello, Olmedo, Heredia, José Bonifacio de Andrada e Silva, Juan Cruz Varela, Francisco Acuña de Figueroa, Mariano Melgar, Felipe Pardo, Irisarri, Batres Montúfar, Domingo Del Monte, Ochoa, Navarrete, Quintana Roo, Ortega, Pesado, and even Fernández de Lizardi (see Chapters IV and V). The *Diario de México* (1805–1817), for instance, printed many local translations from Horace, Ovid, Catullus, and Martial (as well as from Sappho). After the romantic movement, the literatures of classical antiquity received less attention than before; the art of translation, however, was not lost — witness, besides Pagaza and Caro, the Mexicans Montes de Oca and Roa Bárcena (see Chapter V), José María Vigil (1829–1909), who made a masterly version of Persius, Joaquín Diego Casasús (1858–1916), translator of Catullus, Tibullus, and Propertius, Ambrosio Ramírez (1859–1913), and Father Federico Escobedo, the Guatemalan Juan José Micheo (1847–1869), the Venezuelans Jesús María Morales Marcano (1830–1888) and Diego Jugo Ramírez (1836–1903), the Colombian Rafael Pombo (1833–1912), the Peruvian Juan de Arona (pen-name of Pedro Paz Soldán y Unanue, 1839–1895), the Chilean Salvador Sanfuentes (1817–1860), the Argentines Bartolomé Mitre (see Chapter V) and Carlos Guido Spano (mentioned in this chapter), the Brazilians Antonio José de Lima Leitão, Manoel Odorico Mendes (1799–1865), who translated the *Aeneid* (1854), the *Iliad,* and the *Odyssey* into Portuguese, Juan Gualberto Ferreira dos Santos, Manoel Ignacio Soares Lisboa, and Juan Nunes de Andrade. On these and other translators, cf. M. Menéndez y Pelayo, *Horacio en España* (Madrid, 1877; enlarged, 1885), *Biblioteca hispano-latina clásica,* unfinished (Madrid, 1902), and notes to editions of Homer and Virgil in the *Biblioteca Clásica* of Madrid; Gabriel Méndez Plancarte, *Horacio en México* (Mexico, 1937); Antonio Castro Leal and Enrique Díez Canedo, in *Revista de Literatura*

Mexicana, I (1940), 134–148, 318–347, and 363–369; Juan Augusto Perea and Salvador Perea, "Horacio en Puerto Rico," in the review *Indice*, of San Juan, 1930.

In recent times, we may mention as examples of the fruit of classical studies the translations of Greek plays by the Chilean Juan R. Salas and the refined Bolivian poet Gregorio Reynolds, the biographies *Cicerón* (Santiago de Chile, 1933), *Horacio* (Santiago, 1938), and *Juvenal* (Santiago, 1940) by Father Alejandro Vicuña, the books of the Mexican Alfonso Reyes (see Chapter VIII) on *La crítica en la edad ateniense* (Mexico, 1941) and *La antigua retórica* (Mexico, 1942), the translation of Lucretius and the books on Horace and Virgil by the Colombian José María Restrepo Millán, and, in Argentina, the version of many portions of the *Iliad* and the *Odyssey* by Lugones (see Chapter VII), the historical studies of Abraham Rosenvasser (whose studies on Egypt are of even greater importance) and José Luis Romero, and the investigations of María Rosa Lida on the fortunes of certain classical themes in Spanish literature as well as her essay on Sophocles (Buenos Aires, 1944).

17. On the influence of Bécquer, frequently combined with that of Heinrich Heine, whose *Buch der Lieder* was translated by Pérez Bonalde, cf. Max Henríquez Ureña, *El retorno de los galeones* (Madrid, 1930), pp. 23–27. To the names he mentions we may add Federico Rivas Frade (1858–1922), of Colombia, Enrique Henríquez (1859–1940), of Santo Domingo, and José Rosas Moreno (1838–1883), of Mexico. William Cullen Bryant translated into English several fables of Rosas Moreno.

18. Tobías Barreto was not only a poet but a philosopher too, profoundly versed in German thought. His friend Silvio Romero (1851–1914) was a philosopher and a literary critic.

19. Cf. the end of the fourth chapter. The followers of Del Monte include, in Cuba, Ramón Vélez Herrera (1808–1886), Ramón de Palma (1812–1860), Miguel Teurbe Tolón (1820–1858), and El Cucalambé (pen-name of Juan Cristóbal Nápoles Fajardo, 1829–1862); in Santo Domingo, Félix María Del Monte (1819–1899), Nicolás Ureña de Mendoza (1822–1875), and José María González Santín (1830–1863); in Puerto Rico, Manuel Antonio Alonso (1822–1889), better known as an author of *cuadros de costumbres* than as a poet (on the sketches of customs, see Chapter V). They all wrote narrative and descriptive poems of country life. To these are related a number of delightful poems in praise of nature and in praise of women, written by Plácido, José Jacinto Milanés, and later on by Diego Vicente Tejera (1848–1903). In Colombia, after Gutiérrez González (see Chapter V), Rafael Pombo, one of the best poets of the country (already mentioned as a Latinist in note 16), occasionally wrote on *criollo* subjects such as the *bambuco*, one of the national dances.

20. Prieto's *Musa callejera* (1883) is only one of his several poetical works. Next in significance comes his *Romancero nacional* (1885), already mentioned in Chapter V. His *cuadros de costumbres* and his *Memoirs* are as picturesque as his ballads.

21. It should be said, incidentally, that the gaucho dialect differs from the language of cities in Spain and Spanish America only in a few phonetic changes, mostly suppressions; but such changes are known to city people everywhere, because they exist in popular speech on both sides of the Atlantic. In vocabulary, the only divergences from standard Spanish are a few archaisms and Indian words.

22. Cf. F. M. Page, " 'Fausto,' a gaucho poem," introduction, Spanish text, translation and notes, in *Publications of the Modern Language Association*, vol. XI, 1896; also the recent translation into English verse by Mr. Walter Owen (Buenos Aires, 1943).

After *Fausto* and just before *Martín Fierro*, in 1872, a *gauchesco* poem — which Hernández read and praised, although its merit is not very high — appeared in Montevideo, *Los tres gauchos orientales*, by Antonio Lussich (1848–1928), and it was followed by *El matrero Luciano Santos* (1873). The Uruguayan contribution to the literature of the gaucho includes, besides, the poem *Celiar* (1852) and the novel *Caramurú* (1854) of Alejandro Magariños Cervantes (1825–1893), in normal Spanish.

To the literature on gaucho subjects in Argentina must be added the novels of Eduardo Gutiérrez (1853–1890), written in journalistic prose: *Juan Moreira* (1880), *Juan Cuello* (1880), *Santos Vega* (1881), etc. The gaucho plays begin in the circus in 1884 with the pantomime *Juan Moreira* arranged by Gutiérrez, to which José Podestá added words in 1886. This literature survives in the twentieth century with the inevitable changes brought about by the changes in country life, in the plays of the Uruguayan Florencio Sánchez and the Argentines Martín Coronado (1850–1919) and Martiniano Leguizamón (1858–1935) as well as in the stories of the Argentines Benito Lynch, Ricardo Güiraldes, Enrique Larreta, and the Uruguayans Javier de Viana and Carlos Reyles (cf. last chapter).

The gaucho exists also in Brazil, but has not received as much attention there as in Argentina and Uruguay. We may recall, besides Alencar's novel *O gaúcho*, the poems of Mucio Teixeira and some of the stories of Afonso Arinos (1868–1916).

23. Alejandro Korn, *Influencias filosóficas en la evolución nacional*, chap. iv (see *Obras* (La Plata, 1940), III, 192–193).

24. As an exception among the Argentines, before Unamuno wrote on *Martín Fierro*, we might mention Joaquín V. González (1863–1923); in his book *La tradición nacional* (1888) he praises *Fausto* with enthusiasm, side by side with Obligado's *Santos Vega*; he mentions *Martín Fierro* only in passing, lumping it together with *Lázaro*

and *La fibra salvaje* (1860), two mediocre poems by Ricardo Gutiérrez. At least, González was not afraid of coupling dialect poetry with poetry written in "cultured language."

There is an English translation, in verse, of Hernández's poem, *The gaucho Martín Fierro*, by Walter Owen (London and New York, 1936). Cf. also Henry Alfred Holmes, *Martín Fierro, an Epic of the Argentine* (New York, 1923), and G. W. Umphrey, "The Gaucho Poetry of Argentina," in *Hispania*, May, 1931.

25. *Martín Rivas* has been translated into English by Mrs. Charles Whitman, New York, 1918. It is said that there is also an English translation of *El ideal de un calavera*.

Blest Gana published nine novels between 1855 and 1863, then four between 1897 and 1912. From 1867 to 1897 he was busy in important diplomatic posts and did not write literature; incidentally, he never returned to his native country. His most important works are (besides *Martín Rivas*) *La aritmética en el amor* (1860), which won the first prize given by the University of Chile to the best novel "on a Chilean subject," *El ideal de un calavera* (1863), *Durante la reconquista* (1897), a historical novel about the war for independence, which he began in Chile before 1867 and rewrote in Europe, *Los transplantados* (1904), about South Americans in Paris, and *El loco Estero* (1909), which contains many memories of his childhood. Cf. Raúl Silva Castro, *Alberto Blest Gana* (Santiago de Chile, 1941) and Alone (pen-name of Hernán Díaz Arrieta), *Alberto Blest Gana* (Santiago de Chile, 1941); in English W. C. E. Wilson, "The Historical Element in the Novels of Alberto Blest Gana," in *University of Washington Digests of Theses* (1914–1931), pp. 243–251.

Cirilo Villaverde's novel *Cecilia Valdés* (1830–1882) has been translated into English by M. J. Lorente under the title *The Quadroon* (Boston, 1935).

26. Machado de Assis published several volumes of poems, essays, plays, and short stories, and nine novels. The most important are *Iaiá Garcia* (1878), *Memorias postumas de Braz Cubas* (1881), *Quincas Borba* (1891), *Don Casmurro* (1900), *Esaú e Jacob* (1904), and *Memorial de Ayres* (1908). Some of the short stories were translated into English by Isaac Goldberg in the volume *Brazilian Tales* (Boston, 1921).

Aluizio de Azevedo's *O cortiço* (1890) has been translated into English by Harry W. Brown under the title *A Brazilian Tenement* (New York, 1926).

Other Brazilian storytellers of this period were the imitators of Balzac, and the "novelists of the *sertão*," Bernardo da Silva Guimarães (1827–1885), Franklin Távora (1842–1888), and Alfredo d'Escragnolle Taunay (1843–1899), whose *Inocencia* might be called the Brazilian equivalent of Isaacs's *María* (see next note), with an added strain of tragedy ending in crime (there is an English translation by James W. Wells).

The sociologist and literary critic José Verissimo (1857–1916) wrote many descriptions of nature and customs: *Quadros paraenses* (1877), *Viagem ao sertão* (1878), *Cenas da vida amazônica* (1886), *A pesca na Amazonia* (1893).

27. There is an English translation of *María* published in New York around 1890. It was reprinted in 1918 and in 1925.

28. Some of Palma's *Tradiciones* have appeared in English translations in the *Andean Monthly*, September and November, 1938, and in *Inter-America*, February, 1920; April, 1922; June, 1923; and April, 1924.

Cf. G. W. Umphrey, "Palma: Tradicionista," in *Hispania*, May, 1924, and Sturgis E. Leavitt, "Ricardo Palma." in *The Hispanic American Historical Review*, III (1920), 63–67.

29. Cf. notes 23, 27, 30, and 38 of Chapter V.

30. There is an English translation of *Tabaré* by Ralph Walter Huntington (Buenos Aires, 1934).

31. Several books were written during this period about conflicts with the Indians: for instance, in Argentina, *Costumbres de los Indios pampas*, by Federico Barbará (1856), and *Fronteras de las pampas del Sud*, by Álvaro Barros (1872); in Chile, *Crónica de la Araucanía*, a history of the Araucanians, by Horacio Lara (1889), and *La guerra a muerte*, by the eminent historian Benjamín Vicuña Mackenna.

32. This group of "fighters and builders" includes other men — José Hernández, Joaquim Nabuco (1849–1910), of Brazil, who fought side by side with Ruy Barbosa in the abolitionist campaigns and later on developed into a complete statesman and an accomplished critic and historian, Manuel Sanguily (1848–1925) of Cuba, a brilliant orator, historian, and critic, who devoted his life to the independence of his native island and to the diffusion of culture, or Federico Henríquez y Carvajal (1848–) of Santo Domingo, orator, poet, journalist, and educator, who has taken part in every cultural movement of the country since 1873.

The group includes women, too, like Salomé Ureña de Henríquez, who after "fighting against war" — against civil war — in her patriotic poems, from 1873 to 1880, became the founder of higher education for women in Santo Domingo (1881), and Clorinda Matto de Turner (1854–1909), who described in her novel *Aves sin nido* (1889) the social system that makes the downtrodden Indian of Peru a prey and a victim of any sort of greed.

The last man of this group is really José Martí, the liberator of Cuba, but he belongs to the next chapter because of his connection with the literary revolution of the eighties.

33. Only a small part of the writings of Ruy Barbosa are purely literary. But he wrote, besides short essays and articles, a long essay on Swift (1887), whom he defended against Taine (incidentally giving a very acute appraisal of the French thinker who exerted a powerful influence at that time in Hispanic America), and books on Alexandre Herculano, the Portuguese historian and novelist (1877), and the abolitionist poet Castro Alves (1881).

34. García Moreno has found admirers among European believers in the tenet that the end justifies the means, however foul they may be, and several books have been written about him in two or three different languages. Let it be said, incidentally, that García Moreno was a man of letters who wrote good prose and tolerable verse, and had taught physics and chemistry at the University of Quito; during his administration he established a number of schools and gave to the country its first railroad. And, of course, he was strictly honest in pecuniary matters — that was still the custom in his times. The Venezuelan Cecilio Acosta (1818–1881) was similar to Montalvo in knowledge of the Spanish classics and mastery of style, but not as a fighting spirit.

35. Cf. José Enrique Rodó's essay "Montalvo," a true masterpiece, in his book *El mirador de Próspero* (1813), and Gonzalo Zaldumbide, "Montalvo," in his volume *Montalvo y Rodó* (New York, 1938).

36. Shortly after González Prada began his campaign, Clorinda Matto de Turner wrote *Aves sin nido* (cf. note 32).

37. Cf. J. H. Cutler, "Manuel González Prada, Precursor of a Modern Peru," with translations of many of his pages, a Harvard dissertation, 1936, mimeographed, in the Harvard Library, and Isaac Goldberg, "A Peruvian Iconoclast," in *The American Mercury*, November, 1935. In Spanish: Luis Alberto Sánchez, *Don Manuel* (Lima, 1930; second edition, Santiago de Chile, 1937).

38. The most distinguished men of the island were devoting their efforts to making it free or at least making it autonomous within the Spanish empire — José Julián de Acosta (1825–1892), Román Baldorioty de Castro (1822–1889), Ramón Emeterio Betances (1827–1898), Francisco Mariano Quiñones (1830–1908), and Segundo Ruiz Belvis (1829–1867).

39. Hostos went to Washington in 1899, as a member of a delegation, to ask from President McKinley the freedom of Puerto Rico. His disappointment was, naturally, very keen.

40. The *Obras completas* of Hostos, in twenty volumes, was published in Havana, 1939. His essay on *Hamlet*, in an English translation by Mariesta Dodge Howland and Guillermo Rivera, appears in the Bulletin no. 12 of the Hostos Centenary Commission.

Cf. Juan Bosch, *Hostos, el sembrador* (Havana, 1939), Rafael Esténger, *Hostos* (Havana, 1942), Camila Henríquez Ureña, *Las ideas pedagógicas de Hostos* (Santo Domingo, 1932), and Antonio Salvador Pedreira, *Hostos, ciudadano de América* (Madrid, 1932).

41. Sanguily has been mentioned already in note 32. Piñeyro's book *El romanticismo en España* has been translated into English by E. Allison Peers (Liverpool, 1934).

42. Cf. *Homenaje a Enrique José Varona* (Havana, 1935).

43. Justo Sierra's *Political Evolution of Mexico* exists in a very imperfect English translation, 1900–1902. On Justo Sierra, cf. Irma Wilson, *Mexico: A Century of Educational Thought* (New York, 1941).

NOTES TO CHAPTER 7

1. Rafael María de Mendive (1821–1886), a refined poet, translated Byron and Thomas Moore. An English version of his poem *La sonrisa de la virgen* is attributed to Longfellow.

2. During his first visit to New York, in 1880, before he settled there in 1881, Martí wrote articles in English for the *Sun* (he was a friend of Charles A. Dana) and for the magazine *The Hour*.

3. The publication of the complete works of Martí was first attempted by his friend Gonzalo de Quesada y Aróstegui; it began in Washington, 1900, and went on in different cities until 1919, when it had reached fifteen volumes. At present this collection derives its highest value from the large number of articles on Martí that appear at the beginning of each volume. The edition of complete works was attempted again by Néstor Carbonell, in Havana, and reached eight volumes (1918–1920); again by Alberto Ghiraldo, in Madrid, and reached seven volumes (1925–1929); again in Paris, and reached only two volumes (1925) — all remained incomplete, of course. A more methodical attempt is that of Gonzalo de Quesada y Miranda, who began his collection of *Obras completas* in Havana, 1936; it is still in progress and already comprises fifty volumes (May, 1943).

There is already a very extensive literature on Martí, and it is augmented every day. The most important books and pamphlets on him are by Néstor Carbonell (Havana, 1923), Antonio Iraizoz (Havana, 1924), Raimundo Lazo (Havana, 1928), Emilio Roig de Leuchsenring (several publications: Havana, 1927, 1932, 1935, 1938, 1941), Gonzalo de Quesada y Miranda (Havana, 1929), Alfonso Hernández Catá (Madrid, 1929), Jorge Mañach (Madrid, 1931), Emeterio S. Santovenia (several books: Havana, 1934, 1936, 1938, 1940, and Buenos Aires, 1943), Gabriela Mistral (Havana, 1935), Mauricio Magdaleno (Mexico, 1940), Antonio Martínez Bello (Havana, 1940), Félix Lizaso (Buenos Aires, 1940), Luis Rodríguez Émbil (Havana,

1941), M. Isidro Méndez (Havana, 1941), Carlos Márquez Sterling (Havana, 1942), the collective volumes *Vida y pensamiento de Martí* (Havana, begun in 1942), and the review *Archivo de Martí*, edited by Félix Lizaso at Havana, since 1940. In English: Anna Maria Barnes, *Martí, A Story of the Cuban War* (Chicago, 1899).

4. The decisive French sources were Théophile Gautier, Théodore de Banville, the Parnasse, Baudelaire, and the symbolists, particularly Verlaine.

Even the American poets who were popular among us owed it partly to France, especially Poe, who had been praised and translated into French by Baudelaire and Mallarmé. But there were, of course, direct contacts between the United States and Hispanic America. Longfellow found many translators among us, including Bartolomé Mitre, Rafael Pombo, Rafael María Merchán, the Chilean Carlos Morla Vicuña (1846–1901), and the Mexican Joaquín Diego Casasús (1858–1916). The translation of Poe's *The Raven* by Pérez Bonalde and *The Bells* by the Guatemalan Domingo Estrada (*ca.* 1858–1901) enjoyed a wide diffusion. Martí, besides, wrote innumerable articles on American literature, and Varona a fine essay on Emerson. And there are many more examples of direct acquaintance with American literature in other writers. Cf. John Eugene Englekirk, *Edgar Allan Poe in Hispanic Literature* (New York, 1934), and John DeLancey Ferguson, *American Literature in Spain* (New York, 1916) — and my review, with many new data, in the *Revista de Filología Española*, VII (1920), 62–71.

Essays and books on poets and writers of foreign tongues were then, and are still, much more common in Spanish America than in Spain.

5. Cf. Chapter VI.

6. Manuel José Othón (1858–1906) unites romantic imagination and passion with classical finish in style. Several of his poems are vast frescoes of Mexican landscape. Salvador Díaz Mirón (1853–1928) began as a romantic poet in the declamatory manner of Victor Hugo; after his volume *Lascas* (1901) he adopted a complex and highly polished style, and then grew more and more exacting with the years. In his twenties and thirties he took an active part in politics, as a congressman; he also wrote two magnificent poems on political events, *Sursum* and *Voces interiores*. After 1892 his political activity becomes merely nominal. Francisco Asís de Icaza (1863–1925), who spent most of his life in Europe as a diplomat, especially in Spain, wrote delicate poetry of sentiment. He was also a well-known critic, and his book on the *Exemplary Novels* of Cervantes (1901) remained for many years the best on the subject. Almafuerte (pen name of Pedro Bonifacio Palacios, 1854–1917) was always an impetuous romantic in temper and in his carelessness regarding form, but his style was full of originality and novelty, now felicitous, now otherwise. Gastón Fer-

nando Deligne (1861–1913) had a keen philosophical mind and a crisp style, not averse to picturesque detail; a number of his poems may be called psychological short stories in verse and the most original of them is the story of a forgotten country-house invaded by wild plants. His brother Rafael Alfredo Deligne (1863–1902) wrote good poetry and very good prose. Francisco Gavidia (b. 1863), of El Salvador, well read in many literatures, wrote poems on Indian subjects and made experiments in metre which influenced his friend Rubén Darío.

In Spain, Manuel Reina, Ricardo Gil, and Salvador Rueda had begun to move away from romanticism around 1890, and Rueda may be counted as a *modernista* after he came in contact with Darío in 1892; but there was no general "movement" until after 1898.

7. On Casal, and the rest of the *modernistas*, cf. Isaac Goldberg, *Studies in Spanish American Literature* (New York, 1920), Cecil Knight Jones's essay in the collective work *Modern Hispanic America*, edited by Alva Curtis Wilgus (New York, 1933), and G. Dundas Craig, *The Modernist Trend in Spanish American Poetry*, with Spanish texts and English translations (University of California, 1934). In Spanish, Rufino Blanco Fombona, *El modernismo y los poetas modernistas* (Madrid, 1929), Roberto Meza Fuentes, *De Díaz Mirón a Rubén Darío* (Santiago de Chile, 1940), Arturo Torres Rioseco, *Precursores del modernismo* (Madrid, 1925), and Federico de Onís, introduction and critical notes to his *Antología de la poesía española e hispanoamericana* (1882–1932) (Madrid, 1934).

8. The famous *Nocturno* has been translated into English at least three times: by Muna Lee, in *Pan American Magazine*, May, 1928, by Margaret P. Ruscoe, in *Mexican Life*, July, 1926, and by Alice Jane MacVan, in the collective volume *Translations from Hispanic Poets* (New York: The Hispanic Society of America, 1938).

9. Cf. Nell Walker, *The Life and Works of Manuel Gutiérrez Nájera* (The University of Missouri Studies, 1927); Dorothy Schons, "An Interpretation of 'La Serenata de Schubert'" (a poem by Gutiérrez Nájera), with musical notations, in *Hispania*, XIX (1936), 437–440; Erwin K. Mapes, "The First Published Writings of Manuel Gutiérrez Nájera," in the *Hispanic Review*, V (1937), 225–240.

10. All these writers deserve special study, but space forbids it here. There are still others who merit attention — for instance, César Zumeta (b. 1860), Pedro Emilio Coll (b. 1872), and Luis Manuel Urbaneja Achelpohl (1874–1937), in Venezuela; Santiago Pérez Triana (1858–1916), Ismael Enrique Arciniegas (1865–1937), Cornelio Hispano (pen name of Ismael López, b. 1880), Julio Flórez (1869–1923), and Víctor Manuel Londoño (1876–1936), in Colombia; Américo Lugo (b. 1871), Fabio Fiallo (1866–1942), and Tulio Manuel Cestero

(b. 1877), in Santo Domingo; Luis Bonafoux (1855–1925), in Puerto Rico; Manuel Márquez Sterling (1872–1934), in Cuba; Clemente Palma (b. 1872), in Peru; Remigio Crespo Toral (1860–1939), in Ecuador; Franz Tamayo (b. 1879), in Bolivia; Manuel Ugarte, in Argentina; Alejandro Guanes, in Paraguay; Álvaro Armando Vasseur (b. 1878), in Uruguay; Balbino Dávalos (b. 1866), in Mexico; Alberto Masferrer (d. 1932), in El Salvador; Santiago Argüello (1871–1940), in Nicaragua; Juan Ramón Molina (1875–1908) and Froilán Turcios (1878–1943), in Honduras; Roberto Brenes Mesén (b. 1874), in Costa Rica; Darío Herrera (1871–1914), in Panama; Justo A. Facio (1859–1931), of Panama and Costa Rica. The women poets of this period will be mentioned in the last chapter.

11. A very small number of writers who belong to this period held important political posts and even became presidents: Cecilio Báez and Manuel Gondra in Paraguay, Francisco Henríquez y Carvajal in Santo Domingo, and Alfredo Baquerizo Moreno in Ecuador; they are true men of letters, but their writings deal mainly with social and political problems and have no direct connection with the *modernista* movement. In Puerto Rico, two men of letters, José de Diego (1868–1918) and Luis Muñoz Rivera (1859–1916), were the leaders of the political movement that demanded a measure of autonomy for the island and insisted upon preserving its Hispanic type of culture.

12. The chief books of Rubén Darío are *Azul*, verse and prose (Santiago de Chile, 1888); *Prosas profanas*, verse (Buenos Aires, 1896); *Los raros*, essays in criticism (Buenos Aires, 1896); *La España contemporánea*, "crónicas" and literary portraits (Paris, n. d. [1901]); *Peregrinaciones*, travel sketches (Paris, n. d. [1901]); *La caravana pasa*, "crónicas" (Paris, n. d. [1903]); *Tierras solares*, travel sketches (Madrid, 1904); *Cantos de vida y esperanza*, verse (Madrid, 1905); *Oda a Mitre*, verse (Paris, 1906); *Opiniones*, prose (Paris, n. d. [1906]); *El canto errante*, verse (Madrid, 1907); *El viaje a Nicaragua*, verse and prose (Madrid, 1909); *Poema del otoño y otros poemas*, verse (Madrid, 1910); *Canto a la Argentina*, verse (Buenos Aires, 1910). Three attempts have been made in Madrid to publish his *Obras completas*, but no collection is complete, or even carefully edited. Many scattered writings of his have been collected and published from time to time by Professor Erwin K. Mapes, Regino E. Boti, Raúl Silva Castro, Armando Donoso, Joaquín García Monge, Julio Saavedra Molina, and others. Many books about him have been published in Spanish; the most important are by José Enrique Rodó (Montevideo, 1899), Andrés González Blanco (Madrid, 1908), Tulio Manuel Cestero (Havana, 1916), Max Henríquez Ureña (Havana, 1918), Gustavo Alemán Bolaños (Guatemala, 1923), Leopoldo Lugones (Buenos Aires, 1919), Lauxar, pen name of Osvaldo Crispo Acosta (Monte-

video, 1924), Máximo Soto Hall (Buenos Aires, 1925), Guillermo Díaz Plaja (Barcelona, 1930), Francisco Contreras (Barcelona, 1930), Raúl Silva Castro (Santiago de Chile, 1930), Arturo Torres-Rioseco (Cambridge, Massachusetts, 1931), and Arturo Marasso (La Plata, 1934). In Portuguese: by Elisio de Carvalho (Rio de Janeiro, 1906). In French: Erwin K. Mapes, *L'influence française dans l'œuvre de Rubén Darío* (Paris, 1925). Articles by Juan Valera, in his *Cartas americanas*, vol. I (Madrid, 1899); Miguel Santos Oliver, in his *Hojas del sábado*, vol. II (Barcelona, 1918); Armando Donoso, in the review *Nosotros*, of Buenos Aires, 1919; Ventura García Calderón, in his *Semblanzas de América* (Madrid, 1919); Enrique Díez Canedo, in his *Conversaciones literarias* (Madrid, 1921).

English translations: *Eleven Poems*, by Thomas Walsh and Salomón de la Selva (New York, 1916); *Prosas profanas and other poems*, by Charles B. McMichael (New York, 1922); many other poems, in all the anthologies of Spanish and Spanish American poetry. On Darío, in English, cf. James Fitzmaurice-Kelly, *Some Masters of Spanish Verse* (Oxford, 1924); Elijah Clarence Hills, *Some Spanish American Poets* (1915), reprinted in his *Hispanic Studies* (Stanford University, 1929); Isaac Goldberg, in *The Bookman*, XLIX (1919), 563–568; S. Griswold Morley, in *The Dial*, LXII (1917), 509–511; G. W. Umphrey, in *Hispania*, II (1919), 64–81; E. K. Mapes, in *Publications of the Modern Language Association*, vol. XLIX (1934), and in *Philological Quarterly*, January, 1935. Cf., in addition, Henry Grattan Doyle, *A Bibliography of Rubén Darío* (Cambridge: Harvard University Press, 1935), and review by E. K. Mapes, in the *Hispanic Review*, IV (1936), 298–300.

13. It may seem surprising that at this very period of prosperity our men of letters should have become so pessimistic. There were particular causes, of course, in each case — for example, Casal and Silva — but there was a general cause too: these men found the situation of the writer suddenly diminished as soon as he ceased to take an active part in public life; they saw that their elders were still great national figures — Mitre and Miguel Antonio Caro and Justo Sierra and others — but that no such future lay ahead for them. Their elders, we know, did not attain their eminence solely as writers, and these young men were held in high esteem by their readers — in fact, literature still gives more prestige to a man in Hispanic America than in most other countries. But the shock due to the new situation was evidently great, and gave them a sense of frustration.

14. Aquileo Echeverría (1866–1909), of Costa Rica, with *Concherías*; Francisco Lazo Martí (1864–1912), of Venezuela, with his *Silva criolla*; Arturo Pellerano Castro (1865–1916), of Santo Do-

mingo, with his *Criollas* (1907); Elías Regules (1860–1929), of Uruguay, with his *Versitos criollos* (1893); *El Viejo Pancho*, pen name of José Alonso y Trelles (1860–1925), who was born in Spain but lived most of his life in Uruguay (his volume of poems *Paja brava*, 1916, has run into many editions); to them we may add the Chilean Carlos Pezoa Velis, already mentioned in the text, and the Venezuelan Udón Pérez (1868–1925), who also wrote poems on Indian subjects. In Brazil, Catulo Cearense, who writes delightfully in the dialect of Ceará. In a later group, the *criollo* subjects reappear under several guises in Miguel Andrés Camino (1877–1944), Evaristo Carriego (1883–1912), of Argentina, Luis Carlos López (b. 1883), of Colombia, Ramón López Velarde (1888–1921), of Mexico, Fernán Silva Valdés (b. 1887), of Uruguay, occasionally in Fernández Moreno (b. 1886) and Jorge Luis Borges (b. 1899), of Argentina, and in many others. Carriego describes the poor suburbs (*barrios*) of a large city, Buenos Aires; Luis Carlos López and Ramón López Velarde the small towns; the rest, both town and country.

The Indian and Negro subjects, so much in vogue these last twenty-five years, are parallel to but different from the *criollo* subjects. As a forerunner of the recent masters of Negro poetry in Cuba and Puerto Rico we may mention Candelario Obeso (1849–1884), of Colombia, whose *Cantos populares de mi tierra* appeared in 1877.

15. On the verse forms of the *modernistas*, cf. Lauxar, *Rubén Darío y José Enrique Rodó* (Montevideo, 1924), and my own book *La versificación irregular en la poesía castellana* (Madrid, 1920; second edition, 1933), chap. v, sections 12 to 17.

16. Cf. Isaac Goldberg, *Brazilian Literature*.

17. English translation of Rodó: *Ariel*, by F. J. Stimson, with an introduction (Boston and New York, 1922); *Motives of Proteus*, by Ángel Flores (New York, 1928). Cf. articles by Havelock Ellis, in his book *The Philosophy of Conflict* (London, 1919), and Isaac Goldberg, in his *Studies in Spanish American Literature*. In Spanish, cf. books by Gonzalo Zaldumbide (first in *Revue Hispanique*, 1918; later reprinted separately several times: the latest such reprint appearing in the volume *Montalvo y Rodó*, New York, 1938), Víctor Pérez Petit (Montevideo, 1918), Max Henríquez Ureña (Havana, 1918) and Lauxar (Montevideo, 1924). The volume *Rodó y sus críticos*, edited by Hugo Barbagelata (Paris, 1920), contains appreciations by Unamuno, Juan Valera, Clarín (Leopoldo Alas), Rubén Darío, Francisco García Calderón, Ricardo Rojas, Jesús Castellanos, Francis de Miomandre, Camille Le Senne, and others. Cf. also, Ventura García Calderón, in his *Semblanzas de América*, Federico García Godoy, in his books *La hora que pasa* (Santo Domingo, 1910), *De aquí y de allá* (Santo Domingo, 1916), and *Americanismo literario* (Madrid, n. d.

[1918]), Rufino Blanco Fombona, in his book *Grandes escritores de América* (Madrid, 1917), and my own lecture "La obra de José Enrique Rodó," in *Conferencias del Ateneo de la Juventud* (Mexico City, 1910).

18. Eduardo Prado's book *A ilusão americana* was printed in 1895, but the Brazilian government did not allow it to circulate. In 1902, after the author's death, it was given to the public.

19. See Oliveira Lima's *Pan americanismo* (Rio de Janeiro, 1907); *América latina e América inglesa* (Rio de Janeiro, n. d.). His book *The Evolution of Brazil* was translated by Percy Alvin Martin (Stanford University, 1914). Professor Martin also translated the *History of Brazil* written by another Brazilian scholar, João Pandiá Calogeras (New York, 1939).

20. A minor replica of the Brazilian tragedy of Canudos happened in the north of Mexico in the last decade of the nineteenth century. The story was told in *Tomóchic* (1894) by Heriberto Frías (1870–1928), himself one of the cadets who took part in the attack against the fanatics. Euclides da Cunha did not personally take part in the Canudos campaign – he went there as a journalist; but he had also received a military education.

21. Euclides da Cunha, although a military engineer by profession, chose the career of journalist. As such he described the Canudos campaign, on which he wrote afterwards his great book. His diary of the campaign was published in 1939. Another of his books is a study of *Castro Alves e seu tempo* (Rio de Janeiro, 1908). A translation of *Os sertões* into English by Samuel Putnam, with introduction and notes, has just been published under the title *Rebellion in the Backlands* by the University of Chicago Press (1944). R. B. Cunninghame Graham's book, *A Brazilian Mystic* (New York, 1925), is largely based on *Os sertões*.

22. There are already collections of *Obras completas* of Ingenieros and Korn, published in Argentina.

The philosophical movement grows in the next generation with such men as Francisco García Calderón (b. 1883) and Víctor Andrés Belaúnde (b. 1883) in Peru, Antonio Caso (b. 1883) and José Vasconcelos (b. 1881) in Mexico, Francisco Romero in Argentina.

Many of the younger men, born since 1900, are devoting their efforts to philosophy, both to original research and to criticism of classical and modern thought.

In this period there is practically no religious literature. The last classicists and the romantics who had not lost their faith still wrote religious poetry (for example, José Joaquín Pesado, José Eusebio Caro, and Gertrudis Gómez de Avellaneda). Among the poets of the first group of *modernistas*, Gutiérrez Nájera, Casal, and Darío invoke God when in distress; afterwards, even the name of God disappears from poetry. The one important exception is Amado Nervo, not a very orthodox Catholic, since his belief took a strong Oriental hue, but at least a Christian. Cf. Esther Turner Wellman, *Amado Nervo: Mexico's Religious Poet* (New York, 1937), Elijah Clarence Hills, in *Hispania*, December, 1941, and John Eugene Englekirk, in *New Mexican Quarterly*, II (1932), 53–65; translations: *Plenitude*, by William F. Rice (Los Angeles, 1928), *Confessions of a Modern Poet*, by Dorothy Margaret Kress (Boston, 1935); many anthologies. In recent years, a few poets have revived religious subjects — for example, Francisco Luis Bernárdez, in Argentina, and Jorge de Lima, in Brazil.

23. Larreta's *La gloria de Don Ramiro* has been translated into English by L. B. Walton (New York, 1924). There is a French translation by Remy de Gourmont.

Cf. Amado Alonso, *Ensayo sobre la novela histórica* (Buenos Aires, 1943). Among the authors of historical or epical novels, we may recall Pedro César Dominici (b. 1872), of Venezuela, whose *Dionisos* is laid in Greece, and Ángel de Estrada (1872–1923), of Argentina, who drew his subjects from classical antiquity or from the Middle Ages or the Renaissance.

24. Raul Pompeia (1863–1895), the author of *O Atheneu* (1898), an autobiographical novel of college life, is also counted in the first group of Brazilian "naturalists," although he is rather a somber psychologist and a master of poetical description. The second group of "naturalists" includes Henrique Coelho Netto (1864–1934), José Joaquim de Medeiros e Albuquerque (1867–1934), and Xavier Marques (b. 1861). José Pereira de Graça Aranha (1868–1931) belongs to the same generation, but a new type of novel begins with his work (see next chapter).

Aluizio de Azevedo's *O cortiço* (1890) has been translated into English by Harry W. Brown under the title *A Brazilian Tenement* (New York, 1926).

25. The first group of *modernistas* essayed the novel, but without persistence. Martí wrote in his youth *Amistad funesta* and made an abridged translation of Helen Hunt Jackson's *Ramona*, improving the style of the original. Rubén Darío, when barely twenty, wrote *Emelina* (1887) in Chile, in collaboration with Eduardo Poirier; much later he began, but never finished, *El hombre de oro* and *Oro de Mallorca*. Silva lost in a shipwreck the only novel he wrote. In the second group of *modernistas* they were more assiduous — most of the work of Larreta, Reyles, Quiroga, Díaz Rodríguez, and Urbaneja Achelpohl, and part of that of Lugones, Blanco Fombona, Nervo, Cestero, and Clemente Palma, is in fiction. English translations: short stories by Lugones, Quiroga and others, in *Tales from the Argentine*, translated by Anita

Brenner (New York, 1930); Horacio Quiroga's *South American Jungle Tales*, by Arthur Livingston (New York, 1922; reprinted 1942); Reyles' *Castanets* (original title, *El embrujo de Sevilla*), by Jacques LeClercq (New York, 1929), Blanco Fombona's *The Man of Gold*, by Isaac Goldberg (New York, 1920). There are also French translations of Lugones, Quiroga, Reyles, and Blanco Fombona.

26. The outstanding names in the history of our realistic novel, after the period of Blest Gana and Cuéllar, are, in Mexico, José López Portillo y Rojas (1850–1923), Rafael Delgado (1853–1914), Federico Gamboa (1864–1939), in whom there is some influence of the *modernista* taste, and Emilio Rabasa (1856–1930), far more distinguished as a writer on political science (in his constitutional history of Mexico, *La Constitución y la dictadura*, 1912, political doctrines move and face one another like characters in a novel); in Cuba, Nicolás Heredia (born in Santo Domingo, *ca.* 1849–1901) and Carlos Loveira (1882–1928); in Puerto Rico, Manuel Zeno Gandía (1855–1930); in Venezuela, Gonzalo Picón Febres (1860–1918), Manuel Vicente Romerogarcía, and Miguel Eduardo Pardo (1865–1905); in Colombia, Lorenzo Marroquín (1856–1918), and Tomás Carrasquilla (1858–1940); in Peru, Clorinda Matto de Turner (see chap. vi, notes 32 and 36), Mercedes Cabello de Carbonera (*ca.* 1847–1909), who also wrote essays on the modern art of fiction (1892) and on Tolstoy; in Chile, Luis Orrego Luco (b. 1866), Baldomero Lillo (1867–1923), Federico Gana (1867–1926), and Emilio Rodríguez Mendoza (b. 1873); in Uruguay, Eduardo Acevedo Díaz (1851–1921) and Javier de Viana (1872–1927); in Argentina, besides Cambaceres and Payró, Lucio Vicente López (1848–1893), José Miró (1867–1896), who wrote under the pseudonym of Julián Martel the once famous novel *La bolsa*, on the financial crisis of 1890, Carlos María Ocantos (b. 1860), Manuel Podestá (1853–1920), Francisco Sicardi (1856–1927), Martiniano Leguizamón (1858–1935), and José Sixto Álvarez, better known by his pen name Fray Mocho (1858–1903). Viana and Fray Mocho, like Magón, of Costa Rica (pen name of Manuel González Zeledón, 1864–1936), wrote mainly short stories.

English translations: Lorenzo Marroquín's *Pax* (1907), by Isaac Goldberg and W. V. Schierbrand (New York, 1920).

There is a study in English on one of these novelists: *Carlos María Ocantos*, by Theodore Andersson (Yale University Press, 1934). Cf., besides, Dillwyn F. Ratcliff, *Venezuelan Prose Fiction* (New York, 1933).

27. Leguizamón's *Calandria* (1896) was translated into English and published by the Hispanic Society of America (New York, 1932).

28. English translations: *Three Plays of the Argentine*, translated by Jacob S. Fassett, with an introduction by Edward Hale Bierstadt (New York, 1920); the plays included are Silverio Manco's *Juan Moreira*,

Luis Bayón Herrera's *Santos Vega* — not the old circus play by Nosiglia — and Julio Sánchez Gardel's *The Witches' Mountain*, a great success of 1912.

Cf., Ruth Richardson, *Florencio Sánchez and the Argentine Theatre* (New York, 1933); Madaline Wallis Nichols, "The Argentine Theatre," in *Bulletin Hispanique*, XLII (1940), 39–53; Cyrus Townsend Brady, Jr., "Lively Theatre in Buenos Aires," and Edith R. Isaacs, "Argentine Drama," in *Theatre Arts Monthly*, May, 1939; Willis Knapp Jones, " 'La gringa' Theme in River Plate Drama" (*La gringa* is a play — 1904 — by Florencio Sánchez), in *Hispania*, XXV (1942), 326–332.

The plays of Florencio Sánchez may be divided into two classes: rural and urban; the rural are the best, and include *Barranca abajo* (*Down the Hill*), *La gringa*, and *M'hijo el dotor*, his first success (1903); the urban plays include *En familia* (1905), *Los muertos* (1905), *Los derechos de la salud* (1907), and *Nuestros hijos* (1907).

Other interesting Uruguayan dramatists were Ernesto Herrera (1887–1917), author of *El león ciego* and *La moral de Misia Paca*, and Samuel Blixen (1869–1911), who was also a good critic.

The leading dramatists of the Argentine group are Martín Coronado (1850–1919), a good romantic poet whose rural plays are in verse; Payró, the novelist; Gregorio de Laferrere (1867–1913), who wrote the best comedies; Enrique García Velloso (1880–1938); Julio Sánchez Gardel (1879–1937); Emilio Berisso (1878–1922), César Iglesias Paz (d. 1922), José León Pagano (b. 1875), Roberto Gache (b. 1892), and José Antonio Saldías (b. 1891). The Italian dramatist Dario Niccodemi (1874–1934) spent part of his youth in Buenos Aires, where he wrote dramatic criticism during the early years of this century, and gave to the stage his first play (in Spanish), *Duda suprema* (1900).

On the Teatro del Pueblo, in which the *régisseur* is a writer, Leónidas Barletta (b. 1902), cf. John Erskine, "The People's Theatre," in the magazine *Tomorrow*, March, 1943. Recent dramatists include Samuel Eichelbaum (b. 1894), the poet and humorist Conrado Nalé Roxlo (b. 1898), and Román Gómez Masía, whose *El Señor no está en casa* is a good theological-socialistic farce in the manner of Bernard Shaw.

During the last half of the nineteenth century Mexico, besides the traditional religious play (which survives also in Peru, in Central America, and other places, including New Mexico), had a sort of folk drama in which the main characters were outlaws, as in Argentina — *Chucho el Roto* was the most popular of them. But this drama did not develop into a national theatre.

Many efforts have been made by men of letters in most countries of Hispanic America to create a stable "national drama," organizing dramatic companies and special seasons (cf. Rodolfo Usigli, *Caminos del teatro en México*, Mexico, 1933, and Antonio Magaña Esquivel, *Imagen del teatro*, Mexico, 1940). So far, only Brazil approaches the River

Plate countries in its development, having permanently progressed beyond the phase of those short farces, with or without music, that exist practically everywhere. In Brazil the drama has maintained itself with a measure of assured success since the times of Martins Penna. The outstanding names are Joaquim José da França, the younger (1838–1890), Agrario de Menezes (1834–1863), Arthur Azevedo (1855–1908), Valentin Magalhães (1859–1903), Claudio de Souza, Oduvaldo Vianna, and Jovacy Camargo. The novelists Alencar, Macedo, Aluizio de Azevedo, and Coelho Netto were also successful dramatists. Cf. Lafayette Silva, *Historia do teatro brasileiro* (Rio de Janeiro, 1938).

NOTES TO CHAPTER 8

1. Two anecdotes — it is said that in Colombia, during a presidential election, two rival parades were ready to come to blows in front of the house of the poet Guillermo Valencia, who was one of the candidates, when they were appeased by the demand, made by a voice from the crowd, that he read one of his famous poems — a demand with which he complied. The story may be fanciful, but it is typical. I can vouch for the truth of the other anecdote. In commercial Buenos Aires, Fernández Moreno bought a house in 1940, and both the real estate agent and the firm that undertook the cleaning and disinfection of the building declined to collect their accounts because the buyer was a well-known poet.

2. To this transitional generation belong the essayist Ricardo Rojas (b. 1882), the philosopher Francisco Romero (b. 1891), the poets Evaristo Carriego, Enrique Banchs (b. 1888), Arturo Capdevila (b. 1889), Baldomero Fernández Moreno (b. 1886), Rafael Alberto Arrieta (b. 1889), Oliverio Girondo (b. 1891), and Alfonsina Storni (1892–1938), the literary critics Roberto Fernando Giusti (b. 1887) and Julio Noé (b. 1893), the novelists Benito Lynch (b. 1885), Ricardo Güiraldes (1886–1927), Manuel Gálvez (b. 1882), and Alberto Gerchunoff (b. 1884), who is also a distinguished journalist, and the very original essayist and poet Ezequiel Martínez Estrada, in Argentina (b. 1895); the dramatist Ernesto Herrera, the poets Delmira Agustini (1887–1914), Juana de Ibarbourou (b. 1895), Fernán Silva Valdés, Emilio Oribe (b. 1893), and Carlos Sabat Ercasty (b. 1887), the socialist orator and poet Emilio Frugoni (b. 1880), in Uruguay; the historian Efraim Cardoso and the poets Eloy Fariña Núñez (1885–1929) and Juan Emiliano O'Leary (b. 1880), in Paraguay; Gabriela Mistral (b. 1889), the fanciful novelist and poet Pedro Prado (b. 1886), the literary critics Armando Donoso (b. 1887) and Hernán Díaz Arrieta (b. 1891), the novelists Eduardo Barrios (b. 1884), Mariano Latorre (b.

1886), Jenaro Prieto (b. 1889), and Joaquín Edwards Bello (b. 1888), the poet Pablo de Rokha (pen name of Carlos Díaz Loyola, b. 1894), in Chile; the novelists Alcides Arguedas (b. 1879) and Armando Chirveches (1883–1926) and the poets Gregorio Reynolds (b. 1882) and José Eduardo Guerra (1893–1943), in Bolivia; the brothers Francisco and Ventura García Calderón, Víctor Andrés Belaúnde, Abraham Valdelomar (1888–1919), author of picturesque short stories on native subjects, the poets José María Eguren (1882–1942), José Gálvez (b. 1885), and Alberto Hidalgo (b. 1897), the novelist Angélica Palma (1883–1935), the historian of literature José de la Riva Agüero (1885–1944), the essayists José Carlos Mariátegui (1891–1930), and Luis Alberto Sánchez (b. 1900), in Peru; the literary critic Gonzalo Zaldumbide (b. 1885) and the poet Medardo Ángel Silva (1898–1919), in Ecuador; the novelist José Eustasio Rivera (1888–1928), the poets Luis Carlos López, Rafael Maya (b. 1898), León de Greiff (b. 1895), and Miguel Ángel Osorio (ca. 1883–1942), known under the pen names Ricardo Arenales and Porfirio Barba Jacob, the essayist Luis López de Mesa (b. 1884), in Colombia; the poets Alfredo Arvelo Larriva (1883–1934) and J. T. Arreaza Calatrava, the novelists José Rafael Pocaterra (b. 1890) and Rómulo Gallegos (b. 1884), in Venezuela; the poets Salomón de la Selva (b. 1893), who published in English his first book of poems, *Tropical Town* (New York, 1919), Rafael Heliodoro Valle (b. 1891), and Rafael Arévalo Martínez (b. 1884), also a novelist of a most unusual type, and the essayist Omar Dengo (1888–1928), in Central America; Octavio Méndez Pereira (b. 1887) and Ricardo Miró (1883–1940), in Panama; Ramón López Velarde, the poet and essayist Alfonso Reyes (b. 1889), the philosophers Antonio Caso and José Vasconcelos, the archaeologist Alfonso Caso (b. 1896), the novelists Carlos González Peña (b. 1885), José Rubén Romero (b. 1890), Genaro Estrada (1887–1937) and Martín Luis Guzmán (b. 1887), the essayists Julio Torri (b. 1889) and Antonio Castro Leal, the historian of art Manuel Toussaint, in Mexico; the subtle essayist Francisco José Castellanos (1892–1920), the poets Mariano Brull (b. 1891), Agustín Acosta (b. 1887), and Juan Marinello (b. 1899), the novelists Jesús Castellanos (1879–1912) and Alfonso Hernández Catá (1885–1940), the essayists José María Chacón y Calvo (b. 1893), Jorge Mañach (b. 1898), and Félix Lizaso (b. 1891), in Cuba; the poets Olegario Marianno (b. 1889), Filipe d'Oliveira (1891–1933), Raul de Leoni (1895–1926), Guilherme de Almeida (b. 1890), Alvaro Moreyra, Menotti del Picchia (b. 1892), the poet and critic Ronald de Carvalho (1893–1935), the literary critics Alcides Maya (1878–1944) and Agrippino Grieco (b. 1888), the essayists Jackson de Figueiredo (1891–1928) and Renato Almeida, the short-story writer Humberto de Campos (1886–1934), the novelists Alfonso Henriques de Lima Barreto (1881–1922), Afranio Peixoto (b. 1876), and Monteiro Lobato (b. 1883), the philosopher Tristão de Athayde (pen name of Alceu Amoroso Lima, b. 1893), and the *cronista* João do Rio (pen name of Paulo Barreto, 1881–1921), in Brazil.

3. The sonnet "Tuércele el cuello al cisne" of González Martínez appears, in an English translation by John Peale Bishop, on the first page of the *Anthology of Contemporary Latin American Poetry* edited by Dudley Fitts. Several poets mentioned in this chapter are represented in that collection.

González Martínez had a large following in Mexico between 1915 and 1925, among the poets who were young then.

Similar to González Martínez in their tendencies are Magallanes Moure, of Chile, already mentioned in the last chapter, and Rafael Alberto Arrieta, of Argentina.

On most of the poets mentioned in this chapter, cf. the excellent critical notes of Federico de Onís in his *Antología*.

4. The Cuban Juana Borrero (1877–1896) wrote two exquisite poems ("¿Quieres sondear la noche . . .?" and "Yo he soñado en mis lúgubres noches . . .") amid much indifferent verse. Her sister Dulce María Borrero (1883–1945), with less intensity, attained a more finished style, and her *Nueva vida* is one of the rare poems which succeed in the expression of a joyful emotion. But Juana died very young and Dulce María wrote very little after her single book of poems (1912), so the part they played in the literary movement is very restricted.

The Mexican poetess María Enriqueta Camarillo de Pereyra (b. 1875), who signs María Enriqueta, began to publish when nearly thirty. Her work is uneven; in her best poems (*Paisaje*; *Sendero olvidado*) she reaches a somber depth with very simple means.

In Brazil, Francisca Julia (1874–1920) became a disciple of the Parnassians.

5. María Eugenia Vaz Ferreira (1875–1924), in her style at least, strove to attain serenity and with a feigned Parnassian calm drew the portrait of her ideal of manly strength (*El cazador de estrellas*). But her solitary life broke forth at last into lament and protest, envying the happy who can still dream. Delmira Agustini was the first who spoke frankly and freely of passion; her exalted youthful temperament made her life a tragedy. Alfonsina Storni was original and uneven; one of the signs of her originality was her habit of analyzing (in verse) men she happened to see in the street, inferring the soul from the body; there is another sign in her *Versos a la tristeza de Buenos Aires*, in which she discloses the invincible sadness of the proud city that, according to Lugones, "with each golden day approached a new happiness." Juana de Ibarbourou, the youngest of the group, began her

literary career as a happy rebel — her poetry had the youthful freshness of an untrammelled life; but the passing of time brought her the melancholy of *El afilador* — the day, with its whetstone and its twelve silver knives, that cuts her wings.

There are hundreds of followers of these poets, especially in Argentina and Uruguay; at the same time, new types of women have appeared in our literature: Victoria Ocampo, Silvina Ocampo, María Rosa Lida, Nora Lange, Margarita Abella Caprile, María Alicia Domínguez, María de Villarino, and María Rosa Oliver, in Argentina; Sara de Ibáñez and Selva Márquez, in Uruguay; Amanda Labarca, Ana M. Berry (who has written several books in English and published them in London), María Luisa Bombal, Marta Brunet, and Magdalena Petit, in Chile; Rosa Arciniega and Magda Portal, in Peru; María Villar Buceta, Carolina Poncet, Lydia Cabrera, and Dulce María Loynaz, in Cuba; Camila Henríquez Ureña, in Santo Domingo; the delightful novelist Teresa de la Parra (1891–1936), and Enriqueta Arvelo Larriva, in Venezuela; Rachel de Queiroz, Cecilia Meirelles, Lidia Besouchet, Carolina Nabuco, Lucia Miguel Pereyra, Heloisa Alberto Torres, and Adalgisa Nery, in Brazil.

6. Ricardo Rojas published in 1909 his book *La restauración nacionalista*, which deals mainly with public education; in 1916, *La argentinidad* (he coined the word); from 1917 to 1922 his history of *La literatura argentina*; in 1924, *Eurindia* (another word he coined, from "European" and "Indian"), an "essay on aesthetics"; in 1927, *El Cristo invisible* (there is an English translation by W. E. Browning, New York, 1930); in 1933 his biography of San Martín, *El santo de la espada*; in 1942, *Archipiélago*, written in Tierra del Fuego, in 1934, when he was imprisoned as a leader of the opposition; his biography of Sarmiento is soon to be given to the press. The subjects of most of his works are drawn from South America and especially from Argentina — for instance, his short stories in *El país de la selva* (1907) and his plays *Ollántay* (1939) and *La Salamanca* (1943). His devotion to Spain, besides, is shown in his book *El alma española* (1908) and *Retablo español* (1938).

Cf. J. A. Mackay, *The Other Spanish Christ* (London, 1932).

7. Cf. *La Reforma Universitaria*, edited by Gabriel del Mazo, 6 vols. (Buenos Aires, 1926–1927; second edition, in 3 vols., La Plata, 1941).

8. The best known members of the Ateneo are Antonio Caso, Alfonso Reyes, José Vasconcelos, Martín Luis Guzmán, Carlos González Peña, Mariano Silva Aceves, Julio Torri (cf. note 2 of this chapter), the composer Manuel M. Ponce, the architects Jesús Tito Acevedo (*ca.* 1880–1918) and Federico E. Mariscal, and the painters Diego Rivera and Ángel Zárraga. The poet González Martínez, though of an older

generation, joined the society. Several members have been active in politics, especially Vasconcelos, Isidro Fabela, Alfonso Cravioto, and Alberto J. Pani, the first president of the Universidad Popular (the second and last was Dr. Alfonso Pruneda). The present writer, though not a native of Mexico, also belonged to the Ateneo, was the first secretary of the Universidad Popular and, before that, a member of the staff of *El Antireeleccionista*, the organ of the party that opposed the reëlection of Porfirio Díaz and eventually elected Madero president; the paper was suppressed by the Díaz government in 1910. Cf. my article "The Revolution in Intellectual Life," in *Survey Graphic*, May, 1924, and, in Spanish, Alfonso Reyes, *Pasado inmediato* (Mexico, 1941).

9. Similar to Haya de la Torre in his philosophical education and in his style is the Mexican labor leader Vicente Lombardo Toledano (b. 1894).

On the connection between literature and politics in Peru, cf. José Carlos Mariátegui's *Siete ensayos de interpretación de la realidad peruana* (Lima, 1928) and Luis Alberto Sánchez, last chapter of *La literatura del Perú* (Buenos Aires, 1939).

10. It is significant that few writers of the first rank, among those born after 1880, belong to conservative parties. As one of the exceptions we may recall José de la Riva Agüero, who has been a member of the cabinet in Peru. I do not count diplomatic posts as political; it is not unusual for a diplomat to hold political opinions which differ, to a greater or lesser extent, from those of the government he represents.

11. Banchs published four books of poems from his nineteenth to his twenty-third year and then ceased to write for the public — a problem that intrigues his many admirers to this day. Around 1928, however, he gave to the daily *La Prensa*, in which he edits a page for children, four sonnets in which, without giving up his accustomed mastery of form, he vents romantic emotions (especially in "Si en el mar de la vida soy estela . . .").

12. Ramón López Velarde died when he had published only two books of poems. He also wrote excellent prose and good criticism, which appear in the posthumous collection of his works.

On Herrera, cf. Thomas Walsh, "Julio Herrera y Reissig, a Disciple of Poe," in *Poet Lore*, XXXIII (1922), 601–607.

13. Our new movement was, of course, part of an international movement that includes expressionism, surrealism, and many minor tendencies. Cf., for instance, Mr. Edmund Wilson's *Axel's Castle* (New York, 1931) on important aspects of the movement in English and French, and Mr. C. M. Bowra's *The Heritage of Symbolism*, on five European poets (London and New York, 1943). For Spain, and partly

Spanish America, Guillermo de Torre's *Literaturas europeas de van-guardia* (Madrid, 1925).

14. Vicente Huidobro (b. 1893) has published books in verse and in prose, both in Spanish and in French. Two of his works have been translated into English and published in New York and London; *Mirror of a Mage* [Cagliostro] (1926), and *Portrait of a Paladin* [the Cid] (1929). On his poetry, cf. Henry Alfred Holmes, "The Creationism of Vicente Huidobro," in *The Spanish Review*, March, 1934.

15. Cf. the essay of Alfonso Reyes on "Las jitanjáforas" (1929), in his volume *La experiencia literaria* (Buenos Aires, 1942).

16.   I shall say to my soft cloud:
        Hound of my thought, return to the river.
        Walk back over thy foams.
        Die in the dew,   •
        in the gold, in the blood and in the cold.

17. It was while this movement was in full swing that José Ortega y Gasset wrote his famous essay on what he called "dehumanized art," including, of course, all forms of art and not merely literature.

18. Nativism was, naturally, more common in fiction than in poetry; even during the romantic period, we know, while the drama often drew its plots from the history or the legends of the Old World, the novel generally preferred the local subjects.

Besides Madrid, the two centers of the "vanguard" movement in Spanish were Buenos Aires, with Borges (b. 1899), Güiraldes, Girondo, Francisco Luis Bernárdez (b. 1900), Leopoldo Marechal (b. 1900), and Ricardo Molinari (b. 1898), and Mexico, with Carlos Pellicer (b. 1897), Jaime Torres Bodet (b. 1902), José Gorostiza (b. 1901), Enrique González Rojo (1899–1939), Bernardo Ortiz de Montellano (b. 1899), Salvador Novo (b. 1904), Xavier Villaurrutia (b. 1903), and the branch of the *estridentistas* Manuel Maples Arce (b. 1898) and Germán List Arzubide; Octavio Paz (b. 1914), among many others, belongs to a later group.

Brazil is a world by itself, and maintains a much slighter connection with Portugal than Spanish America with Spain (besides, since the civil war of 1936 the majority of the best Spanish writers live in the New World). In recent years, as many as six literary cities may be counted in Brazil, from north to south: Belem do Para, San Salvador de Bahia, Recife de Pernambuco, Rio de Janeiro, São Paulo, and Porto Alegre in Rio Grande do Sul. Rio de Janeiro and São Paulo are the leading centers.

The leading Brazilian poets of the groups that appeared after 1922 are, together with Manuel Bandeira and Mario de Andrade, Jorge de Lima, Murilo Mendes, Oswald de Andrade, Raul Bopp, Cecilia Meirelles, Ribeiro Couto, Carlos Drummond de Andrade, Adalgisa Nery, and the youngest of the masters Augusto Frederico Schmidt. Cf. "La moderna poesía brasileña," by Vinicius de Moraes, himself one of the best of the young poets, in the magazine *Sur*, of Buenos Aires, September, 1942.

19. On Neruda, cf. Amado Alonso, *Poesía y estilo de Pablo Neruda* (Buenos Aires, 1940).

20. A clear notion of the contrast may be drawn, in Brazil itself, from a comparison between Euclides da Cunha's *Os sertões* (mentioned in the seventh chapter) and Gilberto Freyre's *Casa-grande e senzala* (mentioned in the second) or his *Sobrados e mucambos* or his *Nordeste*, or else the sociological studies of Arthur Ramos. Both Freyre and Ramos have outgrown what may be called "the nineteenth-century mentality" on race.

21. Graça Aranha's *Canaan* was translated into English by Mariano J. Lorente (Boston, 1920), with a preface by Guglielmo Ferrero. Cf. Ernesto Montenegro's article on it in the *New York Times Book Review*, June 1, 1923 (in the same magazine there are other articles by Montenegro on Hispanic American literature: see especially issues of February 18, 1923; March 9, 1924; June 7, 1925; June 10, 1928; and March 30, 1941).

22. Rudyard Kipling, *Brazilian Sketches*, collected in a volume (London and New York, 1941).

23. Cf. Stuart Chase, *Mexico*, written in collaboration with Marian Tyler (New York, 1935), and Robert Redfield, *Tepoztlan* (Chicago, 1930).

24. A fine example among many: Miguel Asturias, *Leyendas guatemaltecas*; there is a French translation with a preface by Paul Valéry. Antonio Mediz Bolio's *The Land of the Pheasant and the Deer*, based on Maya traditions, has appeared in English translation (Mexico City, 1935). Drama in native languages exists in Mexico, too, especially in Yucatan..

Many more examples may be found among Peruvian writers, in the stories of Valdelomar, Enrique López Albújar (b. 1872), Luis Eduardo Valcárcel (b. 1891), Ernesto Reyna, Ventura García Calderón (whose volume of tales *La venganza del cóndor*, 1924, has been translated into English by Richard Phibbs under the title *The White Llama*, London, 1938), and in the poems of Alejandro Peralta (b. 1899), Guillermo Mercado (b. 1900), Gamaliel Churata, Eustakio Aweranka, and Luis Fabio Xammar (b. 1911). Churata and Aweranka write in both Spanish and native languages. There is, besides, the more militant literature of César Vallejo (1895–1938), César Falcón, Serafín Delmar, and Ciro Alegría (b. 1909).

In Paraguay, also, there are men of letters who use both Spanish and their native Guarani in poetry (Juan Natalicio González, a well-known historian and essayist; Manuel Ortiz Guerrero, Narciso Colman) and in drama (Julio Correa).

Even in Argentina there is a literature on the Indians and *mestizos* of the northwestern part of the country (Juan Carlos Dávalos, Pablo Rojas Paz, Fausto Burgos, Carlos B. Quiroga, Rafael Jijena Sánchez).

25. The most important poets (the majority of whom are white) of the *poesía negra* are, in Puerto Rico, Luis Palés Matos (who is said to have started the movement) and Tomás Blanco; in Cuba, Nicolás Guillén, Emilio Ballagas, José Zacarías Tallet (b. 1893), Rafael Esténger (b. 1899), Alejo Carpentier (b. 1904), Regino Pedroso (b. 1897), Ramón Guirao (b. 1908), José Antonio Portuondo (b. 1911), Marcelino Arozarena (b. 1912), and Vicente Gómez Kemp (b. 1914); in Santo Domingo, Manuel del Cabral and Tomás Hernández Franco.

Some of their poems appear in English translations in the recent anthologies mentioned in the bibliography at the end of this book. Nicolás Guillén's *Velorio de Papá Montero*, translated by Langston Hughes, appears in the *Anthology of Contemporary Latin American Poetry* edited by Dudley Fitts; six more of his poems have been translated by H. R. Hays in his anthology *Twelve Spanish American Poets*.

In Brazil there is no "movement" of *poesía negra*, but there is very good poetry on Negro subjects by Menotti del Picchia (*Juca Mulato*, 1917), Jorge de Lima, Mario de Andrade, and Cassiano Ricardo. There are a few poets elsewhere interested in the subject — e.g., Ildefonso Pereda Valdés in Uruguay.

26. "Indian, you till the land for a master. Do you not know that it ought to be yours, because of your blood and the sweat of your face? Do you not know that greed deprived you of it, centuries ago? Do you not know that you are the master?" "Perhaps, who knows!"

Aimé F. Tschiffely, the well-known traveler who rode on horseback from Buenos Aires to Washington (on the Argentine horses Mancha and Gato), describes the attitude of the Indians in his recent book *Coricancha* (London, 1943): "Indians continue to sit in their huts, listening intently, hoping and praying that the second part of their forefathers' prophecy as to ultimate deliverance from white men, will be fulfilled."

27. César Vallejo is considered "essentially Indian" by his Peruvian admirers, although the subjects of his poems are not predominantly Indian. His poetry expresses the old sadness of native life far more frequently than the protest against oppression. But he is frankly militant in his novel *Tungsteno* (1930). He visited the Soviet Republics and wrote there a book entitled *Rusia en 1931*. The last poems he wrote were on the Spanish civil war (*España, aparta de mí este cáliz*). Cf. Edna Worthley Underwood, "César Vallejo," in *The West Indian Review*, July, 1939.

Poems of Vallejo, Carrera Andrade (b. 1903) and Fombona Pachano (b. 1901) appear with English translations in H. R. Hays's anthology *Twelve Spanish American Poets*.

On the Indianist poets, cf. Aída Cometta Manzoni, *El indio en la poesía de América española*.

A very interesting addition to the Indianist militancy was that of the great Spanish novelist and poet Ramón del Valle-Inclán (1869–1936) with his poem *Nos vemos*, written in Mexico in 1921 (with the admonition: "Hang the *encomendero!*"), and his novel of political life in Spanish America *Tirano Banderas* (1926; English translation, New York, 1929), in which the characters speak a cleverly contrived "synthetic Spanish American language," mixing Cuban, Mexican, Argentine, and other forms of local speech.

28. Azuela's *Los de abajo* was translated into English by Enrique Munguía under the title *The Under Dogs* and published in New York, 1929. It has been translated also into French, German, Czech, Russian, Yiddish, Portuguese, and Japanese. His *Mala yerba* was translated by Anita Brenner under the title of *Marcela* and published in New York, 1932.

The Eagle and the Serpent (1928), by Martín Luis Guzmán (b. 1887), translated by Harriet de Onís (New York, 1930), is often mistaken for a novel but it is really a brilliant and amazing record of the actual experiences of the author during the revolt of Carranza against the usurper Huerta; all the events and the names are strictly historical. Guzmán afterwards wrote a novel, *La sombra del caudillo*, and the *Memorias de Pancho Villa*. He has been translated into French, German, Dutch, and Czech, besides English.

There are many other novels on the Mexican Revolution, written by José Rubén Romero, Xavier Icaza, Gregorio López y Fuentes, Rafael Muñoz, José Mancisidor, and the Nicaraguan Hernán Robleto (and plays by Mauricio Magdaleno and Juan Bustillo Oro). After the Revolution became wholly a thing of the past, these authors turned their attention to different subjects, such as the "reconstruction" that was the logical sequel of the Revolution, the application of the agrarian laws, and other problems that frequently concern the Indian. Robleto has presented in fiction the revolutions of Nicaragua and the intervention of the United States (notably in *Sangre en el trópico*). On revolutions elsewhere: *Fiebre*, by the Venezuelan Miguel Otero Silva (b. 1908); *La mañosa* (1936), by the Dominican Juan Bosch (b. 1909). On the Chaco war: *Aluvión de fuego* (1935) by Oscar Cerruto and *Sangre de mestizos* (1936) by Augusto Céspedes, both Bolivians.

A fine historical novel on the revolution of independence in Venezuela is *Las lanzas coloradas* (1931), by Arturo Uslar Pietri (b. 1905).

Cf. Berta Gamboa de Camino, "The Novel of the Mexican Revolution," in *Renascent Mexico*, edited by Hubert Herring and Herbert Weinstock (New York, 1935); Ernest R. Moore, "Influence of the Modern Mexican Novel on the American Novel," in *Revue de Littérature Comparée*, January–March, 1939.

On the most recent novelists, cf. Octavio Paz, "Una Nueva Novela Mexicana," in *Sur*, July, 1943.

29. The most numerous groups of social novelists, besides that of Mexico, are the Ecuadorian and the Peruvian. The group of Ecuador includes, besides Icaza, Chaves and Gil Gilbert, José de la Cuadra, Demetrio Aguilera Malta, Humberto Salvador, Alfredo Pareja Díez Canseco, Pablo Palacio, Adalberto Ortiz, Gerardo Gallegos, and Joaquín Gallegos Lara. The group of Peru, besides Vallejo, Falcón, and Alegría, includes Serafín Delmar, also known as a poet (his real name is Óscar Bolaños, b. 1900), José María Arguedas, Pedro Barrantes Castro, Julio Garrido Merino, José Díez Canseco, Fernando Romero, and Juan Seoane.

Cf. Arturo Torres-Rioseco, "Social Trends in the Latin American Novel," in the *Quarterly Journal of Inter-American Relations*, January, 1939; and *Bibliografía de novelistas de la revolución mexicana* (Mexico City, 1941), with many indications about articles in English; Esther Crooks, "Contemporary Ecuador in the Novel and Short Story," in *Hispania*, February, 1940.

Translations into English: Ciro Alegría's prize novel *El mundo es ancho y ajeno* (*Broad and Alien is the World*), by Harriet de Onís (New York, 1941) — a dramatization by Stephen Vincent Benét and Lucía Alzamora was broadcast from New York — and *La serpiente de oro* (*The Golden Serpent*), also by Harriet de Onís (New York, 1943); Enrique Gil Gilbert's *Nuestro pan* (*Our Daily Bread*), by Dudley Poore (New York, 1943); Gregorio López y Fuentes' *El indio* (1935), by Anita Brenner (Indianapolis–New York, 1937); Miguel Ángel Menéndez's *Nayar*, by Ángel Flores (New York, 1942).

30. Cf. Samuel Putnam, "The Brazilian Social Novel, 1935–40," in the *New Mexican Quarterly*, II (1940), 5–12.

English translations of Brazilian fiction, whether of social problems or not: Érico Verissimo's *Crossroads*, by L. C. Kaplan (New York, 1943); Monteiro Lobato's *Brazilian Short Stories*, by Isaac Goldberg (Girard, Kansas, 1925); Mario de Andrade's *Fräulein* (original title: *Amar, verbo intransitivo*), by Margaret Richardson Hollingsworth (New York, 1933). A *Marqueza dos Santos* (1924), of Pablo Setubal (1893–1937), has been translated by Margaret R. Coward under the title of *Domitila* (New York, 1930).

I am informed that José Lins do Rego's novels of the "sugar-cane cycle" are in course of translation.

31. José Eustasio Rivera's *La vorágine* was rendered into English, under the title of *The Vortex*, by Earle K. James (New York, 1935). It has also been translated into German and Russian. Cf. Eduardo Neale-Silva, "The Factual Bases of 'La Voragine'," in *Publications of the Modern Language Association*, 1939.

32. There is a translation of Gallegos' *Doña Bárbara* by Robert Malloy (London, 1931).

33. Ricardo Güiraldes' *Don Segundo Sombra* has appeared in an English translation by Harriet de Onís under the title of *Shadows in the Pampas* (New York, 1935). There is an excellent French translation by Marcelle Auclair with a preface by Valéry Larbaud, and a German version by H. Ollerich. Güiraldes wrote, besides *Don Segundo Sombra*, poems, tales, and three other novels, one of them, *Xaimaca* (1923), a delicate psychological story.

Another novelist of the pampa, the Uruguayan Enrique Amorim, may be read in the English translation of *The Horse and His Shadow*, by Richard L. O'Connell and James Graham Lujan (New York, 1943).

34. Other translations of Spanish American fiction: Jenaro Prieto, of Chile, *Partner* (1928), by Blanca de Roig and Guy Dowler (London, 1931); Ricardo Fernández Guardia, *Cuentos Ticos: Short Stories of Costa Rica*, by Gray Casement (Cleveland, Ohio, 1925); Mauricio Magdaleno, of Mexico, *Sunburst*, by Anita Brenner; Diomedes de Pereyra, of Bolivia, *The Land of the Golden Scarabs* (*El Valle del Sol*) (Indianapolis, 1928), and *The Golden Web* (*La trama de oro*, 1928) (New York, 1938); Magdalena Petit, of Chile, *La Quintrala* (New York, 1943); Jaime Torres Bodet, of Mexico, *Margaret* (*Margarita de Niebla*, 1927), by Abel Plenn, serially in the magazine *Mexican Life*, January to April, 1930, and *Death of Proserpina* (*Proserpina, rescatada*, 1931), by Abel Plenn, also in *Mexican Life*, January to April, 1931; Benjamín Subercasseaux, of Chile, *From East to West* (five short stories), by John Garret Underhill (New York, 1940) — Subercasseaux's essay *Chile: a Geographic Extravaganza* has been translated by Ángel Flores (New York, 1943); Manuel Gálvez, *Nacha Regules* (1919), by Leo Ongley (New York, 1922), and *Holy Wednesday* (1930), by Warren B. Wells (New York, 1934) — Gálvez has also been translated into French, Italian, Portuguese, German, Yiddish, Swedish, Russian, Czech, and Bulgarian; Hugo Wast (Gustavo Adolfo Martínez Zuviria), *Black Valley* (1918) (New York, 1928), and *Peach Blossom* (1911) (New York, 1929) translated by Herman and Miriam Hespelt; *The Stone Desert* (1925) (New York, 1925) and *The Strength of Lovers* (*Lucía Miranda*, 1929) (New York, 1930) translated by Louis Imbert and Jacques LeClercq; and *The House of the Ravens* (1916) (London, 1924).

35. English translations of Mallea's works: *Fiesta in November*, by Ángel Flores and Dudley Poore (New York, in 1942); *The Bay of Silence*, by Stuart E. Grummon (New York, 1943).

The novel poetically conceived is still in vogue. Fine examples of it may be found in the works of the Mexicans Jaime Torres Bodet (see note 34), Xavier Villaurrutia, and Gilberto Owen, the Argentine Enrique Anderson Imbert, and the Chilean María Luisa Bombal.

Germán Arciniegas, of Colombia, is another of the best essayists. His biography of the conqueror Gonzalo Jiménez de Quesada has been translated by Mildred Adams under the title of *The Knight of El Dorado* (New York, 1942), and his historical essay *Germans in the Conquest of America* by Ángel Flores (New York, 1943).

36. Cf. Chapter III and notes 8 to 11. There are surprising proofs of the wide diffusion that the old music had in Hispanic America. In my native Santo Domingo, during the nineteenth century, two popular songs were based on melodies by Mozart, and a hymn of the priestesses of Diana in Gluck's *Iphigenia in Tauris* became very well known in an adaptation as a hymn to the Virgin Mary. The composer Gustavo E. Campa heard in a remote Mexican village a song based on one of the themes used by Beethoven in his Seventh Symphony.

37. Cf. Chapter VI and notes 9 to 15.

38. I quote from Virgil Thomson's article "Revueltas Evening" in the *New York Herald Tribune*, March 5, 1941.

On our modern composers, see the bibliography at the end of this book and in Chapters III and VI; Mario Sánchez de Fuentes, *Panorama actual de la música cubana* (Havana, 1940); also, Mario de Andrade, *Ensaio sob a musica brasileira* (São Paulo, 1928), and Adolfo Salazar, last chapter of *La música moderna* (Buenos Aires, 1944).

In English, *Composers of To-Day*, compiled and edited by David Ewen (New York, 1934); it includes Juan José Castro, b. 1895, Carlos Chávez, b. 1899, and Heitor Vila-Lobos, b. 1881, besides the Venezuelan-Parisian Reynaldo Hahn; *The Book of Modern Composers*, edited by David Ewen (New York, 1942), which includes Chávez and Vila-Lobos; Aaron Copland, article on Chávez, in his book *Our New Music* (New York, 1941); Nicolas Slonimsky, *Music Since 1900* (New York, 1938); Henry Cowell, article on Chávez, in his book *American Composers on American Music*; Nicolas Slonimsky, "South American Composers," in *Musical America*, February 10, 1941, and article on Vila-Lobos in *Great Modern Composers*, edited by Oscar Thomson; Otto Mayer-Serra, article on Silvestre Revueltas (1899–1940), in the *Musical Quarterly*, April, 1941; articles by Carlos Chávez in *The Genius of Mexico*, edited by Hubert Herring and Katherine Terrill (New York, 1931), and in *Renascent Mexico*, edited by Hubert Herring and Herbert Weinstock, and his book *Toward a New Music* (New York, 1937).

39. On art in Hispanic America (painting as well as sculpture and architecture), from the sixteenth to the nineteenth century, cf. Chapter II and notes 17, 33, 34, and 43 to 49; Chapter III and notes 48 to 52; Chapter V and notes 5 to 7; Chapter VI and notes 6 to 8; on the art of the twentieth, cf. the bibliography at the end of this book.

BIBLIOGRAPHY

BIBLIOGRAPHY

A GOOD SYNTHETIC BOOK on Hispanic America is Francisco García Calderón's *Les démocraties latines de l'Amérique* (Paris, n. d. [1912]); it has been translated into English under the title *Latin America, Its Rise and Progress* (London, 1913); it contains three chapters on cultural history. There are similar chapters in William Robert Shepherd's *Central and South America* (London: Home University Library, 1914), published in New York with the title *Latin America*; Mary Wilhelmina Williams' *The People and Politics of Latin America* (Boston, 1930); James Fred Rippy's *Historical Evolution of Latin America* (New York, 1932).

There is a warm appreciation of our cultural life in Waldo Frank's *America Hispana* (New York, 1931), and in J. B. Trend's *South America, with Mexico and Central America* (London: Oxford University Press, 1941).

A classical work of the period immediately preceding independence is the *Voyage aux régions équinoxiales du Nouveau Continent*, by Alexander von Humboldt and Aimé Bonpland, in thirty volumes (Paris, 1807–1834); parts of it have been translated into English — *Political Essay on the Kingdom of New Spain* (London, 1811–1822).

On cultural history and recent developments, *The Civilization of the Americas*, by Herbert Ingram Priestley, Leslie Byrd Simpson, Carleton Beals, and others (Lectures arranged by the University of California at Los Angeles, Committee on International Relations, published by the University of California, Berkeley, 1938); *Hispanic American Culture*, by Víctor Andrés Belaúnde, published by the Rice Institute (Houston, Texas, 1923); J. A. Mackay, *The Other Spanish Christ: A Study in the Spiritual History of Spain and Spanish America* (London, 1932); *Modern Hispanic America*, edited by Alva Curtis Wilgus (Washington, 1933); *Colonial Hispanic America*, edited by Alva Curtis Wilgus (Washington, 1936); *Concerning Latin American Culture*, edited by Charles Carroll Griffin (New York, 1940); *Fifteen Years of Intellectual Progress in the Americas*, published by the Pan American Union (Washington, 1940); *Academic Culture in the Spanish Colonies*, by John Tate Lanning (New York, 1940); *Latin America and the Enlightenment*, edited by Arthur P. Whitaker (New York, 1942); *Hispanic American Essays: A Memorial to James Alexander Robertson* (Chapel Hill: University of North Carolina, 1942).

On individual countries: Manoel de Oliveira Lima, *The Evolution of Brazil*, translated by Percy Alvin Martin (Stanford University, 1914);

Marie Robinson Wright, *Brazil* (Philadelphia, 1901); Lilian E. Elliott (Lilian Elwyn Joyce), *Brazil Today and Tomorrow* (New York, 1922); Anita Brenner, *Idols Behind Altars* (New York, 1929); *The Genius of Mexico*, edited by Hubert Herring and Herbert Weinstock (New York, 1935); Nathaniel and Sylvia Weil, *The Reconquest of Mexico* (New York, 1939); Agustín Edwards, *My Native Land* [Chile] (London, 1929). *Life in Mexico*, by Mme. Calderón de la Barca (Frances Erskine Inglis, 1765–1833), published in Boston, 1843, is a classic in its way (recent edition in Everyman).

In English, the only general work on our literature was, for twenty-five years, Professor Alfred Coester's *Literary History of Spanish America* (New York, 1916), later reissued with additions. It was the first attempt, in any language, at a complete survey of the field, if we except a few previous unsystematic efforts in Spanish, such as *La poesía y la historia en la América latina*, by the Colombian Arcesio Escobar (1861) and the *Ensayo literario sobre la poesía lírica en América*, by the Peruvian Manuel Nicolás Corpancho (Mexico, 1862). The Instituto Internacional de la Literatura Americana published in 1941 *An Outline History of Spanish American Literature*, written in collaboration by John A. Crow, John Eugene Englekirk, E. Herman Hespelt, Irving A. Leonard and John T. Reid. Professor Arturo Torres-Rioseco's *The Epic of Latin American Literature* (lectures at Bryn Mawr College) was published in 1942. Nina Lee Weisinger's *Guide to Studies in Spanish American Literature* (Boston, 1940) is written for beginners in the field. In Professor J. D. M. Ford's *Main Currents of Spanish Literature* (New York, 1919), the last chapter deals with Spanish American writers. On Brazil, not included in any of these books, cf. Isaac Goldberg, *Brazilian Literature* (New York, 1922). Carlos González Peña's *History of Mexican Literature* has just been published in an English translation (New York, 1944).

Among the literary histories of Spanish America that now exist in Spanish the best known are by Isaac J. Barrera (Quito, 1935) and Luis Alberto Sánchez (Santiago de Chile, 1937). Marcelino Menéndez y Pelayo's *Historia de la poesía hispanoamericana* (first issued as a series of prefaces to the *Antología de poetas hispano-americanos*, published by the Spanish Academy in Madrid, 1893–1895) is already a classic, both by age and by quality.

There are, besides, innumerable works on individual countries — on Argentina, by Enrique García Velloso (1914) and Ricardo Rojas (1917–1922); on Paraguay by José Segundo Decoud (1889); on Uruguay by Carlos Roxlo (1912) and Alberto Zum Felde (1921); on Chile by Adolfo Valderrama (1866) and Domingo Amunátegui Solar (1915); on Bolivia by Santiago Vaca Guzmán (1883), José Eduardo Guerra,

Rosendo Villalobos (1936), and Enrique Finot (1943); on Peru by Javier Prado (1918), Raúl Porras Barrenechea (1918), and Luis Alberto Sánchez (1921–1926); on Ecuador by Pablo Herrera (1860), Juan León Mera (1868), Francisco Váscones (1919), Isaac J. Barrera (1924), and Augusto C. Arias (1936); on Colombia by José María Vergara y Vergara (1866), J. J. Ortega (1935), and Antonio Gómez Restrepo (in progress since 1938); on Venezuela by Gonzalo Picón Febres (1906) and Mariano Picón Salas (1941); on Santo Domingo by Abigaíl Mejía de Fernández (1936); on Cuba by Aurelio Mitjans (1890), Juan J. Remos y Rubio (1925), Salvador Salazar (1929); on Guatemala by Ramón A. Salazar (1897); on Central America as a whole by Leonardo Montalbán (1929); on Mexico by Francisco Pimentel (1876), Carlos González Peña (1928) and Julio Jiménez Rueda (1928).

Because of the slight linguistic difference between Spanish and Portuguese, Brazil has so far been excluded from the general literary histories of Hispanic America, but there are more books on Brazilian literature than on the literature of any one of the Spanish-speaking countries. The pioneers in the field were Ferdinand Denis, with the brief sketch he added to his *Résumé de l'histoire littéraire de Portugal* (Paris, 1826), and the eminent German scholar Ferdinand Joseph Wolf, with *Le Brésil littéraire* (Berlin, 1863). Later, in Portuguese, there are the works of Joaquim Caetano Fernandes Pinheiro (1862), Carlos Ferreira França (1879), Silvio Romero (1888, reprinted with additions and corrections in 1902; a new work in 1905; a compendium, written in collaboration with João Ribeiro, 1909), Alexandre José Mello de Moraes filho (1902), José Verissimo (1916), Ronald de Carvalho (1919), Afranio Peixoto (1921), Arthur Motta (1930 . . .), Agrippino Grieco (1932–1933), Nelson Werneck Sodré (1938), José Ossorio de Oliveira (Lisbon, 1939), E. Veríssimo, *Brazilian Literature* (1945).

The anthology *América literaria* published by Francisco Lagommaggiore in Buenos Aires, 1890, contains extensive articles on the literature of most of the Hispanic American countries — e.g., on Cuba by Manuel de la Cruz.

The *Revue Hispanique*, of Paris, began to publish in 1914 a series of literary histories of the several Hispanic American countries; eventually, only five appeared (Peru, Uruguay, Santo Domingo, Colombia, Bolivia); two of them were remarkable critical efforts, "La literatura peruana," by Ventura García Calderón, and "La literatura uruguaya," by Ventura García Calderón and Hugo Barbagelata.

The Instituto de Cultura Latino-americana, of the University of Buenos Aires, began publishing a collection in 1939 under a similar plan.

The only complete group of literary histories of Hispanic America by separate countries, so far, is the series of *ampliaciones* by Pedro Calmon, Roberto Fernando Giusti, José María Chacón y Calvo, Pedro Henríquez-Ureña, etc., added to the Spanish translation of Giacomo Prampolini's *Storia universale della letteratura*, volumes XI and XII, published at Buenos Aires, 1941.

Finally, there are many studies of periods or of genres, such as José Enrique Rodó's masterly essay "Juan María Gutiérrez y su época," in his book *El mirador de Próspero* (Montevideo, 1913); Federico de Onís' critical appreciations in his *Antología de la poesía moderna española e hispanoamericana* (Madrid, 1934), which constitute a connected whole; José Toribio Medina's *Historia de la literatura colonial de Chile* (Santiago de Chile, 1882); Manoel de Oliveira Lima's *Aspectos da literatura colonial brasileira* (Leipzig, 1896); Martín García Mérou's *El Brasil intelectual* (Buenos Aires, 1900); Elisio de Carvalho's *As modernas correntes estheticas na literatura brasileira* (Paris, 1907); Benedicto Costa's *Le roman au Brésil* (Paris, 1918); Arturo Torres-Rioseco's *La novela en la América hispana*, 3 vols. (Berkeley: University of California, 1939–1943).

In English there are a few works of this type: Bernard Moses's *Spanish Colonial Literature in South America* (New York, 1922), and *The Intellectual Background of the Revolution in South America* (New York, 1926), Isaac Goldberg's *Studies in Spanish American Literature* (on the *modernista* period) (New York, 1920), Dillwyn F. Ratcliff's *Venezuelan Prose Fiction* (New York, 1933), Ruth Richardson's *Florencio Sánchez and the Argentine Theatre* (New York, 1933), J. Lloyd Read's *The Mexican Historical Novel, 1826–1910* (New York, 1939), John Eugene Englekirk's *Edgar Allan Poe in Hispanic Literature* (mostly on Spanish America) (New York, 1934), Elijah Clarence Hills' "Some Spanish American Poets," in his *Hispanic Studies* (Stanford University, 1929), Alva Curtis Wilgus' *Historians and Histories of Hispanic America* (New York, 1937; revised edition 1942), David Miller Driver's *The Indian in Brazilian Literature* (New York, 1942).

Then, many articles in *Hispania*, organ of the American Association of Teachers of Spanish, in course of publication since 1918; in the *Hispanic American Historical Review*, published by Duke University at Durham, North Carolina, since 1920; in the *Inter-American Monthly*, published at Washington since 1939 (its former titles were the *Quarterly Journal of Inter-American Relations* and the *Inter-American Quarterly*); in the *New Mexican Quarterly*, organ of the University of New Mexico; in the *University of Miami Hispanic American Studies*, published at Coral Gables, Florida, since 1939; in *Books Abroad*, published by the University of Oklahoma at Norman; in *Poet Lore*; in the *Saturday Review of Literature*; in *Theatre Arts Monthly*; in the *Nation*; in the *New York Times Book Review*, since 1923; in the *West Indian Re-*

view, published at Kingston, Jamaica (it contains many translations of Hispanic American literature by Miss Edna Worthley Underwood); in the various publications — most of them in mimeographed form — of the Pan American Union at Washington; also in the learned journals that deal with Hispanic philology and literature, especially the *Hispanic Review*, the *Romanic Review* and the *Publications of the Modern Language Association*.

Periodicals especially devoted to Hispanic America are, among others, *Brazil*, published in New York since about 1940; the *Andean Monthly*, published in Santiago de Chile since 1938; *Mexican Life*, published in Mexico City since 1924; *Mexican Art and Life*, in Mexico City, 1937–1938; *Mexican Folkways*, edited by Frances Toor, in Mexico City, 1925–1933.

Anthologies of English translations of Hispanic American literature are scarce. As collections of poetry in translation that give examples from Hispanic America we may mention *The Poets and Poetry of Europe*, with a preface by Longfellow (which contains translations from Heredia and Claudio Manoel da Costa); *Modern Poets and Poetry of Spain*, by James Kennedy (London, 1852); *Selections from the Best Spanish Poets* (New York, 1856); Thomas Walsh's *Hispanic Anthology* (New York, 1920), and the Hispanic Society of America's *Translations from Hispanic Poets* (one from Brazil and several from Spanish America are included) (New York, 1938).

Concerning Hispanic America alone, *Mexican and South American Poems*, translated by Ernest Green and H. von Lowenfels (San Diego, California, 1892); Alice Stone Blackwell's *Some Spanish American Poets* (New York, 1929), new edition with introduction and notes by Isaac Goldberg (Philadelphia: University of Pennsylvania, 1937); Edna Worthley Underwood, *Anthology of Mexican Poets* (New York, 1932); *The Modernist Trend in Spanish American Poetry*, translations with commentaries by George Dundas Craig (Berkeley: University of California, 1934); *Three Spanish American Poets* [Jorge Carrera Andrade, Carlos Pellicer, Pablo Neruda], translated by Joseph Leonard Grucci, Lloyd Mallan, C. V. Vicker, and May Vicker (Albuquerque, 1942); Patrick Gannon and Hugo Manning, *Argentine Anthology of Modern Verse* (Buenos Aires, 1942); *An Anthology of Contemporary Latin American Poetry*, translations from ninety-five poets, edited by Dudley Fitts (Norfolk, Connecticut: New Directions, 1942); *Twelve Spanish American Poets*, translated by H. R. Hays (New Haven: Yale University Press, 1943).

In prose: *Brazilian Tales*, translated, with an introduction, by Isaac Goldberg (Boston, 1921); *Tales from the Argentine*, translated by Anita Brenner, with a preface by Waldo Frank (New York, 1930);

Three Plays of the Argentine, translated by Jacob S. Fassett, with an introduction by Edward Hale Bierstadt (New York, 1920); *Contemporary Spanish Americans,* selections from seventeen authors, edited by Henry Alfred Holmes (New York, 1942); *Fiesta in November,* twelve South American novels and short stories, edited by Ángel Flores and Dudley Poore, with an introduction by Katherine Anne Porter (New York, 1942).

On translations, cf. the bibliography *Latin American Literature: References to Material in English,* published in mimeographed form by the Pan American Union (Washington, 1941).

For philosophy, see the *Philosophical Abstracts* published by D. D. Runes.

On Hispanic American architecture, sculpture, and painting the only general survey, so far, is in Spanish: Miguel Solá's *Historia del arte hispano-americano* (Barcelona, 1935); it deals only with colonial art, and omits Brazil, although language is no barrier in this case. Brief summaries, in English, are given by Robert Chester Smith in the recent *New World Guides to the Latin American Republics* (New York, 1943).

As happens with literature, there are many works on individual countries. The earliest are Miguel Luis Amunátegui's "Apuntes sobre lo que han sido las bellas artes en Chile," in the *Revista de Santiago,* 1869; José Bernardo Couto's *Diálogos sobre la historia de la pintura en México* (Mexico, 1872); and Verissimo José do Bom Sucesso (1842–1886), *As artes e as letras no Brasil* (Rio de Janeiro, 1874). In English there are already many books and innumerable articles, especially on Mexico, beginning with the pioneer work of Robert H. Lanborn, *Mexican Painting and Painters* (New York, 1891), followed by the splendid collection of Sylvester Baxter, *Spanish Colonial Architecture in Mexico,* 11 vols., one of text and ten of illustrations (Boston, 1901). Then: Alfred C. Bossom, *An Architectural Pilgrimage in Old Mexico* (New York, 1924); Atlee B. Ayres, *Mexican Architecture* (New York, 1926); Walter H. Kilham, *Mexican Architecture of the Vice-Regal Period* (New York, 1927); Ernestine Evans, *The Murals of Diego Rivera* (New York, 1929); H. P. J. Wiessing, *Diego Rivera* (New York, 1930); Richard G. Garrison and George W. Rustay, *Mexican Houses* (New York, 1930); Federico E. Mariscal, *Colonial Architecture in Mexico* (New York, 1931); Emily Edwards, *Frescoes of Diego Rivera in Cuernavaca* (Mexico, 1932); Hans Tietze, *José Clemente Orozco as a Graphic Artist* (Vienna, 1933); *José Clemente Orozco,* with an introduction by Alma Reed (New York: Delphic Studios, 1933); Bertram D. Wolfe, *Portrait of America* (New York, 1934); and *Portrait of Mexico* (1937), both with many reproductions of paintings by Diego Rivera;

Agustín Velázquez Chávez, *Index of Contemporary Mexican Painting* (Mexico, 1935); Carlos Mérida, *Modern Mexican Painters* (New York, 1937); Bertram D. Wolfe, *Diego Rivera, His Life and Times* (New York, 1939); Ann L. Murphy Vhay and David Vhay, *Architectural Byways in New Spain* (New York, 1939); Laurence E. Schmeckebier, *Modern Mexican Art* (Minneapolis, 1939); MacKinley Helm, *Modern Mexican Painters* (New York, 1941); *Orozco's Frescoes in Guadalajara* (Mexico, 1940); *Twenty Centuries of Mexican Art,* published by the Museum of Modern Art (New York, 1940); Esther Born, *The New Architecture in Mexico* (New York, 1940); Alexander von Warthenau, *Tepozotlán* (originally in German), English translation by E. H. Hathaway (Mexico, 1941) — first volume of the series *Art and Color in Mexico*; Sacheverell Sitwell, chapters in *Southern Baroque Art* (London, 1926), and in *Spanish Baroque Art* (London, 1931); *Contemporary Art of the Western Hemisphere, Sculpture of the Western Hemisphere, Arte contemporáneo del hemisferio occidental,* and *Arte gráfico del hemisferio occidental* (New York: International Business Machines Corporation, 1941); Lincoln Kirstein, *The Latin-American Collection of the Museum of Modern Art* (New York, 1943); F. Violish, *Latin American Cities* (from the point of view of architecture) (New York, 1943); *Candido Portinari* [Brazilian], *His Life and Art,* with an introduction by Rockwell Kent (Chicago: University of Chicago, 1940); Philip L. Goodwin, *Brazil Builds: Architecture New and Old* (New York: Museum of Modern Art, 1943); J. Uriel García, *Artistic and Historical Guide of Peru* (Lima, 1935); *Contemporary Argentine Art* (Washington: American Federation of Arts, 1940); Eugenio Pereira Salas, "Chilean Contemporary Art," introduction to catalogue, Toledo, Ohio, 1942 (Toledo Museum of Art); the series of *Documentos de arte argentino,* in course of publication, with Spanish, French, and English texts; the portfolio *Thirteen Mexican Artists.*

Articles by Walter Pach, Robert Chester Smith, and others, in the *Studio,* the *Art Quarterly,* the *Art Bulletin,* the *Architectural Record,* the *Arts, Art Work, Creative Art,* and many other journals. There are also a few books and many articles in English on applied and folk art.

A few of the general histories of art published in Europe have begun to include Hispanic America: Karl Woerman, *Geschichte der Kunst aller Zeiten und Völker* (Berlin, 1905–1920), and José Pijoán, *Historia del arte,* 3 vols. (Barcelona, 1915–1917).

See also C. Hallenbeck, *Spanish Missions of the Old Southwest* (New York, 1927); Rexford Newcomb, *Spanish Colonial Architecture in the United States* (New York, 1937); George Kubler, *The Religious Architecture of New Mexico* (Colorado Springs, 1940); Arthur Durward Williams, *Spanish Colonial Furniture* [in Texas, Arizona, and New Mexico, with Indian influence] (Milwaukee, 1941).

On music there is no literature comparable in quantity to that concerning architecture and painting. Most of the writings in English refer to folk music and dances. Cf. Eleanor Hague, *Latin American Music, Past and Present*, with bibliography (Santa Ana, California, 1934); Lazare Saminsky, *Music of Our Day* (New York, 1940) — the last chapter deals with Hispanic American music; Gilbert Chase, *The Music of Spain* (New York, 1941) — chap. xvii deals with "Hispanic Music in the Americas"; *Mission Music of California*, transcribed and edited by Owen de Silva (Los Angeles, 1941); *Mexican Music*, notes by Herbert Weinstock and Carlos Chávez (New York: Museum of Modern Art, 1940); *Popular Cuban Music*, with an introductory essay by Emilio Grenet, translated into English by R. Phillips (Havana, 1939); Rodney Gallop, *Mexican Mosaic* (London, 1939); articles by Nicholas Slonimsky, Rodney Gallop, Herbert Weinstock, and others, in *Modern Music, Etude, Musical America*, the *Musical Quarterly*. On writings in Spanish and in Portuguese, cf. notes 9 to 11 of Chapter III, 12 of Chapter VI, and 38 of Chapter VIII.

A systematic bibliography of material about Hispanic America appears yearly in the *Handbook of Latin American Studies* published under the auspices of the American Council of Learned Societies by the Harvard University Press since 1936.

The Harvard Council of Hispano-American Studies published from 1931 to 1937 a series of bibliographies of the several countries of Hispanic America, including Puerto Rico; each country had one volume, except the five republics of Central America, which had one for the whole group, and one for Rubén Darío alone, and Mexico, for which there is one concerning the novel and one concerning poetry (no more appeared, I believe). A special volume deals with *Hispano-American Literature in the United States* (1932).

Cf. also Raymond L. Grismer, *A Reference Index to Twelve Thousand Spanish American Authors* (New York, 1939; new issue, with additions and corrections, New York, 1941), and *A New Bibliography of the Literature of Spain and Spanish America*, vols. I and II (letter A only), which was preceded by *A Bibliography of Articles and Essays on the Literatures of Spain and Spanish America* (Minneapolis, 1935); José Toribio Medina, *Biblioteca hispano-americana*, 7 vols. (Santiago de Chile, 1898–1907) — books on Spanish America, published in Europe from 1493 to 1810; Hayward Keniston, *List of Works for the Study of Hispanic-American History* (New York: The Hispanic Society of America, 1920); Alva Curtis Wilgus, *Histories and Historians of Hispanic America: a Bibliographical Essay* (Washington, 1937; new and revised edition 1942), and the bibliographies compiled under the direction of Concha Romero James at the Pan American Union and distributed in mimeographed form.

On language alone: Madaline Wallis Nichols, *Bibliographical Guide to Materials on American Spanish* (Cambridge: Harvard University Press, 1941).

On folk-lore: Ralph S. Boggs, *Bibliography of Spanish-American Folk-Lore* (New York, 1940).

On music: Gilbert Chase, *Bibliography of Latin American Folk Music*, in mimeographed form (Library of Congress, Washington, 1942).

A bibliography of bibliographies: Cecil Knight Jones, *Latin American Bibliographies* (Cambridge: Harvard University Press, 1932; new edition, 1940).

INDEX

INDEX

A la limón (song), 110
Abad, Father Diego José (Mexico; 1727–1779), 84
Abbeville, Claude d', 25
Abella Caprile, Margarita (Argentina; b. 1901), 276
Aben Tofail, 22
Abrantès, Duchess of, 96
Abravanel, Judah, 64
Abreu, Casimiro de (Brazil; 1837–1860), 122
Abreu, João Capistrano de (Brazil; 1853–1927), 244
Acevedo, Jesús Tito (Mexico; *ca.* 1880–1918), 188, 276
Acevedo Díaz, Eduardo (Uruguay; 1851–1921), 271
Acosta, Augustín (Cuba; b. 1887), 196, 274
Acosta, Cecilio (Venezuela; 1818–1881), 262
Acosta, Joaquín (Colombia; 1800–1852), 244
Acosta, Father José de (Spain; 1539–1600), 55, 219, 221
Acosta, José Julián de (Puerto Rico; 1825–1892), 262
Acuña, Cristóbal de (Spain; 1597–1675?), 220, 221
Acuña, Manuel (Mexico; 1849–1873), 128, 170, 249
Acuña de Figueroa, Francisco (Uruguay; 1790–1862), 109, 257
Adams, Henry, 247
Adams, John, 96, 235
Adams, John Quincy, 99
Adams, Mildred, 284
Adams, Samuel, 95

Aguado, Friar Pedro de (Spain; d. after 1589), 219
Agüero, Juan Miguel de (Spain; 16th cent.), 219
Aguilera Malta, Demetrio (Ecuador; 20th cent.), 282
Aguirre, Father Juan Bautista (Ecuador; 1725–1786), 84
Aguirre, Julián, 201
Agustini, Delmira (Uruguay; 1887–1914), 186, 273, 275
Aires, Matias (Brazil; 1705–before 1770), 232
Alamán, Lucas (Mexico; 1792–1853), 244, 248
Alarcón, *see* Ruiz de Alarcón, Juan
Alas, Leopoldo, 268
Alba Ixtlilxóchitl, Fernando de (Mexico; *ca.* 1568–*ca.* 1648), 36, 55, 214
Alberdi, Juan Bautista (Argentina; 1810–1884), 125, 132, 137, 251, 252
Alberini, Coriolano (Italy-Argentina; b. 1886), 253
Alberto Torres, Heloisa (Brazil; 20th cent.), 276
Albizu Campos, Pedro (Puerto Rico; 20th cent.), 188
Alcedo, Antonio de (Ecuador; 1735–1812), 233
Alcocer, Canon Luis Jerónimo de (Santo Domingo; 1598–1664), 82, 231
Alconedo, *see* Rodríguez Alconedo, José Luis
Aldao, Friar José Félix, 132
Alegre, Friar Francisco Javier (Mexico; 1729–1788), 84

Alegría, Ciro (Peru; b. 1909), 197, 282

Aleijadinho, see Lisboa, Antonio Francisco

Alemán, Mateo (Spain; 1547–after 1614), 46, 108, 220

Alemán Bolaños, Gustavo (Nicaragua; 20th cent.), 266

Alencar, José de (Brazil; 1829–1877), 122, 125, 130, 140, 248, 250, 259, 273

Alessio, Matteo Piero d' (Italy; 1547–1600), 47

Allende, Humberto (Chile; b. 1885), 201

Almafuerte, see Palacios, Pedro Bonifacio

Almeida, Guilherme de (Brazil; b. 1890), 190, 274

Almeida, Manoel Antonio de (Brazil; 1830–1861), 147–148, 182

Almeida, Renato (Brazil; 20th cent.), 226, 274

Almeida Garret, 121

Alone, see Díaz Arrieta, Hernán

Alonso, Amado (Spain-Argentina; b. 1896), 215, 218, 270, 279

Alonso, Manuel Antonio (Puerto Rico; 1822–1889), 258

Alonso Getino, Luis G., 209

Alonso y Trelles, José (Spain-Uruguay; 1860–1925), 173, 268

Alphonso the Wise, 11

Alsop, R., 234

Altamirano, Ignacio Manuel (Mexico; 1834–1893), 115, 138, 242

Alvarado Tezozómoc, Hernando (Mexico; ca. 1520–ca. 1600), 36, 55, 214

Alvarenga Peixoto, Ignacio José de (Brazil; 1744–1793), 86

Alvares de Azevedo, Manoel Antonio (Brazil; 1831–1852), 128

Alvarez, Agustín (Argentina; 1868–1913), 252

Alvarez, José Sixto (Argentina; 1858–1903), 271

Alvarez de Arenales, Juan Antonio, 86

Alzamora, Lucia, 282

Alzate, Father José Antonio (Mexico; 1729–1799), 88, 233

Amado, Jorge (Brazil; b. 1912), 198

Amarilis (Peru; 17th cent.), 75, 222

Amat, Manuel (Spain; 18th cent.), 149

Amorim, Enrique (Uruguay; b. 1900), 283

Amoroso Lima, Alceu (Brazil; b. 1893), 275

Ampíes, Juan de, 46

Amunátegui, Miguel Luis (Chile; 1828–1888), 235, 238, 244, 292

Amunátegui Solar, Domingo (Chile; b. 1860), 220, 288

Anchieta, Father José de (Spain; 1530–1597), 55, 220

Andagoya, Pascual de (Spain; 1495–1548), 219, 221

Anderson, W., 229

Anderson Imbert, Enrique (Argentina; b. 1910), 284

Andersson, Theodore, 271

Andrada e Silva, José Bonifacio de (Brazil; 1765–1838), 99, 116, 118, 234, 242, 257

Andrada e Silva, José Bonifacio de, the second (Brazil; 1827–1886), 152

Andrade, Mario de (Brazil; 1893–1945), 188, 190, 278, 280, 282, 284

Andrade, Oswald de (Brazil; 20th cent.), 278

Andrade, Olegario Víctor (Argentina; 1839–1882), 143, 256
Andrade, Canon Vicente de Paul (Mexico; 19th cent.), 217
Angulo, Friar Pedro de, 31
Antonelli, the brothers, builders, 49
Anunciación, Friar Diego de, see Reinoso, Friar Diego de
Aquino, Marcos or Andrés de (Mexico; 16th cent.), 215
Arango y Parreño, Francisco de (Cuba; 1765–1837), 233
Araujo Porto Alegre, Manoel de (Brazil; 1806–1879), 122
Arboleda, Julio (Colombia; 1817–1861), 115, 116, 121, 127, 130, 150, 250
Arciniega, Claudio de (Spain; 16th cent.), 219
Arciniega, Rosa (Peru; b. 1909), 276
Arciniegas, Germán (Colombia; b. 1900), 213, 224
Arciniegas, Ismael Enrique (Colombia; 1865–1937), 265, 284
Arenales, see Alvarez de Arenales, Juan Antonio
Arenales, Ricardo, see Osorio, Miguel Ángel
Arévalo Martínez, Rafael (Guatemala; b. 1884), 274
Argensola, see Leonardo de Argensola, Bartolomé
Arguedas, Alcides (Bolivia; b. 1879), 197, 274
Arguedas, José María (Peru; 20th cent.), 282
Argüello, Santiago (Nicaragua; 1871–1940), 266
Arias, Augusto C. (Ecuador; 20th cent.), 289
Arinos, Afonso (Brazil; 1868–1916), 259

Ariosto, Ludovico, 72
Aristophanes, 71
Aristotle, 78, 108
Arona, Juan de, see Paz Soldán y Unanue, Pedro
Arozarena, Marcelino (Cuba; b. 1912), 280
Arreaza Calatrava, José Tadeo (Venezuela; 20th cent.), 274
Arrieta, Rafael Alberto (Argentina; b. 1889), 252, 273, 275
Arrué or de Rúa, Juan de (Mexico; 16th cent.), 215
Art of Stealing (Arte de furtar) (17th cent.), 229
Arteaga, Sebastián de (Spain-Mexico; 17th cent.), 47, 91
Arvelo Larriva, Alfredo (Venezuela; 1883–1934), 274
Arvelo Larriva, Enriqueta (Venezuela; 20th cent.), 276
Ascasubi, Hilario (Argentina; 1807–1875), 116, 143-144, 244, 246
Asturias, Miguel Ángel (Guatemala; b. 1899), 279
Atahualpa, 64
Athayde, Tristão de, see Amoroso Lima, Alceu
Atkinson, Geoffrey, 209
Auclair, Marcelle (Chile-France; 20th cent.), 283
Aulnoy, Mme. d', 40
Austin, Mary, 224
Avellaneda, La, see Gómez de Avellaneda, Gertrudis
Avellaneda, Nicolás (Argentina; 1837–1885), 137, 243, 252, 253
Avendaño, Father Diego de (Peru; 17th cent.), 33, 212
Ávila y Cadena, Antonio de, 72
Aweranka, Eustakio (Peru; 20th cent.), 279
Ayres, Atlee B., 292

Ayres do Casal, Manoel (Brazil; d. after 1821), 234
Azevedo, Aluizio de (Brazil; 1857–1913), 147, 182, 260, 270, 273
Azevedo, Arthur (Brazil; 1855–1908), 273
Aznar, Luis (Spain-Argentina; b. 1902), 253
Azorín, see Martínez Ruiz, José
Azuela, Mariano (Mexico; b. 1873), 188, 197, 281

Baca-Flor, Carlos (Peru; 1869–1941), 254
Bach, J. S., 140, 201, 226
Bacon, Francis, 15
Báez, Cecilio (Paraguay; b. 1862), 243, 266
Bailey, Richard Eugene, 247
Bain, Alexander, 158
Balbuena, see Valbuena, Bernardo de
Baldorioty de Castro, Román (Puerto Rico; 1822–1889), 262
Ballagas, Emilio (Cuba; b. 1908), 196, 280
Ballivián, Adolfo (Bolivia; 1831–1874), 243
Balzac, Honoré de, 148, 200, 260
Banchs, Enrique (Argentina; b. 1888), 189, 273, 277
Bandeira, Manuel (Brazil; b. 1886), 190, 278
Banville, Théodore de, 264
Baptista, Mariano (Bolivia; 1832–1907), 243
Baquerizo Moreno, Alfredo (Ecuador; b. 1859), 243, 266
Baquíjano y Carrillo, José de (Peru; 18th cent.), 98, 214, 234
Baralt, Rafael María (Venezuela-

Spain; 1810–1860), 127, 244, 246
Barba, Father Álvaro Alonso (Spain; ca. 1561–after 1638), 46, 220
Barba Jacob, Porfirio, see Osorio, Miguel Ángel
Barbagelata, Hugo (Uruguay; b. 1887), 268, 289
Barbará, Federico (Argentina; 1828–1893), 261
Barbosa, Ruy (Brazil; 1849–1923), 116, 151–152, 157, 261, 262
Barbosa Lage, Domingos Vidal (Brazil; 1761–1793), 86
Bardin, James C., 222
Barker, Granville, 69
Barletta, Leónidas (Argentina; b. 1902), 272
Barnes, Anna Maria, 264
Barrantes Castro, Pedro (Peru; 20th cent.), 282
Barreda, Gabino (Mexico; 1818–1881), 159
Barrenechea y Albis, Friar Juan de (Chile; d. 1707), 231
Barrera, Isaac J. (Ecuador; b. 1884), 288, 289
Barreto, Paulo (Brazil; 1881–1921), 275
Barreto, Tobias (Brazil; 1839–1889), 115, 143, 258
Barrios, Eduardo (Chile; b. 1884), 273
Barros, Álvaro (Argentina; 1827–1892), 261
Barros, Bernardo G. (Cuba; 1890–1922), 255
Barros Arana, Diego (Chile; 1830–1907), 244, 252
Barrutia, Salvador (Guatemala; 1842–1899), 250

Bartolache, José Ignacio (Mexico; 1739–1790), 233
Bascuñán, see Núñez de Pineda Bascuñán, Francisco
Bataillon, Marcel, 213
Battle Ordóñez, José (Uruguay; 1854–1930), 243
Batres Montúfar, José (Guatemala; 1809–1844), 109, 149, 250, 256
Baudelaire, Charles, 127, 264
Bausate, Jaime (Peru; 18th cent.), 44
Bauzá, Francisco (Uruguay; 1849-1899), 244
Baxter, Sylvester, 292
Bayón Herrera, Luis (Argentina; 20th cent.), 272
Beals, Carleton, 287
Becerra, Francisco (Spain; 16th cent.), 48, 219
Bécquer, Gustavo Adolfo, 142, 169, 258
Bedón, Friar Pedro (Ecuador; d. 1621), 215
Beethoven, L. von, 226, 284
Behn, Aphra, 24
Bejarano, Lázaro (Spain; 16th cent.), 46, 218
Belaúnde, Víctor Andrés (Peru; b. 1883), 237, 269, 274, 287
Belgrano, Manuel (Argentina; 1770–1820), 104, 135
Belin Sarmiento, Augusto (Argentina; d. 1936), 252
Bell, Aubrey Fitz-Gerald, 232
Bello, Andrés (Venezuela; 1781–1865), 4, 99–105, 107, 116, 120, 129, 142, 151, 192, 237, 238, 245, 250, 257
Bello, Atanasio (Venezuela; 18th cent.), 226
Bello, Luis, 93

Belmonte, Luis de (Spain; ca. 1580–ca. 1650), 46, 220
Benavente, Friar Toribio de (Spain; d. 1568), 31, 219
Benét, Stephen Vincent, 282
Benítez, Bibiana (Puerto Rico; 1783–1875), 250
Bergamín, José, 69
Bergson, Henri, 180
Berisso, Emilio (Argentina; 1878–1922), 272
Beristáin de Souza, José Mariano (Mexico; 1756–1817), 233
Berkeley, George, 102
Berlanga, Friar Tomás de (Spain; d. 1551), 31, 209
Bernárdez, Francisco Luis (Argentina; b. 1900), 270, 278
Berrien, William, 202
Berro, Bernardo Prudencio (Uruguay; 1803–1868), 243
Berruguete, Alonso, 90
Berry, Ana M. (Chile; 20th cent.), 276
Bertaux, Émile, 53
Besouchet, Lidia (Brazil; b. 1909), 276
Betances, Ramón Emeterio (Puerto Rico; 1827–1898), 262
Betancur, Cayetano (Colombia; 20th cent.), 253
Betanzos, Friar Domingo de (Spain; d. 1549), 31, 209
Betanzos, Friar Juan de (Spain; d. 1576), 220
Bevilaqua, Clovis (Brazil; b. 1859), 253
Bierstadt, Edward Hale, 271, 292
Beyle, Henri, 148
Bilac, Olavo (Brazil; 1865–1918), 175–177
Bilbao, Francisco (Chile; 1823–1865), 125, 248

Bilbao, Manuel (Chile; 1827–1895), 250

Billini, Francisco Gregorio (Santo Domingo; 1844–1898), 243

Bishop, John Peale, 275

Bissell, Benjamin, 210

Bizet, Georges, 141

Blackwell, Alice Stone, 230, 291

Blanco, Eduardo (Venezuela; 1840–1912), 244

Blanco, Tomás (Puerto Rico; 20th cent.), 280

Blanco Fombona, Rufino (Venezuela; 1874–1944), 246, 265, 269, 270, 271

Blanes, Juan Manuel (Uruguay; 1830–1901), 255

Blest Gana, Alberto (Chile; 1830–1920), 147–148, 182, 246, 260, 271

Blixen, Samuel (Uruguay; 1869–1911), 272

Bocanegra, Friar Matías de (Mexico; 1612–1668), 84

Boétie, see La Boétie

Boggs, Ralph Steele, 295

Boiardo, Matteo Maria, 101

Boito, Arrigo, 140

Bolaños, Oscar (Peru; b. ca. 1900), 279, 282

Bolet Peraza, Nicanor (Venezuela; 1838–1906), 248

Bolívar, Simón (Venezuela; 1783–1830), 41, 99, 103, 107, 173, 180, 233, 236, 237, 241

Bom Sucesso, Verissimo José do (Brazil; 1842–1886), 292

Bombal, María Luisa (Chile; b. 1910), 276, 284

Bonafoux, Luis (Puerto Rico; 1855–1925), 246, 266

Bonaparte, Napoléon, 96, 97, 236

Bonpland, Aimé, 238, 287

Bopp, Franz, 248

Bopp, Raul (Brazil; 20th cent.), 278

Borda, José Joaquín (Colombia; 1835–1878), 248

Borges, Jorge Luis (Argentina; b. 1899), 185, 191, 192, 268, 278

Born, Esther, 293

Borrero [de Luján], Dulce María (Cuba; b. 1883), 275

Borrero, Juana (Cuba; 1877–1896), 275

Borrero Echeverría, Esteban (Cuba; 1849–1906), 158

Bosch, Juan (Santo Domingo; b. 1909), 263, 281

Bossom, Alfred C., 292

Boswell, James, 209

Botelho de Oliveira, Manoel (Brazil; 1636–1711), 85

Boti, Regino Eladio (Cuba; b. 1878), 266

Botzaris, Marco, 127

Bougainville, Louis Antoine de, 25

Bourland, Caroline Brown, 227

Bowra, C. M., 277

Brady, Cyrus Townsend, Jr., 272

Brainard, John Gardner Calkins, 240

Bramón, Francisco (Mexico; 17th cent.), 221

Brasseur de Bourbourg, the Abbé, 223

Brau, Salvador (Puerto Rico; 1842–1913), 249

Brébeuf, Jean de, 25

Brémond, the Abbé, 170

Brenes Mesén, Roberto (Costa Rica; b. 1874), 266

Brenner, Anita, 271, 281, 282, 283, 288, 291

Brinton, Daniel Garrison, 223

Brown, Harry W., 260, 270

Browning, W. E., 276

Brull, Mariano (Cuba; b. 1891), 190, 274

Brunet, Marta (Chile; b. 1901), 161, 276

Brutus, 152

Bryant, William Cullen, 240, 258

Bryce, James, 214

Bunge, Carlos Octavio (Argentina; 1874-1918), 252

Bürger, Gottfried August, 118

Burgos, Fausto (Argentina; 20th cent.), 280

Burle Marx, Walter (Brazil; 20th cent.), 202

Buschiazzo, Mario J. (Argentina; 20th cent.), 222, 223

Bustamante, Carlos María de (Mexico; 1774-1848), 44

Bustamante Carlos Inca, Calixto (Peru; 18th cent.), 214

Bustillo Oro, Juan (Mexico; 20th cent.), 281

Bustos, Hermenegildo (Mexico; 1832-1907), 254

Byron, George Gordon, Lord, 101, 110, 121, 127, 128, 263

Caballero, Father José Agustín (Cuba; 1762-1835), 233

Cabello de Balboa, Miguel (Spain; 16th cent.), 220

Cabello de Carbonera, Mercedes (Peru; ca. 1847-1909), 271

Cabeza de Vaca, see Núñez Cabeza de Vaca, Álvaro

Cabral, Manuel del (Santo Domingo; b. 1907), 280

Cabrera, Friar Alonso de (Spain; ca. 1549-1606), 220

Cabrera, Lydia (Cuba; 20th cent.), 276

Cabrera, Miguel (Mexico; 1695-1768), 36, 215, 230

Cabrera Quintero, Cayetano (Mexico; d. 1775), 84

Caesar, Julius, 59

Caicedo Rojas, José (Colombia; 1816-1898), 124, 249, 250

Caillet-Bois, Julio (Argentina; b. 1910), 224

Calancha, Friar Antonio de la (Bolivia; 1584-1654), 231

Calcaño, José Antonio (Venezuela; 1827-1897), 127, 248

Calcaño, José Antonio (Venezuela; 20th cent.), 227

Caldas, Francisco José de (Colombia; 1771-1816), 87, 233

Calderón, Fernando (Mexico; 1809-1845), 245, 249

Calderón de la Barca, Mme. (Frances Erskine Inglis), 288

Calderón de la Barca, Pedro, 57, 68, 80, 87, 101, 169, 191

Calleja, Friar Diego de (Mexico; 17th cent.), 76

Calmon, Pedro (Brazil; b. 1902), 32, 211, 212, 216, 228, 290

Camargo, Joracy (Brazil; 20th cent.), 273

Camargo Guarnieri (Brazil; b. 1907), 202

Camarillo de Pereyra, María Enriqueta (Mexico; b. 1875), 275

Cambaceres, Eugenio (Argentina; 1843-1900), 182, 271

Camino, Miguel Andrés (Argentina; 1877-1944), 268

Camoëns, Luis de, 12, 46

Campa, Arthur Leon, 224

Campa, Gustavo E. (Mexico; 1863-1935), 284

Campanella, 14

Campo, Ángel de (Mexico; 1868-1908), 248

Campo, Estanislao del (Argentina; 1834-1880), 144

Campos, Humberto de (Brazil; 1886–1934), 274

Candía, Pedro de, 36

Cané, Miguel (Argentina; 1851–1905), 252

Cañete, Pedro Vicente, 234

Capdevila, Arturo (Argentina; b. 1889), 139, 186, 273

Carbonell, Néstor (Cuba; b. 1884), 263

Cárdenas, Juan de (Spain; 16th cent.), 59

Cardim, Father Fernão (Portugal; 1540–1625), 61, 220

Cardoso, Efraim (Paraguay; b. 1906), 273

Cardoso, Lucio (Brazil; b. 1913), 198

Cardoza y Aragón, Luis (Guatemala; b. 1902), 191

Carlos, Father (Ecuador; 17th cent.), 91

Carlyle, Thomas, 241

Carnegie, Andrew, 35

Carneiro da Cunha, Olegario Marianno (Brazil; b. 1889), 274

Caro, José Eusebio (Colombia; 1817–1853), 115, 121, 127, 129, 250, 269

Caro, Manuel Antonio (Chile; 1835–1903), 254

Caro, Miguel Antonio (Colombia; 1843–1909), 239, 243, 256–257, 267

Carpentier, Alejo (Cuba; b. 1904), 280

Carranza, Antonio José (Venezuela; 19th cent.), 254

Carranza, Venustiano, 281

Carrasquilla, Tomás (Colombia; 1858–1940), 271

Carreño, Alberto María (Mexico; b. 1875), 232

Carreño, Cayetano (Venezuela; 18th cent.), 226

Carreño, Teresa (Venezuela; 1853–1917), 201, 246

Carrera Andrade, Jorge (Ecuador; b. 1903), 191, 197, 280, 291

Carriego, Evaristo (Argentina; 1883–1912), 268, 273

Carrillo Ramírez, Salomón (Central America; 20th cent.), 253

Cartas chilenas (18th cent.), 86

Carvajal, Luis de (Spain; ca. 1566–1596), 46, 218

Carvajal, Micael de (Spain; 16th cent.), 46, 210, 220

Carvajal y Robles, Rodrigo de (Spain; 16th cent.), 220

Carvalho, Elisio de (Brazil; 1880–1925), 267, 290

Carvalho, Ronald de (Brazil; 1893–1935), 32, 176, 190, 212, 274

Carvallo y Goyeneche, Vicente (Chile; 1740–1816), 231

Casal, Julián del (Cuba; 1863–1893), 166–167, 168, 170, 171, 172, 173, 181, 265, 267, 269

Casasús, Joaquín Diego (Mexico; 1858–1916), 257, 264

Casement, Gray, 283

Caso, Alfonso (Mexico; b. 1896), 274

Caso, Antonio (Mexico; b. 1883), 156, 269, 274, 276

Caspicara, see Chilli, Manuel

Castañeda, Carlos Eduardo, 223

Castell-dos-Ríus, Manuel Oms, Marquis of (Spain; d. 1710), 62, 220, 226

Castellanos, Francisco José (Cuba; 1892–1920), 274

Castellanos, Jesús (Cuba; 1879–1912), 268, 274

Castellanos, Juan de (Spain-Co-

lombia; 1522–1607), 12, 27, 50, 61, 208, 219
Casti, Giovanni Battista, 110
Castiglione, Baldassare, 64
Castillo, Juan del (Spain; d. 1793), 234
Castillo, "la Madre" (Colombia; 1671–1742), 75
Castro, Diego de, see Cusi Yupanqui, Tito
Castro, Juan José (Argentina; b. 1895), 201, 202, 284
Castro Alves, Antonio de (Brazil; 1847–1871), 115, 143, 250, 262
Castro Leal, Antonio (Mexico; 20th cent.), 228, 257, 274
Catherine the Great, 96
Catullus, 257
Caturla, see García Caturla, Alejandro
Caviedes, see Valle Caviedes, Juan del
Cavo, Father Andrés (Mexico; 1739–ca. 1795), 231
Cearense, Catulo da Paixão (Brazil; 20th cent.), 268
Cellini, Benvenuto, 153, 180
Centeno de Osma, Gabriel (Peru; 16th cent.), 231
Cepeda, Lorenzo de (Spain; d. 1580), 35, 220
Cerda, Luis de la (Mexico; 17th cent.), 215
Cerda, Matías de la (Spain; d. after 1621), 48
Cernicchiaro, Vincenzo, 226
Cerruto, Oscar (Bolivia; b. 1907), 281
Cervantes, Ignacio (Cuba; 1847–1905), 142, 201
Cervantes, Miguel de, 35, 47, 61, 63, 69, 149, 152, 158, 226, 264
Cervantes de Salazar, Francisco

(Spain; ca. 1514-1575), 46, 219
Céspedes, Augusto (Bolivia; 20th cent.), 281
Cestero, Tulio Manuel (Santo Domingo; b. 1877), 265, 266, 270
Cetina, Gutierre de (Spain; ca. 1518–ca. 1554), 45, 220
Cevallos, Pedro Fermín (Ecuador; 1812–1893), 244
Chabrier, Emmanuel, 142
Chacón y Calvo, José María (Cuba; b. 1893), 208, 209, 274, 290
Champlain, Samuel de, 25
Channing, William Ellery, 237
Chanson de Roland, 103, 238
Chapman, Charles Edward, 231
Charles V, 15, 20, 42, 46, 224
Charles IX of France, 23
Charles III of Spain, 88, 94
Charles IV of Spain, 97
Charlevoix, Father Pierre François Xavier de, 25
Chase, Gilbert, 294, 295
Chase, Stuart, 279
Chassériau, Théodore (Santo Domingo-France; 1818–1856), 242
Chateaubriand, Vicomte François René de, 239, 240
Chaves, Fernando (Ecuador; 20th cent.), 197, 282
Chaves, Nuflo de, 53
Chávez, Agustín Velásquez, 293
Chávez, Carlos (Mexico; b. 1899), 201, 202, 284, 294
Chénier, André, 129
Chesterton, Gilbert Keith, 153
Chilli, Manuel (Ecuador; 18th cent.), 215
Chimalpahin Quauhtlehuanitzin, Domingo Francisco de, see San Antón Muñoz
Chinard, Gilbert, 210

Chirveches, Armando (Bolivia; 1883–1926), 274

Chocano, José Santos (Peru; 1875–1934), 168, 172, 174, 175, 185, 192, 197

Choquehuanca, José Domingo (Bolivia; 18th–19th cent.), 215

Christina of Sweden, 74

Chucho el Roto (play), 272

Churata, Gamaliel, see Peralta, Arturo

Churriguera, José (Spain; 1650–1725), 92

Cicero, 258

Cid, Poem of the, 103

Cienfuegos, Nicasio Alvarez de, 106

Cieza de León, Pedro de (Spain; 1518–1560), 20, 45, 50, 67, 220, 221

Cípac, see Aquino, Marcos or Andrés de

Cisneros, Luis Benjamín (Peru; 1837–1904), 250

Clarín, see Alas, Leopoldo

Clarinda (Peru; 17th cent.), 75

Claver, Saint Pedro, 33

Clavijero, Father Francisco Javier (1731–1787), 233

Cobo, Father Bernabé (Spain; 1582–1657), 28, 61, 220

Coelho Netto, Henrique (Brazil; 1864–1934), 270, 273

Coello, Sánchez, 47

Coester, Alfred, 288

Cole, M. R., 223

Coll, Pedro Emilio (Venezuela; b. 1872), 265

Colman, Narciso Ramón (Paraguay; b. 1878), 279

Columbus, Christopher (Italy; 1451–1506), 4–10, 21, 24, 27, 29, 45, 49, 171, 219

Columbus, Diego (Portugal; 1476–1526), 16, 60

Columbus, Ferdinand (Spain; 1488–1539), 10

Cometta Manzoni [de Herrera], Aída (Argentina; 20th cent.), 219, 245, 251, 281

Commager, Henry S., 213, 235

Concepcion, Sor Francisca Josefa de la, see Castillo, "la Madre"

Concha, José Vicente (Colombia; 1867–1929), 243

Concolorcorvo (Peru; 18th cent.), 214

Condillac, Etienne de, 42

Condorcet, Antoine-Nicolas de, 26

Condori, José (Peru; 17th cent.), 215

Conselheiro, Antonio, 181

Contreras, Francisco (Chile; 1877–1933), 267

Copland, Aaron, 284

Cordero, Luis (Ecuador; 1833–1912), 243

Córdoba, Friar Pedro de (Spain; 1482–1521), 15–17, 31, 208, 209

Corelli, Arcangelo, 226

Corneille, Pierre, 70, 71, 87, 227

Cornelio Hispano, see López, Ismael

Cornyn, J. H., 224

Coronado, Martín (Argentina; 1850–1919), 259, 272

Corpancho, Manuel Nicolás (Peru; 1830–1863), 249, 288

Correa, Julio (Paraguay; 20th cent.), 279

Correa, Raimundo (Brazil; 1860–1911), 175–177

Corretjer, Juan Antonio (Puerto Rico; 20th cent.), 188

Cortés, Hernán (Spain; 1485–

1547), 20, 40, 45, 50, 53, 66, 160, 219

Cortina, José Antonio (Cuba; 1852–1884), 158

Cortina, Count de la, see Gómez de la Cortina, José

Cosco, Leandro de, 7

Cossío, Francisco de, 93

Costa, Benedicto, 290

Costa, Claudio Manoel da (Brazil; 1728–1789), 86, 191

Costa, Zeferino da (Brazil; 1840–1915), 255

Cotarelo y Mori, Emilio, 226

Couto, José Bernardo (Mexico; 1803–1862), 235, 248, 292

Coward, Margaret R., 282

Cowell, Henry, 284

Craig, George Dundas, 265, 291

Cravioto, Alfonso (Mexico; b. 1884), 277

Crespo, "el Crespillo" (Mexico; 16th cent.), 215

Crespo Toral, Remigio (Ecuador; 1860–1939), 266

Crispo Acosta, Osvaldo (Uruguay; b. 1884), 266, 268

Croce, Benedetto, 158

Crooks, Esther, 282

Cross, St. John of the, 47, 191

Crow, John Armstrong, 288

Cruz, Juan de la (Mexico; 16th cent.), 215

Cruz, Manuel de la (Cuba; 1861–1896), 253, 289

Cruz, Sor Juana Inés de la (Mexico; 1651–1695), 56, 76–82, 90, 110, 222, 229–231

Cruz e Sousa, João de (Brazil; 1862–1898), 175–177

Cuadra, José de la (Ecuador; 1903–1941), 282

Cuauhtémoc, 140

Cucalambé, El, see.. Nápoles Fajardo, Juan Cristóbal

Cuéllar, José Tomás de (Mexico; 1830–1894), 147–148, 271

Cuervo, Rufino José (Colombia; 1844–1911), 39, 215–216, 246, 257

Cueva, Juan de la (Spain; 1543–1610), 27, 46, 220

Cuitláhuac, 36

Cunha, Euclides da (Brazil; 1866–1909), 41, 180, 269, 279

Cunninghame Graham, Robert B., 221, 269

Curie, Marie, 79

Cusi Yupanqui, Tito (Peru; 16th cent.), 36, 214

Cuthbertson, Stuart, 245

Cutler, J. H., 262

Dana, Charles Anderson, 263

Dante Alighieri, 191

Darío, Rubén (Nicaragua; 1867–1916), 165, 166, 168, 169–175, 176, 177–178, 179, 181, 192, 208, 246, 264, 265–267, 268, 269, 270, 294

Dati, Giuliano, 8

Dávalos, Balbino (Mexico; b. 1866), 176, 266

Dávalos, Juan Carlos (Argentina; b. 1887), 280

Dávila, Pedro Francisco (Ecuador; d. 1785), 233

Dávila Padilla, Friar Agustín (Mexico; 1562–1604), 52

Decoud, José Segundo (Paraguay; 1848–1909), 288

Delacroix, Eugène, 242

Delano, Lucile K., 229

Delgadina (ballad), 110

Delgado, Rafael (Mexico; 1853–1914), 271

Deligne, Gastón Fernando (Santo Domingo; 1861–1913), 165, 265

Deligne, Rafael Alfredo (Santo Domingo; 1863–1902), 265

Delmar, Serafín, see Bolaños, Oscar

Del Monte, Domingo (Venezuela-Cuba; 1804–1853), 105, 110, 143, 157, 257, 258

Del Monte, Félix María (Santo Domingo; 1819–1899), 244, 258

Dengo, Omar (Costa Rica; 1888–1928), 274

Denis, Ferdinand, 210, 289

De Quincey, Thomas, 153

Descartes, René, 42, 78, 86

de Soto, Hernando, 65

Deústua, Alejandro (Peru; b. 1849), 181

Dialogues on the greatness of Brazil (17th cent.), 62

Dias, Father Francisco (Portugal; 16th cent.), 48

Dias, Theophilo (Brazil; 1857–1889), 143, 175

Díaz, José (Ecuador; 17th cent.), 215

Díaz, Leopoldo (Argentina; b. 1862), 168

Díaz, Porfirio, 138, 160, 188, 254, 277

Díaz Arrieta, Hernán (Chile; b. 1891), 260, 273

Díaz de Gamarra, Father Juan Benito (Mexico; 1745–1783), 233

Díaz de Guzmán, Ruy (Paraguay; ca. 1554–1629), 36, 52, 214

Díaz de León, Francisco (Mexico; b. 1897), 255

Díaz del Castillo, Bernal (Spain; 1496–1584), 20, 45, 50, 215, 219, 221

Díaz Gebuta Quej, Francisco (Guatemala; 16th cent.), 214

Díaz Loyola, Carlos (Chile; b. 1894), 274

Díaz Mirón, Salvador (Mexico; 1853–1928), 165, 264

Díaz Parrado, Flora (Cuba, 20th cent.), 161

Díaz Plaja, Guillermo, 267

Díaz Rodríguez, Manuel (Venezuela; 1868–1927), 168, 178, 179, 181, 182, 270

Diderot, Denis, 26, 89, 234

Diego, José de (Puerto Rico; 1868–1918), 266

Díez Canedo, Enrique, 93, 257, 267

Díez Leiva, Fernando (Spain; 17th cent.), 82

Domingo, Brother (Ecuador; 17th cent.), 215

Domínguez, María Alicia (Argentina; b. 1908), 276

Domínguez Camargo, Hernando (Colombia; 1601–1656), 84

Dominici, Pedro César (Venezuela; b. 1872), 270

Donoso, Armando (Chile; b. 1887), 252, 266, 267, 273

Dorantes de Carranza, Baltasar (Mexico; 16th cent.), 52

Dos Aguas, Marquis of, 92

Dowler, Guy, 283

Doyle, Henry Grattan, 267

Driver, David Miller, 232, 245, 248, 251, 290

Drummond de Andrade, Carlos (Brazil; b. 1902), 191, 278

Dryden, John, 25

Ducasse, Isidor (Uruguay-France; 1846–1870), 246

Dumas the elder, Alexandre, 121

Duquesne, José Domingo (Colombia; 18th cent.), 233
Durán, Friar Diego (Spain-Mexico; before 1538–1588), 55, 219
Durão, Friar José de Santa Rita (Brazil; 1722–1784), 85–86, 91
Du Tertre, Jean Baptiste, 25

Eberling, Frances, 227
Eça de Queiroz, José Maria, 200
Ecclesiasticus, 18
Echagüe, Juan Pablo (Argentina; b. 1877), 252
Echave family (Spain and Mexico; 16th–17th cent.), 91
Echave Orio, Baltasar de (Spain; 1548–1620), 47
Echeverría, Aquileo (Costa Rica; 1866–1909), 173, 267
Echeverría, Esteban (Argentina; 1805–1851), 117–119, 120, 125, 142, 165, 192, 244, 245
Eckhout, Albert, 48
Eden, Richard, 208
Edwards, Agustín (Chile; b. 1878), 288
Edwards, Emily, 292
Edwards Bello, Joaquín (Chile; b. 1888), 274
Eguiara, Father Juan José de (Mexico; 1706–1763), 233
Eguívar, Hermenegildo de (Argentina; 17th cent.), 215
Eguren, José María (Peru; 1882–1942), 189, 274
Eichelbaum, Samuel (Argentina; b. 1894), 272
El Greco, 36, 163
Elhúyar, Fausto de (Spain; 1757–1833), 43, 234
Eliot, Thomas Stearns, 101, 189
Elliott, Lillian Estelle, 288

Ellis, Havelock, 268
Elórduy, Ernesto (Mexico; 1853–1912), 142
Emerson, Ralph Waldo, 100, 153, 237, 251, 264
Emiro Kastos, see Restrepo, Juan de Dios
Encina, Juan del, 103, 111
Encina, Juan de la, see Gutiérrez, Ricardo (Spain)
Encyclopédie, 88, 241
Englekirk, John Eugene, 224, 264, 270, 288, 290
Enriquillo, 15
Erasmus, 46, 213
Erauso, Catalina de (Spain; 1585–ca. 1635), 45
Ercilla, Alonso de (Spain; 1533–1594), 12, 27, 45, 46, 49–50, 51, 150, 207, 219, 220
Erskine, John, 272
Escobar, Arcesio (Colombia; 1837–1867), 288
Escobar, Eloy (Venezuela; 1824–1889), 127, 248, 249
Escobedo, Father Federico (Mexico; 20th cent.), 232, 257
Espadero, see Ruiz Espadero, Nicolás
Espaillat, Ulises Francisco (Santo Domingo; 1823–1878), 243
Espejo, see Santa Cruz Espejo, Francisco Eugenio
Espinel, Vicente, 59, 108
Espinosa, Aurelio Macedonio, 224
Espinosa, Friar Alonso de (Spain; 16th cent.), 220, 221
Espinosa, José María (Colombia; 19th cent.), 254
Espinosa, Pedro, 72
Espinosa de los Monteros, Juan (Peru; 17th cent.), 91
Espinosa Medrano, Juan de (Peru; ca. 1640–1682), 36, 83, 214, 216

Espronceda, José de, 121, 128
Esquilache, Francisco de Borja, Prince of (Spain; 1581–1658), 62, 220
Esténger, Rafael (Cuba; b. 1899), 263, 280
Estrada, Ángel de (Argentina; 1872–1923), 270
Estrada, Domingo (Guatemala; ca. 1858–1901), 264
Estrada, Genaro (Mexico; 1887–1937), 274
Estrada, José María (Mexico; 19th cent.), 254
Estrada, Santiago (Argentina; 1841–1891), 252
Eugénie, Empress, 246
Evans, Ernestine, 292
Evia, Father Jacinto de (Ecuador; 17th cent.), 84
Évreux, Yves d', 25
Ewen, David, 284

Fabela, Isidro (Mexico; b. 1882), 277
Facio, Justo A. (Panama-Costa Rica; 1859–1931), 266
Fagundes Varella, Luis Nicolau (Brazil; 1841–1875), 115, 128
Fairchild, Hoxie Neale, 210
Falcón, César (Peru; 20th cent.), 197, 279, 282
Fallon, Diego (Colombia; 1834–1905), 255
Farías Brito, Raimundo de (Brazil; 1862–1917), 181
Fariña Núñez, Eloy (Paraguay; 1885–1929), 273
Fariña Núñez, Porfirio (Paraguay; d. 1937), 252
Fassett, Jacob S., 271, 292
Favart, Charles-Simon, 89
Fénelon, François de Salignac de la Mothe, 221

Ferdinand the Catholic, 17
Ferdinand VII of Spain, 97
Ferguson, John DeLancey, 264
Fernandes, Lorenzo (Brazil; b. 1897), 202
Fernandes Pinheiro, Canon Joaquim Caetano (Brazil; 1825–1876), 289
Fernández, Carmelo (Venezuela; d. 1877), 254
Fernández, Diego, "el Palentino" (Spain; 16th cent.), 220
Fernández, Juan Rómulo (Argentina; b. 1884), 252
Fernández, Justino (Mexico; 20th cent.), 212
Fernández de Enciso, Martín (Spain; 16th cent.), 219
Fernández de Lizardi, José Joaquín (Mexico; 1776–1827), 108, 182, 221, 257
Fernández de Oviedo, Gonzalo (Spain; 1478–1557), 12, 32, 45, 49, 207, 219, 221
Fernández de Piedrahita, Bishop Lucas (Colombia; 1624–1688), 214, 231
Fernández de Quirós, Pedro (Portugal; 1565–1615), 220, 221
Fernández de Santa Cruz, Bishop Manuel, 77
Fernández Guardia, Ricardo (Costa Rica; b. 1867), 283
Fernández Moreno, Baldomero (Argentina; b. 1886), 186, 268, 273
Ferreira, Alexandre (Brazil; 1765–1815), 234
Ferreira dos Santos, Juan Gualberto (Brazil), 257
Ferreira França, Carlos (Brazil; 19th cent.), 289
Ferrero, Guglielmo, 279

Fiallo, Fabio (Santo Domingo; 1866–1942), 265
Fierro, Pancho (Peru; 1803–1879), 140
Figari, Pedro (Uruguay; 1861–1938), 204
Figueiredo, Jackson de (Brazil; 1891–1928), 274
Figueiredo, Pedro Americo (Brazil; 1843–1905), 255
Figueroa, Bartolomé de (Peru; 17th cent.), 215
Finney, R. V., 227
Finot, Enrique (Bolivia; b. 1891), 289
Fitts, Dudley, 275, 280, 291
Fitzmaurice-Kelly, James, 69, 267
Fitzmaurice-Kelly, Julia, 227
Flaubert, Gustave, 28
Flores, Ángel (Mexico; 20th cent.), 268, 282, 283, 284, 292
Flores, Juan José (Venezuela-Ecuador; 1800–1864), 233, 243
Flores Jijón, Antonio (Ecuador; b. 1833), 243
Flórez, José (Guatemala; 1758–1814), 233
Flórez, Julio (Colombia; 1869–1923), 265
Florian, 25
Florio, John, 25, 210
Fombona Pachano, Jacinto (Venezuela; b. 1901), 197, 280
Fonteneau, Jean, see Saintonge, Jean Alphonse de
Ford, Jeremiah Denis Matthias, 288
Foster, Stephen, 147
Foxá, Francisco Javier (Santo Domingo; 1816–ca. 1865), 123, 249
Fracastoro, Girolamo, 12, 207
Frampton, J., 3

Franca, Leonel (Brazil; 20th cent.), 253
França, the younger, José Joaquim (Brazil; 1838–1890), 273
France, Anatole, 151
Francia, Dr., see Rodríguez de Francia, José Gaspar
Francisca Julia, see Silva, Francisca Julia da
Francovich, Guillermo (Brazil; 20th cent.), 253
Frank, Waldo, 242, 287, 291
Fray Mocho, see Álvarez, José Sixto
Freire, Laudelino (Brazil; 1873–1937), 235
Freyre, Gilberto (Brazil; b. 1900), 33, 211, 212, 214, 216, 247, 279
Freyre de Jaimes, Carolina (Peru; d. 1916), 250
Frías, Heriberto (Mexico; 1870–1928), 269
Frias de Albornoz, Bartolomé (Spain; 17th cent.), 212
Frugoni, Emilio (Uruguay; b. 1880), 273
Fucilla, Joseph G., 228
Fuenleal, see Ramírez de Fuenleal, Sebastián
Fugger, Johann, 224
Funes, Dean Gregorio (Argentina; 1749–1829), 234
Furness, Horace Howard, 3

Gache, Roberto (Argentina; b. 1892), 272
Gade, Niels, 142
Galafre, 154
Galdós, see Pérez Galdós, Benito
Galileo, 42, 78
Galindo, Miguel (Mexico; b. 1881), 227

Gallardo, Lino (Venezuela; 18th cent.), 226

Gallego, Juan Nicasio, 142

Gallegos, Gerardo (Ecuador; 20th cent.), 282

Gallegos, Rómulo (Venezuela; b. 1884), 198–199, 274, 283

Gallegos Lara, Joaquín (Ecuador; 20th cent.), 282

Gallop, Rodney, 294

Galván, Manuel de Jesús (Santo Domingo; 1834–1910), 149, 250

Gálvez, José (Peru; b. 1885), 274

Gálvez, Manuel (Argentina; b. 1882), 273, 283

Gama, José Basilio da (Brazil; 1740–1795), 85–86, 91, 232

Gamarra, Abelardo (Peru; 1857–1924), 248

Gamarra, see Díaz de Gamarra, Father Juan Benito

Gamboa, Federico (Mexico; 1864–1939), 233, 271

Gamboa, Francisco Javier (Mexico; 1717–1794), 87

Gamboa de Camino, Berta (Mexico; 20th cent.), 281

Gana, Federico (Chile; 1867–1926), 271

Gannon, Patrick, 291

Gante, Friar Pedro de (Belgium; ca. 1479–1572), 31, 47, 212

Garcés, Enrique (Portugal; 16th cent.), 46, 220

García, José Uriel (Peru; b. 1891), 293

García Calderón, Francisco (Peru; b. 1883), 246, 253, 268, 269, 274, 287

García Calderón, Ventura (Peru; b. 1887), 246, 267, 268, 274, 279, 289

García Caturla, Alejandro (Cuba; 1906–1940), 201

García de Ascucha, Ignacio (Spain; 16th cent.), 48

García de Quevedo, José Heriberto (Venezuela; 1819–1871), 246, 249

García del Río, Juan (Colombia; 1794–1856), 99, 100

García Godoy, Federico (Santo Domingo; 1857–1924), 268

García Granados, Rafael (Mexico; 20th cent.), 222

García Heria, Luis (Venezuela; 19th cent.), 254

García Icazbalceta, Joaquín (Mexico; 1825–1894), 215, 217, 244, 248

García Mérou, Martín (Argentina; 1862–1905), 252, 290

García Monge, Joaquín (Costa Rica; b. 1881), 188, 266

García Moreno, Gabriel (Ecuador; 1821–1875), 152, 243, 262

García Tassara, Gabriel, 123

García Velloso, Enrique (Argentina; 1880–1938), 272, 288

Garcilaso de la Vega, the conqueror, 63

Garcilaso de la Vega, the Inca (Peru; 1539–1616), 20, 36, 50, 55, 56, 63–67, 72, 126, 169, 214, 223, 227

Garcilaso de la Vega, the poet, 126, 169

Garçon Rivière, Philippe, 254

Garrido Merino, Julio (Peru; 20th cent.), 282

Garrison, Richard G., 292

Gates, Eunice Joiner, 229

Gautier, Théophile, 167, 175, 264

Gavidia, Francisco (El Salvador; b. 1863), 265

Gavilán, Baltasar (Peru; 18th cent.), 215

Geiger, Maynard, 222

Geraldini, Bishop Alessandro (Italy; 1455-1524), 12, 61, 207

Gerchunoff, Alberto (Argentina; b. 1884), 273

Gerineldo (ballad), 110

Ghiraldo, Alberto (Argentina; b. 1875), 263

Gil Ricardo, 265

Gil Fortoul, José (Venezuela; 1862-1943), 244

Gil Gilbert, Enrique (Ecuador; 20th cent.), 197, 282

Giotto, 203

Giraudoux, Jean, 29

Girondo, Oliverio (Argentina; b. 1891), 273, 278

Giusti, Roberto Fernando (Argentina; b. 1887), 252, 273, 290

Gluck, Christoph Willibald von, 63, 201, 284

Godoy Alcayaga, Lucila (Chile; b. 1889), 161, 186-187, 263, 273

Goethe, Johann Wolfgang von, 80, 129, 194

Goicoechea, see Liendo Goicoechea, Friar José Antonio

Goldberg, Isaac, 245, 248, 260, 262, 265, 267, 268, 271, 282, 288, 290, 291

Gómara, see López de Gómara, Francisco

Gomes, Carlos (Brazil; 1836-1896), 140, 201, 255-256

Gómez, José Antonio (Mexico; 19th cent.), 256

Gómez, Máximo (Santo Domingo-Cuba; 1836-1905), 162

Gómez Carrillo, Enrique (Guatemala; 1873-1927), 178, 179, 246

Gómez de Avellaneda, Gertrudis (Cuba-Spain; 1814-1873), 123, 127, 129, 240, 246, 247, 249, 250, 269

Gómez de la Cortina, Count de la Cortina, José (Mexico; 1799-1860), 248

Gómez de Mora, Juan, 219

Gómez de Orozco, Federico (Mexico; 20th cent.), 223

Gómez de Vidaurre, Felipe (Chile; 1740-1818), 234

Gómez Farías, Valentín, 112

Gómez Kemp, Vicente (Cuba; b. 1914), 280

Gómez Masía, Román (Argentina; 1903-1944), 272

Gómez Restrepo, Antonio (Colombia; b. 1869), 231, 289

Gonçalves Crespo, Antonio (Brazil-Portugal; 1847-1883), 142, 246

Gonçalves de Magalhães, José Domingos (Brazil; 1811-1882), 121, 122, 246

Gonçalves Dias, Antonio (Brazil; 1823-1864), 115, 122, 127, 130, 245, 249, 250

Gonçalves Teixeira e Sousa, Antonio (Brazil; 1812-1861), 222

Gondra, Manuel (Paraguay; b. 1872), 243, 266

Góngora, Luis de, 52, 72, 80, 83, 101, 111, 169, 194, 228, 232

Góngora Marmolejo, Alonso de (Spain; 1536-1575), 220

Gonzaga, Thomaz Antonio (Portugal-Brazil; 1744-1810), 86

González, Joaquín V. (Argentina; 1863-1923), 252, 259, 260

González, Juan Francisco (Chile; 19th-20th cent.), 254

González, Juan Natalicio (Paraguay; 20th cent.), 279

González, Juan Vicente (Venezuela; 1811-1866), 244, 245
González, Manuel, 254
González Arrili, Bernardo (Argentina; b. 1892), 252
González Blanco, Andrés, 266
González Dávila, Gil, 91, 213, 235
González de Nájera, Alonso (Spain; d. after 1614), 220
González del Valle, José Zacarías (Cuba; 1820-1851), 253
González Laguna, Father Francisco (Peru; 18th cent.), 234
González Martínez, Enrique (Mexico; b. 1871), 168, 171, 186, 275, 276
González Peña, Carlos (Mexico; b. 1885), 220, 274, 276, 288, 289
González Prada, Manuel (Peru; 1848-1918), 151, 154-155, 165, 177, 188, 196, 246, 262
González Rojo, Enrique (Mexico; 1899-1939), 278
González Santín, José María (Santo Domingo; 1830-1863), 258
González Suárez, Bishop Federico (Ecuador; 1844-1917), 244
González Zeledón, Manuel (Costa Rica; 1864-1936), 271
Goodwin, Philip L., 235, 254, 293
Goríbar, Nicolás Javier de (Ecuador; 17th cent.), 215
Gorjón, Hernando de (Spain; d. 1547), 42
Gorostiza, José (Mexico; b. 1901), 278
Gorostiza, Manuel Eduardo de (Mexico; 1789-1851), 245, 278
Gottschalk, Louis Moreau, 256
Gounod, Charles François, 144
Gourmont, Remy de, 38, 270
Gove, Philip Babcock, 209

Goya, Francisco de, 91
Goyena, Pedro (Argentina; 1843-1892), 252
Gozzoli, Benozzo, 12
Graça Aranha, José Pereira de (Brazil; 1868-1931), 190, 194-195, 270, 279
Gracián, Baltasar, 22, 90, 163
Grant, Ulysses S., 164
Gray, Thomas, 238
Green, Ernest, 291
Greiff, León de (Colombia; b. 1895), 274
Grenet, Emilio (Cuba; 20th cent), 294
Grétry, André, 226
Grieco, Agrippino (Brazil; b. 1888), 274
Griffin, Charles Carroll, 216, 287
Grismer, Raymond Leonard, 294
Groot, José Manuel (Colombia; 1800-1878), 244
Grotius, Hugo, 19
Groussac, Paul (France-Argentina; 1848-1929), 245, 252
Grucci, Joseph Leonard, 291
Grummon, Stuart E., 283
Guadalupe y Téllez, Francisco Pío de, 38
Guanes, Alejandro (Paraguay; 19th-20th cent.), 266
Guardia, Heraclio Martín de la (Venezuela; 1829-1908), 248
Guarín, José David (Colombia; 1830-1890), 248
Guarín, José Joaquín (Colombia; 1825-1854), 255
Guedalla, Philip, 242
Güegüence, El (play), 56, 223
Guerra, Friar García, 47
Guerra, José Eduardo (Bolivia; 1893-1943), 274, 288
Guerra, José Guillermo (Chile; 19th cent.), 252

Guerrero, Vicente, 241
Guevara, Andrés de (Mexico; 18th cent.), 233
Guevara, Friar Antonio de, 21
Guevara, Friar Juan de (Mexico; 16th cent.), 55, 80
Guevara, Friar Miguel de (Mexico; d. ca. 1640), 232
Guido, Ángel (Argentina; b. 1896), 223
Guido Spano, Carlos (Argentina; 1827–1918), 139, 257
Guillachamin, Gabriel (Ecuador; 17th cent.), 215
Guillén, Nicolás (Cuba; b. 1904), 196, 280
Guimarães, Bernardo da Silva (Brazil; 1827–1855), 260
Guimarães, Luis (Brazil; 1847–1898), 143, 175
Güiraldes, Ricardo (Argentina; 1886–1927), 199–200, 259, 273, 278, 283
Guirao, Ramón (Cuba; b. 1908), 280
Gusmão, Father Bartolomeu Lourenço de (Brazil; 1685–1724), 234
Gutiérrez, Eduardo (Argentina; 1853–1890), 183, 244, 259
Gutiérrez, Juan María (Argentina; 1809–1878), 99, 119, 217, 242
Gutiérrez, Ricardo (Argentina; 1836–1896), 138, 139, 260
Gutiérrez, Ricardo (Spain), 93
Gutiérrez, Zeferino (Mexico; 19th cent.), 254
Gutiérrez Coll, Jacinto (Venezuela; 1836–1901), 127, 248
Gutiérrez de Luna, Cristóbal (Spain; 16th cent.), 223
Gutiérrez de Piñeres, Germán (Colombia; 1816–1872), 250

Gutiérrez de Santa Clara, Pedro (Cuba or Mexico; 16th cent.), 52, 214
Gutiérrez González, Gregorio (Colombia; 1826–1872), 127, 129–130, 170, 258
Gutiérrez Nájera, Manuel (Mexico; 1859–1895), 160, 166, 167, 168, 170, 171, 172, 173, 177, 178, 181, 265, 269
Guzmán, Antonio Leocadio (Venezuela; 1800–1884), 125
Guzmán, Martín Luis (Mexico; b. 1887), 188, 246, 274, 276, 281

Habig, Marion Alphonse, 212
Hague, Eleanor, 227, 294
Hahn, Reynaldo (Venezuela-France; b. 1874), 246, 284
Hallenbeck, C., 293
Hamilton, Alexander, 96
Hamilton, Earl Jefferson, 211
Hamilton, Sir William, 102
Hanke, Lewis, 212
Harcourt, Raoul and Marguerite d', 225
Haring, Clarence Henry, 211, 213
Hartzenbusch, Juan Eugenio, 67, 228
Harvey, William, 42
Hathaway, E. H., 293
Haya de la Torre, Víctor Raúl (Peru; b. 1895), 188, 277
Haydn, Franz Josef, 140, 201, 226
Hays, H. R., 280, 291
Heine, Heinrich, 258
Helm, MacKinley, 293
Hennepin, Louis, 25
Henríquez, Enrique (Santo Domingo; 1859–1940), 258
Henríquez, Father Camilo (Chile; 1769–1845), 98

Henríquez de Camporredondo, Pero Ansúrez, 48
Henríquez de Guzmán, Alonso (Spain; 1500–after 1544), 45, 218, 221
Henríquez Ureña, Camila (Santo Domingo; b. 1894), 263, 276
Henríquez Ureña, Max (Santo Domingo; b. 1885), 258, 266, 268
Henríquez y Carvajal, Federico (Santo Domingo; b. 1848), 261
Henríquez y Carvajal, Francisco (Santo Domingo; 1859–1935), 243, 266
Herculano, Alexandre, 262
Herder, Johann Gottfried von, 117
Heredia, José Francisco (Santo Domingo; 1776–1820), 106
Heredia, José María (wrote in Spanish; Cuba; 1803–1839), 85, 105–107, 116, 121, 129, 142, 151, 157, 239, 240, 291
Hérédia, José Maria de (wrote in French; Cuba-France; 1842–1905), 208, 246
Heredia, Nicolás (Santo Domingo-Cuba; ca. 1849–1901), 271
Hernández, Daniel (Peru; 1856–1932), 254
Hernández, José (Argentina; 1834–1886), 144–147, 191, 259, 261
Hernández Arana Xahilá, Francisco (Guatemala; 16th cent.), 214
Hernández Catá, Alfonso (Cuba-Spain; 1885–1940), 263, 274
Hernández Franco, Tomás (Santo Domingo; b. 1904), 280
Herodotus, 67
Herrera, Antonio de, 65

Herrera, Darío (Panama; 1871–1914), 266
Herrera, Ernesto (Uruguay; 1887–1917), 272, 273
Herrera, Juan de, 92
Herrera, Pablo (Ecuador; 1820–1896), 289
Herrera y Obes, Julio (Uruguay; 1842–1912), 243
Herrera y Reissig, Julio (Uruguay; 1875–1910), 168, 189, 276
Herring, Hubert, 281, 284, 288
Herschfeld, Dorothy, 224
Hespelt, Ernest Herman, 283, 288
Hespelt, Miriam, 283
Hidalgo, Alberto (Peru; b. 1897), 274
Hidalgo, Bartolomé (Uruguay; 1788–1823), 110, 111, 143
Hidalgo, Father Miguel (Mexico; 1753–1811), 98, 173, 241
Hill, Thomas, 252
Hills, Elijah Clarence, 224, 238, 240, 267, 270, 290
Hinojosa, Eduardo de, 209
Hobbes, Thomas, 26
Hojeda, Friar Diego de (Spain-Peru; ca. 1570–1615), 46, 220
Hole, Myra Cadwalader, 217
Holland, Lord, 102
Hollingworth, Margaret Richardson, 282
Holmes, Henry Alfred, 260, 278, 292
Holmes, Oliver Wendell, 237
Homer, 257
Horace, 4, 100, 105, 106, 108, 115, 126, 158, 194, 256, 257, 258
Hostos, Eugenio María (Puerto Rico; 1839–1903), 151, 155–157, 158, 160, 163, 178, 262
Howland, Mariesta Dodge, 262

Huaican, Juan (Peru; 17th–18th cent.), 215
Huaman, Melchor (Peru; 17th cent.), 215
Huaman Poma de Ayala, Felipe (Peru; 16th cent.), 36, 214
Huayna Cápac, 103
Hudson, William Henry, the naturalist (Argentina-England; 1841–1922), 118, 199, 228, 246
Huerta, Victoriano, 281
Hughes, Langston, 280
Hugo, Victor, 28, 101, 120, 123, 124, 127, 130, 194, 264
Huidobro, Vicente (Chile; b. 1893), 190, 278
Húmara, Rafael, 247
Humboldt, Alexander von, 8, 91, 232, 238, 287
Hume, David, 102
Huntington, Ralph Walter, 261
Hurtado de Mendoza, Diego, 47, 50
Hurtado de Mendoza, García, 49
Hurtado de Toledo, Luis, 210
Huxley, Aldous, 27

Ibáñez, Sara [Iglesias] de (Uruguay; 20th cent.), 191, 276
Ibarbourou, Juana [Fernández] de (Uruguay; b. 1895), 186, 273, 275
Ibarguren, Carlos (Argentina; b. 1877), 239
Icaza, Francisco Asís de (Mexico; 1863–1925), 165, 246, 264
Icaza, Jorge (Ecuador; b. 1906), 197, 282
Icaza, Xavier (Mexico; b. 1892), 281
Iglesias Paz, César (Argentina; d. 1922), 272
Imbert, Louis, 283

Inca, Simón (Peru; 17th cent.), 215
Incháustegui Cabral, Héctor (Santo Domingo; b. 1912), 191
Ingenieros, José (Argentina; 1877–1925), 181, 237, 252, 253, 269
Ingres, Jean Auguste Dominique, 242
Iradier, Sebastián (Spain; d. ca. 1865), 141
Iraizoz, Antonio (Cuba; b. 1890), 263
Irala, see Martínez de Irala, Domingo
Irisarri, Antonio José de (Guatemala; 1786–1868), 109, 257
Isaacs, Edith J. R., 272
Isaacs, Jorge (Colombia; 1837–1895), 149, 170, 261
Isabella the Catholic, 30, 79
Isla, Andrés de (Mexico; 18th cent.), 230
Itaparica, Friar Manoel de Santa Maria (Brazil; 1704–after 1768), 85
Ituarte, Julio (Mexico; 1845–18–), 256
Iturbide, Agustín de, 112, 115
Ixtlilxóchitl, see Alba Ixtlilxóchitl, Fernando de

Jackson, Helen Hunt, 270
Jaimes Freyre, Ricardo (Bolivia; 1868–1933), 168, 171
James, Concha Romero, see Romero (de) James, Concha
James, Earle K., 282
James, Henry, 228
James, Jesse, 164
Jane, Cecil, 207
Jarnés, Benjamín, 212
Jáuregui, Agustín de, 214
Jeffers, Robinson, 146

Jefferson, Thomas, 99
Jerez, Francisco de (Spain; 1504–1539), 20, 45, 220, 221
Jijena Sánchez, Rafael (Argentina), 280
Jiménez, José Manuel (Cuba; 1855–19–), 256
Jiménez, Juan Ramón, 169
Jiménez de Quesada, Gonzalo (Spain; ca. 1499–1579), 53, 219, 284
Jiménez Rueda, Julio (Mexico; b. 1896), 214, 228, 289
João IV of Portugal, 74
João VI of Portugal, 236
João do Rio, see Barreto, Paulo
Job, Book of, 17
Jodelle, Étienne, 23
John of Austria, 64
Johnson, Harvey Leroy, 218
Johnson, Samuel, 4, 26, 209
Jones, Cecil Knight, 265, 295
Jones, Willis Knapp, 272
José "el Indio" (Argentina, 18th cent.), 215
Jotabeche, see Vallejo, José Joaquín
Juan "el Indio" (Argentina; 17th cent.), 215
Juárez, Benito, 138, 248
Juárez, Father Gaspar (Argentina; 1731–1804), 234
Juárez family (Mexico; 17th–18th cent.), 91
Jugo Ramírez, Diego (Venezuela; 1836–1903), 257
Junqueira Freire, Luis José (Brazil; 1832–1855), 128
Juvenal, 108

Kabiyú, J. M. (Paraguay; 17th cent.), 215
Kaplan, L. C., 282
Keats, John, 194

Keiser, Albert, 210
Kelly, Edith Louise, 247
Keniston, Hayward, 221, 294
Kennedy, James, 291
Kent, Rockwell, 293
Keyserling, Count Hermann, 10
Kilham, Walter H., 292
Kipling, Rudyard, 194, 242, 279
Kirstein, Lincoln, 210, 255, 293
Knox, Henry, 96
Koeller, Julio Frederico, 254
Korn, Alejandro (Argentina; 1860–1936), 181, 237, 253, 259, 269
Kotzebue, August Friedrich Ferdinand von, 211
Kowalewska, Sonia, 79
Kress, Dorothy Margaret, 270
Kubler, George, 222, 293

La Boétie, Étienne de, 12, 207
La Condamine, Charles Marie de, 25
La Fontaine, Jean de, 110
La Granja, Luis Antonio de Oviedo, Count of (Spain-Peru; 1636–1717), 220
La Llave, Father Pablo de (Mexico; 1773–1833), 233
Labarca Hubertson, Amanda [Pinto de] (Chile; b. 1886), 242, 276
Lacerda, Francisco de (Brazil; 1750–1798), 234
Lacunza, Father Manuel (Chile; 1731–1801), 231
Lafayette, Marie Joseph, Marquis de, 95
Laferrere, Gregorio de (Argentina; 1867–1913), 272
Laforgue, Jules (Uruguay-France; 1860–1887), 246
Lagommaggiore, Francisco, 289
Lahontan, Baron de, 25

Lamartine, Alphonse Marie Louis de, 121

Lamas, Andrés (Uruguay; 1820–1891), 244

Lamas, José Ángel (Venezuela; d. 1814), 226

Lampérez y Romea, Vicente, 54, 222

Lanborn, Robert H., 292

Landa, Friar Diego de (Spain; 1524–1579), 219, 221

Landívar, Father Rafael (Guatemala; 1731–1793), 84–85, 90, 91, 107, 256

Landor, Walter Savage, 153

Lange, Francisco Curt, 227

Lange [de Girondo], Nora (Argentina; 20th cent.), 276

Lanning, John Tate, 217, 287

Lara, Horacio (Chile; 19th cent.), 261

Larbaud, Valéry, 283

Larra, Mariano José de (Spain; 1809–1837), 121

Larrañaga, Dámaso (Uruguay; 1771–1846), 234

Larrazábal, Felipe (Venezuela; 1817–1873), 244

Larreta, Enrique [Rodríguez] (Argentina; b. 1875), 168, 181, 246, 259, 270

Las Casas, Friar Bartolomé (Spain; 1474–1566), 5, 15, 17–20, 21, 25, 31, 32, 33, 49, 50, 208, 219, 221

Lasso, Francisco (Peru; d. ca. 1868), 254

Lastarria, José Victorino (Chile; 1817–1888), 120, 245

Latorre, Mariano (Chile; b. 1886), 273

Laura Victoria, see Peñuela de Segura, Laura Victoria

Lautréamont, Comte de, see Ducasse, Isidor

Lauxar, see Crispo Acosta, Osvaldo

Lavalle, José Antonio de (Peru; 1833–1893), 216, 250, 252

Lavardén, Manuel de (Argentina; 1754–1809), 251

Lawrence, David Herbert, 26, 27

Lazo, Raimundo (Cuba; b. 1904), 263

Lazo Martí, Francisco (Venezuela; 1864–1912), 173, 263, 267

Lea, Henry Charles, 212

Leal, Father Francisco Luis dos Santos (Brazil; 1740–1820), 234

Leavitt, Sturgis E., 261

Lecky, William J., 113

LeClercq, Jacques, 271, 283

Lecuona, Ernesto (Cuba; b. 1895), 201

Lee [de Muñoz Marín], Muna, 230, 265

Leguizamón, Martiniano (Argentina; 1858–1935), 183, 259, 271

Lehmann-Nitsche, Robert, 244

Leite, Serafim, 212

Leite filho, Solidonio (Brazil; 20th cent.), 213

Lejarza, Juan José (Mexico; 1785–1824), 226, 233

Lejeune, Louis François, 25

León Hebreo, see Abravanel, Judah

León, Francisco de, 44

León, Friar Luis de, 22, 47, 126, 169, 191

León, Nicolás (Mexico), 217

León y Gama, Antonio (Mexico; 1735–1802), 87, 233

Leonard, Irving Albert, 221, 232, 288

Leonardo de Argensola, Bartolomé, 62, 200

Leoni, Raul de (Brazil; 1895–1926), 274

Leonidas, 126

Leopardi, Giacomo, 105

Lerdo de Tejada (Mexico; 1827–1889), 138, 243

Léry, Jean de, 23

Lescarbot, Marc, 25

Le Senne, Camille, 268

Leslie, John Kenneth, 246

Lessing, Gotthold Ephraim, 44, 246

Levene, Ricardo (Argentina; b. 1885), 211

Lida, María Rosa (Argentina; 20th cent.), 257, 276

Liendo, Rodrigo Gil de (Spain; 16th cent.), 48

Liendo Goicoechea, Friar José Antonio de (Costa Rica-Guatemala; 1735–1814), 233

Liévana, Pedro de (Spain; d. 1602), 220

Lillo, Baldomero (Chile; 1867–1923), 271

Lima, Jorge de (Brazil; b. 1895), 191, 270, 278, 280

Lima Barreto, Afonso Henriques de (Brazil; 1881–1922), 274

Lima Leitão, Antonio José (Brazil; 19th cent.), 257

Lincoln, Abraham, 133

Lins do Rego, José (Brazil; b. 1901), 198, 282

Lira, Pedro (Chile; 1845–1912), 254

Lisboa, Antonio Francisco, the Aleijadinho (Brazil; 1730–1814), 91

Lisboa, Antonio José (Brazil; 1705–1739), 232

List Arzubide, Germán (Mexico; 20th cent.), 278

Livingston, Arthur, 271

Lizardi, see Fernández de Lizardi, José Joaquín

Lizárraga, Friar Reginaldo de (Spain; 1545–1615), 220

Lizaso, Félix (Cuba; b. 1891), 263, 264, 274

Llano de Zapata, José Eusebio (Peru; ca. 1724–after 1780), 233

Llauqui, see Zangurima, Gaspar

Llerena, Cristóbal de (Santo Domingo; 16th cent.), 52

Llona, Numa Pompilio (Ecuador; 1832–1907), 249

Llorens Castillo, Vicente, 225

Lobo, Gerardo, 84

Locke, John, 26, 42

Lohmann Villena, Guillermo (Peru; 20th cent.), 218, 240

Lollis, Cesare de, 8, 207

Lombardo Toledano, Vicente (Mexico; b. 1894), 277

Londoño, Víctor Manuel (Colombia; 1876–1936), 265

Longfellow, Henry Wadsworth, 252, 263, 264

Longinus, 233

Lope de Vega, see Vega

Lopes, Bernardino (Brazil; 1859–1916), 175–177

Lopes de Sousa, Pero (Portugal; 16th cent.), 45, 220

López, Ismael (Colombia; b. 1880), 265

López, Lucio Vicente (Argentina; 1848–1893), 186, 271

López, Luis Carlos (Colombia; b. ca. 1880), 268, 274

López, Vicente Fidel (Argentina; 1815–1903), 119, 215, 250
López Albújar, Enrique (Peru; b. 1872), 279
López de Gómara, Francisco, 65, 210
López de Mesa, Luis (Colombia; b. 1884), 274
López de Santa Anna, Antonio, 112
López Portillo y Rojas, José (Mexico; 1850–1923), 271
López Velarde, Ramón (Mexico; 1888–1921), 189, 268, 274, 277
López y Fuentes, Gregorio (Mexico; b. 1895), 197, 281, 282
López y Planes, Vicente (Argentina; 1783–1856), 239, 243 279
Lorente, Mariano Joaquín, 260,
Loureda, Ignacio, 232
Louverture, Toussaint, 127
Loveira, Carlos (Cuba; 1882–1928), 271
Lovejoy, Arthur Oncken, 211
Lowenfels, H. von, 291
Loynaz, Dulce María (Cuba; b. 1901), 276
Lozano, José Tadeo (Colombia; 1771–1816), 233
Luca, Esteban de (Argentina; 1786–1824), 239
Lucretius, 128, 258
Lugo, Américo (Santo Domingo; b. 1871), 265
Lugones, Leopoldo (Argentina; 1874–1938), 147, 168, 171, 174, 175, 181, 185, 189, 192, 252, 258, 266, 270, 271, 275
Lujan, James Graham, 283
Lully, Jean Baptiste, 63
Luna y Victoria, Father Francisco

Javier de (Panama; d. 1777), 216
Lussich, Antonio (Uruguay; 1848–1928), 259
Luz y Caballero, José de la (Cuba; 1800–1862), 157
Lynch, Benito (Argentina; b. 1885), 259, 273

MacClelland, I. L., 244
Macedo, Joaquim Manoel de (Brazil; 1820–1882), 125, 273
Maceo, Antonio, 162
Machado, Antonio,, 169
Machado, Gilka (Brazil; b. 1893), 186
Machado de Assis, Joaquim María (Brazil; 1839–1908), 143, 147–148, 175, 260
Machiavelli, Niccolò, 14
Mackay, J. A., 276, 287
McKinley, William, 262
MacLeish, Archibald, 221
McMichael, Charles B., 267
MacNutt, Francis Augustus, 208
MacVan, Alice Jane, 265
Madero, Francisco (Mexico; 1873–1913), 243, 277
Madiedo, Manuel María (Colombia; 1815–1888), 249
Madison, James, 99
Maffei, Scipione, 89
Magalhães, Valentin (Brazil; 1859–1903), 273
Magalhães Gandavo, Pero de, 218
Magallanes Moure, Manuel (Chile; 1878–1924), 168, 275
Magaña Esquivel, Antonio (Mexico; 20th cent.), 272
Magariños Cervantes, Alejandro (Uruguay; 1825–1893), 259
Magdaleno, Mauricio (Mexico; b. 1906), 263, 281, 283

Magón, *see* González Zeledón

Maitín, José Antonio (Venezuela; 1804–1874), 128, 245

Maldonado, Father Francisco Severo (Mexico; *ca.* 1770–1832), 98

Maldonado, Pedro Vicente (Ecuador; 1704–1748), 233

Malinowski, Marta, 246

Mallan, Lloyd, 291

Mallarmé, Stéphane, 126, 171, 264

Mallea, Eduardo (Argentina; b. 1903), 200, 283

Malloy, Robert, 283

Mancera, Marquis and Marchioness of, 76, 79

Mancisidor, José (Mexico; b. 1894), 281

Manco, Silverio (Argentina; 20th cent.), 271

Mann, Mary (Mrs. Horace), 251

Mann, Thomas, 194

Manning, Hugo, 291

Mansilla, Lucio Victorio (Argentina; 1837–1913), 150, 252

Mañach, Jorge (Cuba; b. 1898), 263, 274

Mapes, Erwin Kempton, 265, 266, 267

Maples Arce, Manuel (Mexico; b. 1898), 278

Marasso, Arturo (Argentina; b. 1890), 267

Marechal, Leopoldo (Argentina; b. 1900), 278

María Enriqueta, *see* Camarillo de Pereyra, María Enriqueta

Marianno, Olegario, *see* Carneiro da Cunha, Olegario Marianno

Mariátegui, José Carlos (Peru; 1891–1930), 274, 277

Marilia de Dirceu, 86

Marín, Francisco Gonzalo (Puerto Rico; 1863–1897), 116

Marín de Solar, Mercedes (Chile; 1804–1866), 115

Marinello, Juan (Cuba; b. 1898), 274

Mariño de Lobera, Pedro (Spain; 1536–1595), 220

Mariscal, Federico E. (Mexico; b. 1881), 188, 276, 292

Markham, Sir Clements Robert, 221, 222, 224, 227

Mármol, José (Argentina; 1817–1871), 116, 120, 245, 249

Marmontel, Jean François, 25, 89

Marques, Xavier (Brazil; b. 1861), 270

Marques Pereira, Nuno (Brazil; 1652–1728), 85

Marques Rebelo (Brazil; 20th cent.), 198

Marquette, Jacques, 25

Márquez, Father Pedro José (1741–1820), 233

Márquez, Selva (Uruguay; 20th cent.), 276

Márquez Sterling, Carlos (Cuba; b. 1899), 264

Márquez Sterling, Manuel (Cuba; 1872–1934), 266

Marrero, Baltasar (Venezuela; 18th cent.), 233

Marroquín, José Manuel (Colombia; 1827–1908), 124, 243

Marroquín, Lorenzo (Colombia; 1856–1918), 271

Martel, Julian, *see* Miró, José

Martí, José (Cuba; 1853–1895), 116, 162–166, 168, 173, 177, 178, 181, 192, 196, 261, 263, 270

Martial, 257

Martin, Gregory, 208

Martin, John Lewis, 250

Martín, Lorenzo (Spain; 16th cent.), 53
Martin, Percy Alvin, 251, 269, 287
Martín de la Plaza, Luis, 72
Martínez, Friar Melchor (Chile; 19th cent.), 98
Martínez Bello, Antonio (Cuba; 20th cent.), 263
Martínez de Irala, Domingo, 38
Martínez del Río, Pablo (Mexico; b. 1892), 218
Martínez Estrada, Ezequiel (Argentina; b. 1895), 273
Martínez Montoya, Andrés (Colombia; 1869–1933), 227
Martínez Ruiz, José, 169, 177
Martínez Vela, Bartolomé (Bolivia; 1645–1702), 231
Martínez Zuviría, Gustavo Adolfo (Argentina; b. 1883), 283
Martins Penna, Luis Carlos (Brazil; 1815–1848), 123, 249, 273
Mascarenhas, Pedro, 74
Masferrer, Alberto (El Salvador; d. 1932), 266
Mass, Otto, 212
Matiz, Francisco Javier (Colombia; 1774–1851), 91
Matta, Guillermo (Chile; 1829–1899), 248
Matto de Turner, Clorinda (Peru; 1854–1909), 196, 261, 271
Mattos, Annibal (Brazil; b. 1886), 235
Mattos, Gregorio de (Brazil; 1633–1696), 58, 85
Maximilian of Hapsburg, 112, 115, 138, 254
Maya, Alcides (Brazil; 1878–1944), 274
Maya, Rafael (Colombia; b. 1898), 191, 274

Mayer-Serra, Otto, 256, 284
Mazade, Charles de, 252
Maziel, Juan Baltasar (Argentina; 1721–1788), 234
Mazo, Gabriel Carlos del (Argentina; b. 1898), 276
Medeiros e Albuquerque, José Joaquim de (Brazil; 1868–1934), 270
Medina, José Toribio (Chile; 1852–1930), 213, 217, 220, 290, 294
Medinilla, Jerónimo de, 22
Mediz Bolio, Antonio (Mexico; b. 1884), 279
Medoro, Angelo or Angelico (Italy; 16th cent.), 47
Meireles, Victor (Brazil; 1832–1903), 255
Meirelles, Cecilia (Brazil; 20th cent.), 191, 276, 278
Mejía, Diego (Spain; ca. 1565–ca. 1620), 46, 75, 220
Mejía, José (Ecuador; 1777–1813), 97
Mejía de Fernández, Abigaíl (Santo Domingo; 1896–1941), 289
Meléndez, Concha (Puerto Rico; 20th cent.), 248, 251
Meléndez, Friar Juan (Peru; 17th cent.), 231
Meléndez Valdés, Juan, 142
Melgar, Mariano (Peru; 1791–1815), 108, 214, 257
Mello, Francisco Manoel de (Portugal; 1608–1666), 46, 90, 163, 220
Mello de Moraes, Alexandro (Brazil; 1816–1882), 244
Mello de Moraes filho, Alexandre José (Brazil; 1844–1919), 289
Mello Franco, Afonso Arinos de (Brazil, 20th Cent.), 211

Mena, Juan de, 53
Menander, 71
Mendes, Manoel Odorico (Brazil; 1799–1865), 257
Méndez, Manuel Isidro (Spain-Cuba; b. 1887), 263
Méndez Pereira, Octavio (Panama; b. 1887), 274
Méndez Plancarte, Gabriel (Mexico; 20th cent.), 257
Mendieta, Friar Jerónimo de (Spain; 1525–1604), 219
Mendive, Rafael María de (Cuba; 1821–1886), 162, 263
Mendoza, Antonio de, 212
Mendoza, Daniel (Venezuela; 1823–1867), 124, 248
Mendoza, Elvira de (Santo Domingo; 16th cent.), 52
Mendoza, Friar Domingo de (Spain; 16th cent.), 209
Mendoza, Miguel de (Mexico; 17th cent.), 215
Menéndez, Miguel Ángel (Mexico; 20th cent.), 282
Menéndez Pidal, Ramón, 207
Menéndez y Pelayo, Marcelino, 8, 63, 71, 90, 101, 147, 160, 209, 217, 220, 234, 239, 245, 247, 257, 288
Menezes, Agrario de (Brazil; 1834–1863), 273
Menotti del Picchia, Paulo (Brazil; b. 1892), 274, 280
Mera, Juan León (Ecuador; 1832–1894), 149, 250, 289
Mercado, Guillermo (Peru; b. 1900), 279
Merchán, Rafael María (Cuba; 1844–1905), 158, 264
Mérida, Carlos (Guatemala; b. 1893), 293
Mérimée, Prosper, 149, 167
Meriño, Archbishop Fernando Arturo de (Santo Domingo; 1833–1907), 243
Mestre, José Manuel (Cuba; 1832–1886), 253
Meza Fuentes, Roberto (Chile; b. 1899), 265
Michelangelo, 47, 180
Michelena, Arturo (Venezuela; 1863–1898), 254
Micheo, Juan José (Guatemala; 1847–1869), 257
Micrós, see Campo, Ángel de
Mier, Friar Servando Teresa de (Mexico; 1765–1827), 108
Mignone, Francisco (Brazil; b. 1877), 202
Miguel Pereyra, Lucia (Brazil; 20th cent.), 276
Milanés, José Jacinto (Cuba; 1814–1863), 249, 258
Mill, James, 102
Mill, John Stuart, 102, 158
Milla, José (Guatemala; 1822–1882), 250
Milton, John, 194
Mina, Francisco Javier, 86
Miomandre, Francis de, 268
Miralla, José Antonio (Argentina; 1790–1825), 238
Miranda, Francisco de (Venezuela; 1750–1816), 94–97, 98, 104, 235
Miró, José (Argentina; 1867–1896), 271
Miró, Ricardo (Panama; 1883–1940), 274
Mistral, Gabriela, see Godoy Alcayaga, Lucila
Mitjans, Aurelio (Cuba; 1863–1889), 289
Mitre, Bartolomé (Argentina; 1821–1906), 119, 137, 151, 173, 215, 243, 251, 253, 257, 264, 267

Mociño, José Mariano (Mexico; ca. 1750–1821), 233

Mocquet, Jean, 25

Moctezuma, 171

Mogrovejo, Saint Toribio Alfonso de (Spain; 1534–1606), 31

Molière, Jean Baptiste, 71, 87, 98

Molina, Cristóbal de, "of Cuzco" (Peru; 16th cent.), 52, 214, 222

Molina, Cristóbal de, "of Santiago" (Spain; 1494–1578), 220

Molina, Juan Ignacio de (Chile; 1740–1829), 234

Molina, Juan Ramón (Honduras; 1875–1908), 266

Molinari, Ricardo E. (Argentina; b. 1898), 278

Moll, Aristides A., 234

Moncayo, Pedro (Ecuador; 1804–1888), 244

Montaigne, Michel de, 23–26, 65, 153, 210

Montalbán, Leonardo (Nicaragua; b. 1887), 289

Montalván, Juan Pérez de, 69

Montalvo, Juan (Ecuador; 1832–1889), 142, 151, 152–154, 155, 163, 180, 246, 262

Montaña, Luis (Mexico; 1755–1820), 232

Montañés, Juan Martínez, 90

Monteagudo, Bernardo de (Argentina; ca. 1787–1825), 99

Monteiro Lobato, José Bento (Brazil; b. 1883), 275, 282

Montenegro, Ernesto (Chile; 20th cent.), 279

Montes de Oca, Bishop Ignacio (Mexico; 1840–1921), 115, 257

Montes del Valle, Agripina (Colombia; 1844–1915), 240

Montesinos, Friar Antón de (Spain; 16th cent.), 15–17, 31, 208, 209

Montesinos, Fernando de (Spain; 1593–1655), 220

Montesquieu, Charles Louis de Secondat, 94, 211

Monteverde, Manuel de (Santo Domingo; 1793–1871), 233

Montgolfier, the brothers, 234

Montijo, Eugenia, see Eugénie, Empress

Montoro, Rafael (Cuba; 1852–1933), 158

Montt, Manuel, 131, 138

Montúfar, Juan Pío, Marquis of Selva Alegre (18th–19th cent.), 233

Moore, Ernest Richard, 281

Moore, Thomas, 263

Mora, José María Luis (Mexico; 1794–1850), 244

Moraes, Vinicius de (Brazil; 20th cent.), 279

Moraes e Silva, Antonio de (Brazil; 1756–1824), 234

Morales, Juan Bautista (Mexico; 1788–1856), 248

Morales, Melesio (Mexico; 1838–1909), 256

Morales de los Ríos, Adolfo (Brazil; 20th cent.), 254

Morales Marcano, Jesús María (Venezuela; 1830–1888), 257

More, Sir Thomas, 14, 22, 31

Morel, Carlos (Argentina; 1813–1894), 255

Morel Campos, Juan (Puerto Rico; 1857–1896), 142, 201

Morell de Santa Cruz, Bishop Pedro Agustín (Santo Domingo; 1694–1768), 231

Morelos, José María, 115

Moreno, Gabriel (Peru; 18th cent.), 233

Moreno, Gabriel René (Bolivia; 1834–1908), 244
Moreno, Ignacio (Peru; 1817–1876), 254
Moreno, Mariano (Argentina; 1778–1811), 99, 104
Moreno Villa, José, 223
Moreyra, Alvaro (Brazil; b. 1888), 190, 274
Morgan, John Pierpont, 254
Morison, Samuel Eliot, 207, 213, 235
Morla Vicuña, Carlos (Chile; 1846–1901), 264
Morley, S. Griswold, 227, 267
Moses, Bernard, 220, 221, 237, 290
Mota Padilla, Father Matías de la (Mexico; 1688–1776), 231
Motolinía, see Benavente, Friar Toribio de
Motta, Arthur (Brazil; b. 1879), 289
Mozart, Wolfgang Amadeus, 201, 226, 284
Mumford, Lewis, 208
Munguía, Enrique (Mexico; d. 1940), 281
Muñiz, Francisco Javier (Argentina; 1795–1871), 133
Muñoz, Rafael (Mexico; b. 1899), 281
Muñoz Camargo, Diego (Mexico; ca. 1526–ca. 1600), 214
Muñoz Del Monte, Francisco (Santo Domingo; 1800–1865), 106
Muñoz Marín, Luis (Puerto Rico; b. 1898), 188
Muñoz Rivera, Luis (Puerto Rico; 1859–1916), 266
Murillo, Bartolomé Esteban, 47
Murillo, Gabriel (Spain; 1655–after 1682), 47

Murilo Mendes (Brazil; b. 1902), 278
Murray, Gilbert, 193
Musset, Alfred de, 194
Mutis, José Celestino (Spain; 1732–1808), 234

Nabuco, Carolina (Brazil; 20th cent.), 276
Nabuco, Joaquim (Brazil; 1849–1910), 212, 261
Nalé Roxlo, Conrado (Argentina; b. 1898), 272
Napoleon, see Bonaparte
Nápoles Fajardo, Juan Cristóbal (Cuba; 1829–1862), 258
Nariño, Antonio (Colombia; 1765–1823), 94, 98
Narváez, Alonso de (Spain; 16th cent.), 47
Nascentes, Antenor (Brazil; b. 1886), 215
Navarrete, Friar Manuel de (Mexico; 1768–1809), 107, 257
Nazareo, Pablo (Mexico; 16th cent.), 214
Neal, John, 240
Neale-Silva, 282
Nebrija, Antonio de, 27, 103
Neruda, Pablo, see Reyes, Neftalí Ricardo
Nervo, Amado (Mexico; 1870–1919), 168, 181, 186, 246, 270
Nery, Adalgisa (Brazil; 20th cent.), 276, 278
Newcomb, Rexford, 293
Nibelungenlied, 101
Niccodemi, Dario (Italy-Argentina; 1874–1934), 272
Nichols, Madaline Wallis, 241, 251, 272, 295
Nigli, Josephine, 224
"No me mueve, mi Dios . . . ," sonnet (17th cent.), 232

Nóbrega, Father Manoel da (Portugal; d. 1570), 220

Noé, Julio (Argentina; b. 1893), 273

Noel, Martín S. (Argentina; b. 1888), 223

Nolasco, Flérida [García] de (Santo Domingo; b. 1891), 227

Noreña, Miguel (Mexico; 19th cent.), 140

Northup, George Tyler, 207

Norton, Charles Eliot, 3

Nosiglia, Juan C. (Argentina; 19th cent.), 244, 272

Novo, Salvador (Mexico; b. 1904), 278

Numa Pompilius, 154

Nun Ensign, see Erauso, Catalina de

Nunes de Andrade, Juan (Brazil; 19th cent.), 257

Núñez, Rafael (Colombia; 1825–1894), 243

Núñez Cabeza de Vaca, Álvar (Spain; 1507–1559), 38, 45, 221

Núñez de Pineda Bascuñán, Francisco (Chile; 1607–1682), 83, 150

Nys, Ernest, 209

Obeso, Candelario (Colombia; 1849–1884), 268

Obligado, Rafael (Argentina; 1851–1920), 147, 244, 259

Obregón, Baltasar de (Mexico; 16th cent.), 52

Ocampo [de Bioy Casares], Silvina (Argentina; 20th cent.), 276

Ocampo [de Estrada], Victoria (Argentina; b. 1891), 276

Ocantos, Carlos María (Argentina; b. 1860), 246, 271

Ochoa, Anastasio de (Mexico; 1783–1833), 108, 257

O'Connell, Richard L., 283

O'Gorman, Edmundo (Mexico; 20th cent.), 212

Olavarría y Ferrari, Enrique (Spain-Mexico; 1844–1918), 218

Olavide, Pablo de (Peru; 1725–1804), 88–89, 234

O'Leary, Juan Emiliano (Paraguay; b. 1880), 273

Olivares, Father Miguel de (Chile; 1674–1788), 231

Olivares, Juan Manuel (Venezuela; 18th cent.), 226

Oliveira, Alberto de (Brazil; 1857–1937), 175–177

Oliveira, Filipe d' (Brazil; 1891–1933), 274

Oliveira Lima, Manoel de (Brazil; 1867–1928), 180, 269, 287, 290

Oliver, María Rosa (Argentina; b. 1900), 276

Oliver, Miguel Santos, 267

Ollántay (play), 57, 224

Ollerich, H., 283

Olmedo, José Joaquín de (Ecuador 1780–1847), 103–105, 107, 116, 129, 142, 239, 243, 257

Olmos, José (Ecuador, 17th cent.), 215

Onetti, Carlos María (Uruguay; 1895–1940), 252

Ongley, Leo, 283

Onís, Federico de, 162, 265, 275, 290

Onís, Harriet de, 281, 282, 283

Oña, Pedro de (Chile; 1570–ca. 1643), 51, 219, 222

Oré, Luis Jerónimo de (Peru; ca. 1554–1627), 52, 222

Orgaz, Raúl A. (Argentina; b. 1888), 252

Oribe, Emilio (Uruguay; b. 1893), 273

Oro, Domingo de, 132

Oro, Father José de, 131

Orozco, José Clemente (Mexico; b. 1883), 203

Orozco y Berra, Manuel (Mexico; 1816–1881), 244, 248

Orrego Luco, Luis (Chile; b. 1866), 271

Orrego Vicuña, Eugenio (Chile; b. 1900), 239

Ortega, Aniceto (Mexico; 1823–1875), 256

Ortega, Francisco (Mexico; 1793–1849), 115

Ortega, J. J. (Colombia; 20th cent.), 289

Ortega y Gasset, José, 38, 50, 169, 216, 257, 278

Ortiguera, Friar Toribio de (Spain; 16th cent.), 220

Ortiz, Adalberto (Ecuador; 20th cent.), 282

Ortiz, Diego de (Spain; 16th cent.), 48

Ortiz, Fernando (Cuba; b. 1881), 216

Ortiz, José Joaquín (Colombia; 1814–1892), 250

Ortiz de Montellano, Bernardo (Mexico; b. 1899), 278

Ortiz Guerrero, Manuel (Paraguay; 20th cent.), 279

Osorio, Miguel Angel (Colombia; 1883–1942), 186, 274

Ospina, Mariano (Colombia; 1805–1885), 243

Ossorio de Oliveira, José, 289

Oteiza, Juan José de (Mexico; 1777–1810), 2

Otero Silva, Miguel (Venezuela; b. 1908), 281

Othón, Manuel José (Mexico; 1858–1906), 165, 264

Ots Capdequí, José María, 212, 214

Ovalle, Father Alonso de (Chile; d. 1650), 231

Ovando, Sor Leonor de (Santo Domingo; d. after 1609), 52, 222

Ovid, 107, 257

Oviedo, see Fernández de Oviedo, Gonzalo

Owen, Arthur L., 227, 260

Owen, Gilberto (Mexico; 20th cent.), 284

Owen, Walter, 259

Pach, Walter, 293

Pachacuti Yamqui Salçamayhua, Juan de Santa Cruz, see Santa Cruz Pachacuti

Pagano, José León (Argentina; b. 1875), 272

Pagaza, Bishop Joaquín Arcadio (Mexico; 1839–1918), 256, 257

Page, F. M., 258

Paine, Thomas, 99

Pájara pinta (song), 110

Palacio, Pablo (Ecuador; 20th cent.), 282

Palacios, Pedro Bonifacio (Argentina; 1854–1917), 165, 264

Palacios Sojo, Father Pedro (Venezuela; 18th cent.), 226

Palafox, Bishop Juan de (Spain; 1600–1659), 50, 220

Palcos, Alberto (Argentina; b. 1894), 252

Palés Matos, Luis (Puerto Rico; b. 1898), 196, 280

Palestrina, Pierluigi, 140, 201, 226

Paley, William, 131

Palma, Angélica (Peru; 1883–1935), 255, 274

Palma, Clemente (Peru; b. 1872), 266, 270

Palma, Ramón de (Cuba; 1812–1860), 258

Palma, Ricardo (Peru; 1833–1919), 142, 149, 250, 261

Pampite, see Olmos, José

Pandiá Calogeras, João, 169

Pane, Friar Ramón (Spain; 15th cent.), 45

Pani, Alberto J. (Mexico; b. 1878), 277

Pardo, Felipe (Peru; 1806–1868), 115, 123, 125, 246, 248, 257

Pardo, Francisco Guaicaipuro (Venezuela; 1829–1882), 127, 248

Pardo, Miguel Eduardo (Venezuela; 1865–1905), 271

Paredes, Countess of, 79

Pareja Díez Canseco, Alfredo (Ecuador; b. 1908), 282

Parra, Félix (Mexico; 1845–1919), 254

Parra Pérez, C., 225

Parra, Teresa de la (Venezuela; 1891–1936), 246, 276

Parrington, Vernon Louis, 213

Paso y Troncoso, Francisco de Borja del (Mexico; 1842–1916), 215, 223

Pater, Walter, 160, 177

Patiño Ixtolinque, Pedro (Mexico; 1765–1835), 215

Paul III, Pope, 42

Payne, Edward John, 213

Payno, Manuel (Mexico; 1810–1894), 124, 248

Payró, Roberto José (Argentina; 1867–1928), 182, 271, 272

Paz, Alonso de la (Guatemala; 1605–1676), 91

Paz, Juan Carlos (Argentina; b. 1897), 202

Paz, Octavio (Mexico; b. 1914), 278, 282

Paz Soldán y Unanue, Pedro (Peru; 1839–1895), 257

Pazós Kanki, Vicente (Bolivia; 1780–1851?), 215

Pech, An Nakuk (Mexico; 16th cent.), 214

Pederneiras, Mario (Brazil; 1868–1915), 186

Pedreira, Antonio Salvador (Puerto Rico; 1899–1939), 263

Pedro I of Brazil and IV of Portugal, 236

Pedro II of Brazil (1825–1891), 122, 138, 148, 236

Pedro Americo, see Figueiredo

Pedroso, Regino (Cuba; b. 1897), 280

Peers, E. Allison, 243, 244, 263

Péguy, Charles, 41

Peixoto, Afranio (Brazil; b. 1876), 74, 99, 275

Pellerano Castro, Arturo (Santo Domingo; 1865–1916), 173, 267

Pellegrini, Carlos (Argentina; 1845–1906), 252

Pellicer, Carlos (Mexico; b. 1897), 278, 291

Peña, David (Argentina; 1863–1930), 252

Peñuela de Segura, Laura Victoria (Colombia; b. 1910), 161

Peón Contreras, José (Mexico; 1843–1908), 250

Peralta, Alejandro (Peru; b. 1899), 279

Peralta, Arturo (Peru; b. ca. 1901), 279

Peralta Barnuevo, Pedro de (Peru; 1663–1743), 87, 231, 232

Perea, Juan Augusto, and Salvador (Puerto Rico; 20th cent.), 258
Pereda Valdés, Ildefonso (Uruguay; b. 1899), 280
Pereira da Silva, João Manoel (Brazil; 1817–1898), 222
Pereira Salas, Eugenio (Chile; b. 1904), 227, 293
Pereyns, Simon (Belgium-Mexico; 16th cent.), 47
Pereyra, Carlos (Mexico; 1871–1942), 246
Pereyra, Diomedes de (Bolivia; 20th cent.), 283
Pérez, Francisco de Sales (Venezuela; 1836–1926), 248
Pérez, José Joaquín (Santo Domingo; 1845–1900), 41, 149, 250–251
Pérez, Lázaro María (Colombia; 1824–1892), 250
Pérez, Santiago (Colombia; 1830–1900), 243, 249, 250
Pérez, Udón (Venezuela; 1868–1925), 268
Pérez Bonalde, Juan Antonio (Venezuela; 1846–1892), 128, 240, 258, 264
Pérez de Casteñeda, Alonso, 219
Pérez de Hita, Ginés, 247
Pérez de Zambrana, Luisa (Cuba; 1837–1923), 128
Pérez Freire, Osmán (Chile; 1878–1930), 201
Pérez Galdós, Benito, 148, 200
Pérez Petit, Víctor (Uruguay; b. 1871), 268
Pérez Ramírez, Juan (Mexico; 16th cent.), 52
Pérez Rosales, Vicente (Chile; 1807–1886), 244, 248
Pérez Triana, Santiago (Colombia; 1858–1916), 265

Perricholi, La, see Villegas, Micaela
Persius, 257
Pesado, José Joaquín (Mexico; 1801–1861), 109, 248, 257, 269
Pessoa, Epitacio, 243
Peter Martyr of Anghera, 12–14, 21, 207
Petit, Magdalena (Chile; 20th cent.), 276, 283
Petrarch, Francesco, 46
Pettoruti, Emilio (Argentina; b. 1894), 203
Pezoa Velis, Carlos (Chile; 1879–1908), 168, 268
Phibbs, Richard, 279
Philip II of Spain, 181
Philip IV of Spain, 40
Phillips, R., 294
Picasso, Pablo, 189
Picón Febres, Gonzalo (Venezuela; 1860–1918), 271, 289
Picón Salas, Mariano (Venezuela; b. 1901), 289
Pierce, Frank, 218
Pigafetta, Francesco Antonio (Italy; 1491–1534), 219
Pijoán, José, 293
Pimentel, Francisco (Mexico; 1832–1893), 289
Piñeyro, Enrique (Cuba; 1839–1911), 158, 244, 246, 247, 263
Pitt, William (1759–1806), 96
Pizarro, Francisco, 50, 53
Pizarro, Gonzalo, 20, 21
Pizarro, Pedro (Spain; ca. 1514–1571), 45, 220
Plácido, see Valdés, Gabriel de la Concepción
Plancarte, Friar José Antonio (Mexico; 1735–1815), 84
Plato, 156, 160

Plautus, 4, 101
Plaza, José Antonio de (Colombia; 1809–1854), 250
Plaza, Ramón de la (Venezuela; d. 1896), 227
Plenn, Abel, 283
Pliny, the naturalist, 8, 207
Plutarch, 152
Pocaterra, José Rafael (Venezuela; b. 1890), 274
Podestá, José (Argentina; *ca.* 1858–1937), 183, 244, 259
Podestá, Manuel T. (Argentina; 1853–1920), 271
Poe, Edgar Allan, 178, 194, 263
Poey, Felipe (Cuba; 1799–1891), 233
Poirier, Eduardo (Chile; 19th cent.), 270
Polo, Marco, 8,
Polo de Ondegardo, Juan (Spain; d. *ca.* 1571), 45, 220, 221
Pomar, Juan Bautista (Mexico; 16th cent.), 214
Pombo, Rafael (Colombia; 1833–1912), 240, 257, 258, 264
Pompeia, Raul (Brazil; 1863–1895), 147, 270
Ponce, Aníbal (Argentina; d. 1938), 252
Ponce, Manuel Antonio (Chile; 19th cent.), 252
Ponce, Manuel M. (Mexico; b. 1886), 201, 276
Ponce de León, José María (Colombia; 1846–1882), 255, 256
Poncet, Carolina (Cuba; b. 1880), 276
Ponchielli, Amilcare, 140
Poore, Dudley, 282, 283, 292
Pope, Alexander, 105, 129
Porras Barrenechea, Raúl (Peru; b. 1897), 289

Portal, Magda (Peru; 20th cent.), 276
Portales, Diego, 115, 138
Porter, Katherine Anne, 240, 292
Portinari, Candido (Brazil; b. 1903), 293
Portuondo, José Antonio (Cuba; b. 1911), 280
Posada, José Guadalupe (Mexico; 1851–1913), 140, 255
Posada Gutiérrez, Joaquín (Colombia; 1797–1881), 244
Post, Franz Janszoon (Holland-Brazil; 1612–1682), 47
Prado, Eduardo (Brazil; 1860–1901), 180, 212, 269
Prado, Pedro (Chile; b. 1886), 273
Prado y Ugarteche, Javier (Peru; 1871–1921), 289
Prescott, William Hickling, 65, 66
Prampolini, Giacomo, 290
Prestage, Edgar, 218
Price, Enrique (Colombia; 1819–1863), 142
Priego, Marquis of, 64
Priestley, Herbert Ingram, 209, 287
Prieto, Guillermo (Mexico; 1818–1897), 115, 138, 143, 240, 248, 259
Prieto, Jenaro (Chile; b. 1889), 274, 283
Propertius, 257
Proust, Marcel, 151
Pruneda, Alfonso (Mexico; b. 1879), 277
Psalms, 89
Puente y Apezechea, Fermín de la (Mexico; 1821–1875), 246
Pueyrredón, Prilidiano Paz (Argentina; 1823–1870), 255
Purcell, Henry, 63
Putnam, Samuel, 269, 282

Queiroz, Rachel de (Brazil; 20th cent.), 197, 276
Quesada, Ernesto (Argentina; 1858–1934), 252
Quesada y Aróstegui, Gonzalo de (Cuba; 1868–1915), 263
Quesada y Miranda, Gonzalo de (Cuba; b. 1900), 263
Quevedo, Francisco de, 22, 70, 80, 111, 149, 163, 169, 194
Quevedo Arvelo, Julio (Colombia; 1829–1897), 255
Quintana, Manuel José, 129, 142
Quintana Roo, Andrés (Mexico; 1787–1851), 105, 129, 257
Quiñones, Francisco Mariano (Puerto Rico; 1830–1908), 250, 262
Quiroga, Bishop Vasco de (Spain; ca. 1470–1565), 31
Quiroga, Carlos B. (Argentina; b. 1890), 280
Quiroga, Facundo, 132
Quiroga, Horacio (Uruguay; 1879–1937), 168, 198, 270, 271
Quispe Tito, Diego (Peru; 17th cent.), 215

Rabasa, Emilio (Mexico; 1856–1930), 271
Rabelais, François, 20
Rabello, Laurindo (Brazil; 1826–1864), 128
Rabinal Achí (play), 56
Racine, Jean, 89, 98, 223
Rafael, Rafael de (Mexico; 1817–1882), 248
Raimundo, Jacques (Brazil; 20th cent.), 216
Rameau, Jean Philippe, 63
Ramírez, Ambrosio (Mexico; 1859–1913), 257

Ramírez, Carlos María (Uruguay; 1848–1898), 244
Ramírez, Ignacio (Mexico; 1818–1879), 115, 127, 128, 138, 178, 249
Ramírez, José Fernando (Mexico; 1804–1871), 242, 244, 248
Ramírez de Fuenleal, Bishop Sebastián (Spain; d. 1547), 42
Ramos, Arthur (Brazil; b. 1903), 279
Ramos, Graciliano (Brazil; 20th cent.), 198
Ramos, Samuel (Mexico; b. 1897), 253
Ramos, Silvio (Brazil; 1851–1914), 253, 258, 289
Rangel, Nicolás (Mexico; 1864–1935), 239
Raphael, 29
Ratcliff, Dillwyn Fristchel, 271, 290
Ravel, Maurice, 142
Ravelo, José de Jesús (Santo Domingo; 20th cent.), 255
Raynal, the Abbé, 26
Read, J. Lloyd, 247, 290
Rebull, Santiago (Mexico; 1829–1902), 254
Redfield, Robert, 279
Reed, Alma, 292
Reed, Frank Otis, 227
Regnard, Jean François, 89
Regules, Elías (Uruguay; 1860–1929), 183, 268
Reid, John T., 288
Reina, Casiodoro de, 213
Reina, Manuel, 265
Reinalte Coelho, Pedro de (Spain; 16th cent.), 47
Reinoso, Friar Diego de (Guatemala; 16th cent.), 214
Remesal, Friar Antonio de (Spain; 17th cent.), 220

Remos y Rubio, Juan José (Cuba; b. 1896), 289
René Moreno, Gabriel (Bolivia; 1834–1908), 244
Rengifo, Marcos (Peru; 17th–18th cent.), 215
Restrepo, José Manuel (Colombia; 1782–1863), 244
Restrepo, Juan de Dios (Colombia; 1825–1894), 248
Restrepo Millán, José María (Colombia; 20th cent.), 258
Restrepo Tirado, Ernesto (Colombia; b. 1862), 244
Revueltas, Silvestre (Mexico; 1899–1940), 201, 202, 284
Reyes, Alfonso (Mexico; b. 1889), 189, 228, 246, 258, 274, 276, 277, 278
Reyes, Neftalí Ricardo (Chile; b. 1904), 185, 191, 193, 278, 291
Reyles, Carlos (Uruguay; 1868–1938), 168, 182, 246, 259, 270, 271
Reyna, Ernesto (Peru; 20th cent.), 279
Reynolds, Gregorio (Bolivia; b. 1882), 258, 274
Ribeiro, João (Brazil; 1860–1934), 244, 289
Ribeiro, Julio (Brazil; 1845–1900), 182
Ribeiro Couto, Ruy (Brazil; b. 1898), 278
Ribeiro Rocha, Manoel (Brazil; 18th cent.), 33, 212
Ribera, Luis de [poet] (Spain; 17th cent.), 220
Ricardo, Cassiano (Brazil; b. 1895), 280
Rice, William F., 270
Richard Lavalle, Enrique (Argentina; 19th–20th cent.), 252
Richardson, Ruth, 272, 290

Ricke, Friar Jodoco (Belgium–Ecuador; 16th cent.), 48
Rimbaud, Jean Arthur, 127
Río, Andrés Mariano del (Spain; 1765–1849), 43, 234
Rioja, Francisco de, 72
Rippy, James Fred, 287
Riva Agüero, José de la (Peru; 1885–1944), 220, 227, 274, 277
Riva Palacio, Vicente (Mexico; 1832–1896), 115, 138, 242
Rivadavia, Bernardino, 112, 138, 253
Rivas, Duke of, 118, 123
Rivas Frade, Federico (Colombia; 1858–1922), 258
Rivera, Agustín (Mexico; 1824–1916), 253
Rivera, Diego (Mexico; b. 1886), 202–203, 255, 276, 292
Rivera, Guillermo, 262
Rivera, José Eustasio (Colombia; 1888–1928), 198, 274, 282
Rivera, Luis de, sculptor (Spain; 16th cent.), 48
Roa Bárcena, José María (Mexico; 1827–1908), 115, 257
Robertson, William Spence, 235
Robespierre, Maximilien Marie Isidore, 96
Robles, Diego de (Spain; 16th cent.), 48, 53
Robleto, Hernán (Nicaragua; 20th cent.), 281
Roca, Ramón (Spain; d. 1820), 239
Rocafuerte, Vicente (Ecuador; 1783–1847), 243
Rocha Pitta, Sebastião da (Brazil; 1660–1738), 85, 231
Rodin, Auguste, 140
Rodó, José Enrique (Uruguay; 1871–1917), 165, 168, 178,

179–180, 192, 196, 245, 262, 266, 268, 290

Rodríguez Alconedo, José Luis (Mexico; 18th–19th cent.), 91

Rodríguez de Francia, José Gaspar, 112, 134, 241

Rodríguez de Mendoza, Toribio (Peru; 1750–1825), 234

Rodríguez de Sosa, Tomás (Santo Domingo; 17th cent.), 38

Rodríguez Demorizi, Emilio (Santo Domingo; 20th cent.), 231

Rodríguez Embil, Luis (Cuba; b. 1879), 263

Rodríguez Freile, Juan (Colombia; 1566–1638), 52

Rodríguez Galván, Ignacio (Mexico; 1816–1842), 250

Rodríguez Mendoza, Emilio (Chile; b. 1873), 271

Roig, Blanca de, 283

Roig de Leuchsenring, Emilio (Cuba; b. 1889), 263

Rojas, Arístides (Venezuela; 1826–1894), 244

Rojas, Cristóbal (Venezuela; 19th cent.), 254

Rojas, Fernando de, 90

Rojas, Juan Ramón (Argentina; d. 1824), 239

Rojas, Ricardo (Argentina; b. 1882), 41, 187, 224, 252, 268, 273, 276, 288

Rojas Garciadueñas, José (Mexico; 20th cent.), 218

Rojas Paz, Pablo (Argentina; b. 1896), 280

Rokha, Pablo de, see Díaz Loyola, Carlos

Roldán, Amadeo (Cuba; b. 1900), 202

Román, Friar Jerónimo, 210

Roman de Berthe, 238

Romero, Fernando (Peru; 20th cent.), 216, 282

Romero, Francisco (Spain-Argentina; b. 1891), 253, 269, 273

Romero, José Luis (Argentina; b. 1909), 258

Romero, José Rubén (Mexico; b. 1890), 274, 281

Romero, Silvio, see Ramos, Silvio

Romero [de] James, Concha (Mexico; b. 1901), 295

Romero de Terreros, Manuel, Marquis of San Francisco (Mexico; b. 1880), 93

Romerogarcía, Manuel Vicente (Venezuela; 1865–1917), 271

Ronsard, Pierre de, 23

Ros de Olano, Antonio (Venezuela-Spain; 1802–1887), 246

Rosales, Friar Diego de (Spain; 1603–1677), 220, 231

Rosas, Juan Manuel de, 112, 115, 116, 119, 120, 132, 137, 150

Rosas, Juventino (Mexico; d. 1895), 201

Rosas, Moreno, José (Mexico; 1838–1883), 258

Rosas de Oquendo, Mateo (Spain; 16th cent.), 220, 226

Rose of Lima, Saint (Peru; 1586–1617), 75

Rosenblat, Ángel (Argentina; b. 1902), 213, 234

Rosenvasser, Abraham (Argentina; 20th cent.), 258

Rotea, Agustín (Mexico; d. 1788), 233

Rousseau, Jean Jacques, 26, 88, 94, 108, 211, 241

Roxlo, Carlos (Uruguay; 1860–1926), 288

Rúa, Juan de, see Arrué, Juan de

Rubens, Carlos, 235

Rubens, Peter Paul, 29

Rueda, Salvador, 265
Ruiz, Hipólito (Peru; 18th cent.), 234
Ruiz de Alarcón, Juan (Mexico; ca. 1580-1639), 35, 63, 67-71, 72, 78, 90, 227-228, 246
Ruiz Belvis, Segundo (Puerto Rico; 1829-1867), 262
Ruiz Espadero, Nicolás (Cuba; 1833-1890), 256
Ruiz de León, Francisco (Mexico; 18th cent.), 84
Runes, Dagobert D., 292
Ruscoe, Margaret P., 265
Ruskin, John, 163
Rustay, George W., 292
Rycaut, Sir Paul, 227

Saavedra, Hernandarias de, 60
Saavedra Fajardo, Diego de, 163
Saavedra Molina, Julio (Chile; 20th cent.), 266
Sabat Ercasty, Carlos (Uruguay; b. 1887), 186, 273
Sabugosa, Vasco Fernandes, Count of (Portugal; 18th cent.), 62, 220
Saco, José Antonio (Cuba; 1797-1879), 157, 212, 233, 244
Sagard, Gabriel, 25
Sahagún, Friar Bernardino de (ca. 1500-1590), 20, 55, 219
Saint Gelais, Mellin de, 8, 12, 207
Saint Paul, 13
Saint-Saëns, Camille, 142
Saint Theresa, 35, 75, 79, 163, 232
Saintonge, Jean Alphonse de, 12
Salas, Eugenio (Colombia; 1823-1853), 255
Salas, Juan R. (Chile; 20th cent.), 257
Salas, Manuel de (Chile; 1755-1841), 234

Salaverry, Carlos Augusto (Peru; 1831-1890), 250
Salazar, Adolfo, 284
Salazar, Eugenio de (Spain; ca. 1530-1602), 27, 46, 52, 220
Salazar, Ramón A. (Guatemala; 19th cent.), 289
Salazar, Salvador (Cuba; b. 1892), 289
Saldías, José Antonio (Argentina; b. 1891), 272
Saldívar, Gabriel (Mexico; 20th cent.), 227
Salvador, Humberto (Ecuador; b. 1906), 282
Salvador, Friar Vicente do (Brazil; 17th cent.), 85, 228, 231
Saminsky, Lazare, 294
San Antón Muñoz Chimalpahin Quauhtlehuanitzin, Domingo Francisco de (Mexico; 16th cent.), 37, 214
San Juan de Buena Vista, Marquis of, 54
San Martín, Cosme (Chile; 19th cent.), 254
San Martín, José de, 104, 143, 236, 276
Sánchez, Florencio (Uruguay; 1875-1910), 183, 259, 272
Sánchez, Gabriel or Rafael, 8
Sánchez, Luis Alberto (Peru; b. 1900), 220, 227, 274, 277, 288, 289
Sánchez, Mariquita (María Sánchez de Thompson; later de Mendeville) (Argentina; 1786-1868), 254
Sánchez Coello, Alonso, 47
Sánchez de Fuentes, Eduardo (Cuba; b. 1876), 201, 225, 256
Sánchez de Fuentes, Mario (Cuba; 20th cent.), 284

Sánchez Gardel, Julio (Argentina; 1879–1937), 272
Sánchez Reulet, Aníbal (Argentina; b. 1910), 253
Sánchez Valverde, Antonio (Santo Domingo; 1729–1790), 233
Sancho de Hoz, Pedro (Spain; d. 1547), 220, 221
Sandoval, Alfonso de, 212
Sanfuentes, Salvador (Chile; 1817–1860), 249, 250, 257
Sanguily, Manuel (Cuba; 1848–1925), 158, 261, 263
Sanín Cano, Baldomero (Colombia; b. 1860), 38, 168, 179
Santa Anna, see López de Santa Anna, Antonio,
Santa Cruz Espejo, Francisco Eugenio de (Ecuador; 1747–1795), 98, 214, 233
Santa Cruz Pachacuti Yamqui Salcamayhua, Juan de (Peru; 16th cent.), 36, 55, 214
Santa Cruz Wilson, Domingo (Chile; b. 1899), 201, 202
Santa Eulalia, Father José María de (Spain; 18th cent.), 255
Santángel, Luis de, 8
Santayana, George, 159, 170
Santiago, Isabel de (Ecuador; 17th cent.), 215
Santiago, Miguel de (Ecuador; d. 1673), 91, 215
Santisteban del Puerto, Count of (Spain; 17th cent.), 220
Santovenia, Emeterio S. (Cuba; b. 1889), 252, 263
Sanz, Elena, 256
Sanz, Miguel José (Venezuela; 18th cent.), 233
Sappho, 257
Sarmiento, Domingo Faustino (Argentina; 1811–1888), 116, 125, 131–136, 137, 139, 140, 150, 151, 159, 180, 199, 242, 243, 251–252, 253, 276
Sarmiento, Domingo Fidel (Dominguito), 133
Sarmiento de Gamboa, Pedro (Spain; ca. 1530–1592), 45, 220, 221
Saumell, Manuel (Cuba; 1817–1870), 256
Schierbrand, W. V., 271
Schiller, Friedrich, 130
Schmeckebier, Laurence E., 293
Schmidt, Augusto Frederico (Brazil; b. 1906), 278
Schons, Dorothy, 227, 228, 265
Schopenhauer, Arthur, 249
Scott, James Brown, 209
Scott, Sir Walter, 121, 124, 126
Segall, J. B., 227
Segura, Manuel Ascensio (Peru; 1805–1871), 123, 125, 248
Selva, Salomón de la (Nicaragua; b. 1893), 267, 274
Seneca, 108
Seoane, Juan (Peru; 20th cent.), 282
Sepúlveda, Juan Ginés de, 46
Serrano, Mary J., 245
Serrano Redonnet, Antonio Ernesto (Argentina; 20th cent.), 221
Sessé, Martín de (Spain; d. 1809), 234
Setubal, Pablo (Brazil; 1893–1937), 282
Shakespeare, William, 24, 69, 71, 156, 194
Shaw, George Bernard, 71, 153, 156, 272
Shelley, Percy Bysshe, 80, 126, 194, 230
Shepherd, William Robert, 287
Sheridan, Frances, 221
Sheridan, Richard Brinsley, 211

Sicardi, Francisco Anselmo (Argentina; 1856–1927), 271
Sierra, Justo (Mexico; 1848–1912), 37, 151, 159–160, 178, 211, 244, 263, 267
Sigourney, Mrs., 240
Sigüenza y Góngora, Carlos de (Mexico; 1645–1700), 86–87
Siloe, 92
Silva, Francisca Julia da (Brazil; 1874–1920), 275
Silva, José Asunción (Colombia; 1865–1896), 166, 167, 168, 170, 171, 173, 175, 265, 267, 270
Silva, Lafayette (Brazil; 20th cent.), 273
Silva, Medardo Ángel (Ecuador; ca. 1898–1921), 274
Silva, Owen de, 294
Silva, Teresa Margarita da (Brazil; 18th cent.), 221
Silva Aceves, Mariano (Mexico; 1887–1937), 276
Silva Alvarenga, Manoel Ignacio da (Brazil; 1749–1814), 86
Silva Castro, Raúl (Chile; b. 1903), 260, 266, 267
Silva Valdés, Fernán (Uruguay; b. 1887), 268, 273
Silveira Bueno, Barbara da (Brazil; 18th cent.), 86
Simón, Friar Pedro (Spain; 1574–ca. 1630), 220, 221
Simpson, Leslie Byrd, 218, 287
Sitwell, Sacheverell, 93, 235, 293
Sívori, Eduardo (Argentina; 1847–1918), 255
Skelton, Thomas, 29, 211
Slonimsky, Nicolas, 284, 294
Smith, Adam, 99
Smith, G. Elliot, 27
Smith, Robert Chester, Jr., 218, 235, 292, 293

Soares Lisboa, Manoel Ignacio (Brazil; 19th cent.), 257
Soares de Sousa, Gabriel (Portugal; 1540–1591), 45, 220
Socrates, 126, 157
Sodré, Nelson Werneck (Brazil; 20th cent.), 289
Solá, Miguel (Argentina; 20th cent.), 218, 223, 234, 292
Solano, Saint Francisco (Spain; 1549–1610), 31
Solórzano Pereira, Juan de (Spain; 1575–1654), 214
Sombart, Werner, 211
Somerscales, Tomás (Chile; 1842–1927), 254
Sophocles, 258
Soto, Friar Domingo de, 18, 212
Soto, Marco Aurelio (Honduras; 1846–1908), 243
Soto de Rojas, Pedro, 72
Soto Hall, Máximo (Guatemala; 1871–1944), 267
Sotomayor Valdés, Ramón (Chile; 1830–1903), 244
Sousa, Rita Joana de (Brazil; 1696–1718), 75
Souza, Claudio de (Brazil; 19th–20th cent.), 273
Spell, Jefferson Rea, 237, 240, 248
Spencer, Herbert, 158
Spenser, Edmund, 73
Staël, Mme. de, 117
Steck, F. B., 221
Steele, Richard, 227
Stein, Gertrude, 126
Stendhal, see Beyle, Henri
Stiles, Ezra, 96
Stimson, F. J., 268
Storni, Alfonsina (Switzerland-Argentina; 1892–1938), 186, 273, 275
Stravinsky, Igor, 189

340 INDEX

Suárez, José Bernardo (Chile; 1822-1912), 252
Suárez, Marco Fidel (Colombia; 1855-1927), 243
Suárez de Peralta, Juan (Mexico; 16th cent.), 225
Subercasseaux, Benjamín (Chile; 20th cent.), 283
Sucre, Antonio José de, 236
Sue, Eugène, 124
Supervielle, Jules (Uruguay-France; b. 1884), 246
Swift, Jonathan, 24, 262
Swinburne, Algernon, 169
Symonds, John Addington, 218
Syrkin, Marie, 214

Tablada, José Juan (Mexico; 1871-1945), 168
Taine, Hippolyte, 262
Tallet, José Zacarías (Cuba; b. 1893), 280
Tamayo, Franz (Bolivia; b. 1879), 266
Tamberlick, 256
Tapia, Alejandro (Puerto Rico; 1827-1882), 249, 250
Taunay, Alfredo d'Escragnolle (Brazil; 1843-1899), 260
Távora, Franklin (Brazil; 1842-1888), 260
Teixeira, Mucio (Brazil; 1857-1926), 259
Teixeira Pinto, Bento (Brazil; 1545-ca. 1619), 46, 218, 220
Tejeda, Luis de (Argentina; 1604-1680), 82, 84
Tejera, Diego Vicente (Cuba; 1848-1903), 258
Ten Kate, H. F. C., 210
Terence, 71
Terrazas, Francisco de (Mexico; 16th cent.), 51, 58
Terrill, Katherine, 284

Teurbe Tolón, Miguel (Cuba; 1820-1858), 258
Tezozómoc, see Alvarado Tezozómoc, Hernando
Theocritus, 73, 115
Thévet, André, 22
Thomas, Isaiah, 43
Thompson, G. A., 233
Thomsen, Thomas, 218
Thomson, Oscar, 284
Thomson, Virgil, 202, 284
Tibullus, 257
Ticknor, George, 252
Tietze, Hans, 292
Tintoretto, 163
Tipan, Francisco (Ecuador; 17th cent.), 215
Tiradentes, 236
Tirso de Molina (Spain; 1584-1648), 21, 46, 47, 68, 69, 71, 111, 220
Titian, 29
Tito Yupanqui, Francisco (Peru; 16th cent.), 215
Tolstoy, Leo, 144, 200
Tomás, Juan (Peru; 17th cent.), 215
Tomé, Narciso, 92
Toor, Frances, 255, 291
Toro, Alfonso (Mexico; 20th cent.), 255
Toro, Fermín (Venezuela; 1807-1865), 125, 245
Toro, Julio del, 227
Torquemada, Friar Juan de (Spain; ca. 1563-1624), 219
Torre, Guillermo de, 278
Torre, Juana de la, 11
Torre Revello, José (Argentina; b. 1893), 217
Torres Bodet, Jaime (Mexico; b. 1902), 278, 283
Torres Homem (Brazil; 19th cent.), 121

Torres Méndez, Ramón (Colombia; 19th cent.), 254
Torres Rioseco, Arturo (Chile; b. 1897), 265, 267, 282, 288, 290
Torri, Julio (Mexico; b. 1889), 274, 276
Toussaint, Manuel (Mexico; 20th cent.), 92, 215, 218, 219, 222, 223, 235, 255, 274
Tovar, Martín (Venezuela; 1828–1902), 254
Trend, John Brande, 287
Trejo y Sanabria, Bishop Hernando de (Paraguay; 16th–17th cent.), 60
Tresguerras, Francisco Eduardo (Mexico; 1745–1833), 93
Trueba y Cosío, Telesforo, 247
Tschiffely, Aimé F., 280
Tschudi, J. J. von, 224
Túpac Amaru, 57, 94
Túpac Yupanqui, 64
Turcios, Froilán (Honduras; 1878–1943), 266
Tyler, Marian, 279

Ugarte, Manuel (Argentina; b. ca. 1875), 266
Uhrbach, Carlos Pío (Cuba; 1872–1897), 116
Ulloa, Francisco (Colombia; 18th cent.), 233
Umphrey, George Wallace, 230, 260, 261, 267
Unamuno, Miguel de, 34, 147, 169, 251, 259, 268
Unanue, Hipólito (Peru; 1755–1833), 234
Underhill, John Garret, 283
Underwood, Edna Worthley, 230, 280, 291
Urbaneja Achelpohl, Luis María (Venezuela; 1874–1937), 265, 270

Urbina, Luis Gonzaga (Mexico; 1868–1934), 168, 181, 239, 246
Ureña de Henríquez, Salomé (Santo Domingo; 1850–1897), 256, 261
Ureña de Mendoza, Nicolás (Santo Domingo; 1822–1875), 258
Urquiza, Justo José de, 132, 133
Urueta, Jesús (Mexico; 1868–1920), 178
Uscamaita, José (Peru; 17th cent.), 215
Usigli, Rodolfo (Mexico; b. 1905), 272
Uslar Pietri, Arturo (Venezuela; b. 1905), 281

Vaca Guzmán, Santiago (Bolivia; 19th cent.), 288
Valadés, Friar Diego de (Spain; 16th cent.), 47
Valbuena, Bishop Bernardo de (Spain-Mexico; ca. 1562–1627), 12, 44, 60, 71–73, 90, 150, 208, 221, 228
Valcárcel, Luis Eduardo (Peru; b. 1891), 279
Valdelomar, Abraham (Peru; 1888–1919), 188, 274, 279
Valderrama, Adolfo (Chile; 1834–1902), 288
Valderrama, Friar Domingo de (Ecuador; d. ca. 1615), 59
Valdés, Alfonso de, 21
Valdés, Gabriel de la Concepción (Cuba; 1809–1844), 116, 130, 163, 239, 250, 258
Valdés, José Manuel (Peru; 1767–1843), 216, 234
Valdés, Juan de, 21
Valdivia, Pedro de, 53
Valencia, Guillermo (Colombia;

1873–1943), 168, 171, 174, 178, 185, 273

Valenzuela Puelma, Alfredo (Chile; 1856–1908), 254

Valera, Father Blas (Peru; *ca.* 1538–1598), 52, 55, 214

Valera, Cipriano de, 213

Valera, Juan, 124, 247, 267, 268

Valéry, Paul, 25, 279

Valle, Aristóbulo del (Argentina; 1845–1896), 252

Valle, José Cecilio del (Honduras; 1780–1834), 233, 237

Valle, Rafael Heliodoro (Honduras; b. 1891), 274

Valle Caviedes, Juan del (Spain-Peru; *fl.* 1683–1691), 109, 240

Valle Inclán, Ramón del, 168, 281

Vallejo, César (Peru; 1895–1938), 197, 279, 280, 282

Vallejo, José Joaquín (Chile; 1811–1858), 124

Valverde Téllez, Bishop Emeterio (Mexico; 19th cent.), 253

Van Horne, John, 219, 221, 228

Varela, Father Félix (Cuba; 1788–1853), 157, 233

Varela, Juan Cruz (Argentina; 1794–1839), 105, 116, 237, 257

Varela, Mariano (Argentina; 1834–1902), 133, 157

Vargas Ugarte, Father Rubén (Peru; 20th cent.), 231

Varnhagen, Francisco Adolfo de (Brazil; 1816–1878), 244

Varona, Enrique José (Cuba; 1849–1933), 151, 157–160, 177, 253, 264

Vasconcelos, José (Mexico; b. 1881), 269, 274, 276, 277

Váscones, Francisco (Ecuador; 20th cent.), 289

Vassallo, Angel (Argentina; 20th cent.), 253

Vasseur, Álvaro Armando (Uruguay; b. 1878), 266

Vauthier, Louis Léger, 247

Vaz Ferreira, Carlos (Uruguay; b. 1873), 181

Vaz Ferreira, María Eugenia (Uruguay; 1875–1924), 186, 275

Vázquez, Gregorio (Colombia; 1638–1711), 91

Vega, Carlos (Argentina; b. 1898), 256

Vega, Florentino (Colombia; 18th cent.), 233

Vega, Lope de, 22, 46, 57, 63, 68, 69, 71, 72, 75, 80, 111, 169, 226, 232

Vega, Ventura de la (Argentina-Spain; 1807–1865), 123, 246, 249

Veitia, Mariano [Fernández de Echeverría] (Mexico; 1718–*ca.* 1779), 231

Velasco, Father Juan de (Ecuador; 1727–1792), 231

Velasco, José María (Mexico; 1840–1912), 254

Velázquez, Diego Rodríguez, 90

Velázquez, José Francisco (Venezuela; 18th cent.), 226

Velázquez, Father José Guadalupe (Mexico; 1856–1920), 255

Velázquez Chávez, Agustín (Mexico; 20th cent.), 293

Velázquez de Cárdenas y León, Joaquín (Mexico; 1732–1786), 84, 231, 233

Velázquez de León, Joaquín (Mexico; 1803–1882), 233

Vélez Herrera, Ramón (Cuba; 1808–1886), 258

Velloso, Friar Conceição (Brazil; 1742–1811), 234

Verdi, Giuseppe, 140
Vergara y Vergara, José María
(Colombia; 1831–1872), 248,
289
Verissimo, Érico (Brazil; 20th
cent.), 198, 282, 289
Verissimo, José (Jose Verissimo
Dias de Mattos), 261, 289
Verlaine, Paul, 176, 264
Vértiz, Juan José de, 45, 59
Vespucci, Amerigo (Italy; 1451–
1512), 10, 14, 21, 29, 45, 219
Vhay, Ann L. Murphy, 293
Vhay, David, 293
Viana, Javier de (Uruguay; 1872–
1927), 259, 271
Vianna, Oduvaldo (Brazil; 20th
cent.), 273
Vicente, Gil, 90, 111
Vicker, C. V., 291
Vicker, May, 291
Victoria, Tomás Luis de, 140, 201,
226
Vicuña, Father Alejandro (Chile;
20th cent.), 258
Vicuña Mackenna, Benjamín
(Chile; 1831–1886), 244, 261
Vieira, Father Antonio (Portugal-
Brazil; 1606–1697), 33, 73–74,
85, 212, 228–229
Viejo Pancho, el, see Alonso y
Trelles, José
Vigil, José María (Mexico; 1829–
1909), 257
Vigil, Father Francisco de Paula
(Peru; 1792–1875), 249
Vila-Lobos, Heitor (Brazil; b.
1881), 201, 202, 284
Villalobos, Mariano (Ecuador;
18th cent.), 233
Villalobos, Rosendo (Bolivia; b.
1859), 289
Villanueva, Felipe (Mexico; 1863–
1893), 142, 201

Villar Buceta, María (Cuba; b.
1898), 276
Villarino, María [Bellini] de (Ar-
gentina; 20th cent.), 276
Villarroel, Friar Gaspar de (Ec-
uador; ca. 1587–1665), 82–83
Villasana, José María (Mexico;
19th cent.), 140
Villaseñor, José Antonio (Mexico;
18th cent.), 233
Villate, Gaspar (Cuba; 1851–
1891), 256
Villaurrutia, Jacobo de (Santo
Domingo; 1757–1833), 221
Villaurrutia, Xavier (Mexico; b.
1903), 44, 278, 284
Villaverde, Cirilo (Cuba; 1812–
1894), 147, 260
Villegaignon, Nicolas Durand de,
22
Villegas, Micaela, 149
Violish, F., 293
Virgil, 59, 73, 83, 100, 126, 194,
256, 257, 258
Vitier, Medardo (Cuba; b. 1886),
253
Vitoria, Friar Francisco de, 18,
209
Vivanco, Marchioness of (Mexi-
co; 18th–19th cent.), 229
Vives, Luis, 19, 209
Voltaire, François Marie Arouet
de, 25, 26, 49, 89, 94
Vossler, Karl, 19, 80, 230

Walewski, Countess, 120
Walker, Nell, 265
Wallace, Elizabeth, 230
Walsh, Thomas, 229, 230, 267,
277, 291
Walton, L. B., 270
Warthenau, Alexander von, 293
Washington, George, 95, 99, 107,
124

Wast, Hugo, *see* Martínez Zuviría, Gustavo
Waxman, Samuel Montefiore, 227
Webster, Noah, 237
Weil, Nathaniel, 288
Weil, Sylvia, 288
Weinstock, Herbert, 281, 284, 288, 294
Weisinger, Nina Lee, 288
Wellman, Esther Turner, 270
Wells, Herbert George, 194
Wells, James W., 261
Wells, Warren B., 283
Weyl, Nathaniel, 288
Weyl, Sylvia, 288
Whitaker, Arthur P., 232, 287
White, Edward Lucas, 241
White, José (Cuba; 1836–1918), 142, 201
Whitehead, Alfred North, 129
Whitman, Mrs. Charles, 260
Whitman, Walt, 164, 171, 194
Wiessing, H. P. J., 292
Wilde, Oscar, 158
Wilder, Thornton, 149
Wilgus, Alva Curtis, 216, 245, 265, 287, 290, 294
Williams, Arthur Durward, 293
Williams, Edwin Bucher, 247
Williams, Mary Wilhelmina, 287
Wilson, Edmund, 277
Wilson, Irma, 217, 242, 263
Wilson, W. C. E., 260
Wilson, William E., 212
Winckelmann, Johann Joachim, 44
Woerman, Karl, 293
Wolf, Ferdinand Joseph, 69, 289
Wolfe, Bertram D., 292, 293
Woolf, Virginia, 28
Wordsworth, William, 127, 129
Wright, Marie Robinson, 288

Xammar, Luis Fabio (Peru; b. 1911), 279
Ximenes, Friar Francisco (Spain-Guatemala; 1666–*ca.* 1722), 220
Xiu *or* Herrera, Gaspar Antonio (Mexico; 16th cent.), 214

Yapuguay *or* Yaparaguey, Nicolás (Paraguay; 18th cent.), 215
Yepes, José Ramón (Venezuela; 1822–1881), 127, 248
Yupanqui, Dionisio Inca (Peru; 19th cent.), 97
Yupanqui, *see* Tito Yupanqui, Francisco

Zafra, builder (Spain; 15th cent.), 48
Zaldumbide, Gonzalo (Ecuador; b. 1885), 262, 274
Zaldumbide, Julio (Ecuador; 1833–1887), 246, 256, 268
Zamora, Friar Alonso de (Colombia; 1635–1717), 214
Zangurima, Gaspar (Ecuador; 18th cent.), 215
Zapata, Dámaso, 251
Zapata Inga, Juan (Peru; 17th cent.), 36, 215
Zárate, Agustín de (Spain; d. after 1560), 220, 221
Zarlino, Gioseffo, 79
Zárraga, Angel (Mexico; b. 1886), 276
Zárraga y Heredia, Agustín (Venezuela; 19th cent.), 123
Zavala, Lorenzo de (Mexico; 1788–1836), 244
Zavala, Silvio (Mexico; b. 1909), 209, 212
Zea, Francisco Antonio (Colombia; 1770–1822), 99, 233

Zea, Leopoldo (Mexico; 20th cent.), 253

Zegarra, Pedro (Peru; d. 1839), 223

Zenea, Juan Clemente (Cuba; 1832–1871), 116

Zeno Gandía, Manuel (Puerto Rico; 1855–1930), 271

Zola, Émile, 182

Zorita, Alonso de (Spain; 1512–ca. 1586), 45, 219

Zorrilla, José, 191

Zorrilla de San Martín, Juan (Uruguay; 1857–1931), 121, 149, 165, 191, 251

Zum Felde, Alberto (Uruguay; b. 1890), 288

Zumárraga, Friar Juan de (Spain; d. 1548), 31, 212

Zumaya, Father Manuel (Mexico; 18th cent.), 226

Zumaya, Francisco de (Spain; 16th cent.), 47

Zumeta, César (Venezuela; b. 1860), 265

Zurbarán, Francisco de, 90

Zuviría, José María (Argentina; 1830–1891), 252

Zweig, Stefan, 74